Personality, Human Development, and Culture

International Perspectives on Psychological Science (Volume 2)

This is the second of two volumes which together present the main contributions from the 29th International Congress of Psychology, held in Berlin in 2008, written by international leaders in psychology from around the world. The authors present a variety of approaches and perspectives that reflect cutting-edge advances in psychological science.

Personality, Human Development, and Culture provides an overview of advances in several areas of the field such as clinical, health, social, developmental, and cross-cultural psychology. One section of the volume is dedicated solely to emotions and health, and addresses state-of-the art work on the regulation of self, health, social relations, and emotions such as passion. Other sections deal with development and personality issues as well as conceptual, cultural, and ethnic approaches to modern psychology. The global perspective of this collection illustrates research being undertaken on all five continents and emphasizes the cultural diversity of the contributors.

This book will be an invaluable resource for researchers, professionals, teachers, and students in the field of psychology

Ralf Schwarzer is Professor of Psychology at the Freie University of Berlin, Germany. He has been President of the Stress and Anxiety Research Society (STAR), the European Health Psychology Society (EHPS), and Division 8 of the International Association for Applied Psychology (IAAP). His research is on stress, coping, social support, self-efficacy, and health behaviours.

Peter A. Frensch is Dean of the Faculty of Mathematics and Natural Sciences II, at Humboldt-University, Berlin. He is also president-elect of the German Society of Psychology, and a member of the Executive Committee of the International Union of Psychological Science. His research is concerned with the cognitive mechanisms underlying different facets of learning.

Personality, Human Development, and Culture

International Perspectives on Psychological Science (Volume 2)

**Edited by Ralf Schwarzer &
Peter A. Frensch**

Psychology Press
Taylor & Francis Group
HOVE AND NEW YORK

First published 2010
by Psychology Press
27 Church Road, Hove, East Sussex BN3 2FA

Simultaneously published in the USA and Canada
by Psychology Press
270 Madison Avenue, New York NY 10016

Psychology Press is an imprint of the Taylor & Francis Group, an Informa business

© 2010 International Union of Psychological Science

Typeset in Times by RefineCatch Limited, Bungay, Suffolk
Printed and bound in Great Britain by
TJ International Ltd, Padstow, Cornwall
Cover design by Andrew Ward
Cover image: Laurenatclemson

This publication has been produced with paper manufactured to strict environmental standards and with pulp derived from sustainable forests.

British Library Cataloguing in Publication Data
A catalogue record for this book is available
from the British Library

Library of Congress Cataloging-in-Publication Data
International Congress of Psychology (29th : 2008 : Berlin)
    Invited lectures presented at the XXIXth International Congress
    of Psychology (Berlin 2008) / edited by Ralf Schwarzer &
    Peter A. Frensch.
        p. cm.
    Includes bibliographical references and index.
    1.Psychology—Congresses.   I.Schwarzer,Ralf.   II.Frensch,PeterA.
    III. Title
    BF2O.I616 2008
    150—dc22
                                                    2009053354

ISBN: 978–1–84872–023–7 (hbk)

Contents

Contributors to Volume 2

Henk Aarts, Department of Social and Organizational Psychology, Utrecht University, Heidelberglaan 1, 3508 TC Utrecht, The Netherlands

Ruben Ardila, National University of Colombia, Bogota, D.C., Colombia

Daniel Bar-Tal, School of Education, Tel Aviv University, Tel Aviv 69978, Israel

Michael Harris Bond, Department of Psychology, Chinese University of Hong Kong, 3rd Floor, Sino Building, Shatin, N.T., Hong Kong, China

Noémie Carbonneau, Research Laboratory on Social Behavior (RLSB), Université du Québec à Montréal, P.O. Box 8888, Succursale Centre-Ville, Montréal, QC H3C 3P8, Canada

Charles S. Carver, Department of Psychology, University of Miami, Coral Gables, FL 33124–0751, USA

Bor-Shiuan Cheng, Department of Psychology, National Taiwan University, No. 1, Sec. 4, Roosevelt Road, Taipei 106, Taiwan

Shirley Y. Y. Cheng, Department of Psychology, University of Illinois at Urbana-Champaign, 603 East Daniel Street, Champaign IL 61820, USA

Chi-yue Chiu, Nanyang Business School, Nanyang Technological University, S3–01C-81 Nanyang Avenue, Singapore 639798

Norman Duncan, Department of Psychology, School of Human and Community Development, University of the Witwatersrand, Johannesburg, South Africa

Maria Cristina Ferreira, Universidade Salgado de Oliveira, R. Marechal Deodoro, 211, 2° andar, Centro Niteroi RJ, Brazil CEP 24030–060

Nico H. Frijda, Faculty of Social and Behavioural Sciences, Department of Psychonomics, University of Amsterdam, Roetersstraat 15, 1018 WB Amsterdam, The Netherlands

Michaela Gummerum, Max-Planck Institute for Human Development, Lentzeallee 94, 14195 Berlin, Germany

Monika Keller, Max-Planck Institute for Human Development, Lentzeallee 94, 14195 Berlin, Germany

Marc-André Lafrenière, Research Laboratory on Social Behavior (RLSB), Université du Québec à Montréal, P.O. Box 8888, Succursale Centre-Ville, Montréal, QC H3C 3P8, Canada

Adela Leibovich de Duarte, Facultad de Psicología, Secretaria de Investigaciones, Universidad de Buenos Aires, Av. Independencia 3065, Ciudad de Buenos Aires, C1225AAM, Argentina

Yi-Cheng Lin, Department of Psychology, National Taiwan University, No. 1, Sec. 4, Roosevelt Road, Taipei 106, Taiwan

Girishwar Misra, Department of Psychology, Arts Faculty Extension Building, University of Delhi, Delhi – 110 007, India

A. Bame Nsamenang, Human Development Resource Centre, Bamenda, Université de Yaoundé I, B.P. 337 Yaoundé, Cameroon

Esther K. Papies, Department of Psychology, Utrecht University, P.O. Box 80140, 3508 TC Utrecht, The Netherlands

Tuuli Pitkänen, A-Clinic Foundation, Järvenpää Addiction Hospital, Kuusitie 36, 04480 Haarajoki, Finland

Lea Pulkkinen, Department of Psychology, University of Jyväskylä, P.O. Box 35 (MaC), 40014 Jyväskylä, Finland

Emilio Ribes-Iñesta, Centro de Estudios e Investigaciones en Comportamiento, Universidad de Guadalajara, Francisco de Quevedo 180, 44130 Guadalajara, México

Bernard Rimé, Faculté de Psychologie, University of Louvain (UCL) at Louvain-la-Neuve, Place du Cardinal Mercier, 10, 1348 Louvain-la-Neuve, Belgium

Wolfgang Stroebe, Department of Social and Organizational Psychology, Utrecht University, P.O. Box 80140, 3508 TC Utrecht, The Netherlands

Masanori Takezawa, Max-Planck Institute for Human Development, Lentzeallee 94, 14195 Berlin, Germany

Robert J. Vallerand, Research Laboratory on Social Behavior (RLSB), Université du Québec à Montréal, P.O. Box 8888, Succursale Centre-Ville, Montréal, QC H3C 3P8, Canada

Liqi Zhu, Institute of Psychology, Chinese Academy of Sciences, Beijing, 4A Datun Road, Chaoyang District, Beijing 100101, China

Roderick Fulata Zimba, Department of Educational Psychology and Inclusive Education, University of Namibia, Private Bag 13301, Windhoek, Namibia

Editors

Peter A. Frensch, Department of Psychology, Humboldt-Universität zu Berlin, Rudower Chaussee 18, 12489 Berlin, Germany

Ralf Schwarzer, Health Psychology Department, Freie Universität Berlin, Habelschwerdter Allee 45, 14195 Berlin, Germany

Committees

Executive Committee
Peter A. Frensch (President), Carola Brücher-Albers (Vice-President), Barbara Schauenburg (Secretary-General), Michel Denis (IUPsyS Liaison), Arthur M. Jacobs, Heinz-Jürgen Rothe, Rainer K. Silbereisen, Marcus Hasselhorn, Ralf Schwarzer

Scientific Committee
Arthur M. Jacobs (Chair), Jens B. Asendorpf, Jürgen Baumert, Niels Birbaumer, Anke Ehlers, Michael Eid, Michael Frese, Joachim Funke, Gerd Gigerenzer, Peter M. Gollwitzer, Kurt Hahlweg, Christoph Klauer, Rainer H. Kluwe, Ulman Lindenberger, Gerd Lüer, Frank Rösler, Wolfgang Schneider, Lael Schooler, Sabine Sonnentag, Ursula M. Staudinger, Elsbeth Stern, Hannelore Weber, Hans Westmeyer

Organizing Committee
Heinz-Jürgen Rothe (Chair), Robert Gaschler, Matthias Jerusalem, Helmut Jungermann, Ulf Kieschke, Dietrich Manzey, Michael Niedeggen, Herbert Scheithauer, Peter Walschburger, Hartmut Wandke, Jochen Ziegelmann

International Advisory Committee
Rainer K. Silbereisen (Chair), Conny H. Antoni, Merry Bullock, Avshalom Caspi, Erik De Corte, Nancy Eisenberg, Rocio Fernandez-Ballesteros, James D. Georgas, Esther R. Greenglass, Buxin Han, Jutta Heckhausen, Michael Knowles, Howard Leventhal, Gerold Mikula, Walter Mischel, Elizabeth Nair, Lars-Göran Nilsson, Arne Öhman, Meinrad Perrez, José M. Prieto, Marc Richelle, Sir Michael Rutter, Juan Jose Sanchez-Sosa, Christiane Spiel, Ingrid Schoon, Wolfgang Stroebe, Richard E. Tremblay, Endel Tulving, Alexander von Eye, Kan Zhang

IUPSyS Executive Committee (2004–2008)
J. Bruce Overmier (President), Saths Cooper (Vice-President), Ingrid Lunt (Vice-President), Michel Denis (Past President), Pierre Ritchie (Secretary-General), Michel Sabourin (Treasurer), Merry Bullock (Deputy

Secretary-General), Helio Carpintero, James Georgas, Hassaim Khan, Sunoko Kuwano, Patrick Lemaire, Elizabeth Nair, Juan-Jose Sánchez-Sosa, Rainer K. Silbereisen, Barbara Tversky, Kan Zhang

Preface

The 29th International Congress of Psychology took place in Berlin, Germany, July 20–25, 2008, under the auspices of the International Union of Psychological Science (IUPsyS). It has been the largest event in the long series of world congresses, with more than 9,000 scientific contributions from all parts of the globe. Volumes 1 and 2 of *International Perspectives on Psychological Science* present a selection of invited chapters from the 29th International Congress. These expert contributions include the Presidential address, the Keynote presentations, and State-of-the-Art lectures. They are written by international leaders in psychology from many countries and regions around the world. The chapters reflect a variety of topics and perspectives, creating an invaluable overview of the discipline of psychological science around the world today.

The first volume, *Cognition and Neuropsychology*, is dedicated to summarizing and characterizing the current scientific state of affairs in three substantive content areas: (I) Perception, Attention, and Action, (II) Social Cognition, and (III) Learning, Memory, and Development. While some of the contributions focus on relatively narrow areas of research, others adopt a much broader stance, trying to understand and explain many different facets of behaviour across widely differing situations. Some contributions even try to bridge the fundamental gap between behavior and genetics. The final part of the volume contains two chapters that discuss Fundamental General Issues in psychology, such as the fate of mentalism and the significance of phenomenal analyses. All chapters offer fascinating insights into modern and current theorizing on the mind and are written by some of the best-known scholars of our time.

The second volume, *Personality, Human Development, and Culture*, provides an overview of advances in several areas of psychology such as clinical, health, social, developmental, and cross-cultural psychology. The first section, which is dedicated to Emotions and Health, addresses state-of-the-art work on the regulation of self, health, social relations, and emotions such as passion. Other sections deal with developmental and personality issues as well as with cultural, ethnic, and conceptual approaches to modern psychology. The emphasis of this collection of chapters lies on a world perspective illustrating which kind of research is being done in all five continents rather than an in-depth analysis of a narrow subject matter. Thus, cultural diversity is addressed in the majority of the contributions.

The chapters of the two volumes constitute only a small selection of the total congress contributions. Readers might also want to refer to the 9,000+ abstracts that are published in Volume 43, Issue 3/4, of the *International Journal of Psychology*.

We do hope that these two volumes may spark further interest in psychological research around the world and may stimulate readers to submit their own contributions to the upcoming conferences.

Ralf Schwarzer, Peter A. Frensch (*Editors*)

Section I

Emotions and health

1 Affects and self-regulation

Charles S. Carver

Human behavior has been viewed from many perspectives over the years. This chapter outlines a view in which behavior is viewed through the lens of feedback control processes. Two layers of control processes, which manage two different aspects of behavior, are postulated. The layers work jointly to attain goals and to permit management of multiple goals across time – that is, they underlie the transforming of simultaneous motives into a stream of actions that shifts repeatedly from one goal to another.

The view described here has long been identified with the term *self-regulation* (Carver & Scheier, 1981, 1998). The connotations of this term vary. It is used here to convey the sense of purposive processes, involving self-corrective adjustments that originate within the person. This view is applied both to the regulation of action and to the regulation of affect.

Behavior as goal-directed and feedback-controlled

A basic concept in this view is the feedback loop. An easy way to approach this concept is to start with goals. Everyone knows what a goal is: a mental representation of a state the person is trying to attain. People have many goals, at varying levels of abstraction and of varying importance. Most goals can be reached in many ways, and a given action can create movement toward very different goals.

Feedback processes

Approaching a goal illustrates the principle of feedback control. A feedback loop has several sub-functions (Miller, Galanter, & Pribram, 1960; Powers, 1973): an input, a reference value, a comparison, and an output. Think of the input as perception: input is information about present circumstances. A reference value is a goal. The input is compared to the reference value. Any discrepancy detected is an "error signal." The output is behavior, though sometimes the behavior is internal.

If the comparison detects no discrepancy, the output remains as it was. How detection of a discrepancy influences output depends on the kind of loop it is. In a discrepancy-reducing loop, the output acts to reduce the discrepancy. Such an effect is seen in attempts to reach a goal, maintain a desired condition, or conform to a standard. In discrepancy-enlarging loops, the reference value is avoided rather than approached. The value in this case is a threat or an "anti-goal": for example, a feared or disliked possible self (Carver, Lawrence, & Scheier, 1999; Ogilvie, 1987). A discrepancy-enlarging loop compares existing conditions to the anti-goal, and enlarges the discrepancy.

In living systems, effects of discrepancy-enlarging processes are typically constrained by discrepancy-reducing processes. Put differently, acts of avoidance often lead into other acts of approach. A person escaping a threat may spot an approach goal that also distances the person from the threat. The avoidance of the threat is then joined by the approach of that goal. This pattern of dual influence defines active avoidance: an organism facing a feared stimulus picks a safer location to escape to and approaches that location.

Feedback processes are ubiquitous in living systems. The feedback concept is readily applied to physiological systems, such as the homeostatic systems that maintain blood pressure and body temperature. We have argued, however, that the same structural elements underlie behaviors at the level of abstraction of interest to personality and social psychologists.

Further points

It is easy to portray the elements of a feedback loop conceptually. In some cases (e.g., in electronic systems), it is also easy to point to them. In other cases, this is more difficult. For example, some feedback loops have no explicit representation of a reference value. The system regulates around a value, but no value is represented as a goal (Berridge, 2004; Carver & Scheier, 2002).

Another point concerns homeostasis as an illustration of feedback processes. Some infer that feedback loops act only to create and maintain steady states. Not so. Some goals *are* static states. Others are dynamic and evolving (e.g., the goal of taking a week's vacation). In such cases, the "goal" is the process of traversing the changing trajectory of the activity, not just to be the end point. Feedback processes apply perfectly well to moving targets (Beer, 1995).

Another point is that goals vary in abstractness. You may have the goal of being a good citizen, but you can also have the goal of recycling, a narrower goal that contributes to being a good citizen. To recycle entails concrete action goals: placing newspapers into containers and moving them to a pick-up location. Thus goals seem to form a hierarchy (Carver & Scheier, 1998; Powers, 1973; Toates, 2006; Vallacher & Wegner, 1987). Abstract goals are attained by achieving the concrete goals that help to define them.

Feedback and affect

Physical behavior is important, but it is not everything. Another important aspect of life is affects, feelings, emotions. What is affect? Where does it come from? It pertains to one's desires and whether they are being met (Clore, 1994; Frijda, 1988; Ortony, Clore, & Collins, 1988). But by what internal mechanism do they arise? Answers range from the neurobiological (e.g., Davidson, 1992) to the cognitive (Ortony et al., 1988).

We posed an answer (Carver & Scheier, 1990, 1998), using feedback control again as an organizing principle but now focusing on a different quality than before. We suggested that feelings arise as a consequence of a feedback process that operates simultaneously with the behavior-guiding process and in parallel to it. It operates automatically and without supervision. The easiest characterization of what this second process is doing is that it is checking on how well the first one is doing. The input for this second loop thus is the *rate of progress in the action system over time*.

Action implies change between states. Thus, behavior is analogous to the physical property of distance. If the affect loop assesses the action loop's progress, then the affect loop is controlling the psychological analog of velocity, the first derivative of distance over time (Hsee & Abelson, 1991). If this analogy is meaningful, the perceptual input to the affect loop would be the first derivative over time of the input used by the action loop.

Input per se does not create affect; a given rate of progress has different affective effects in different contexts. We think that the input is compared to a reference value (cf. Frijda, 1988), as in other feedback systems. In this case, the reference is an acceptable or expected rate of behavioral discrepancy reduction. As in other feedback loops, the comparison checks for deviation from the standard. If there is a discrepancy, the output function changes.

We believe that the error signal in this loop is manifested as affect with positive or negative valence. Progress below the criterion creates negative affect. Progress exceeding the criterion creates positive affect. In essence, feelings with a positive valence mean that you are doing better at something than you need to, and feelings with a negative valence mean that you are doing less well than you need to (Carver & Scheier, 1998).

What determines the criterion for the velocity loop? There are, surely, many influences. Framing the action to oneself in different ways may change the criterion (Brendl & Higgins, 1996). If the activity is unfamiliar, what is used as a criterion is probably quite flexible. If the activity is familiar, however, then the criterion probably reflects accumulated experience, an expected rate. Whether "expected" or "desired" or "needed" rate is the best depiction may depend strongly on the context.

The criterion can also change, though this probably occurs relatively slowly in a relatively familiar behavioral domain. Repeated overshoots result automatically in an upward drift, repeated undershoots result in a downward drift (see Carver & Scheier, 2000). An ironic consequence of such a recalibration would be to keep the balance of a person's emotional experience (positive to negative, aggregated across a span of time) relatively similar, even when the rate criterion changes considerably.

Two kinds of behavioral loops, two dimensions of affect

So far the focus has been on approach loops, but the same logic applies to avoidance loops. Positive feeling exists when a behavioral system is making rapid progress *doing what it is organized to do*. If a system organized to *avoid* is making rapid progress attaining its ends, there should be positive affect. If it is doing poorly, there should be negative affect. In this view, both approach and avoidance have the potential to induce positive feelings (by doing well), and both have the potential to induce negative feelings (by doing poorly).

But doing well at approaching an incentive is not quite the same as doing well at avoiding a threat. There may be differences between the two positives and between the two negatives. In line with Higgins (e.g., 1987, 1996), we argued for two dimensions, one concerning approach, the other concerning avoidance (Carver, 2001; Carver & Scheier, 1998). Approach yields such positive affects as elation, eagerness, and excitement, and such negative affects as frustration, anger, and sadness (Carver, 2004). Avoidance yields such positive affects as relief, serenity, and contentment and such negative affects as fear, guilt, and anxiety.

Merging affect and action

This portrayal implies a natural link between affect and action. That is, if the input of the affect loop is rate of progress in action, then the output function of the affect loop must be a change in rate of that action. Thus, the affect loop has a direct influence on what occurs in the action loop.

Some changes in rate are straightforward, others are less so. The rates of many "behaviors" reflect not the pace of physical actions but choices among potential actions. For example, increasing rate of progress on a project at work may mean choosing to spend a weekend working rather than playing. Increasing your rate of being kind means choosing to do an act that reflects kindness when an opportunity arises. Thus, change in rate is often translated into terms such as concentration or allocation of time and effort.

The idea of two layers of feedback systems functioning together is common in control engineering (e.g., Clark, 1996). Engineers have long recognized that having two systems – one controlling position, one controlling velocity – permits the device they control to respond in a way that is both quick and stable (without overshoots and oscillations). The combination of quickness and stability is desirable in devices engineers deal with, but it is also desirable in living beings. A person with very reactive emotions overreacts, and oscillates behaviorally. A person who is emotionally unreactive is slow to respond even to urgent events. A person whose reactions are between those extremes responds quickly but without oscillation. Being able to respond quickly yet accurately confers a clear adaptive advantage. This combination of quick and stable responding may be a consequence of having both behavior-managing and affect-managing control systems.

Divergent view of the dimensional structure of affect

The ideas outlined up to this point have a certain degree of internal coherence, but this view differs in several ways from other views bearing on emotion. At least two differences appear to be important.

One concerns dimensionality of affect. Some theories (though not all) treat affects as aligned along dimensions, as does ours. As outlined above, we argue that affect relating to approach has the potential to be either positive or negative and that affect relating to avoidance has the potential to be either positive or negative. This view differs from most other dimensional models of affect.

The idea that eagerness, excitement, and elation relate to approach and that fear and anxiety relate to avoidance is widely accepted (Cacioppo, Gardner, & Berntson, 1999; Davidson, 1992, 1998; Depue & Collins, 1999; Gray, 1994a, 1994b; Watson, Wiese, Vaidya, & Tellegen, 1999). But on the opposite poles consensus breaks down. For example, Gray (e.g., 1990, 1994b) held that the inhibition (or avoidance) system is engaged by cues of punishment and also by cues of frustrative non-reward. It is thus linked to negative feelings pertaining to approach as well as avoidance. Similarly, he held that the approach system is engaged by cues of reward and cues of escape or avoidance of punishment. It thus is linked to positive feelings pertaining to avoidance as well as to approach.

That view, then, is one in which each system is responsible for affect of one and only one hedonic tone. That theory yields two unipolar affective dimensions (neutral to negative, and neutral to positive), each linked to the functioning of a separate behavioral system. A similar position has been taken by others (e.g., Cacioppo & Berntson, 1994; Cacioppo et al., 1999; Lang, Bradley, & Cuthbert, 1990; Watson et al., 1999). In that respect, our dimensional view is quite different from these.

Evidence of negative affects relating to approach

What kinds of evidence would favor one view over the other? Links from the approach system to negative affects would support our viewpoint, as would links from the avoidance system to positive affects. I focus here on approach and on affect that arises when the person is "doing poorly" in approach. I address only a few examples, but a substantial literature exists on the question (Carver & Harmon-Jones, 2009).

My studies have used an individual-differences strategy to examine the issue. In one case (Carver, 2004, Study 1), participants were led to believe that they could obtain a desired reward if they performed well on a task. There was no penalty for doing poorly – only a chance of reward for doing well. Participants had been pre-assessed on the sensitivity of their approach and avoidance systems (Carver & White, 1994). All received feedback that they had not done well, and they thus failed to obtain the reward. Reports of sadness and discouragement at that point related to pre-measured sensitivity of the approach system, but not to sensitivity of the avoidance system.

Another source of information on sadness is the literature on self-discrepancy theory. Many studies have shown that sadness relates uniquely (i.e., controlling for anxiety) to discrepancies between people's actual and ideal selves (see Higgins, 1987, 1996, for reviews). Ideals are qualities a person intrinsically desires: aspirations, hopes, positive wishes for the self. There is evidence that pursuing an ideal is an approach process (Higgins, 1996). Thus, this literature also suggests that sadness stems from a failure of approach.

There is also evidence linking the approach system to the negative affect of anger. Harmon-Jones and Allen (1998) studied individual differences in trait anger. Higher anger related to higher left frontal activity (and to lower right frontal activity). This suggests a link between anger and the approach system, because the approach system has been linked to activation of the left pre-frontal cortex (e.g., Davidson, 1992). Later, Harmon-Jones and Sigelman (2001) induced anger in some persons but not in others, then examined cortical activity. They found elevations in left frontal activity, suggesting again that anger relates to greater engagement of the approach system.

Further evidence comes from research (Carver, 2004) in which people indicated the feelings they experienced in response to hypothetical events (Study 2) and after the destruction of the World Trade Center (Study 3). Participants had been pre-assessed on approach and avoidance sensitivities. Reports of anger related to pre-measured sensitivity of the approach system, whereas reports of anxiety related instead to sensitivity of the avoidance system.

A good deal of other evidence from a variety of sources, using divergent methodologies, makes a similar case regarding anger (reviewed by Carver & Harmon-Jones, 2009). Anger seems to relate to the approach system.

Need for a conceptual mechanism

This issue matters because it appears to have implications for the attempt to identify a conceptual mechanism underlying creation of affect. Theories positing unipolar dimensions seem to assume that greater activation of a system translates directly to more affect of that valence (or greater potential for affect of that valence). If the approach system relates instead both to positive and to negative feelings, this direct transformation of system activation to affect is not tenable.

A conceptual mechanism is needed that naturally addresses both positive and negative feelings within the approach function (and, separately, the avoidance function). One such mechanism was described earlier. There may be others, but this one has advantages. For example, its mechanism fits nicely with the fact that feelings occur continuously throughout the attempt to reach an incentive, not just at the point of its attainment. Indeed, feelings rise, wane, and change valence, as progress varies from time to time along the way forward.

Divergent functions of anger and depression

The last section described evidence linking approach to both sadness and anger. Yet sadness and anger are quite different experiences. How do they relate to each other? Anger and sadness are both potential consequences of doing poorly at approach, but which of them emerges as dominant is presumed to be at least partly a function of how poorly this approach is going and thus whether the reward seems attainable or not (see also Rolls, 1999).

In theory, inadequate movement forward (or no movement, or going backward) initially gives rise to frustration, irritation, and anger (Figure 1.1). These feelings (or the mechanism underlying them) engage effort more completely, to overcome obstacles and enhance current progress. If the situation is one in which more effort (or better effort) can improve progress, progress goes up, and the incentive may be attained.

Sometimes, however, continued efforts do not produce adequate movement forward. Indeed, if the situation involves loss, movement forward is precluded, because the incentive is out of reach. When failure seems – or is – assured, there are feelings of sadness, depression, despondency, grief, and hopelessness (cf. Finlay-Jones & Brown, 1981). Behaviorally, the person tends to disengage from – give up on – further effort toward the incentive (Klinger, 1975; Lewis, Sullivan, Ramsay, & Allessandri, 1992; Mikulincer, 1988; Wortman & Brehm, 1975).

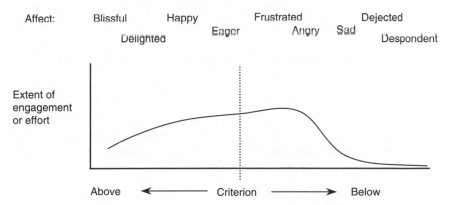

Figure 1.1 Hypothesized approach-related affects as a function of doing well versus doing poorly compared to a criterion velocity. A second (vertical) dimension indicates the degree of behavioral engagement posited to be associated with affects at different degrees of departure from neutral. Adapted from C. S. Carver, Negative affects deriving from the behavioral approach system. *Emotion*, 2004, *4*, 3–22.

Thus there is a bifurcation in the behavioral responses to inadequate movement forward. In some cases the response is continued, or even enhanced, in a struggle to make headway. In other cases the response is disengagement. Both have adaptive properties. In the first situation – when the person falls behind, but the goal is not seen as lost – feelings of frustration and anger can be adaptive because the struggle fosters goal attainment. In the second situation, when effort is futile, reducing effort can be adaptive (Carver & Scheier, 2003; Wrosch, Scheier, Miller, Schulz, & Carver, 2003). It conserves energy rather than waste it in pursuit of the unattainable (Nesse, 2000). If reducing effort also helps diminish commitment to the goal (Klinger, 1975), it eventually readies the person to take up other incentives in place of the unachieved one.

This bifurcation also makes an important point about the Carver and Scheier (1998) view. That view is dimensional in the sense of being predicated on a dimension of variability in system functioning (from very well to very poorly); however, the affects themselves do not form a simple linear dimension (i.e., depressed affect is not a more intense state of frustration or anger). The affects may be thought of as nonlinear consequences of linear variation in system functioning.

Priority management in behavior

One more aspect of this viewpoint deserves at least brief attention. This view has an additional counterintuitive implication, which pertains to positive feelings. Positive feelings occur when progress is greater than needed (or expected). If affect reflects the error signal in a feedback loop, however, affect is a signal to adjust rate – whether the affect is positive or negative. If affect is part of a self-regulating system, a consequence of positive affect should be to permit rate to slow, such that it returns to the criterion level. A behavioral consequence of this principle is that people should pull back a little on the effort exerted toward that goal – that is, should "coast" a little. An experiential consequence is that positive feelings do not persist for very long.

There is not much evidence on this idea. To test it, a study must assess coasting with respect to the same goal as underlies the affect. Many studies have created positive affect in one context and assessed its influence on another task. However, that does not test this question. Suggestive evidence has been reported by Mizruchi (1991) and by Louro, Pieters, and Zeelenberg (2007), but the issue remains relatively open.

Coasting and multiple goals

Why would a process that limits positive feelings – indeed, dampens them – be built in? One interpretation begins with the fact that people have multiple simultaneous goals (Carver, 2003; Carver & Scheier, 1998; Frijda, 1994). Given multiple goals, people generally do not optimize on any one goal, but rather "satisfice" (Simon, 1953) – do a good enough job on each to deal with it satisfactorily.

A tendency to coast would virtually define satisficing on that goal – that is, reduction in effort prevents one from attaining the best possible outcome on that goal. A tendency to coast would also foster satisficing on a broader set of goals. That is, if progress in one domain yields a tendency to coast there, it would be easy to shift to another domain, at little or no cost. This would help to ensure satisfactory goal attainment in the other domain and ultimately across multiple domains.

This line of argument begins to imply positive feelings in a broad function within the organism, which deserves much further consideration: shifting from one goal to another as focal in behavior (Dreisbach & Goschke, 2004; Shallice, 1978). This critical phenomenon is often disregarded. Many goals are pursued simultaneously, but only one can have top priority at a given moment. People need to shift flexibly among goals.

Many years ago, Simon (1967) addressed the problem of priority management as follows: at any given moment, most of people's goals are largely beyond their awareness. Only the one with the highest priority has full access to consciousness. Sometimes events occur during the pursuit of that top-priority goal that create problems for another, lower-priority goal. Indeed, the mere passing of time can create a problem for the second goal. If the second goal is also important, an emerging problem considering its attainment needs to be registered and taken into account. If the situation seriously threatens the second goal, some mechanism is needed for changing priorities, so that the second goal replaces the first one as focal.

Simon (1967) proposed that emotions are calls for re-prioritization. He suggested that emotion arising with respect to a goal that is out of awareness eventually causes people to interrupt their behavior and give that goal a higher priority than it had previously. The stronger the emotion, the stronger is the claim being made that the unattended goal should have higher priority than the presently focal goal. The affect is what pulls the out-of-awareness into awareness.

Simon's analysis applies readily to negative feelings, but by strong implication it deals only with negative feelings. However, there is another way in which priority ordering can shift: The goal that is currently in focus can *relinquish its place*. Positive feelings may foster priority change by reducing the priority of the goal to which the feeling pertains. Positive feelings in approach (happiness, joy) indicate that an incentive is being attained. If it is fully attained, effort can cease; if it is not yet attained, the affect signals that one could temporarily put this goal aside because one is doing so well (Carver, 2003).

If a focal goal diminishes in priority, what follows? It depends partly on what is waiting in the wings, but partly also on whether the context has changed in any important way while one was busy with the focal goal. That is, opportunities for incentives sometimes appear unexpectedly, and people put aside their plans to take advantage of them (Hayes-Roth & Hayes-Roth,

1979; Payton, 1990). It seems reasonable that people with positive affect should be more prone to shift goals at this point if something else needs fixing or doing (a goal that is next in line) or if an unanticipated opportunity for gain has appeared.

Sometimes the next item in line is of fairly high priority in its own right, and sometimes the situation has changed and a new goal has emerged for consideration. At other times, on the other hand, neither of these conditions exists. In that case, no change would occur, because the downgrade in priority of the focal goal does not make it lower than the priorities of the alternatives. Positive affect does not *require* a change in direction. It simply sets the stage for such a change to be more likely. Indirect support for this general line of reasoning is reviewed elsewhere (Carver, 2003).

Concluding comment

This chapter described basic principles of one control-process view of the self-regulation of behavior and affect. The description was by no means exhaustive. As but one example, there was no mention of self-control and the processes involved in overriding impulses. Such processes clearly are important to the fuller understanding of self-regulation (Baumeister & Vohs, 2004; Carver, Johnson, & Joormann, 2008). Nonetheless, I hope the picture sketched here will seem useful in thinking about these topics, and that psychologists of the future will be prompted to seriously consider how self-regulatory functions that appear throughout nature pertain to both action and emotion.

References

Baumeister, R. F., & Vohs, K. D. (Eds.). (2004). *Handbook of self-regulation: Research, theory, and applications*. New York: Guilford Press.

Beer, R. D. (1995). A dynamical systems perspective on agent–environment interaction. *Artificial Intelligence, 72*, 173–215.

Berridge, K. C. (2004). Motivation concepts in behavioral neuroscience. *Physiology and Behavior, 81*, 179–209.

Brendl, C. M., & Higgins, E. T. (1996). Principles of judging valence: What makes events positive or negative? *Advances in Experimental Social Psychology, 28*, 95–160.

Cacioppo, J. T., & Berntson, G. G. (1994). Relationship between attitudes and evaluative space: A critical review, with emphasis on the separability of positive and negative substrates. *Psychological Bulletin, 115*, 401–423.

Cacioppo, J. T., Gardner, W. L., & Berntson, G. G. (1999). The affect system has parallel and integrative processing components: Form follows function. *Journal of Personality and Social Psychology, 76*, 839–855.

Carver, C. S. (2001). Affect and the functional bases of behavior: On the dimensional structure of affective experience. *Personality and Social Psychology Review, 5*, 345–356.

Carver, C. S. (2003). Pleasure as a sign you can attend to something else: Placing positive feelings within a general model of affect. *Cognition and Emotion, 17,* 241–261.

Carver, C. S. (2004). Negative affects deriving from the behavioral approach system. *Emotion, 4,* 3–22.

Carver, C. S., & Harmon-Jones, E. (2009). Anger is an approach-related affect: Evidence and implications. *Psychological Bulletin, 135,* 183–204.

Carver, C. S., Johnson, S. L., & Joormann, J. (2008). Serotonergic function, two-mode models of self-regulation, and vulnerability to depression: What depression has in common with impulsive aggression. *Psychological Bulletin, 134,* 912–943.

Carver, C. S., Lawrence, J. W., & Scheier, M. F. (1999). Self-discrepancies and affect: Incorporating the role of feared selves. *Personality and Social Psychology Bulletin, 25,* 783–792.

Carver, C. S., & Scheier, M. F. (1981). *Attention and self-regulation: A control-theory approach to human behavior.* New York: Springer-Verlag.

Carver, C. S., & Scheier, M. F. (1990). Origins and functions of positive and negative affect: A control-process view. *Psychological Review, 97,* 19–35.

Carver, C. S., & Scheier, M. F. (1998). *On the self-regulation of behavior.* New York: Cambridge University Press.

Carver, C. S., & Scheier, M. F. (2000). Scaling back goals and recalibration of the affect system are processes in normal adaptive self-regulation: Understanding "response shift" phenomena. *Social Science & Medicine, 50,* 1715–1722.

Carver, C. S., & Scheier, M. F. (2002). Control processes and self-organization as complementary principles underlying behavior. *Personality and Social Psychology Review, 6,* 304–315.

Carver, C. S., & Scheier, M. F. (2003). Three human strengths. In L. G. Aspinwall & U. M. Staudinger (Eds.), *A psychology of human strengths: Fundamental questions and future directions for a positive psychology* (pp. 87–102). Washington, DC: American Psychological Association.

Carver, C. S., & White, T. L. (1994). Behavioral inhibition, behavioral activation, and affective responses to impending reward and punishment: The BIS/BAS scales. *Journal of Personality and Social Psychology, 67,* 319–333.

Clark, R. N. (1996). *Control system dynamics.* New York: Cambridge University Press.

Clore, G. C. (1994). Why emotions are felt. In P. Ekman & R. J. Davidson (Eds.), *The nature of emotion: Fundamental questions* (pp. 103–111). New York: Oxford University Press.

Davidson, R. J. (1992). Anterior cerebral asymmetry and the nature of emotion. *Brain and Cognition, 20,* 125–151.

Davidson, R. J. (1998). Affective style and affective disorders: Perspectives from affective neuroscience. *Cognition and Emotion, 12,* 307–330.

Depue, R. A., & Collins, P. F. (1999). Neurobiology of the structure of personality: Dopamine, facilitation of incentive motivation, and extraversion. *Behavioral and Brain Sciences, 22,* 491–517.

Dreisbach, G., & Goschke, T. (2004). How positive affect modulates cognitive control: Reduced perseveration at the cost of increased distractibility. *Journal of Experimental Psychology: Learning, Memory, and Cognition, 30,* 343–353.

Finlay-Jones, R., & Brown, G. W. (1981). Types of stressful life event and the onset of anxiety and depressive disorders. *Psychological Medicine, 11,* 803–815.

Frijda, N. H. (1988). The laws of emotion. *American Psychologist, 43*, 349–358.

Frijda, N. H. (1994). Emotions are functional, most of the time. In P. Ekman & R. J. Davidson (Eds.), *The nature of emotion: Fundamental questions* (pp. 112–126). New York: Oxford University Press.

Gray, J. A. (1990). Brain systems that mediate both emotion and cognition. *Cognition and Emotion, 4*, 269–288.

Gray, J. A. (1994a). Personality dimensions and emotion systems. In P. Ekman & R. J. Davidson (Eds.), *The nature of emotion: Fundamental questions* (pp. 329–331). New York: Oxford University Press.

Gray, J. A. (1994b). Three fundamental emotion systems. In P. Ekman, & R. J. Davidson (Eds.), *The nature of emotion: Fundamental questions* (pp. 243–247). New York: Oxford University Press.

Harmon-Jones, E., & Allen, J. J. B. (1998). Anger and frontal brain activity: Asymmetry consistent with approach motivation despite negative affective valence. *Journal of Personality and Social Psychology, 74*, 1310–1316.

Harmon-Jones, E., & Sigelman, J. D. (2001). State anger and prefrontal brain activity: Evidence that insult-related relative left-prefrontal activation is associated with experienced anger and aggression. *Journal of Personality and Social Psychology, 80*, 797–803.

Hayes-Roth, B., & Hayes-Roth, F. (1979). A cognitive model of planning. *Cognitive Science, 3*, 275–310.

Higgins, E. T. (1987). Self-discrepancy: A theory relating self and affect. *Psychological Review, 94*, 319–340.

Higgins, E. T. (1996). Ideals, oughts, and regulatory focus: Affect and motivation from distinct pains and pleasures. In P. M. Gollwitzer & J. A. Bargh (Eds.), *The psychology of action: Linking cognition and motivation to behavior* (pp. 91–114). New York: Guilford Press.

Hsee, C. K., & Abelson, R. P. (1991). Velocity relation: Satisfaction as a function of the first derivative of outcome over time. *Journal of Personality and Social Psychology, 60*, 341–347.

Klinger, E. (1975). Consequences of commitment to and disengagement from incentives. *Psychological Review, 82*, 1–25.

Lang, P. J., Bradley, M. M., & Cuthbert, B. N. (1990). Emotion, attention, and the startle reflex. *Psychological Review, 97*, 377–395.

Lewis, M., Sullivan, M. W., Ramsay, D. S., & Allessandri, S. M. (1992). Individual differences in anger and sad expressions during extinction: Antecedents and consequences. *Infant Behavior and Development, 15*, 443–452.

Louro, M. J., Pieters, R., & Zeelenberg, M. (2007). Dynamics of multiple-goal pursuit. *Journal of Personality and Social Psychology, 93*, 174–193.

Mikulincer, M. (1988). Reactance and helplessness following exposure to unsolvable problems: The effects of attributional style. *Journal of Personality and Social Psychology, 54*, 679–686.

Miller, G. A., Galanter, E., & Pribram, K. H. (1960). *Plans and the structure of behavior*. New York: Holt, Rinehart, & Winston.

Mizruchi, M. S. (1991). Urgency, motivation, and group performance: The effect of prior success on current success among professional basketball teams. *Social Psychology Quarterly, 54*, 181–189.

Nesse, R. M. (2000). Is depression an adaptation? *Archives of General Psychiatry, 57*, 14–20.

Ogilvie, D. M. (1987). The undesired self: A neglected variable in personality research. *Journal of Personality and Social Psychology*, *52*, 379–385.

Ortony, A., Clore, G. L., & Collins, A. (1988). *The cognitive structure of emotions*. New York: Cambridge University Press.

Payton, D. W. (1990). Internalized plans: A representation for action resources. In P. Maes (Ed.), *Designing autonomous agents: Theory and practice from biology to engineering and back* (pp. 89–103). Cambridge, MA: MIT Press.

Powers, W. T. (1973). *Behavior: The control of perception*. Chicago: Aldine.

Rolls, E. T. (1999). *The brain and emotion*. Oxford, UK: Oxford University Press.

Shallice, T. (1978). The dominant action system: An information-processing approach to consciousness. In K. S. Pope & J. L. Singer (Eds.), *The stream of consciousness: Scientific investigations into the flow of human experience* (pp. 117–157). New York: Wiley.

Simon, H. A. (1953). *Models of man*. New York: Wiley.

Simon, H. A. (1967). Motivational and emotional controls of cognition. *Psychological Review*, *74*, 29–39.

Toates, F. (2006). A model of the hierarchy of behaviour, cognition, and consciousness. *Consciousness and Cognition: An International Journal*, *15*, 75–118.

Vallacher, R. R., & Wegner, D. M. (1987). What do people think they're doing? Action identification and human behavior. *Psychological Review*, *94*, 3–15.

Watson, D., Wiese, D., Vaidya, J., & Tellegen, A. (1999). The two general activation systems of affect: Structural findings, evolutionary considerations, and psychobiological evidence. *Journal of Personality and Social Psychology*, *76*, 820–838.

Wortman, C. B., & Brehm, J. W. (1975). Responses to uncontrollable outcomes: An integration of reactance theory and the learned helplessness model. In L. Berkowitz (Ed.), *Advances in experimental social psychology* (Vol. 8, pp. 277–336). New York: Academic Press.

Wrosch, C., Scheier, M. F., Miller, G. E., Schulz, R., & Carver, C. S. (2003). Adaptive self-regulation of unattainable goals: Goal disengagement, goal re-engagement, and subjective well-being. *Personality and Social Psychology Bulletin*, *29*, 1494–1508.

2 The psychology of dieting and overweight

Testing a goal conflict model of the self-regulation of eating

Wolfgang Stroebe, Esther K. Papies, and Henk Aarts

The last three decades have witnessed a dramatic increase in the prevalence of overweight and obesity in most countries. For example, since 1980 obesity rates have doubled in the United States (Ogden, Carroll, McDowell, Tabak, & Flegal, 2006) and nearly tripled in Great Britain (Rennie & Jebb, 2005). At the same time, obesity rates have also been increasing in many developing countries, motivating the World Health Organization to speak of a global epidemic (WHO, 2000). This is a matter of grave concern, not only because individuals who are overweight or obese are the target of prejudice and discrimination (e.g., Brownell, Puhl, Schwartz, & Rudd, 2005), but also because obesity is associated with an increased risk of morbidity and mortality (McGee, 2005; Stroebe, 2008).

From homeostatic to hedonic theories of eating

The question why some people become overweight or even obese whereas others are able to keep their weight within the normal range has interested psychologists for many decades (e.g., Bruch, 1961; Herman & Polivy, 1984; Kaplan & Kaplan, 1957; Schachter, 1971). Since there is consensus that weight is homeostatically regulated, most psychological theories have answered this question by suggesting a disturbance or breakdown of homeostatic control. It is widely accepted that individuals who are overweight or obese have lost the ability to recognize the internal hunger and satiety signals that are part of homeostatic regulation and respond instead to cues that are unrelated to the physiological needs of their body. For example, externality theory (e.g., Schachter, 1971) assumes that exposure to food-relevant external stimuli (e.g., the presence of tasty food; dinnertime) triggers eating in overweight and obese individuals, while psychosomatic theory (e.g., Bruch, 1961) suggests that overweight and obese individuals are unable to distinguish hunger cues from other states of bodily arousal (e.g., strong emotions). Finally, the boundary model of eating (Herman & Polivy, 1984) argues that individuals with weight problems are often chronic dieters (i.e., restrained eaters) who regulate their food intake according to self-set rules of maximal calorie intake (diet boundary) and who, as a result of their chronic dieting, have lost the ability to recognize bodily hunger and satiety cues. Since the cognitive regulation of eating requires a great deal of cognitive resources, their eating control breaks down when they are distracted by strong emotions or when they are de-motivated as a result of having transgressed their diet boundary.

There can be no doubt that food intake and body weight are to some extent homeostatically controlled and that hormonal and neural signals are critical in the regulation of food intake (e.g., Woods, Schwartz, Baskin, & Seeley, 2000). What is increasingly questioned, however, is the importance of homeostatic regulation for the development of overweight and obesity (Lowe & Butryn, 2007; Pinel, Assanand, & Lehman, 2000; Stroebe, 2000, 2002, 2008). As Pinel and colleagues argued, people in food-rich environments rarely experience energy deficits, but they eat because of the pleasure they expect to derive from food. Along similar lines, Lowe and Butryn suggested a distinction between homeostatic hunger (resulting from a prolonged absence of food intake) and hedonic hunger (determined by the availability of palatable food in people's environment). According to Lowe and Butryn, people experience weight problems if their eating is overly influenced by hedonic rather than homeostatic hunger.

By emphasizing the importance of hedonic eating or eating enjoyment as a determinant of overweight and obesity, these theorists have advanced our understanding of eating regulation among individuals with weight problems. However, they fail to address the question why hedonic hunger or eating enjoyment comes to dominate the regulation of food intake of individuals with weight problems, and how it succeeds in derailing homeostatic regulation and undermining people's motivation to diet. To address these questions, my colleagues and I have developed (and empirically tested) a goal conflict theory of eating that is described in the following section (Papies, Stroebe, & Aarts, 2007, 2008a, 2008b, 2008c; Stroebe, 2008; Stroebe, Mensink, Aarts, Schut, & Kruglanski, 2008a; Stroebe, Papies, & Aarts, 2008b).

Why dieters fail: A theory of hedonic eating

Body weight is strongly determined by genetic factors (e.g., Maes, Neale, & Eaves, 1997). It is therefore plausible to assume that most people who are overweight or obese have a genetic disposition towards weight gain (Bouchard & Rankinen, 2008; Lowe & Kral, 2006). Although this does not alter the fact that ultimately overweight is due to an imbalance of energy input and energy output (i.e., too much food and too little exercise), such a genetic disposition increases the likelihood for an imbalance to arise. Once people have gained substantial amounts of weight and become overweight or even obese, they typically go on weight loss diets in an attempt to shed some of their weight (Serdula et al., 1999). These diets can be successful in the short run and may result in considerable weight loss. However, the majority of individuals regain the lost weight within three to five years (Mann et al., 2007). As a result, these individuals are likely to become chronic dieters (i.e., restrained eaters). The question to be addressed in the remainder of this chapter is why chronic dieters so often fail in their attempt at weight control.

Restrained eating and the breakdown of eating control

According to the goal conflict model of eating, the difficulty of restrained eaters in resisting the attraction of palatable food is due to a conflict between the goals of eating enjoyment and of weight control (Stroebe, 2002, 2008; Stroebe et al., 2008a). Restrained eaters like the pleasure of enjoying palatable food, but at the same time they also want to control their weight (i.e., lose weight or at least not gain it). Unless one loves grilled fish or salads, these two goals are incompatible. Chronic dieters therefore try to shield their weight control goal by avoiding thinking about palatable food. Unfortunately, at least from a dieting perspective, most of us live in food-rich environments, where we are surrounded by cues signalling or symbolizing palatable food. Such cues are likely to prime the goal of eating enjoyment and increase its cognitive accessibility. Once the goal of eating enjoyment has become the focal goal, it inhibits the (incompatible) goal of eating control. This is the reason why we might go to a restaurant with the firm intention of eating only a salad but, after having studied a menu (listing many of our favourite dishes), find ourselves ordering several courses, including dessert. In terms of our conflict model, the menu primed our goal of eating enjoyment up to the point where the goal of eating control became inhibited.

We suggest that restrained eaters' problems in eating regulation might begin with the fact that they are more sensitive to the hedonic properties of food. Due to this increased hedonic sensitivity, the perception of palatable food triggers in restrained eaters a hedonic orientation towards food. As the goal of eating the attractive food remains highly accessible, restrained eaters' cognitive processes will be geared towards pursuing this goal, and, importantly, conflicting goal representations will be inhibited (Aarts, Custers, & Holland, 2007). Since eating enjoyment and eating control are incompatible goals, increasing the accessibility of eating enjoyment should inhibit access to the mental representation of the goal of eating control (Shah, Friedman, & Kruglanski, 2002; Aarts et al., 2007). We tested this hypothesis in a study in which we subliminally primed restrained and unrestrained eaters (measured with the Concern for Dieting subscale of the Restraint Scale; Heatherton, Herman, Polivy, King, & McGree, 1988) either with words reflecting attractive food or with adjectives such as "delicious" or "tasty". Both primes should trigger the goal of eating enjoyment. In a control condition, we used neutral primes (i.e., words unrelated to food). Since each word was presented for only 23 ms on a computer monitor, participants could not consciously process the word. The accessibility of eating control concepts was assessed with a lexical decision task. With this task, participants are presented with either a word or a letter string and have to decide as fast as possible whether the target stimulus is a word. There is empirical evidence that the time taken to recognize a concept reflects the cognitive accessibility of this concept (e.g., Neely, 1991). Thus, we recognize words faster if they are at the top of our minds, compared to unfamiliar and rarely thought-about words. Consistent with predictions, priming with eating-enjoyment words (but not with neutral words) significantly increased the time it took restrained eaters to recognize the dieting words used as existing words (see Figure 2.1). Eating-enjoyment primes had no effect on reaction times of unrestrained eaters.

But why should palatable food items have greater attraction for restrained than for unrestrained eaters? Since the difference does not appear to be due to differences in attitudes towards palatable food (e.g., Roefs, Herman, MacLeod, Smulders, & Jansen, 2005), we reasoned that restrained eaters' difficulty in resisting palatable food could be due to the way in which they represent food items. The work on delay of gratification of Mischel and colleagues (Metcalfe & Mischel, 1999; Mischel & Ayduk, 2004; Mischel, Shoda, & Rodriguez, 1989) suggests that individuals who focus on the "hot" or hedonic features of food items, immediately thinking how the food would taste and how delicious the eating experience would be, have greater

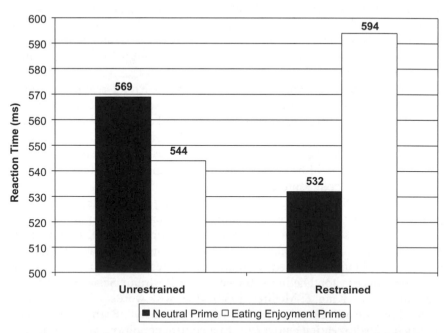

Figure 2.1 Mean reaction time to diet targets of restrained and unrestrained eaters primed with eating-enjoyment (palatable food words) or neutral words. From Stroebe et al., Why dieters fail: Testing the goal conflict model of eating. *Journal of Experimental Social Psychology*, 2008, *44*, 26–36.

difficulties in delaying consumption than do individuals who use a "cool" informational representation of the food.

Indirect support for the assumption that restrained eaters are more likely than unrestrained eaters to focus on the hedonic aspects of palatable food items comes from studies of physiological and affective reactions to the perception of food. The presence or even the smell of palatable food induces more salivation in restrained than in unrestrained eaters (e.g., Brunstrom, Yates, & Witcomb, 2004; LeGeoff & Spigelman, 1987; Tepper, 1992). Furthermore, exposure to palatable food cues elicits stronger cravings in restrained eaters (Fedoroff, Polivy, & Herman, 1997). To assess the presumed difference in the cognitive representation of palatable food items more directly, we conducted a study in which we used the probe recognition task of McKoon and Ratcliff (1986), which allows one to assess the spontaneous activation of concepts during text comprehension (Papies et al., 2007). Restrained and unrestrained eaters were presented with a number of behaviour descriptions, some of which described an actor eating some palatable food. Each behaviour description was immediately followed by a probe word, and participants had to decide as quickly as possible whether the probe word was part of that sentence. With critical trials the probe word could be inferred from a sentence without actually being part of it. If reading the sentence activates the probe word, participants should take slightly longer to decide that the probe word is not part of the sentence. Thus, if restrained eaters who read the sentence "Jim eats a piece of apple cake" immediately think how delicious this cake would taste, they should take slightly longer to decide that the probe word "delicious" was not part of the sentence than would unrestrained eaters reading the same sentence. On sentences that had nothing to do with eating, restrained and unrestrained eaters should not differ in their response times. The findings of our study supported these assumptions. These findings were replicated in a second study, in which activation of concepts during text comprehension was measured with a lexical decision task.

The work of Mischel and colleagues (see Mischel & Ayduk, 2004) points at a second process that contributes to individuals' difficulties in resisting the temptation – namely, attention allocation. Thus, the difficulty of restrained eaters in resisting the temptation of palatable food might be aggravated by the fact that once this food has triggered hedonic thoughts, restrained eaters find it difficult to withdraw their attention from the palatable food item. To test this assumption, we used the probe identification task of MacLeod, Mathews, and Tata (1986). Participants were presented with word pairs on a computer screen. The critical word pairs were food words paired with office-related (neutral) words. After a brief presentation, both words disappeared, and a probe stimulus (arrow) appeared in the location of one of the two words. Participants were asked to use two clearly marked computer keys to indicate as fast as possible whether the arrow pointed up or down. If palatable food attracts the attention of restrained eaters, these individuals should be able to respond more quickly when the probe appeared in the position of the food word rather than the office word. Our results supported this hypothesis, and the effect was moderated by the perceived palatability of the food items. However, the effect could only be demonstrated under conditions where hedonic thoughts had been triggered beforehand with a priming task. Furthermore, it could be interrupted by subsequently (subliminally) priming restrained eaters with dieting words and thus, presumably, re-establishing the dieting goal (Papies et al., 2008a).

Thus, according to our goal conflict model, the breakdown of the eating control of restrained eaters is due to a sequential process: Exposure to palatable food triggers hedonic thoughts in restrained eaters, which result in the allocation of selective attention to these food items and the inhibition of dieting thoughts. Thus, unless they are reminded of their dieting goal, they find it very difficult to withdraw their attention from the palatable food and to resist the temptation to eat the food.

Can restrained eaters be successful in controlling their eating?

Although the moderate correlations between eating restraint and body mass index would allow for the possibility that some restrained eaters are successful in controlling their weight, such an assumption would be alien to the research tradition on restrained eating. After all, restrained eaters have been considered individuals who are characterized by their lapses rather than by their success in eating control (Heatherton et al., 1988). However, a few years ago Fishbach, Friedman, and Kruglanski (2003) suggested that with repeated and successful attempts at self-control in a given domain, an individual might form facilitative associative links between a specific temptation and the overriding goal with which it interferes. For these individuals, the activation of a temptation, even if it occurred without their awareness, might suffice to activate the higher order goal.

Fishbach and colleagues tested this hypothesis in a study in which they measured the importance of dieting and perceived success in dieting with newly constructed self-report scales. Otherwise the study was similar to that of Stroebe et al. (2008a). In support of their predictions, Fishbach et al. (2003) found an interaction between perceived success in dieting and importance of dieting for individuals who were subliminally primed with tempting food words. The more successful participants for whom dieting was important perceived themselves in their attempts at weight control, the faster they were in recognizing dieting words.

Although the Fishbach et al. (2003) study differs somewhat in design and measures from our own study, their findings suggest that our results might only hold for unsuccessful restrained eaters. In order to test this assumption, we replicated the Stroebe et al. study (2008a), but added the Fishbach et al. measure of dieting success (Papies et al., 2008b). With an interaction between eating restraint and dieting success in the conditions with palatable food primes, our findings were consistent with expectations: in replication of our previous results, eating-enjoyment primes inhibited the dieting goal in unsuccessful restrained eaters in the lexical decision task. However, replicating the findings of Fishbach et al. (2003), the opposite pattern emerged for successful restrained eaters: for them, eating-enjoyment primes increased the accessibility of the dieting words.

Critics of social cognition studies might wonder whether a few milliseconds difference in the recognition of dieting words should be considered proof that these self-declared successful restrained eaters are really successful in controlling their weight. To provide further empirical evidence for this assumption, we therefore correlated the success measure with the body mass index (BMI: an index of body weight corrected by height) of our participants. The resulting correlation was significant and negative (−.48): The higher individuals rated themselves on the Fishbach et al. (2003) measure of dieting success, the lower was their BMI (Papies et al., 2008b).

We pursued this issue further in a study in which participants were asked to indicate the strength of their intention to abstain from eating five calorific but exceedingly palatable food items during the following two weeks. When these participants (who did not expect to be contacted again) were asked two weeks later how often they had eaten any of these food items, an interesting pattern emerged. For unrestrained eaters, there was only a main effect of intention on the self-reported frequency of having eaten these food items: The more they intended not to eat them, the less they actually did. The success measure did not predict eating. However, for restrained eaters, a significant Success by Restraint interaction emerged, with intention predicting abstention from eating the forbidden food for successful but not for unsuccessful restrained eaters.

The study of successful restrained eating is obviously in its early stages, and our findings need replication. However, these findings are also rather promising. If we could find out how successful restrained eaters managed to become successful, we should be able to develop intervention strategies that would enable researchers to train unsuccessful restrained eaters to become successful.

Conclusions

With obesity rates increasing at a dramatic rate in most developed and even some developing countries, there is great need for effective programmes of prevention and intervention. Since the development of such programmes is guided or at least informed by our theories of weight regulation, validation of these theories has changed from being merely a theoretical issue to becoming of major practical importance. It is therefore unfortunate that almost all psychological theories of dieting, overweight, and obesity are based on the assumption that weight problems are due to some malfunction in homeostatic feedback. Although there has been increasing criticism of such homeostatic models (e.g., Lowe & Butryn, 2007; Lowe & Levine, 2005; Pinel et al., 2000), eating research is still theoretically dominated by the boundary model of Herman and Polivy (1984), which assumes a malfunction in bodily feedback.

In contrast, the goal conflict model of eating attributes the difficulty of restrained eaters in regulating their food intake to a conflict between two incompatible goals – namely, the goal of weight control and eating enjoyment rather than an inability to recognize bodily cues of hunger and satiation. Weight control is normally the dominant goal, and restrained eaters can go for a long time without ever thinking about eating enjoyment. However, food-rich environments are replete with stimuli that symbolize or signal palatable food, and restrained eaters are highly sensitive to such stimulation. Continued exposure to these food primes should increase the accessibility of the eating-enjoyment goal to such an extent that, at least in unsuccessful restrained eaters, it gains dominance over the goal of weight control. In contrast, in successful restrained eaters, continued exposure to palatable food stimuli, rather than inhibiting dieting thoughts, should increase the accessibility of the dieting goal.

According to Popper (1968), a new theory should replace an older one, if, in addition to accounting for all the findings that were previously explained by the older theory, it can also explain results that are inconsistent with the older theory. It would go beyond the scope of this chapter to demonstrate how our model can account for all the findings accumulated in empirical tests of the boundary model of eating (see Stroebe, 2008 for such a discussion). But, to give one example, we would argue that the preload (e.g., milkshakes; Herman & Mack, 1975) used in studies testing this theory acted as eating-enjoyment primes for restrained eaters. Thus, the subsequent overeating of ice cream by restrained eaters was motivated by a hedonic orientation induced by the tasty milkshakes, rather than by the awareness of having broken their diet rules. This assumption can not only account for all the results of preload studies (for a review, see Stroebe, 2008), it can also explain findings inconsistent with that theory: namely, that even the smell of a tasty preload induced overeating (Jansen & van den Hout, 1991). Since smelling tasty food can hardly be construed as a breach of dietary rules, these findings are inconsistent with the boundary model. Finally, this assumption can also account for the finding that exposing participants to pizza smells before a taste test of various pizzas induced overeating in restrained but not in unrestrained eaters (Fedoroff et al., 1997). We would therefore argue that the goal conflict model offers a more plausible explanation than the boundary model for the failure of restrained eaters to control their weight.

References

Aarts, H., Custers, R., & Holland, R. W. (2007). The nonconscious cessation of goal pursuit: When goals and negative affect are coactivated. *Journal of Personality and Social Psychology*, *92*, 165–178.

Bouchard, C., & Rankinen, T. (2008). Genetics of human obesity: Exciting advances and new opportunities. In K. Clement & T. I. A. Sorensen (Eds.), *Obesity, genetics, and postgenomics* (pp. 549–562). New York: Informa Healthcare.

Brownell, K. D., Puhl, R. M., Schwartz, M. B., & Rudd, L. (Eds.). (2005). *Weight bias: Nature, consequences and remedies.* New York: Guilford Press.

Bruch, H. (1961). The transformation of oral impulses in eating disorders: A conceptual approach. *Psychiatric Quarterly, 35,* 458–481.

Brunstrom, J. M., Yates, H. M., & Witcomb, G. L. (2004). Dietary restraint and heightened reactivity to food. *Physiology and Behavior, 81,* 85–90.

Fedoroff, I. C., Polivy, J., & Herman, C. P. (1997). The effect of pre-exposure to food cues on the eating behavior of restrained and unrestrained eaters. *Appetite, 28,* 33–47.

Fishbach, A., Friedman, R. S., & Kruglanski, A. W. (2003). Leading us not unto temptation: Momentary allurements elicit overriding goal activation. *Journal of Personality and Social Psychology, 84,* 296–309.

Heatherton, T. F., Herman, C. P., Polivy, J., King, G. A., & McGree, S. T. (1988). The (mis)measurement of restraint. An analysis of conceptual and psychometric issues. *Journal of Abnormal Psychology, 97,* 19–28.

Herman, C. P., & Mack, D. (1975). Restrained and unrestrained eating. *Journal of Personality, 43,* 647–660.

Herman, C. P., & Polivy, J. (1984). A boundary model for the regulation of eating. In J. A. Stunkard & E. Stellar (Eds.), *Eating and its disorders* (pp. 141–156). New York: Raven Press.

Jansen, A., & van den Hout, M. (1991). On being led into temptation: "Counterregulation" of dieters after smelling a "preload". *Addictive Behaviors, 16,* 247–253.

Kaplan, H. I., & Kaplan, H. S. (1957). The psychosomatic concept of obesity. *Journal of Mental and Nervous Disease, 125,* 181–201.

LeGeoff, D. B., & Spigelman, M. N. (1987). Salivary response to olfactory food stimuli as a function of dietary restraint and body weight. *Appetite, 8,* 29–35.

Lowe, M. R., & Butryn, M. L. (2007). Hedonic hunger: A new dimension of appetite? *Physiology & Behavior, 91,* 432–439.

Lowe, M. R., & Kral, T. V. E. (2006). Stress-induced eating in restrained eaters may not be caused by stress or restraint. *Appetite, 46,* 16–21.

Lowe, M. R., & Levine, A. S. (2005). Eating motives and the controversy over dieting: Eating less than needed versus less than wanted. *Obesity Research, 13,* 797–806.

MacLeod, C., Mathews, A., & Tata, P. (1986). Attentional bias in emotional disorders. *Journal of Abnormal Psychology, 95,* 15–20.

Maes, H. H. M., Neale, M. C., & Eaves, L. J. (1997). Genetic and environmental factors in relative body weight and human adiposity. *Behavior Genetics, 27,* 325–351.

Mann, T. A., Tomiyama, J., Westling, E., Lew, A.-M., Samuels, B., & Chatman, J. (2007). Medicare's search for effective obesity treatments: Diets are not the answer. *American Psychologist, 62,* 15–20.

McGee, D. L. (2005). Body mass index and mortality: A meta-analysis based on person-level data from twenty-six observational studies. *Annals of Epidemiology, 15,* 87–97.

McKoon, G., & Ratcliff, R. (1986). Inferences about predictable events. *Journal of Experimental Psychology: Learning, Memory, and Cognition, 12,* 82–91.

Metcalfe, J., & Mischel, W. (1999). A hot/cool-system analysis of delay of gratification: Dynamics of willpower. *Psychological Review, 106,* 3–19.

Mischel, W., & Ayduk, O. (2004). Willpower in a cognitive-affective processing system: The dynamics of delay of gratification. In R. F. Baumeister & K. D. Vohs (Eds.), *Handbook of self-regulation* (pp. 99–129). New York: Guilford Press.

Mischel, W., Shoda, Y., & Rodriguez, M. L. (1989). Delay of gratification in children. *Science*, *244*, 933–938.

Neely, J. (1991). Semantic priming effects in visual word recognition: A selective review of current findings and theories. In D. Besner & G. W. Humpreys (Eds.), *Basic processes in reading: Visual word recognition* (pp. 264–336). Hillsdale, NJ: Lawrence Erlbaum Associates, Inc.

Ogden, C. L., Carroll, M. D., Curtin, L. R., McDowell, M. A., Tabak, C. J., & Flegal, K. M. (2006). Prevalence of overweight and obesity in the United States, 1999–2004. *Journal of the American Medical Association*, *295*, 1549–1555.

Papies, E. K., Stroebe, W., & Aarts, H. (2007). Pleasure in the mind: Restrained eating and spontaneous hedonic thoughts about food. *Journal of Experimental Social Psychology*, *43*, 810–817.

Papies, E. K., Stroebe, W., & Aarts, H. (2008a). The allure of forbidden food: On the role of attention in self-regulation. *Journal of Experimental Social Psychology*, *44*, 1283–1292.

Papies, E. K., Stroebe, W., & Aarts, H. (2008b). Healthy cognition: Processes of self-regulatory success in restrained eating. *Personality and Social Psychology Bulletin*, *34*, 1290–1300.

Papies, E. K., Stroebe, W., & Aarts, H. (2008c). Understanding dieting: A social cognitive analysis of hedonic processes in self-regulation. *European Review of Social Psychology*, *19*, 339–383.

Pinel, J. P. J., Assanand, S., & Lehman, D. R. (2000). Hunger, eating, and ill health. *American Psychologist*, *55*, 1105–1116.

Popper, K. R. (1968). *The logic of scientific discovery*. London: Hutchinson.

Rennie, K. L., & Jebb, S. A. (2005). National prevalence of obesity: Prevalence of obesity in Great Britain, *Obesity Reviews*, *6*, 11–12.

Roefs, A., Herman, C. P., MacLeod, C. M., Smulders, F. T. Y., & Jansen, A. (2005). At first sight: How do restrained eaters evaluate high-fat palatable foods? *Appetite*, *44*, 103–114.

Schachter, S. (1971). *Emotion, obesity, and crime*. New York: Academic Press.

Serdula, M. K., Mokdad, A. H., Williamson, D. F., Galuska, D. A., Mendlein, J. M., & Heath, G. W. (1999). Prevalence of attempting weight loss and strategies for controlling weight. *Journal of the American Medical Association*, *282*, 1353–1358.

Shah, J. Y., Friedman, R., & Kruglanski, A. W. (2002). Forgetting all else: On the antecedents and consequences of goal shielding. *Journal of Personality and Social Psychology*, *83*, 1261–1280.

Stroebe, W. (2000). *Social psychology and health* (2nd ed.). Buckingham, UK: Open University Press.

Stroebe, W. (2002). Übergewicht als Schicksal? Die kognitive Steuerung des Essverhaltens [Obesity as fate? Cognitive regulation of eating]. *Psychologische Rundschau*, *53*, 14–22.

Stroebe, W. (2008). *Dieting, overweight, and obesity: Self-regulation in a food-rich environment*. Washington, DC: American Psychological Association.

Stroebe, W., Mensink, W., Aarts, H., Schut, H., & Kruglanski, A. W. (2008a). Why dieters fail: Testing the goal conflict model of eating. *Journal of Experimental Social Psychology*, *44*, 26–36.

Stroebe, W., Papies, E., & Aarts, H. (2008b). From homeostatic to hedonic theories of eating: Self-regulatory failure in food-rich environments. *Applied Psychology: Health and Well-Being, 57*, 172–193.

Tepper, B. J. (1992). Dietary restraint and responsiveness to sensory-based food cues as measured by cephalic phase salivation and sensory specific satiety. *Psychopharmacology, 157*, 67–74.

WHO (2000). *Obesity: Preventing and managing the global epidemic*. Geneva: World Health Organization.

Woods, S. C., Schwartz, M. W., Baskin, D. G., & Seeley, R. J. (2000). Food intake and the regulation of body weight. *Annual Review of Psychology, 51*, 255–277.

3 Psychotherapists at work

Exploring the construction of clinical inferences

Adela Leibovich de Duarte

Introduction

Clinicians in their clinical work attempt to answer questions regarding what is happening to the patient, why it is happening, and how to help cure or alleviate the patient's suffering. It is clear that how a psychotherapist thinks and makes decisions about patients will influence both the treatment process and the outcome.

The pioneering research carried out by Strupp (1960), the subject of his book *Psychotherapists in Action*, along with that of Seitz (1966) on the problem of consensus in psychoanalysis, are landmarks in the bibliography on the contribution of the psychotherapist to the psychotherapeutic situation. Very little empirical research has been done since then, however.

Our usual way of knowing and explaining new facts and situations that deviate from customary patterns rests on inferences for which we have recourse to our previous knowledge and experience.

Theories provide us with cognitive parameters for perceiving, apprehending, and organizing the evidence we gather, offering categories that mediate and facilitate the organization and comprehension of the clinical data and strategies that guide our clinical inferences, which, in turn, make interpretations possible. In addition to these explicit theories, we are, according to Sandler (1983), the bearers of "implicit private theories" that relate directly to our clinical work.

As researchers in the area of human perception point out (Bruner & Tagiuri, 1954), each person has his or her own implicit theory of personality on the basis of which inferences about other people are made involving, consciously or not, stereotypes, schemas, and conventions. We act on the basis of self-fulfilling biases inevitably present in the way we organize, code, and decode data, as well as the way in which we select evidence, attribute to ourselves and others characteristics and intentions, and accept causes and explanations for our own and others' behavior.

In order to establish the context of mutual understanding that makes analytical work possible, analyst and patient must not only share a common language; they also need to have a similar "common sense epistemology"

(Paicheler, 1984). A non-systematic knowledge of the world, which makes it possible to comprehend and predict the behavior of others, is enriched and perfected by systematic and specific kinds of acquired knowledge.

Shared and private codes are present in the dialogue between psychotherapist and patient. In this linguistic context, the therapist attempts to gain access to his or her patient's ideolect or private code of unconscious meaning.

One problem with inferential activity is that, by definition and to a greater or lesser degree, it ignores alternative possibilities, evidence, and references. We constantly have recourse to prior experience when seeking acceptable solutions for situations confronting us in our daily life and when solving new problems. Our way of thinking may influence therapy outcome.

The problem of the kinds of data on which we base our hunches, convictions, and technical-clinical criteria is not a simple one.

Some empirical research has been done regarding the construction of clinical judgments in psychodiagnosis (Garb, 1998; Holt, 1978, 1988; Turk & Salovey, 1988). The effect of cognitive biases on clinical judgment has been examined in a series of studies carried out precisely in the area of psychodiagnosis. Much of the current interest in the cognitive activity in clinical judging was awakened by Chapman's research on "illusory correlations" (Chapman & Chapman, 1967, 1969). Later research found that the phenomenon of illusory correlation is highly resistant to change.

Comprehending the other person's discourse presupposes a complex inferential function that takes us "beyond the information given," as Bruner wrote in 1957. Processing the information we receive when reading a text or listening to others – in our particular case, a patient's discourse – takes place within the context of our preconceived knowledge: that is, there is more information involved in the process than the information that is extracted from the discourse itself (Leibovich de Duarte, 2006).

A psychoanalyst will be looking for latent contents or hidden meanings while listening to a patient, while a cognitive therapist will be seeking out the patient's dysfunctional assumptions.

Clinical inferences are formulations based on specific knowledge elaborated by an expert concerning another person. Descriptively, a clinical inference can be taken to mean the "abductive" process by which clinical data is transformed and new meaning is added to pre-existing information.

Interpreting clinical material is not a question of mechanically applying rules; instead, it depends, above all, on the therapist's skill in discovering, integrating, and explaining significant cues.

In the clinical situation, with the help of our theoretical resources and techniques, we, psychotherapists, attempt to understand and account for the reasons behind our patients' conduct. In order to produce our clinical inferences, we are attentive to the reiteration, convergence, and/or the appearance of new information. In the course of this process we may either confirm our conjectures or go off on a new tack.

We, clinicians, have different ways available for decoding clinical material and discovering consistencies and inconsistencies. There is no doubt that mechanically applying rules for selecting and organizing clues is not the way to formulate a clinical inference. What is required, above all, is a psychotherapist adept at discerning and integrating significant indicators. And this involves not only a theoretical framework and clinical experience, but also personality and cognitive style characteristics.

The patient's verbal and non-verbal messages, in which certain indicators and clues become significant, are complemented by our own impressions and reflections. We construct provisional structures that function as parameters for organizing the accumulating data and for elaborating hypotheses. Certain data only become relevant clues later on, while other details appear that shed new light on prior information. There is also information that adds to and enriches the comprehension of the patient's material, as well as information that will become irrelevant and fade away. Our inferences and hypotheses do not always take the form of verbal interpretations directed at the patient.

The way we listen to a patient is influenced not only by personal characteristics but also strongly by our theoretical orientation, how strongly we adhere to it, and how much clinical experience we have.

Several studies, some empirical and some theoretical–clinical, have approached the problem of the incidence of the therapist's theoretical perspective in our clinical work (Bernardi, 1989, 1993; Bouchard, Lecomte, Carbonneau, & Lalonde, 1987; Fine & Fine, 1990; Hamilton, 1996; Holt, 1988; Hunter, 1994; Jones & Poulos, 1993; Leibovich de Duarte, 2000; Leibovich de Duarte, Duhalde, Huerín, Rutsztein, & Torricelli, 2001; Pulver, 1987; Roussos, Boffi Lissin, & Leibovich de Duarte, 2007; Roussos & Leibovich de Duarte, 2002; Schlesinger, 1994; Stuart Ablon & Jones, 1998). Empirical research on the level of experience in psychotherapy shows that it plays an important role in clinical work (Garb, 1989, 1998; Henry, Strupp, Butler, Butler, & Binder, 1993; Leibovich de Duarte, 1996a, 1996b; Leibovich de Duarte, Huerín, Roussos, Rutsztein, & Torricelli, 2002).

As it is an exploratory study, we did not generate any specific hypotheses, except that we expected to find differences based on theoretical orientation and level of experience. Therefore, these are the research questions posed for this study.

Some research questions

- How do different psychotherapists think about clinical materials?
- Do differences in clinical experience play a significant role in the way in which psychotherapists deal with clinical data and construct clinical inferences?
- Do differences in theoretical orientation play a significant role in the way in which psychotherapists deal with clinical data and construct clinical inferences?

- Are there significant differences among psychotherapists in the time elapsed between the beginning of the session and the moment when they formulate their first inference about the patient?

Method

Participants

The subjects were 28 Spanish-speaking psychotherapists who volunteered to participate: 14 psychoanalysts and 14 cognitive psychotherapists, seven of whom in each group had more than 20 years of clinical experience and seven of whom had less than 10 years.[1]

Materials

1   A tape-recorded first session of a psychotherapeutic treatment (the same for all participants)
2   Verbatim transcript of that tape-recorded first session
3   Semi-structured interview designed to elicit additional information about the participant's inferential processes
4   Theoretical Framework List
5   Psychotherapeutic Goals List
6   Other Technical Resources Questionnaire.

Selection of the stimulus session

The session presented to the participant therapists[2] met several criteria: (1) it was a first session; (2) during the session the treating therapist's interventions were few and did not include any theoretical terminology; (3) it was not a session with a severely disturbed patient.

The main difference between the stimulus session and a standard clinical situation was that the latter included direct observation of the patient, thus making possible the inclusion of non-verbal data that might or might not have corresponded to the patient's words. In this case, the fact that the patient was a young woman could be inferred from her voice. However, except for not seeing the patient – in this case a woman whose youth could be inferred from the inflections of her voice – the psychoanalysts who participated in this study and the treating psychotherapist shared the same information about the patient.

In order to see whether the treating therapist's orientation was recognizable, the selected session was first presented to two cognitive therapists and two psychoanalysts who did not participate in this study. After listening to the session, they were asked to identify the treating therapist's theoretical framework and to indicate whether the session offered enough information for formulating clinical inferences. They stated that they could not determine the treating therapist's theoretical framework and considered the material to contain enough information to work with.

Procedures

Each participating therapist was seen individually by a member of the research team and asked to:

1 listen to the tape-recorded initial session;
2 simultaneously read the verbatim transcript;
3 underline what he or she considers relevant;
4 stop the tape every time she/he has a hunch, a clue, a clinical inference, a comment, or a possible intervention and formulates it to the research team member, who recorded it on a separate tape recorder;
5 answer questions during the semi-structured interview;
6 offer any further reflections and comments elicited by the experience;
7 complete the Theoretical Framework List, the Psychotherapeutic Goals List, and the Other Technical Resources Questionnaire. The analysis and results obtained with the following three instruments are not given in this presentation.

Results

Underlined text

While listening to the tape-recorded session, the psychotherapists were asked to underline relevant parts of the session on the verbatim transcript. The text underlined by cognitive therapists and psychoanalysts was compared. A correlation was run to assess the resemblance of the underlined texts (Kendall tau = 0.49, $p < .001$). The result reflects that there were no large significant differences. The Kendall tau shows a significant level of agreement between the two groups.

Figures 3.1 and 3.2 show the correspondence between those segments of the transcript considered relevant by psychoanalysts and cognitive psychotherapists.

Underlined topics

Next we ascertained which topics were underlined most frequently by both junior and senior cognitive therapists and psychoanalysts. In order to do this, the following set of categories was drawn up by the research team: family in general; mother; father; boyfriend; other interpersonal relations; self-image; dependency–autonomy; suffering; discomfort; need to control; depression; and therapy.

The texts were submitted to an independent group of judges made up of

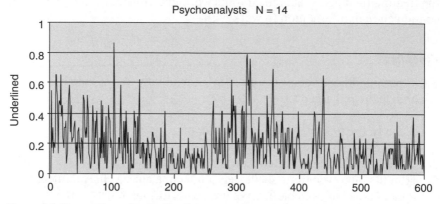

Figure 3.1 Proportion of underlined text.

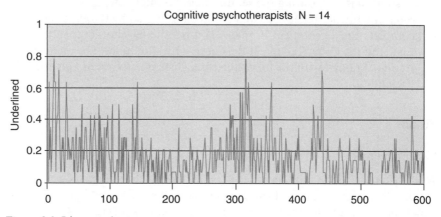

Figure 3.2 Line number.

three psychologists who classified the underlined portions of the session transcript according to the above categories. In cases of disagreement, a consensus was reached. The items most frequently underlined by all four groups of psychotherapists were those referring to interpersonal relations and mother, followed by self-image and boyfriend.

Time elapsed before the formulation of the first clinical inference

The time elapsed before the formulation of the first clinical inference measured chronometrically was very brief. Out of a total number of 28 psychotherapists, 22 required less than 6 minutes to produce their first clinical inference, regardless of theoretical framework and/or level of experience; of those 22, 13 produced their first clinical inference in 2 minutes or less. The extremes were 15 minutes required by one psychotherapist and 30 seconds by three others.

A discrepancy was found between the time that elapsed before producing the first inference, as chronometrically measured, and the *subjective perception* of that period of time. Six psychoanalysts, both senior and junior, and four cognitive therapists who needed less than three minutes to express their inferences were asked later on about their subjective impression regarding the time that had elapsed before their first inference. All of them answered that the time elapsed was no less than 10 minutes (see Figure 3.3).

Clinical inferences classified by content

The content of the clinical inferences was classified by three independent judges according to a set of categories drawn up by the research team. The categories were similar to those used in Leibovich de Duarte et al. (2001). (See Exhibit 3.1.)

The independent judges, three psychologists, had been trained to perform this task. A Kappa (Cohen) was calculated to get interjudge reliability ($K = .88$).

Clinical inferences were classified according to whether they were simple or combined. An inference was classified as simple when only one category from the list was involved, while a combined clinical inference involved two or more (see Figure 3.4).

Table 3.1 shows the number of simple and combined inferences formulated by the participant psychotherapists. Out of a total number of 462 clinical inferences, 265 were simple inferences and 197 were combined. Senior psychoanalysts formulated 88 simple inferences and 96 combined ones, while senior cognitive psychotherapists formulated 72 simple inferences and 49

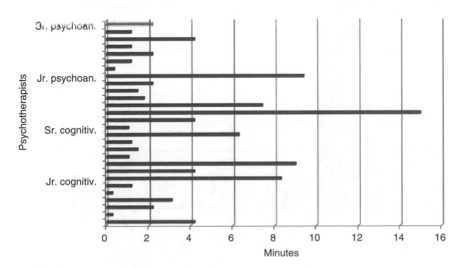

Figure 3.3 Time elapsed before first inference.

Interpersonal: the way the patient relates to peers, family, and others.

Intrapsychic: the patient's internal world: fantasies, unconscious contents, ego and superego aspects. Includes: conflicts, defenses, affects, ways of dealing with anxiety, personal constructs, belief systems.

Family situation: the structure and functioning of the patient's family.
- *Etiological*: the origin or cause of the patient's current psychic situation.
- *Diagnostic*: assigns the patient's symptoms to a diagnostic category.
- *Prognostic*: related to the future course or possible efficacy of the treatment, and the consequences of not starting treatment. Includes the patient's expectations or fantasies of being cured.
- *Viability of treatment*: considerations related to the possibility of initiating psychotherapy and to the existence or not of a request for treatment.

Developmental: related to the stage in the vital cycle through which the patient is currently going. Explains present or past situations within this framework.
- *Psychotherapeutic relationship*: the role in which the patient places the therapist, references to transference and/or countertransference.

Exhibit 3.1 Categories of content of clinical inferences.

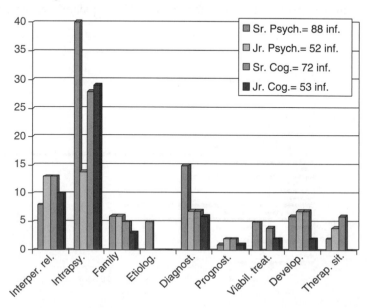

Figure 3.4 Content of clinical inferences.

Table 3.1 Number of formulated inferences

	Psychoanalysts		Cognitive psychotherapists		
	Senior (n = 7)	Junior (n = 7)	Senior (n = 7)	Junior (n = 7)	Total (n = 28)
Simple inferences	88	52	72	53	265
Combined inferences	96	27	49	25	197
Total	184	79	121	78	462

combined ones. Junior psychoanalysts formulated 52 simple inferences and 27 combined ones, while junior cognitive psychotherapists formulated 53 simple and 25 combined ones.

A homogeneous pattern was not found in the total number of clinical inferences because of individual differences within each of the four groups of participating psychotherapists. However, there was a clear tendency on the part of senior psychoanalysts to produce more simple and combined clinical inferences; senior psychoanalysts produced a total of 184, while senior cognitive psychotherapists produced 121. The total number of simple and combined clinical inferences produced by junior psychoanalysts was 79, while junior cognitive psychotherapists produced 78.

As Table 3.1 shows, a difference exists within each theoretical framework between inferences made by senior psychoanalysts and cognitive psychotherapists and those made by the junior members of each group. However, the difference is greater between junior and senior psychoanalysts than between junior and senior cognitive psychotherapists.

Of the total, 42% were in the category "mental processes," 16% in "interpersonal relationships," and 13% in "diagnostic inferences"; the remaining 28% were irregularly distributed in the other six general categories. Out of a total of 197 combined clinical inferences, 96 were formulated by the senior psychoanalysts, almost double the 49 produced by the senior cognitive psychotherapists. The junior psychoanalyst and junior cognitive psychotherapist groups produced 27 and 25 combined clinical inferences, respectively. The general categories most referred to in their combined clinical inferences by the four groups of participating psychotherapists were: 55 in the "mental processes" and "interpersonal process" categories; 21 "mental processes" and "diagnostic inferences", and 17 "mental processes" and "family situation" aspects.

There were 17 combined clinical inferences that included the etiological category and one other. Of these, 16 were formulated by the two senior groups and only one by a junior psychoanalyst.

Results of the semi-structured interview

Participating psychoanalysts and cognitive psychotherapists made the following comments on their clinical inferences:

1   26 out of 28 considered that their clinical inferences were closely related to the data;
2   20 out of 28 indicated that recurrence of topics during the session was an important point of reference for their inferences;
3   23 out of 28 said that prior experience with other patients was relevant to their clinical inferences;
4   28 out of 28 indicated their confidence in their clinical inferences as three or higher on a five point Likert-type scale;
5   28 out of 28 considered that their theoretical framework strongly influenced the data they selected to base their clinical inference on and the interventions they suggested for the patient;
6   in spite of the fact that there were few prognostic considerations in the psychotherapists' clinical inferences (see Figure 3.2), 10 out of 14 senior psychotherapists thought that they had paid considerable attention not only to diagnostic but also to prognostic considerations.

Participating psychoanalysts and cognitive psychotherapists made the following comments on the patient's main problems:

1   24 out of 28 psychotherapists considered that the patient's problems revolved around her interpersonal relationships, expressed in different ways that ranged from vague: "Difficulty in interacting" (Senior Cognitive) to more specific: "Submission, demands and difficulty in overcoming them" (Senior Psychoanalyst);
2   16 out of 28 participating psychotherapists specified that the patient's problem was her relationship with her mother, expressed in different ways that ranged from vague: "relations with mother" (Senior Cognitive) to more specific: "Her battle to separate her mind from her mother's mind, identification with her mother" (Junior Psychoanalyst);
3   8 out of 14 cognitive therapists made reference to the question of dependence and autonomy, a subject that was not explicitly referred to by the psychoanalysts; the latter only mentioned this subject in terms of interpersonal conflict between the patient and her mother, while the cognitive psychotherapists posed it in terms of the construction of an autonomous identity: "The unfolding of the personal script, the development of autonomy" (Cognitive Senior) or "achievement of structures of autonomy" (Junior Cognitive).

Discussion

Psychoanalysts and cognitive psychotherapists tend to underline similar relevant material in the transcript of the patient's initial sessions. They select similar cues.

The short period of time that elapsed between the beginning of the session and the first inference produced by the therapist coincides with the results of the studies previously mentioned, which indicate the importance of the first minutes of an initial clinical interview.

Several studies show that clinicians tend to take very few minutes to arrive at a diagnostic decision in an initial psychiatric or psychological interview (Bourgeois & Rechoulet, 1992; Gauron & Dickinson, 1966, 1969; Helstone & van Zuuren, 1996; Kendell, 1973; Sandifer, Hordern, & Green, 1970). In this regard, Kendell states that professionals can reach accurate diagnoses, "even within the first two minutes" of a clinical interview. In a previous study that used the same stimulus session and whose subjects were Freudian and Lacanian psychoanalysts (Leibovich de Duarte et al., 2001), we obtained similar results; in another study using a different stimulus session we again obtained similar results.

We agree with Garb (1989, 1998), who refers to the fact that mental health professionals, as well as other people, make judgments quickly. This primacy effect "describes the clinical judgment process, but it does not demonstrate that clinicians make invalid judgments" (1998, p. 184).

Adherence to a particular theoretical school of thought was not reflected in the nature of the clues that psychotherapists selected, nor in differences in the quantity, complexity, or nature of the inferences made by psychoanalysts and cognitive therapists. But differences do appear when analyzing the different terminologies utilized according to the theoretical framework of the therapist.

A gap exists within each theoretical framework between the inferences made by seniors and those by juniors; the seniors make more simple, combined, and interpretative inferences than do the juniors. However, the gap is greater between junior and senior psychoanalysts than between junior and senior cognitive therapists. This greater difference can be explained by the nature of the two theoretical models involved as indicated and by how each is used by its practitioners. In the words of Stuart Ablon and Jones (1998): "the cognitive–behavioral therapists applied a good deal in the way of cognitive–behavioral techniques, but did not foster a psychodynamic process. The cognitive–behavioral treatments appeared to follow the cognitive–behavioral model closely. The psychodynamic treatments that were studied clearly included a more diverse set of interventions" (p. 80).

Expertise might account for the fact that senior psychotherapists produced more combined inferences, which, by relating different topics to each other, attempted to explain, relate, and integrate more aspects of the patient's problem into more elaborated clinical inferences. Junior psychotherapists produced inferences that were more limited in scope, less elaborated, and less integrated than their senior colleagues.

Eells and Lombart (2003) mention a "robust characteristic of experts identified by Glaser and Chi (1988): Experts see and represent problems in more abstract and meaningful conceptual categories than do novices, who tend to categorize problems according to more superficial properties. It is possible that the experts understand these patients and their problems better" (p. 200).

As we have seen, adherence to a particular theoretical framework was not reflected in the nature of the clues psychotherapists underlined; however, theoretical variations did appear in the way these clues were organized and explained in their clinical inferences. Differences emerged when the inferences were analyzed regarding the different kinds of specific theory jargon utilized by the psychotherapists. This means that their clinical inferences were different, basically based on their different theoretical framework.

An analysis of the answers to the semi-structured interview, which reflected what participating psychotherapists said they did, shows that their evaluation of their approach to the patient's material did not differ greatly, regardless of their years of experience.

Very few inferences made by participating therapists referred to prognostic aspects. This could be due to the fact that in a first interview it is more difficult to elaborate prognostic considerations regarding a patient than diagnostic ones.

There is a clear tendency to formulate inferences in terms of the patient's interpersonal relationships and mental processes in both simple and combined inferences. The foregoing holds true for both theoretical schools and both senior and junior therapists.

The general principles of the cognitive theoretical framework link the cognitive aspect with emotional and behavioral ones; it is through the cognitive aspect that cognitive therapists gain access to the patient's emotions and behavior. The fact that cognitive therapists include as many affective as cognitive aspects when formulating inference is not surprising, since cognitive psychotherapy assumes a close relationship between thought, emotions, and behavior. In cognitive psychotherapy how people perceive events is seen as influencing their emotions and behavior. For this therapeutic school feelings are determined not by the situation itself but by how the person interprets it. In other words, a person's feelings are associated with the way of thinking and interpreting a situation. It is not the situation itself that directly determines how the person feels (discomfort, for example) but, rather, how the person interprets the situation; thought acts as a filter for producing emotions.

It is in this sense that therapist #16 (SC) indicates that the patient "suffers from her view of things and not from the things themselves; she is to some degree aware that she is constructing this view of things."

Cognitive therapy is usually characterized as an active, directive, structured procedure of pre-established duration. Cognitive therapy focuses on the "here and now," emphasizing the patient's internal experiences like thoughts, feelings, desires, aspirations, and attitudes. The therapist should concentrate on identifying thoughts that are determined by dysfunctional beliefs. The presupposition is that modifying cognition will lead to changes in emotions and behavior, given the fact that a person's emotions and behavior are profoundly determined by how they structure their world.

Final considerations

Even though this was not a truly naturalistic study, I consider that its design comes very close to tapping the process used by clinicians in their everyday clinical work. I expect that this study will help us gain a better understanding of how psychotherapists elaborate their clinical inferences and contribute to make our work and expertise more accessible to others, mainly to young trainees.

Notes

1 The treating therapist was not part of the sample. The participant psychoanalysts and cognitive psychotherapists had received systematic training in Argentinian recognized institutions.
2 The tape-recorded psychotherapeutic session was used with the agreement of both the patient and the treating therapist.

References

Bernardi, R. (1989). The role of paradigmatic determinants in psychoanalytic understanding. *International Journal of Psychoanalysis, 70*, 341–357.

Bernardi, R. (1993). Discussion of "theory in vivo" by Dennis Duncan. *International Journal of Psychoanalysis, 74*, 1167–1173.

Bouchard, M. A., Lecomte, C., Carbonneau, H., & Lalonde, F. (1987). Inferential communications of expert psychoanalytically oriented, gestalt and behavior therapists. *Canadian Journal of Behavioural Science, 19*(3), 275–286.

Bourgeois, M., & Rechoulet, D. (1992). Los primeros minutos. Primer contacto y rapidez diagnóstica en psiquiatría [The first minutes: First contact and quick diagnosis in psychiatry]. In P. Pichot & W. Rein (Eds.), *El abordaje clínico en psiquiatría* (pp. 37–49). Buenos Aires, Argentina: Polemos, 1995.

Bruner, J. S. (1957). Going beyond the information given. In J. S. Bruner, E. Brunswik, L. Festinger, F. Heider, K. F. Meuenzinger, C. E. Osgood, & D. Rapaport, *Contemporary approaches to cognition: A report of a symposium at the University of Colorado, May 12–14, 1955* (pp. 41–69). Cambridge, MA: Harvard University Press.

Bruner, J. S., & Tagiuri, R. (1954). The perception of people. In G. Lindzey (Ed.), *Handbook of social psychology*. Cambridge, MA: Addison-Wesley.

Chapman, L., & Chapman, J. (1967). Genesis of popular erroneous psychodiagnostic observations. *Journal of Abnormal Psychology, 72*, 193–204.

Chapman, L., & Chapman, J. (1969). Illusory correlation as an obstacle to the use of valid psychodiagnostic signs. *Journal of Abnormal Psychology*, *74*, 271–280.

Eells, T. D., & Lombart, K. G. (2003). Case formulation and treatment concepts among novice, experienced, and expert cognitive–behavioral and psychodynamic therapists. *Psychotherapy Research*, *13*(2), 187–204.

Fine, S., & Fine, E. (1990). Four psychoanalytic perspectives: A study of differences in interpretative interventions. *Journal of the American Psychological Association*, *38*, 1017–1048.

Garb, H. (1989). Clinical judgment, clinical training, and professional experience. *Psychological Bulletin*, *105*(3), 387–396.

Garb, H. (1998). *Studying the clinician. Judgment research and psychological assessment*. Washington, DC: American Psychological Association.

Gauron, E. F., & Dickinson, J. K. (1966). Diagnostic decision making in psychiatry. *Archives of General Psychiatry*, *14*, 225–232.

Gauron, E. F., & Dickinson, J. K. (1969). The influence of seeing the patient first on diagnostic decision making in psychiatry. *American Journal of Psychiatry*, *126*(2), 199–205.

Glaser, R., & Chi, M. T. H. (1988). Overview. In M. T. H. Chi, R. Glaser, & M. J. Farr (Eds.), *The nature of expertise* (pp. 15–28). Hillsdale, NJ: Lawrence Erlbaum.

Hamilton, V. (1996). *The analyst's preconscious*. Hillsdale, NJ: Analytic Press.

Helstone, F., & van Zuuren, F. (1996). Clinical decision making in intake interviews for psychotherapy: A qualitative study. *British Journal of Medical Psychology*, *69*(3), 191–206.

Henry, W., Strupp, H., Butler, S., Butler, S. F., & Binder, J. L. (1993). Effects of training in time-limited dynamics psychotherapy: Mediators of therapist's responses to training. *Journal of Consulting and Clinical Psychology*, *61*, 441–447.

Holt, R. R. (1978). Clinical judgement as a disciplined inquiry. In *Methods in clinical psychology* (Vol. 2, pp. 38–54). New York: Plenum Press.

Holt, R. R. (1988). Judgment, inference and reasoning in clinical perspective. In D. Turk & P. Salovey (Eds.), *Reasoning, inference and judgment in clinical psychology*. New York: Free Press.

Hunter, V. (1994). *Psychoanalysts talk*. New York: Guilford Press.

Jones, E. E., & Poulos, S. M. (1993). Comparing the process in psychodynamic and cognitive–behavioral psychotherapy. *Journal of Consulting and Clinical Psychology*, *61*(2), 306–316.

Kendell, R. E. (1973). Psychiatric diagnoses: A study of how they are made. *British Journal of Psychiatry*, *122*, 437–445.

Leibovich de Duarte, A. (1996a). Diferencias individuales en el proceso inferencial clínico [Individual differences in the clinical inferential process]. *Anuario de Investigaciones*, *4*, 249–261 [Facultad de Psicología, UBA].

Leibovich de Duarte, A. (1996b). Variaciones entre psicoanalistas en el proceso inferencial clínico [Variations among psychoanalysts in the clinical inferential process]. *Investigaciones en psicología. Revista del Instituto de Investigaciones*, *1*(1), 27–38 [Facultad de Psicología, UBA].

Leibovich de Duarte, A. (2000). Más allá de la información dada: Cómo construimos nuestras inferencias clínicas ["Beyond the information giving": How do we construct our clinical inferences]. *Revista de la Sociedad Argentina de Psicoanálisis*, *3*, 97–114.

Leibovich de Duarte, A. (2006). Going beyond the information given: Constructing our clinical hypotheses. *Bulletin of the European Psychoanalytic Federation, 60* (online).

Leibovich de Duarte, A., Duhalde, C., Huerín, V., Rutsztein, G., & Torricelli, F. (2001). Acerca del proceso inferencial clínico en psicoanálisis [On the inferential clinical process]. *Vertex. Revista Argentina de Psiquiatría, 12*, 194–203.

Leibovich de Duarte, A., Huerín, V., Roussos, A., Rutsztein, G., & Torricelli, F. (2002). Empirical studies on clinical inference: Similarities and differences in the clinical work of psychotherapists with different theoretical approaches and levels of experience. In P. Fonagy (Ed.), *IPA: An open door review of outcome studies in psychoanalysis* (2nd revised edition, pp. 201–204). London: International Psychoanalytical Association.

Paichcler, H. (1984). La epistemología del sentido común: De la percepción al conocimiento del otro [The epistemology of common sense]. In S. Moscovici (Ed.), *Psicología social*. Buenos Aires, Argentina: Paidós, 1986.

Pulver, S. (1987). How theory shapes technique: Perspectives on a clinical study. *Psychoanalytic Inquiry, 7*(2), 141–299.

Roussos, A., Boffi Lissin, L., & Leibovich de Duarte, A. (2007). The importance of the theoretical framework in the formulation of clinical inferences in psychotherapy. A comparative study of clinical inferences of psychoanalysts and cognitive therapists using the Psychotherapy Q Sort. *Psychotherapy Research, 17*(5), 535–543.

Roussos, A., & Leibovich de Duarte, A. (2002). La incidencia de la Actividad Referencial en el proceso de formulaciones clínicas. La importancia del marco teórico en la formulación de las inferencias clínicas en psicoterapia [The incidence of Referential Activity in the process of formulating clinical inferences by psychotherapists with different theoretical frameworks]. *Intersubjetivo, 1*(4), 45–63.

Sandifer, M. G., Hordern, A., & Green, L. M. (1970). The psychiatric interview: The impact of the first three minutes. *American Journal of Psychiatry, 126*(7), 968–973.

Sandler, J. (1983). Reflections on some relations between psychoanalytic concepts and psychoanalytic practice. *International Journal of Psychoanalysis, 64*, 35–45.

Schlesinger, H. J. (1994). How the analyst listens: The pre-stages of interpretation. *International Journal of Psychoanalysis, 75*, 31–37.

Seitz, P. (1966). The consensus problem in psychoanalytic research. In L. Gottschalk & A. Auerbach (Eds.), *Methods of research in psychotherapy* (pp. 209–225). New York: Appleton-Century-Crofts.

Strupp, H. (1960). *Psychotherapists in action: Explorations of the therapist's contribution to the treatment process*. New York: Grune & Stratton.

Stuart Ablon, J., & Jones, E. (1998). How expert clinicians' prototypes of an ideal treatment correlate with outcome in psychodynamic and cognitive–behavioral therapy. *Psychotherapy Research, 8*(1), 71–83.

Turk, D., & Salovey, P. (Eds.). (1988). *Reasoning, inference and judgment in clinical psychology*. New York: Free Press.

4 Passions

What emotions really are

Nico H. Frijda

Phenomena

I will tell you what emotions really are.

I stole my title – that part of my title – from the philosopher Paul Griffiths (1997), who reacted with that against the very concept-oriented treatments of emotions in philosophy, and he was right. But I think his solutions were not right. Emotions are not innate behavior patterns, as he argued. Then what are they?

In a sense, the better answer is simple. "Emotions" is the plural of a word Descartes coined for them in 1632. And he used it besides other, more general and current words that had been used for ages. Those words were not invented by scientists. They were invented in everyday language because they were useful to denote phenomena that struck people in everyday interaction.

There are many things that may strike people in interaction, and in themselves. Scherer (1984, 2005) characterized emotions as "multicomponential phenomena," and not for nothing. One witnesses actions and reactions that include facial expressions as well as all sorts of other behaviors, including autonomic changes and professions of belief changes and of feelings. There is no component that is always there when several of the others are. People can feel grief without much autonomic arousal; they can be nasty without professing to feeling angry; they can show liking without feeling liking. All this is among the major findings in emotion research over the past few decades.

But four sets of phenomena appear to be common among these multicomponential complexes. These four sets of phenomena, I think, are what gave rise to the old concepts of *pathema* in Greek, *affectus* in Latin, *Leidenschaft* in German, and passion in French and English. These phenomena are not components among the ones just mentioned. They come on top of them. They are features of the *ensemble* of the components as manifest at any particular moment.

The four gross phenomena are these.

1   What we call emotions are responses that engage the entire person.

2   What we call emotions are responses that tend to take control over all functioning.
3   What we call emotions are responses by which the individual relates to the world or to objects, people, and events.
4   What we call emotions are responses that manifest engagement with objects or events and, in particular, engagements qualified by pleasure or displeasure.

I will explain.

First: the responses that we call emotions are responses by the entire person. That is, the responses engage a large number of processes that occur more or less simultaneously, that interact and sustain each other, together forming the action or reaction. They manifest a *synchronization* of component processes (Scherer, 2005), in that the components are tuned to each other. In a reaction called "fear," for instance, not only does the body move away, and bend so as to diminish its vulnerability. Respiration change also occurs: it supplies oxygen for flight. Autonomic activity is enhanced in support. Thoughts arise: "Away!" Attention is focused: "Away from there!" Perception is focused upon the threat and on what it may inflict.

Second: the response exerts what I call *control precedence*. The response as a whole, in its growth as well as in its execution, takes control over acting and attending. While doing so, it overrides other claims for action or attention, which tend to be neglected. The responses we call "emotions" often involve changes in control and changes in priorities for acting. That is in fact where the word passion comes from. They feel as states that one is overcome by: one is passive in their regard. In the past, such responses were interpreted as inspired by spirits or demons, or as sicknesses of the soul.

Third: There are responses that consist of *actions* that establish or modify a relationship between the person and some object. The actions are "about" something. They are "towards" or "away" from something, or they are "between" the person and that something else. A stance is taken towards the object. That is what all component processes together appear to contribute to. As a whole, one goes towards or away from that object. One is open for, or shuts off from. The actions are *to* or *for* or *with* some object, that may on occasion be oneself, as they are in self-love and self-loathing. The third striking aspect of many behaviors is that they manifest people's *engagement* with the world.

And, fourth, particularly striking is the phenomenon that often engagement seeks in some way or other to enhance or weaken the relationship to or the engagement with its object. It combines with people professing feelings of pleasure or displeasure.

Pleasure or displeasure is not an aspect of all engagement. Some engagement merely consists of taking an interest in what happens: watching, knowing, understanding, which can be manifest emotions like interest, surprise, wonder, curiosity, fascination: the non-hedonic emotions. Others are hedonically complex or unspecified: being moved, awe, and nostalgia are examples.

Passion

The aspects are more or less independent. But they often appear together. Together they give a clue to what binds them.

They define "passion": a motive state, with *control precedence* – a state that clamors for action, or on occasion for inaction, or induces the felt impulse for such action or inaction.

The word "passion" has many meanings. But one of these is this: a passion is a *motive state*. It is a state of striving to obtain or retain a particular end. The words "emotion" and "passion" have different implications. In Descartes' day, "*émotion*" meant something like "uproar," and he indeed borrowed the word to stress the uproar of bodily arousal (Rimé, 2005). The older word "passion," by contrast, emphasized the aspect of *striving* that pushes an individual forward or backward, or to remain motionless, as in frozen panic, that can be felt and seen in what others do.

"Emotions are passions": this is of course a rhetorical way of speaking, as both "emotion" and "passion" are just words. The point is this: the core process that underlies most of the phenomena that we call emotions is a motive state with control precedence that clamors for action to achieve or modify one's relation to some object – some person, some event, some issue, some activity, or the world as a whole.

This perspectives places action central in emotions: readiness for action, to relate or stop relating, or else to drop into hopeless apathy or disorganized confusion. This deviates from common alternative views of emotions: as private feelings that are sometimes betrayed by expressions, or as states of bodily upset, or as "body feelings" (Damasio, 2000), or as judgments (Nussbaum, 2001).

But private feelings consist largely of action impulses or action images. Expressions betray readiness for action. Body feelings reflect intentional states and urges that are "about something." And judgments as such neglect why and how these judgments feel so hot, and that they entail priority settings that interrupt other interests, overrule ongoing action, and often call for self-control.

Action readiness

Because of all that, I have called these passionate motive states "states of action readiness." They are states of readiness: of being set for establishing or changing one's relationship to the world or some object. They are not cognitions, not mere wishes, but states of being set for achieving or maintaining a particular relational aim: coming closer, avoiding, preventing interference, fusing with the object, submitting to it, and so forth, to mention some of its modes.

Action readiness occurs in different forms, each characterized by the kind of relation or relational change it aims at. The person who is afraid wants to be safe; the one who is angry wants an interference to stop or an offense to be retaliated; the one who is in love wants to be in close erotic contact. Or, better, one can turn it around: desire to be safe from threat is called fear; desire to forcefully stop interference is often called anger. And, as indicated, some states of action readiness involve action *un*readiness: loss of motivation, or total loss of interest – a motivational state of strength zero.

There are two sides to action readiness. One is their content: the type of relationship aimed at or striven after. Many states of action readiness can be described as *action tendencies*. Felt relational aims and overt behaviors implement action tendencies. Many emotion categories or labels are modeled around them. Self-report questionnaire research has found appreciable correlations between ratings of action tendencies and emotion labels (Frijda, Kuipers, & Terschure, 1989; Frijda, Markam, Sato, & Wiers, 1995) (see Table 4.1).

The other side of action readiness is the *engagement* with whatever the action readiness is about and the restraint or liberty in implementing that engagement. "Engagement" refers to the extent to which the individual's resources are or will be mobilized to shape his or her actions; "restraint and liberty" refers to the degree to which implementing action readiness is or is not controlled, inhibited, or held back. Variations in engagement I call activation modes. I repeat: the emotion names are given as hints or illustrations only. Activation modes constitute the huge variety of degrees of engagement and its flow over time, caught by descriptive terms like "enthusiast," "listless," "tense," "easygoing," "relaxed," "strained," "excited," or "driven." More than discrete emotions, they include emotional states that Stern (1985)

Table 4.1 Action readiness modes.

Attend	Amend
Interest, savor	Undo
Shut off	Hurt
Approach	Reactant
Withdraw	Broaden and build
Reject	Depend
Oppose	Action suspension
Disappear from view	Helpless
Be with	Relaxed
Fuse with	Tense
Dominate	Inhibited
Submit	Apathetic
Possess	Disinterest
Care for	Rest

Data derived from Frijda (2007).

called "vitality affects," and Damasio (2000) "background emotions." They are precisely what the term "vitality affects" says: manifestations of degree of engagement and its control. They are manifest in particular in the "prosody" of behavior and experience – that is, their course over time. Variations in amplitude, speed, variability, smoothness or angularity of transitions, and "fullness" (the degree to which the body participates in an action) (Frijda, 2007) can show emotional content of any sort of action and interaction, from grasping a cup of tea to a smile.

Table 4.1 may suggest that the variety of modes of action readiness is limited. With regard to action tendencies this is the case. Going towards something differs categorically from going against or rejecting something, and so forth. But within each mode there can be infinite variety, because of the implications of the action prepared or done. It may manifest greater or lesser "fullness": partial engagement, or, by contrast, engagement of one's entire body or entire person. That is, the scope of action readiness can vary widely. Take the action readiness for "being with." Being with: how? In order to be close? Or to be intimate? And if intimate, to what extent? How fully, and how naked? Or consider the urge for bodily intimacy. What is aimed for: kissing with the full mouth and tongue, and arms intertwining, or with the lips tenderly touching, and stroking with one's fingertips? Realize the emotional implications of either the one or the other: becoming immersed in desire for intimacy, or desiring to do it in such a fashion that space is left for the other's autonomy and it is being relished as such.

The preceding illustrates that states of action readiness do not indicate or prescribe a particular kind of action. They indicate a particular kind of *aim* or engagement, at some level of specification. Actions may differ. One can seek intimacy by talking and smiling or by kissing and stroking. One can seek to approach by walking, swimming, or ordering someone to come. Fear – that is, the urge to be safe from threat – may induce freezing, running away, hiding in a shelter or behind something, making oneself as inconspicuous as one can be. Behaviors induced by a given state of action readiness show *equifinality*. Equifinality of different behaviors shown in given circumstances is, in fact, the source of the very notion of action readiness: that which actions shown in a given situation have in common. Action readiness, rather than "emotion," is what one perceives at a glance from someone's facial expression: the person is seen to draw back, become strained and tight, and so forth (Frijda & Tcherkassof, 1997).

In view of this divergence between motive state and action, action readiness represents a psychological provision with a remarkable property: its adaptive flexibility. States of motivation can lead to choosing actions that are geared to details of circumstance: the only thing laid down is the aim to be reached. Upon a signal that announces danger, a rat may freeze, jump, run, or hide, depending on what the situation offers or allows. Moreover, it allows learning new actions that have been shown earlier to lead to the aim of action readiness. Flexibility is what passionate emotions developed for. It distinguishes emotions from reflexes.

Reflex-like emotions do exist. Some elementary responses to emotional events are rigid and stereotyped. Examples of this are the startle reflex, freezing, sensory disgust, elementary sexual responses like copulation in non-primate animals. They fit into a simpler and older system architecture that does not allow for motive states. Insects and reptiles show them. They remain in birds and mammals as an elementary part of their emotion repertoire.

Action readiness is not action. States of action readiness can, for a variety of reasons, remain covert – mere readiness, mere inner state, mere feeling.

In fact, on close scrutiny, emotional feelings (Davitz, 1969) are not "private" in all respects. They are not just *qualia*. They largely consist of felt urges toward the world, felt desires, thoughts that embody these, even emotions felt when alone. "I could kill him," "how kissable she is," "I see no way out whatsoever," or "Man delights me not, nor woman for that matter," as Hamlet expressed his sadness after his father's death. Emotional feelings are not just body feelings but the feelings of readiness for given sorts of relational action in relation to the world. Such felt action readiness also forms the substance of thinking about emotional events, of recalled emotions, imagined emotions, and empathy with what someone else is feeling. Only occasionally does such covert emotion crystallize into overt "affect bursts," as Scherer (1994) has labeled them.

Analyzing emotions in terms of states of action readiness makes certain theoretically baffling complexities of emotions transparent. Emotions do *not* consist of the emergence of standard response packages: of responses that include specific expressions and other behaviors, autonomic response patterns, feelings, and other components, as the basic emotions view has proposed (Ekman, 1999; Öhman & Mineka, 2001). No emotion, as defined by some emotion name, can be characterized by such a specific pattern of components. This has appeared to be an untenable hypothesis: such packages are not consistently found (Frijda, 1986; Scherer, 2005). Emotions are states of action readiness, of which the form is implemented in accordance with the actual situation. The optimal level of analysis of the emotional phenomena is at the level of states of action readiness. Modes of action readiness can plausibly be conceived as innate dispositions that may even be stable across species, and of which there may exist a relatively small number, of the order of the table just shown.

There is something lovely in this structure of emotion and emotional behavior. Emotions manifest themselves in behavior, but no piece of behavior indicates one and only one emotion, or one and only one mode of action readiness. Each behavior can serve more than one master – that is, more than one mode of action readiness. These latter all form part of a "hierarchical–heterarchical model" of motivation (Gallistel, 1980) that originated in twentieth-century ethology (Lorenz, Tinbergen, Kortlandt). States of action readiness command a hierarchy of submotives, action programs, and actions, but each action, action program, or subgoal can form part of several different hierarchies. We kiss our children and our lovers, our political associates, and those whom we may betray, if need be.

Processes of passion

Can we get a closer view of the processes that give rise to the phenomena of passion? Yes, we can.

First, action readiness itself: the concept of "action readiness" may appear a puzzling notion: orientation towards some future state, even in the case of unreflective and impulsive action. But the evidence is ample. Central representations of action to come, including its aim, direction, and intended action parameters like force, are evident from the contents and neural manifestations of imagined actions (Jeannerod, 1997). That action representations can occur in the absence of efferent motor innervation is evident from canonical neuron activity while viewing objects of manipulation (Rizzolatti, Fogassi, & Gallese, 2001), as well as from mirror neuron activity when viewing the actions of others.

The proximal mechanism of implicit goal orientation has also become clear, in the findings that gave rise to the so-called efferent copy model of goal-directed action developed by Von Holst and Mittelstaedt (1950). "Efferent copies" are representations of the expected feedback from the final stages of the action to come, or sensory settings that prepare for such feedback. They are produced at the very moment that an action is prepared, when an efferent copy is formed as expectancy of the sensation of the action involved, such as the sensation of an object in hand that guides grasping. In emotion, it is appraisal that generates the efferent copy. Action is guided by decreasing the discrepancy between current perception and the efferent copy.

"Current perception" is usually referred to, in analysis of emotions, as "appraisal"; I will turn to this briefly later. Different appraisals, even of the same events, cause different states of action readiness. A dangerous situation may be appraised as a threat that one may not be able to handle or as a challenge that one feels one can cope with. As Scherer (2004) pointed out, emotion appraisals directly match modes of action readiness, because the efferent copy that selects mode of action readiness stems from how the situation is appraised: as a threat that is close by, for instance, or as a challenge that is to be conquered, or a loss that should not be there, or a desired person who should be in one's arms. Action is guided by the perception of events that includes their character of "affordances" of appropriate possible actions, as suggested by Gibson (1979) and elaborated in the Theory of Event Coding (Hommel, Müsseler, Aschersleben, & Prinz, 2001). Action readiness follows from the appraised affordance: away from a threat, getting at an offender, arms around an attractive person. Action readiness aims at achieving a satisfaction condition, such that efferent copy and perception match.

With all this, something more can be said about what makes action readiness arise. Let us view the context in which emotions arise. Action readiness is called when an event is appraised as being relevant to the individual's concerns. It spells satisfaction or harm to one's goals or sensitivities. Such appraisal implies integration of information from all over the brain, as shown by widespread cerebral coordination, evident in EEG synchronization over large brain regions (Edelman & Tononi, 2000; M. R. Lewis & Todd, 2007; Varela, Thompson, & Rosch, 1991). In this integration, action readiness can plausibly be assigned the organizing role, so that the response becomes a response "by the entire person." All component processes collaborate in contributing to the rationale of the moment's action readiness, and in tuning how one relates to the given event and deals with it. The state of action readiness not only represents readiness for appropriate relational action; it also sets perceptual sensitivities. In fear, for instance, threat signals are detected more rapidly (Crombez, Eccleston, Bayens, & Eelen, 1998; MacLeod, Mathews, & Tata, 1986), and it restricts attention to those stimuli (Easterbrook, 1959). Readiness for forthcoming vigorous action in anticipation activates the autonomic nervous system (Obrist, 1981). Action readiness also activates anticipation of the possible consequences of prepared actions, as evident from regulation of emotion before response appears.

Insight is growing into the mechanisms of such widespread synchrony: those of neurotransmitter and neuropeptide activation, which show a distinct degree of emotion specificity. Some such neurohumors are carried by the bloodstream. Others are secreted by widely branching neurotransmitter systems. It has recently been demonstrated that others again – oxytocin notably – are carried by the extra-neural liquor in the cerebral ventricles and subarachnoidal space (Veening, de Jong, & Barendregt, 2010).

The nature of the dispositions underlying states of action readiness forms one of the major questions for emotion theory. What is it that allows them to emerge? Where do they come from?

One major hypothesis is that they come from biologically prepared dispositions that are activated by events as appraised. That hypothesis is plausible, first, because of the evolutionary continuity in several major kinds of emotion, when defined in terms of the evident relational function or aim of the behaviors linked to eliciting circumstances, and, second, because these major forms of emotion involve activation of circuits in evolutionary old subcortical systems, often referred to as the limbic system. Cruder emotions are retained under decortication as well as under prefrontal cortical damage (Bard, 1934; Damasio, 2000). An fMRI study found somewhat differential subcortical activations during recall of different emotions (Damasio et al., 2000). The limbic circuits found to be involved in emotions show considerable cross-species similarity (Panksepp, 1998).

Panksepp (1998) has advanced evidence for seven subcortical systems that each may correspond to a basic mode of emotional motivation or action readiness: for desire, for anger, for fear, for sorrow, for caring, for lust, and for joy or play. Other investigators have made related proposals (e.g., Damasio, 2000; Depue & Collins, 1999; Gray, 1987; LeDoux, 1996). The systems may or may not correspond to accepted emotion categories, but it seems certain that they are best considered motivational systems, linked on the one hand to sensitivities for particular event contingencies (such as threats) and, on the other hand, to relevant action hierarchies, and their control by prefrontal networks.

The evidence has so far not been sufficiently compelling to convince all investigators, however. Alternative hypotheses remain, such as an organizing role of innate relation-specific action dispositions and the neurotransmitters facilitating them, as well as ad hoc organization of modes of action readiness by individual environment contingencies such as reward opportunities, modes of social interaction, infants to care for, and the like.

Control precedence

Action readiness was passion's first element. Control precedence is the second. It is intuitively defined by the feeling of being overtaken by one's emotion, of attention being preempted by the event, of persistence after obstacles and interruptions, of neglect of risks and other costs.

The phenomena of control precedence in fact index the power or intensity of emotions, also subjectively, as seen in a study by Sonnemans and Frijda (1994). They asked each of a number of subjects to report on six recent emotion experiences. These were also asked to rate how intense the emotion was felt to have been, and they had to rate a number of more specific aspects of each emotion: the effects of the emotion on one's thinking, on one's beliefs regarding the objects or people involved, the felt strength and urgency of action readiness, the recurrence of the event in thought, the felt impact of the event on one's daily conduct of life, the felt bodily arousal, and the emotion's duration. The first five concern control precedence. Most of these ratings correlated significantly with felt emotion intensity. They accounted for about half of the variance of felt intensity ratings in a multiple regression analysis. The control precedence variables contributed to felt intensity independently from felt bodily arousal, which is generally the only variable used to measure emotional intensity. Experienced emotion intensity thus has relatively little to do with Damasio's (2000) somatic markers. It largely comes from the felt impact of the event on daily life and thought.

Control precedence, the push of passion, appears to result from the operation of a major biological mechanism: the midbrain dopamine system, which is fundamental in emotion. It appears implicated in its most fundamental dimension: interest, or engagement in the world. The system has been identified by various names: Reward System (e.g., Shizgal, 1999); Behavioral Activation System (Gray, 1982); Behavior Facilitation System (Depue & Collins, 1999); Seeking System (Panksepp, 1998); or Wanting System (Berridge, 1999, 2007). I call it "the System named Desire." Phasic bursts in dopamine

(DA) firing accompany attention shifts towards valued events; enduring DA increases sustain interest in these events (Leyton, 2009). When the system is blocked, effort to obtain formerly coveted food disappears while signs of liking the food remain (Berridge, 1999). Experiences of craving and urge tend to correlate with activation of part of the system and dopamine release (Panksepp, 2005). Such activation is increased upon unexpected signals for coming satisfaction, during heroin rushes, and when subjects think of the person with whom they are in love (Fisher, 2004). Severe disturbance of the midbrain dopamine system, as in Parkinson's disease, tends to lead to severe general decrease in interest and spontaneous action (Damasio, 2000).

Emotion elicitation: Appraisal

Emotions are aroused by events as appraised by the subject. A given event can be appraised differently and, in consequence, generate different emotions, or no emotion. On appraisal I have to be brief, however.

"Appraisal" is a central notion for understanding emotions. The word is easily misunderstood, however. It does *not* mean conscious evaluation or interpretation. It only means that processes internal to the person intervene between arrival of a stimulus event and the occurrence of emotional response. The processes can be very elementary, as when a sweet taste is liked or an unexpected loud sound triggers a startle reflex, or viewing a baby elicits endearments. They often do involve more complex information, though, such as event context and stored associations, knowledge, and expectations: then, one speaks of "cognitive appraisal."

Appraisal then pertains to a number of different event aspects. It involves appraisal of novelty or familiarity and intrinsic pleasantness or unpleasantness, the most elementary and noncognitive appraisal aspects (Grandjean & Scherer, 2008). It includes what the event might offer or do to the subject, and what the subject can or cannot do to cope or deal with it or to make use of it.

The major appraisal aspect has already been mentioned: appraisal of concern relevance – that is, the relevance of the event for obtaining or not obtaining concern satisfaction. The term *concerns* refers to major motives, needs, interests, and all other dispositions that cause an individual to care about what happens: affective sensitivities, ongoing goals, and attachments. Positive emotions arise when events favor or promise satisfaction of concerns. Emotions are negative when events threaten or harm concern satisfaction. Emotions thus result from the encounter between an event and one or more of an individual's concerns. This holds even for elementary appraisals. A baby looks sweet because one is predisposed to care for babies. Mutilation looks disgusting because it is perceived in terms of one's own bodily integrity. A given event thus has a different meaning and evokes different emotions when it touches on different concerns in different individuals and different cultures (Mesquita & Leu, 2007). Differences in concerns belong to the major sources of cultural and individual differences in what elicits emotions, and how this happens. Indeed, in the aforementioned study by Sonnemans and Frijda (1994), felt emotion strength was found to correlate notably with measures of the prominence and number of the individual's concerns implicated in their reported events. Measures of concern strength accounted for one fourth of the variance of felt intensity ($R^2 = .24$).

The analysis of appraisal thus provides insight into the function of emotions: into what they are for. Emotions, by their appraisal and their states of action readiness and actions, serve to safeguard the individual's concerns.

But a major point needs emphasis. Whether elementary or cognitive, the appraisal processes are essentially nonconscious. One may become aware of their outcomes – the baby looks endearing. Event-as-perceived is a second major component of emotional feeling. But how and why it arises one does not know. This is an old insight: nothing new. It was the main substance of Wundt's (1863–64) theory of emotion, which recently received renewed attention in a careful review by Wassmann (2009). Most appraisal processes also proceed automatically, as has been extensively demonstrated in many subtle experiments by Moors and De Houwer (2006). And even nonconscious appraisal outcomes may still influence subsequent judgments and actions (Bargh, 1994; Berridge, 2004). In exploring why an emotion has emerged, the subject is generally in no better position than any third person. One reconstructs and guesses.

While this is a good, coherent account of emotion arousal, it is not entirely complete. Not all emotions are triggered by events appraised as relevant to concerns. Not all emotions may involve appraisal. Some emotions may be triggered by events directly: those of making emotional movements (e.g., Strack, Martin, & Stepper, 1988), going along with perceived emotional movements in others, and perceiving stimuli that induce such movements. I am hinting at emotional contagion (Hatfield, Cacioppo, & Rapson, 1992) and at emotion induction by miming emotions in dancing and hearing music (e.g., Zentner, Grandjean, & Scherer, 2008). But the actual emotional content of these emotions has hardly been closely examined.

Pleasure and displeasure

Emotions center around pleasure and pain (Russell, 2003). Yet, so far I have hardly said anything about them.

There is a good reason for this: space is limited. But there is another good reason: pleasure and displeasure are impossible to describe, except by repeating that they feel good or bad. In the case of pleasure in particular: when focusing attention on the feeling, it simply evaporates. All that remains is an awareness of the body or the sensory sensation without its gloss of niceness. Pleasure has no phenomenology (Arnold, 1960), except that one would willingly have more of whatever it is a gloss to: the sweetness, the bodily touch, the state one is in.

But this latter is precisely its functional role. Pleasure signals acceptance of an object or event, or of the state one is in. It signals an object or state that one is at ease with, and with which one welcomes increased interaction. It calls to linger with the object or event, if only for a moment. Lingering may extend to behaviors that increase and prolong interaction. I call them "acceptance wriggles" (Frijda, 2007): watching, sniffing, stroking, exposing skin, opening up, curling one's tongue around a delicious candy, or more complex ways to expand interaction. Hence pleasure's vital role in learning. Conscious pleasure appears to be indispensable for learning a novel action for obtaining a given reward. Without conscious pleasure, the link between action and reward will not be laid (Dickinson & Balleine, 2000).

Displeasure can be characterized in a contrasting way. It presses for change and generates readiness to cut interaction short. It represents non-acceptance of the object, event, or state involved. It is an inherently unstable state.

The big question is, of course, what makes certain events pleasant and others unpleasant? For sensory pleasures, evolutionary theory suggests that evolution made it so. But the evidence suggests that the connection may well be more dynamic. Food that feeds well does smell and taste good, for the simple reason that what feeds well accompanies return to homeostasis or equilibrium. Smell and taste as such predict such return. There are various sorts of evidence for this view. Sensory pleasures come from stimuli that match the entry point for systems of behavior, as well as their terminal points. Pleasant tastes make the mouth water. An attractive person sets the sexual system in motion, while orgasm and intimacy make it stop. The link with homeostasis is most evident in the phenomena of *alliesthesia* (Cabanac, 1992): sensory pleasure covaries with one's state of need. Hunger makes raw beans palatable. Sex pictures are liked more after sexual deprivation, and less after six exposures of the same picture (Laan & Everaerd, 1995).

And what is more, these functional relationships also hold for non-sensory pleasures and displeasures; and most of our pleasures and displeasures are non-sensory. They accompany the acts and facts of satisfying concerns, and of encountering their frustration.

Pleasure, in fact, accompanies all progress towards achieving any striven-after goal: recognizing a fitting object; progress as such; overcoming an obstacle on the road; changes in circumstances that render progress more likely. Relief from previous threat, lifting of previous uncertainty, disappearance of pain all belong to the strongest of pleasures. In erotic pleasure, seeing an attractive person, or a sign that he or she recognizes one's interest, a lingering glance, a kiss, going for a drink together, foreplay and the final play all are nice, and they are nice as such – not merely as foresight of the still happier endings.

There also are the pleasures that arise from taking part in activities in which one is skilled. Exerting social skills is generally fun, and avidly sought: chatting in its different senses, communicating with children by cooing and smiling, sitting together with familiar others in the marketplace; or intellectual skills, such as solving crossword puzzles; or the epitome of pleasure: operating at the fringes of one's competence that engenders experiences of "flow," as Csikszentmihalyi (1990) called them.

These observations and findings lead to the following generalization. Pleasure signals that the organism is functioning well (Frijda, 2007). Displeasure results from detecting that it is not functioning well. Both pleasure and displeasure are outcomes of a general provision for monitoring functioning – ill or well. Actually, the monitoring is probably slightly more subtle. Normal everyday adequate functioning carries no affect. It is taken for granted. Why waste monitoring provisions when nothing needs to be done? Pleasure results when functioning well was not self-evident before – when things are going better than expected (Carver & Scheier, 1990). Displeasure results when things go worse; prefrontal-cortically, it results from "error processing" (Holroyd & Coles, 2002).

I think that monitoring functioning well is what affects are for. Such monitoring operates at diverse levels: at the level of simple actions like writing or walking – walking with difficulty, or not being able to walk by oneself, is highly unpleasant. It also operates at the general level of energy depletion or fatigue, and of possessing abundant energy resources. It has powerful motivational consequences for pursuing and expanding current processing, or seeking realignment.

This formulation is not at all novel. Aristotle (*Nicomachean Ethics*; Aristotle, trans. 1941) proposed it: pleasure is the sense of unimpeded functioning. Spinoza (1677/1989) improved on it: pleasure represents "increase in perfection," meaning that one comes closer to exerting of all one's potential capacities.

The hypothesis has interesting implications. It suggests that functioning monitoring is a distributed process: distributed as a component of all function provisions of which the output answers some adequacy criterion. It is no great step to suppose each such provision to generate a signal that is noticed by a more encompassing provision that instigates corrective action in cases of bad functioning, and action continuation in the case of good functioning. It could be a local opiate receptor, a bit like the hedonic hotspots recently discovered for food rewards (Peciña, Smith, & Berridge, 2006), that broadcasts response of pleasure or discomfort; it could also be mediated by anterior cingulate dopamine receptors (Holroyd & Coles, 2002), as well as more generally in the orbitofrontal cortex (Kringelbach, 2005). The whole would imply a bottom-up system of overall monitoring that integrates results from distributed part-monitoring, without a supervising mechanism.

Pleasure and displeasure can be hypothesized to be extraordinarily basic in evolution. They may well represent the most elementary form of consciousness, occurring in early vertebrates, since by themselves they need no representations. They may exist as subcortical states of consciousness, like those analyzed by Merkel (2007), as existing even in children without a cerebral cortex.

Conclusions

Action readiness is not just one of the components of the multicomponential responses called emotions. It is their main functional aspect. It serves satisfying and safeguarding concerns by establishing and modifying relationships. All this forms ample reason for giving passion – action readiness with control precedence – pride of place in analyzing emotions. It is what emotions are for. They form the tools for defending and satisfying concerns.

True, emotions are generally held to have developed in evolution because they served adaptation. But they did not do so only in evolution. They also do so now, in adapting to current opportunities, challenges, dangers, and rivalries.

But adaptation is not the core function of emotions. Serving adaptation is how they survived during evolution, but not what *made* them survive. Their actual function was and is safeguarding concerns.

That function spills over the rims of adaptational basins of attraction. Concerns stretch wider than how the world is at this moment and in one's present niche. Some concerns are adaptive, others destructive: witness the concerns for group identity (Sen, 2007); witness the concern for easy living, with its call on energy expenditure.

Many human concerns are exaptive. People are open to the world. Curiosity may have its evolutionary origin in the benefits of locating food and mates, but the joys of walking around on a sunny morning in a beautiful landscape do not derive from those benefits. Humans – many or most humans – go out to meet and explore, prodded by what one encounters there by way of challenges and invitations for the cognitive emotions of curiosity, interest, and fascination. Exploring a novel situation yields novel aspects that yield exploration that yields novel aspects, and so forth. Play is similarly exaptive. It brings unasked-for challenges; joy has been linked to being open to gratuitous interactions and to broaden and build novel competences. Sexual interaction brings the satisfactions of body warmth and intimacy, as chimpanzees discovered when discovering consortships (Goodall, 1986), as well as discovering the goal of obtaining sexual pleasure as such. Fear does likewise, when successful coping makes one discover the thrills of being able to cope.

Emotions thus also serve exaptation: activation of states of action readiness for novel purposes. It expands one's niche. It may then even become a determinant of morphological or functional change (Gottlieb, 2002; Gould, 1991; Piaget, 1978; Varela et al., 1991) through the advantages of adapting to the expanded niche.

I believe that the preceding provides a coherent story of emotions. It allows an integrative view, by linking observable phenomena and subjective experiences to inferred processes at the subpersonal level of description, linking these processes among themselves and providing occasional pointers from these processes to processes at the neuroscientific level of description.

It has done so with the help of several theoretical constructs.

The central one of these is that of passion – that is, of motive states called states of action readiness, aiming to achieve or modify person–object relationships.

Second to that is the notion of concerns: the dispositions that enable sensitivity to events and the aims of action readiness.

The third is appraisal: the information processes that link observed events to concerns, producing matches or mismatches of representations that elicit action readiness and guide action.

The story has led to a functional interpretation of emotions: safeguarding concerns and their satisfaction in an uncertain and importantly social environment by modifying subject–object relationships.

Then there are those not very theoretical constructs of pleasure and displeasure. These constructs lead one to reflect on their general architectural implications. They indicate major features of the architecture of the human and the animal mind (Sloman, 1999).

Pleasure and displeasure may themselves represent one of the most prominent of these features. One does well to stop to wonder about this amazing capability of humans, and perhaps of all animals: to go at, remain with, or move away from other entities, and to be sensitive to whatever these other entities bring to lead to either the one or the other. Humans possess the sensitivity to respond to almost everything by liking or disliking it, or else by watching out how it might turn out to be.

This hedonic sensitivity is an amazing and amazingly profound property. It makes value enter a world of fact. It is what makes animals into autonomous systems, capable of moving about on their own and fending for themselves.

Hedonic sensitivity is, it would seem, an outgrowth of the more encompassing capabilities for engagement and interest. I mentioned the consequences of severe dopamine dysfunction in advanced Parkinson's disease. Loss of emotional sensitivity, interest, and engagement are also prominent in other severe brain disturbances, such as akinetic mutism (Damasio, 2000) and in the avolition symptoms in schizophrenia (Frith, 2006). Emotional functioning appears to depend on very basic provisions.

Action readiness belongs to the domain of motivation: orientation towards a future state or contingency. Motivation brings enormous flexibility in action, as compared with prewired stereotyped responses.

And, finally: what are emotions really? This may not be a good question.

Scherer (2005) suggests that emotions as phenomena of experience and behavior result from streams of processes running in close but variable reciprocal interactions and irregular sequencing, pretty much as envisaged by M. D. Lewis (2005). "Emotion" is not a coherent category. Sometimes only one process is present – merely affect, as in eating moderately good ice-cream while moderately thirsty; or mere action readiness, as in an irritable mood or lively vital affect. Making a transversal cut through the stream on occasion gives a pattern that one may want to call "an emotion," but it has no sharp or natural boundaries with other patterns in the stream except when the processes fully embody in an affect burst (Scherer, 1994). Otherwise, one does not "have" emotions. One is emoting – sometimes more, sometimes less – by having a somewhat variable set of synchronized processes going on that may include appraisal processes, ongoing action readiness with variable control precedence, feelings stemming from parts of those processes, regulatory interactions coming from expected consequences of some of these processes on other ones. What more should one wish for? It is a beautiful perspective.

References

Arnold, M. B. (1960). *Emotion and personality* (Vol. 1). New York: Columbia University Press.

Bard, P. (1934). On emotional expression after decortication with some remarks on certain theoretical views. Parts I and II. *Psychological Review, 309–329*, 424–449.

Bargh, J. A. (1994). The four horsemen of automaticity: Awareness, intention, efficiency, and control in social cognition. In R. S. Wyer & T. K. Srull (Eds.), *Handbook of social cognition* (pp. 1–40). Hillsdale, NJ: Lawrence Erlbaum Associates, Inc.

Berridge, K. C. (1999). Pleasure, pain, desire, & dread: Hidden core processes of emotion. In D. Kahneman, E. Diener, & N. Schwarz (Eds.), *Foundations of hedonic psychology: Scientific perspectives on enjoyment and suffering* (pp. 525–557). New York: Sage.

Berridge, K. C. (2004). Unfelt affect and irrational desire: A view from the brain. In A. R. S. Manstead, N. H. Frijda, & A. Fischer (Eds.), *Feelings and emotions: The Amsterdam Symposium* (pp. 243–262). Cambridge, UK: Cambridge University Press.

Berridge, K. C. (2007). The debate over dopamine's role in reward: The case for incentive salience. *Psychopharmacology, 191*, 391–431.

Cabanac, M. (1992). Pleasure: The common currency. *Journal of Theoretical Biology, 155*, 173–200.

Carver, C. S., & Scheier, M. F. (1990). Origins and functions of positive and negative affect: A control-process view. *Psychological Review, 97*, 19–35.

Crombez, G., Eccleston, C., Bayens, F., & Eelen, P. (1998). Attentional disruption is enhanced by the threat of pain. *Behaviour Research and Therapy, 36*, 195–204.

Csikszentmihalyi, M. (1990). *Flow: The psychology of optimal experience*. New York: HarperCollins.

Damasio, A. (2000). *The feeling of what happens: Body, emotion, and consciousness*. London: Random House.

Damasio, A. R., Grabowski, D. J., Bechara, A., Damasio, H., Ponto, L. L. B., Parvisi, J., et al. (2000). Subcortical and cortical brain activity during the feeling of self-generated emotions. *Nature Neuroscience, 3*, 1049–1056.

Davitz, J. R. (1969). *The language of emotion*. New York: Academic Press.

Depue, R. A., & Collins, P. F. (1999). Neurobiology of the structure of personality: Dopamine, facilitation of incentive motivation, and extraversion. *Behavioral and Brain Sciences, 22*, 491–517.

Dickinson, A., & Balleine, B. W. (2000). Causal cognition and goal-directed action. In C. Heyes & L. Huber (Eds.), *Evolution of cognition* (pp. 185–204). Cambridge, MA: MIT Press.

Easterbrook, J. A. (1959). The effects of emotion on cue utilization and the organization of behavior. *Psychological Review*, *66*, 183–201.

Edelman, G. M., & Tononi, G. (2000). *Consciousness: How matter becomes imagination*. Harmondsworth, UK: Penguin.

Ekman, P. (1999). Basic emotions. In T. Dalgleish & M. J. Power (Eds.), *Handbook of cognition and emotion*. Chichester, UK: Wiley.

Fisher, H.E. (2004). *Why we love: The nature and chemistry of romantic love*. New York: Holt.

Frijda, N. H. (1986). *The emotions*. Cambridge, UK: Cambridge University Press.

Frijda, N. H. (2007). *The laws of emotion*. Mahwah, NJ: Lawrence Erlbaum Associates, Inc.

Frijda, N. H., Kuipers, P., & Terschure, E. (1989). Relations between emotion, appraisal, and emotional action readiness. *Journal of Personality and Social Psychology*, *57*, 212–228.

Frijda, N. H., Markam, S., Sato, K., & Wiers, R. (1995). Emotion and emotion words. In J. A. Russell, J.-M. Fernández-Dols, A. S. R. Manstead, & J. Wellenkamp (Eds.), *Everyday conceptions of emotion* (pp. 121–144). Dordrecht: Kluwer.

Frijda, N. H., & Tcherkassof, A. (1997). Facial expressions as modes of action readiness. In J. A. Russell & J. M. Fernández-Dols (Eds.), *The psychology of facial expression* (pp. 78–102). Cambridge, UK: Cambridge University Press.

Frith, C. (2006). Interpersonal factors in the disorders of volition associated with schizophrenia. In N. Sebunz & W. Prinz (Eds.), *Disorders of volition* (pp. 233–247). Cambridge, MA: Bradford Books.

Gallistel, C. R. (1980). *The organization of action: A new synthesis*. Hillsdale, NJ: Lawrence Erlbaum Associates, Inc.

Gibson, J. J. (1979). *The ecological approach to visual perception*. Boston: Houghton Mifflin.

Goodall, J. (1986). *The chimpanzees of Gombe: Patterns of behavior*. Cambridge, MA: Belknap.

Gottlieb, G. (2002). Developmental-behavioral initiation of evolutionary change. *Psychological Review*, *109*, 211–218.

Gould, S. J. (1991). Exaptation: A crucial tool for evolutionary psychology. *Journal of Social Issues*, *47*, 43–65.

Grandjean, D., & Scherer, K. R. (2008). Unpacking the cognitive architecture of the emotion process. *Emotion*, *8*, 341–352.

Gray, J. A. (1982). *The neuropsychology of anxiety: An enquiry into the functions of the septo-hippocampal system*. Oxford, UK: Oxford University Press.

Gray, J. A. (1987). *The psychology of fear and stress* (2nd edition). Cambridge, UK: Cambridge University Press.

Griffiths, P. E. (1997). *What emotions really are: The problem of psychological categories*. Chicago: University of Chicago Press.

Hatfield, E., Cacioppo, J. T., & Rapson, R. L. (1992). Primitive emotional contagion. In M. S. Clark (Ed.), *Emotion and social behavior. Review of personality and social psychology* (Vol. 14, pp. 151–177). Newbury Park, CA: Sage.

Holroyd, C. B., & Coles, M. G. H. (2002). The neural basis of human error processing: Reinforcement learning, dopamine, and error-related negativity. *Psychological Review*, *109*, 679–709.

Hommel, B., Müsseler, J., Aschersleben, G., & Prinz, W. (2001). The theory of event coding (TEC): A framework for perception and action planning. *Behavioral and Brain Sciences, 24*, 849–878.

Jeannerod, M. (1997). *The cognitive neuroscience of action.* Oxford, UK: Blackwell.

Kringelbach, M. L. (2005). The human orbitofrontal cortex: Linking reward to hedonic experience. *Nature Reviews: Neuroscience, 6*, 691–702.

Laan, E., & Everaerd, W. (1995). Habituation of female sexual arousal to slides and film. *Archives of Sexual Behavior, 24*, 517–541.

LeDoux, J. (1996). *The emotional brain.* New York: Simon & Schuster.

Lewis, M. D. (2005). Bridging emotion theory and neurobiology through dynamic system modeling. *Behavioral and Brain Sciences, 28*, 105–131.

Lewis, M. R., & Todd, R. M. (2007). The self-regulating brain: Cortical–subcortical feedback and the development of intelligent action. *Cognitive Development, 22*, 406–430.

Leyton, M. (2009). The neurobiology of desire: Dopamine and the regulation of mood and motivational states in humans. In K. Berridge & M. Kringelbach (Eds.), *Pleasures of the brain* (pp. 222–243). New York: Oxford University Press.

MacLeod, C., Mathews, A., & Tata, P. (1986). Attentional bias in emotional disorders. *Journal of Abnormal Psychology, 95*, 15–20.

Merkel, B. (2007). Consciousness without a cerebral cortex: A challenge for neuroscience and medicine. *Behavioral and Brain Sciences, 30*, 63–81.

Mesquita, B., & Leu, J. (2007). The cultural psychology of emotion. In S. Kitayama & D. Cohen (Eds.), *Handbook of cultural psychology.* New York: Guilford Press.

Moors, A., & De Houwer, J. (2006). Automaticity: A theoretical and conceptual analysis. *Psychological Bulletin, 132*, 297–326.

Nussbaum, M. C. (2001). *Upheavals of thought: The intelligence of emotions.* New York: Cambridge University Press.

Obrist, P. A. (1981). *Cardiovascular psychophysiology: A perspective.* New York: Plenum Press.

Öhman, A., & Mineka, S. (2001). Fears, phobias, and preparedness: Toward an evolved module of fear and fear learning. *Psychological Review, 108*, 483–522.

Panksepp, J. (1998). *Affective neuroscience.* Oxford, UK: Oxford University Press.

Panksepp, J. (2005). Affective consciousness: Core emotional feelings in animals and humans. *Consciousness and Cognition, 14*, 81–88.

Peciña, S., Smith, K. S., & Berridge, K. (2006). Hedonic hot spots in the brain. *The Neuroscientist, 12*, 500–511.

Piaget, J. (1978). *Behavior and evolution.* New York: Pantheon Press.

Rimé, B. (2005). *Le partage social des émotions* [Sharing of emotions]. Paris: Presses Universitaires de France.

Rizzolatti, G., Fogassi, L., & Gallese, V. (2001). Neurophysiological mechanisms underlying the understanding and imitation of action. *Nature Reviews: Neuroscience, 2*, 661–670.

Russell, J. A. (2003). Core affect and the psychological construction of emotion. *Psychological Review, 110*, 145–172.

Scherer, K. R. (1984). Emotion as a multicomponent process: A model and some cross-cultural data. In P. Shaver (Ed.), *Review of personality and social psychology* (Vol. 5, pp. 37–63). Beverly Hills, CA: Sage.

Scherer, K. R. (1994). Affect bursts. In S. H. M. Van Goozen, N. E. Van de Poll, & J. A. Sergeant (Eds.), *Emotions: Essays on emotion theory* (pp. 161–196). Hillsdale, NJ: Lawrence Erlbaum Associates, Inc.

Scherer, K. R. (2004). Feelings integrate the central representation of appraisal-driven response organization in emotion. In K. S. Manstead, N. H. Frijda, & A. Fischer (Eds.), *Feelings and emotions: The Amsterdam Symposium*. New York: Cambridge University Press.

Scherer, K. R. (2005). What are emotions? And how can they be measured? *Social Science Information, 44*, 695–729.

Sen, A. (2007). *Identity and violence: The illusion of destiny*. Harmondsworth, UK: Penguin.

Shizgal, P. (1999). On the neural computation of utility: Implications from studies of brain stimulus reward. In D. Kahneman, E. Diener, & N. Schwarz (Eds.), *Foundations of hedonic psychology: Scientific perspectives on enjoyment and suffering* (pp. 500–524). New York: Russell Sage.

Sloman, A. (1999, April). *Why can't a goldfish long for its mother? Architectural prerequisites for various types of emotions*. Paper presented at British HCI Group one-day meeting on the role of emotion in HCI, University College London.

Sonnemans, J., & Frijda, N. H. (1994). The structure of subjective emotional intensity. *Cognition and Emotion, 8*, 329–350.

Spinoza, B. (1989). *Ethica* (G. H. R. Parkinson, Trans.). London: Everyman's Library. (Original work published 1677.)

Stern, D. N. (1985). *Interpersonal world of the infant. A view from psychoanalysis and development psychology*. New York: Basic Books.

Strack, F., Martin, L. L., & Stepper, S. (1988). Inhibiting and facilitating conditions of the human smile: A nonobtrusive test of the facial feedback hypothesis. *Journal of Personality and Social Psychology, 54*, 768–777.

Varela, F. J., Thompson, E., & Rosch, E. (1991). *The embodied mind*. Cambridge, MA: MIT Press.

Veening, J. G., de Jong, T., & Barendregt, H. T. (2010). The regulation of brain states by neuroactive substances distributed via the cerebrospinal fluid: A review. *Cerebrospinal Fluid Research, 7*(1), doi:10.1186/1743-8454-7-1 (online).

Von Holst, E., & Mittelstaedt, H. (1950). Der Reafferenzprinzip. Wechselwirkung zwischen Zentralnervensystem und Peripherie [The reafference principle: Interaction between central nervous system and periphery]. *Naturwissenschaften, 37*, 464–475.

Wassmann, C. (2009). Physiological optics, cognition and emotion: A novel look at the early work of Wilhelm Wundt. *Journal for the History of Medicine and Allied Sciences, 64*(2), 213–249.

Wundt, W. (1863–64). *Vorlesungen über die Menschen- und Thierseele* [Lectures on the human and animal mind]. Berlin: Springer-Verlag, 1990.

Zentner, M., Grandjean, D., & Scherer, K. R. (2008). Emotions evoked by the sound of music: Characterization, classification, and measurement. *Emotion, 8*, 494–521.

5 On living life to the fullest

The role of passion

Robert J. Vallerand,
Noémie Carbonneau, and
Marc-André Lafrenière

Each day, millions, if not billions, of people engage in an activity for which they have a passion. Given the prevalence of the use of the concept of passion in everyday life, it is surprising that so little scientific information exists on its role in people's life. While passion has generated a great deal of attention from philosophers (see Rony, 1990, for a review), until a few years ago the only research on passion in psychology had focused on romantic passion (Hatfield & Walster, 1978). However, recently Vallerand and his colleagues (Vallerand, 2008, 2010; Vallerand et al., 2003; Vallerand & Houlfort, 2003) have developed a model of passion that focuses on activities and has generated increasing research. The purpose of this chapter is to present this theoretical formulation on passion, the Dualistic Model of Passion (Vallerand, 2008; Vallerand et al., 2003), along with supportive evidence. As we shall see, passion plays an important role in the quality of life one experiences.

A dualistic model of passion

In line with Self-Determination Theory (Deci & Ryan, 2000), the Dualistic Model of Passion posits that individuals are motivated to explore their environment in order to grow as individuals. In so doing, they engage in a variety of activities. Of these, only a few will be perceived as particularly enjoyable and important and to have some resonance with how we see ourselves. These activities will turn out to be passionate. Vallerand et al. (2003) define passion as a strong inclination toward a self-defining activity that one likes (or even loves), finds important, and in which one invests time and energy. In fact, these activities come to be so self-defining that they represent central features of one's identity. For instance, those who have a passion for painting, playing the piano, or writing novels do not merely engage in these activities. They *are* "painters," "piano players," and "writers."

Past research has shown that values and regulations concerning non-interesting activities can be internalized in either a controlled or an autonomous fashion (see Deci, Eghrari, Patrick, & Leone, 1994; Sheldon, 2002; Vallerand, Fortier, & Guay, 1997). Similarly, it is posited that activities that people like will also be internalized in the person's identity to the extent that these are highly valued and meaningful for the person. Furthermore, it is proposed that there are two types of passion, obsessive and harmonious, that can be distinguished in terms of how the passionate activity has been internalized into one's identity. Harmonious passion results from an autonomous internalization of the activity into the person's identity. An autonomous internalization occurs when individuals have freely accepted the activity as important for them without any contingencies attached to it. This type of internalization emanates from the intrinsic and integrative tendencies of the self (Deci & Ryan, 2000; Ryan & Deci, 2003). It produces a motivational force to engage in the activity willingly and engenders a sense of volition and personal endorsement about pursuing the activity. When harmonious passion is at play, individuals do not experience an uncontrollable urge to engage in the passionate activity but, rather, freely choose to do so. With this type of passion, the activity occupies a significant but not overpowering space in the person's identity and is in harmony with other aspects of the person's life. In other words, with harmonious passion the authentic integrating self (Deci & Ryan, 2000) is at play, allowing the person to fully partake in the passionate activity with an openness that is conducive to positive experiences (Hodgins & Knee, 2002). Consequently, people with a harmonious passion should be able to focus fully on the task at hand and experience positive outcomes both during (e.g., flow, positive affect, concentration, etc.) and after (e.g., satisfaction, general positive affect, etc.) task engagement. Thus, there should be little or no conflict between the person's passionate activity and his/her other life activities. Furthermore, when prevented from engaging in their passionate activity, people with a harmonious passion should be able to adapt well to the situation and focus their attention and energy on other tasks that need to be done. Finally, with harmonious passion, the person is in control of the activity and can decide when to and when not to engage in the activity. People with a harmonious passion are able to decide not to engage in the activity on a given day if needed or even to eventually terminate the relationship with the activity if they decide it has become a permanent negative factor in their life. Thus, behavioral engagement in the passionate activity can be seen as flexible.

Conversely, obsessive passion results from a controlled internalization of the activity into one's identity and self. A controlled internalization originates from intra- and/or interpersonal pressure typically because certain contingencies are attached to the activity such as feelings of social acceptance or self-esteem, or because the sense of excitement derived from activity engagement is uncontrollable. People with an obsessive passion can thus find themselves in the position of experiencing an uncontrollable urge to partake in the activity they view as important and enjoyable. They cannot help but engage in the passionate activity. Consequently, they risk experiencing conflicts and other negative affective, cognitive, and behavioral consequences during and after activity engagement. It is thus proposed that individuals with an obsessive passion come to display a rigid persistence toward the activity, as often they cannot help but engage in the passionate activity. This is so because ego-invested rather than integrative self processes (Hodgins & Knee, 2002) are at play with obsessive passion, leading the person to eventually develop a dependency on the activity. While such persistence may at times lead to some benefits (e.g., improved performance at the activity over time), it may also come at a cost for the individual, potentially leading to less than optimal functioning within the confines of the passionate activity because of the lack of flexibility that it entails. Furthermore, such a rigid persistence may lead the person to experience conflict with other aspects of his or her life when engaging in the passionate activity (when one should be doing something else, for instance), as well as to frustration and rumination about the activity when prevented from engaging in it. We now turn to research on the Dualistic Model of Passion.

Research on passion

Over the past few years, a number of studies have been conducted on passion. These studies pertain to a variety of activities, settings, participants, and outcomes. Below, we briefly review some of these studies.

On the concept of passion

In our initial work (Vallerand et al., 2003, Study 1), we tested several aspects of the concept of passion. College students ($n = 539$) completed the Passion Scale with respect to an activity that they liked, that they valued, and in which they invested time and energy (i.e., the passion definition), as well as other scales, allowing predictions derived from the model to be tested. Interestingly, 84% of participants indicated that their activity was "a passion" for them. Passionate activities included physical activities and sports, music, watching movies, reading, and many others. Participants reported that they engaged in their passionate activity for an average of 8.5 hours per week and that they had been engaging in that activity for almost 6 years. Thus, clearly, passionate activities are meaningful to people.

The findings provided empirical support for several aspects of the passion conceptualization. Exploratory and confirmatory factor analyses documented the existence of two constructs that correspond to harmonious and obsessive passion. The Passion Scale consists of 2 subscales of 6 items[1] each: the Obsessive (e.g., "I almost have an obsessive feeling toward this activity") and the Harmonious (e.g., "This activity is in harmony with other activities in my life") subscales. Subsequent research has supported the construct validity of the scale in several activities and contexts, including education (Vallerand et al., 2007, Study 2), dramatic arts (Vallerand et al., 2007, Study 1), work (Carbonneau, Vallerand, Fernet, & Guay, 2008; Vallerand & Houlfort, 2003), Internet use (Séguin-Lévesque, Laliberté, Pelletier, Blanchard, & Vallerand, 2003), sports (Vallerand, Rousseau, Grouzet, Dumais, & Grenier, 2006,

Study 1), music (Mageau et al., 2009, Study 3), gambling (Castelda et al., 2007; Rousseau, Vallerand, Ratelle, Mageau, & Provencher, 2002), and hundreds of different types of leisure activities (Vallerand et al., 2003, Study 1). Furthermore, internal consistency analyses have shown that both subscales are reliable.

In addition, the results (i.e., partial correlations, controlling for the common variance between the two types of passion) of the initial study clearly showed that both harmonious and obsessive passions were positively associated with measures of activity valuation and measures of the activity perceived as a "passion," thereby bolstering the definition of passion. In addition, both types of passion were seen as part of one's identity, as manifested by their positive correlation with an inclusion-in-the-self activity measure (Aron, Aron, & Smollan, 1992). Furthermore, only obsessive passion was positively related to a measure of conflict with other life activities. Finally, obsessive (but not harmonious) passion was found to lead to rigid persistence in ill-advised activities such as cycling over ice and snow in winter (Vallerand et al., 2003, Study 3) and pursuing one's engagement in gambling even though it has become pathological in nature (Vallerand et al., 2003, Study 4).

In sum, initial research provided support for the concepts of harmonious and obsessive passion. Let us now turn to different lines of research that have explored some of the outcomes and processes associated with the passion construct.

Passion, affective life, and psychological adjustment

Much research has focused on the affective experiences associated with passion. Thus, Vallerand and his colleagues have shown that controlling for obsessive passion, harmonious passion predicts positive on-task experiences such as flow and positive emotions during activity engagement (Vallerand et al., 2003, Study 1; Vallerand et al., 2006, Studies 2 and 3) and positive emotions and the absence of negative affect following task engagement (Vallerand et al., 2003, Study 1). On the other hand, controlling for harmonious passion, obsessive passion was found to be positively associated with negative emotions (especially shame), both during and following activity engagement. Obsessive passion has also been found to be associated with negative affect (notably shame and anxiety) and rumination when the person is prevented from engaging in the passionate activity, while harmonious passion is unrelated to these negative experiences (Ratelle, Vallerand, Mageau, Rousseau, & Provencher, 2004; Vallerand et al., 2003, Study 1). These findings have been replicated in various life settings, such as work (Vallerand & Houlfort, 2003), sport (Vallerand et al., 2006), and gambling (Mageau, Vallerand, Rousseau, Ratelle, & Provencher, 2005; Ratelle et al., 2004).

But what are some of the other affective consequences of having a passion in one's life? For instance, does passion contribute to general affect and psychological adjustment? Recent research has been conducted in an attempt to investigate these questions. For instance, using a diary study over a two-week period, Mageau and Vallerand (2007) showed that harmonious passion led to increases in general positive affect (as assessed by the PANAS; Watson, Clark, & Tellegen, 1988) on days when people engaged in the passionate activity. On the other hand, obsessive passion predicted decreases in general positive affect on days when they did not engage in the passionate activity. A longitudinal study has further revealed that harmonious passion for football led to an increase in one's general positive affect over the course of an entire American football season. Conversely, obsessive passion for football was shown to lead to an increase of negative affect in one's life during the same period.

So, what about psychological adjustment? A first question pertains to the advantages of being passionate. Are there any? Philippe, Vallerand, and Lavigne (2009b) attempted to answer this question by comparing individuals who are harmoniously passionate, obsessively passionate, or non-passionate on two types of psychological well-being (based on the Vallerand & Houlfort, 2003, method). The results appear in Figure 5.1. As can be seen, on both eudaemonic (e.g., self-growth) and hedonic (e.g., life satisfaction) well-being, harmoniously passionate individuals displayed higher levels of well-being than did obsessively passionate and non-passionate individuals, who did not differ from each other. Thus, being passionate does bring some psychological benefits over being non-passionate, but only if such passion is harmonious in nature. These findings are in line with past research on the relative role of harmonious and obsessive passion in well-being with a variety of populations (e.g., Rousseau & Vallerand, 2003, 2008; Vallerand et al., 2008a, Study 2; Vallerand et al., 2007, Studies 1, 2). For instance, in a study with elderly individuals, Rousseau and Vallerand (2003) showed that harmonious passion

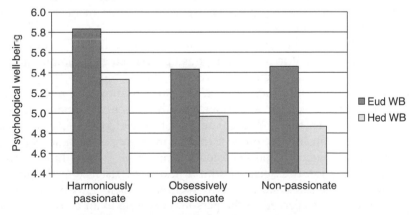

Figure 5.1 A comparison of harmoniously passionate, obsessively passionate, and non-passionate individuals on indices of eudaemonic and hedonic well-being. From F. Philippe, R. J. Vallerand, & G. Lavigne, Passion does make a difference in people's lives: A look at well-being in passionate and non-passionate individuals. *Applied Psychology: Health and Well-Being*, 2009, *1*, 3–22. Reprinted with permission.

positively predicted numerous positive indices of psychological adjustment such as life satisfaction, meaning in life, and vitality. Obsessive passion, on the other hand, was found to be positively associated with anxiety and depression, negatively related to life satisfaction, and unrelated to meaning in life.

If passion affects psychological adjustment, then a second question deals with the issue of the mediating processes at play. At least two different mediating processes are hypothesized to be at play in the relationship between passion and psychological adjustment. In line with Fredrickson (2001), a first process deals with on-task positive affect. Specifically, harmonious passion toward the passionate activity leads to the repeated experience of situational (or state) positive affect during activity engagement, which facilitates psychological adjustment presumably because it gives access to a broader set of cognitive and social skills. Support for this sequence was obtained in a recent study (Rousseau & Vallerand, 2008). This study included three measurement times. At Time 1, participants completed the Passion Scale with respect to physical activity as well as measures of psychological adjustment; at Time 2, they completed situational measures of positive and negative affect following an exercise bout; and at Time 3, they completed measures of psychological adjustment again. Results from structural equation modeling revealed that harmonious passion positively predicted positive affect, which led to increases in psychological adjustment from Time 1 to Time 3. Obsessive passion was found to be unrelated to positive affect but positively related to negative affect, which was not related to psychological adjustment. These findings provide support for the role of situational positive affect experienced during task engagement as a mediator of the effect of harmonious passion on psychological adjustment. These findings have been replicated with middle-aged adults engaged in coaching sports (Lafrenière, Jowett, Vallerand, Donahue, & Lorimer, 2008, Study 2).

The above findings are interesting in that they support the role of positive affect as a key mediator in the relationship between harmonious passion and psychological adjustment. However, they did not identify the processes that mediate the relationship between obsessive passion and psychological adjustment. Indeed, neither situational positive affect nor situational negative affect has been found to mediate the obsessive passion–psychological adjustment relationship. We propose that in obsessive passion another mediating process – namely, rigid persistence – might be at play. Indeed, while harmonious passion is associated with a flexible persistence in the activity, obsessive passion leads individuals to persist in their activity even when important costs are accrued to the person. Persisting in an activity that has become permanently negative for oneself might eventually lead to addiction and to low levels of psychological adjustment. Let us turn to research examining the links between passion and addictive behaviors.

Passion and addictive behaviors

Individuals addicted to an activity come to lose control over it such that they no longer willfully choose to participate but, rather, cannot control their urge to do so. This aspect of dependence is similar to a characteristic of obsessive passion where the individual cannot help but engage in his/her activity as if the activity controlled the person rather than the converse. For some individuals, the passionate activity can have profound negative psychological consequences. For other passionate people, however, exactly the same activity might just be a great source of pleasure, entertainment, and harmless distraction. It is therefore reasonable to suggest that the two types of passion can greatly influence how the engagement in the activity will be experienced. With harmonious passion, the person is in control of the activity. As such, the person can decide when to and when not to engage in the activity and should even be able to drop out of the activity if the latter has become permanently negative for the person. Such is not the case with obsessive passion. Typically, because the activity has taken control of the person, obsessive passion would be expected to lead to rigid persistence, since individuals with this type of passion may stick with the activity regardless of the consequences and even in the absence of positive emotional experience (Vallerand et al., 2003, Study 2).

Research in the realm of gambling provides support for this analysis. Such research has shown that obsessive passion for gambling predicts pathological gambling, higher amounts of money gambled, and more time spent gambling, while harmonious passion is unrelated to these negative outcomes (Ratelle et al., 2004; Rousseau et al., 2002). In addition, obsessive passion was positively associated with negative emotions such as anxiety and guilt as well as with rumination after playing and when prevented from gambling (Ratelle et al., 2004). On the other hand, harmonious passion for gambling was positively related to positive affective experiences while playing (Mageau et al., 2005). Furthermore, other research has shown that obsessive (but not harmonious) passion is higher for pathological gamblers than for at-risk and non-problematic gamblers (Philippe & Vallerand, 2007; Vallerand et al., 2003, Study 4).

This general pattern of results was also found in the domain of problematic Internet use. Using cluster analyses, Wang, Khoo, Liu, and Divaharan (2008) found that passionate individuals for online gaming played more often per week and experienced more flow and positive affect while playing relative to less passionate individuals. However, these findings are not entirely clear, because Wang and colleagues did not differentiate between harmonious and obsessive passion in their cluster analyses. Making the distinction between the two types of passion, Lafrenière, Vallerand, Donahue, and Lavigne (2009) found that while both harmonious and obsessive passion for online gaming were positively associated with the experience of positive affect while playing, only obsessive passion was related to the experience of negative affect while playing and number of weekly hours spent playing. More important,

Lafrenière et al. (2009) and Wang and Chiu (2007) have shown that obsessive passion was positively related to problematic behaviors usually associated with excessive gaming (e.g., Davis, 2001) such as getting irritable or restless when prevented from playing or using video games as a way to escape from problems. Harmonious passion was unrelated to such behaviors. Finally, Wang and Yang (2006) found that obsessive (but not harmonious) passion for online shopping was positively related to online shopping dependency.

The Dualistic Model of Passion (Vallerand, 2008; Vallerand et al., 2003) regards people with an obsessive passion as individuals who cannot resist the urge to engage in their favorite activity as it comes to dominate their lives. Thus, obsessive passion may represent the psychological mechanism responsible for the lack of control observed in addictive behaviors such as gambling and problematic Internet use. Obsessive passion may therefore represent a precursor of addiction. Longitudinal research on the development of passion with respect to problematic behavior is needed in order to shed light on the underlying mechanisms leading individuals to develop pathological gambling and problematic Internet use.

Passion and physical health

The rigid persistence that obsessive passion fosters toward the passionate activity can lead people to engage in risky behaviors. Let us take the example of winter cycling – an activity that is considered a very hazardous affair in the Province of Quebec because the roads are icy and full of snow during this season. Clearly, it would be advisable not to cycle under such conditions as it may lead to falls and injuries. Vallerand et al. (2003, Study 3) posited that obsessively passionate cyclists would be more likely to continue cycling during winter than harmoniously passionate ones. In order to test this hypothesis, they asked 59 cyclists to complete the Passion Scale in August with respect to cycling. Six months later, the cyclists were contacted again to determine whether they were still cycling in the dead of winter (in February). It was found that 30% of participants were still cycling. Further analyses revealed that those persistent cyclists had reported higher levels of obsessive passion 6 months earlier than had those who had wisely stored their bicycles for the winter. These results show that obsessive passion puts people at risk of experiencing injuries when engaging in the passionate activity.

The previous study did not look at injuries directly, but a recent study with dancers did do so (Rip, Fortin, & Vallerand, 2006). In the dance realm, the issue is not whether dancers will get injured or not but, rather, what happens when they do. Since obsessive passion is characterized by a rigid persistence, Rip and colleagues posited that this type of passion would lead dancers to continue dancing even when injured. This would be likely to lead to chronic injuries, since continuing to dance with an injury can increase its severity through further bleeding and tissue damage (Simpson, 2006). In their study with 80 dancers, Rip and colleagues found that obsessive passion was positively related to the number of weeks missed because of chronic injuries, while harmonious passion was unrelated to this measure. In addition, results revealed that unlike harmoniously passionate dancers, obsessively passionate dancers, when injured, ignore the pain, have their pride interfere with treatment, and do not stop dance activities. Clearly such behavior on the part of obsessively passionate dancers puts them at risk of developing chronic injuries.

Another area where obsessive passion for the activity may lead to detrimental effects on health is gaming. Indeed, people who are obsessively passionate about gaming might play for excessively long periods of time, leading them to disregard biological needs such as hunger, eating, and sleep. Over time, such neglect is likely to take its toll on physical health. Conversely, because people with a harmonious passion remain in control of their activity, they should be able to stop when needed and thus prevent hurtful consequences from affecting their health. Results from a recent research (Lafrenière et al., 2009) supported these hypotheses. Obsessive passion for gaming was found to be positively associated with physical symptoms typically related to excessive gaming (e.g., loss of appetite, sleep disorders, etc.), while harmonious passion was unrelated to such physical symptoms. In addition, harmonious passion was found to lead to some positive outcomes such as more positive psychological adjustment (i.e., higher life satisfaction, self-realization, and general positive affect).

In sum, through the different types of persistence and engagement in risky behaviors that they engender, the two types of passion are associated with very different physical health outcomes. Future research should attempt to replicate these findings with more objective measures of injuries, such as medical records.

Passion in sport

Much research has been conducted on passion in sport from the athlete's perspective. Such research provides strong support for the Dualistic Model of Passion (for reviews, see Vallerand, Donahue, & Lafrenière, in press; Vallerand & Miquelon, 2007). However, in addition to athletes, at least three other types of sport participants need to be studied, namely fans, referees, and coaches. Coaches spend a lot of time on their sport. As such, they would be expected to be highly passionate toward coaching. And they are (see Lafrenière et al., 2008, Study 2). Thus, in line with past research, the type of passion that they have toward their coaching should matter greatly with respect to outcomes. One in particular that would appear important is the quality of relationships that coaches develop with their athletes. Indeed, several authors have suggested that the quality of the coach–athlete relationship may represent one of the most important factors affecting athletes' motivation (Mageau & Vallerand, 2003). Waugh and Fredrickson (2006) have shown that the experience of positive emotions in a given context is conducive to high-quality relationships, presumably because positive emotions lead people to open up to others and to engage in positive interpersonal behaviors. Thus, because it leads people to fully immerse themselves in the activity and to experience positive emotions, harmonious passion should foster positive relationships in the purview of the activity. This hypothesis was tested with over 100 coaches involved with team and individual sports (Lafrenière et al., 2008, Study 2). Results from structural equation modeling analyses provided support for the hypotheses. Specifically, harmonious passion predicted the experience of positive emotions, which led to high-quality relationships with athletes. Obsessive passion was unrelated to emotions or to relationship quality. These results are illustrated in Figure 5.2. Thus, the present findings suggest that passion matters with respect to the coach–athlete relationship, with harmonious passion predicting better coach–athlete relationships than obsessive passion. These findings on the quality of relationships have been replicated in other fields (Philippe, Vallerand, Houlfort, Lavigne, & Donahue, in press).

Remarkably, referees have been understudied. This is surprising because referees are sport participants in their own right whose behavior can have an important impact on game outcomes. Coaches and athletes are typically seen as being passionate for their sport, but does this apply also to referees? And if so, are the consequences of passion the same as those experienced by athletes and coaches? These questions have been answered through two studies conducted by Philippe, Vallerand, Andrianarisoa, and Brunel (2009a). With respect to the first question, across the two studies (and more than 450 referees from different sports), 90% of the referees, including professional referees, displayed a passion for their sport (using the passion definition

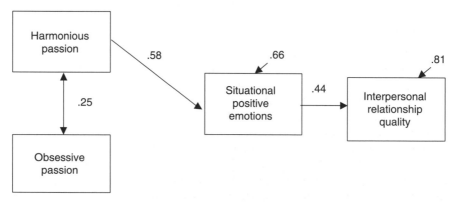

Figure 5.2 The mediating role of positive affect in the harmonious passion interpersonal (coach–athlete) relationship from the coach's perspective. All parameters are significant at *p* < .01. Modified from M.-A. Lafrenière, S. Jowett, R. J. Vallerand, E. G. Donahue, & R. Lorimer, Passion in sport: On the quality of the coach–player relationship. *Journal of Sport and Exercise Psychology*, 2008, *30*, 541–560.

criteria). It thus appears that referees can be just as passionate as athletes and coaches. What about the role of passion in outcomes? Results (Philippe et al., 2009a, Study 1) revealed that harmonious passion for refereeing was positively associated with positive emotions and the experience of flow during games, but unrelated to negative emotions. Conversely, obsessive passion for refereeing was unrelated to positive emotions and flow, but was positively associated with negative emotional experiences during games. Thus, these findings replicate past research with athletes.

Past research has shown that the most important stress factor in refereeing is to make bad calls (e.g., Dorsch & Paskevich, 2007). Referees' reactions and strategies to deal with their own mistakes have been shown to vary drastically, ranging from rumination over the error and feelings of shame to cognitive suppression of the event, and even engaging in make-up calls – or favoring the team that has been unjustly penalized by the poor call (Wolfson & Neave, 2007). In line with the Dualistic Model of Passion (Vallerand et al., 2003), Philippe et al. (2009a, Study 2) hypothesized that passion might account for the different ways in which referees react after having committed an important error. Because with harmonious passion the activity occupies an important, but not overwhelming, space in one's identity, making an error should not be experienced as self-threatening. Consequently, with harmonious passion, it should prove possible to deal with the stressful situation without engaging in repair behaviors and losing concentration on the task at hand. Conversely, with obsessive passion, the activity occupies an overwhelming space in the person's identity, and contingencies are attached to the activity such as doing well on the passionate activity. Therefore, making an error should activate ego-invested structures that should be conducive to a stressful emotional state, negative self-related emotions, and maladaptive cognitive functioning involving rumination over mistakes and concentration problems. Results described by Philippe et al. (2009a) confirmed these hypotheses. Obsessive passion was found to be *positively* associated with negative self-related emotions, rumination, and make-up call decisions subsequent to an error. Conversely, harmonious passion was *negatively* associated with the above variables. Clearly, the two types of passion lead to different affective and cognitive functioning under stress. Future research on the role of coping strategies as mediators in the relationship between passion and cognitive functioning would appear important.

Sport fans are often depicted as highly passionate. Thus, the type of passion they have toward their sport or team should lead to different consequences. Vallerand et al. (2008b, Studies 1 and 2) conducted a series of three studies with football (soccer) fans in both the United Kingdom and Canada. Results revealed that obsessive passion predicted maladaptive behaviors such as missing some very important event (e.g., a wedding, funerals, work, etc.) to go to a game, having trouble concentrating for the whole day when there is a game on that evening, and taunting losing teams' fans. On the other hand, both types of passion were associated with experiencing positive affect and celebrating after one's team victory. Clearly, the type of passion one holds for one's team matters greatly with respect to the type of outcomes a sport fan will experience. Finally, the above findings have clear repercussions for the phenomenon of hooliganism. Future research should seek to determine whether obsessive passion is indeed involved in such unruly and destructive behaviors on the part of sport fans.

Passion and performance

It is generally believed that passionate people reach high levels of performance because they have spent several years of considerable engagement in their favorite activity fine-tuning their skills. But is it really the case? Recent research reveals that it is indeed so. In a study with basketball players (Vallerand et al., 2008a, Study 1), both harmonious and obsessive passion were found to lead to engagement in deliberate practice that, in turn, led to improved sport performance as assessed by athletes' coaches. These findings were replicated in a prospective study in the realm of dramatic arts (Vallerand et al., 2007, Study 1). In this second study, results further showed that while harmonious passion was positively and significantly associated with life satisfaction, obsessive passion was not. These results suggest that while both types of passion lead to enhanced performance through engagement in deliberate practice, obsessive passion is also associated with some sense of "suffering" – or lower levels of life satisfaction than harmonious passion – in the process of pursuing high performance levels.

An additional study (Vallerand et al., 2008a, Study 2) was conducted in order to examine the psychological processes through which passion contributes to deliberate practice and performance. Participants were water-polo players and synchronized swimmers, including some who were part of the junior national Canadian teams. In line with Elliot and Church (1997), Vallerand et al. proposed that achievement goals might represent possible mediators of the relationship between passion and performance. In their study, the achievement goals proposed by Elliot and Church (1997) were assessed: mastery goals (which focus on the development of personal competence and task mastery), performance-approach goals (which focus on the attainment of personal competence relative to others), and performance-avoidance goals (which focus on avoiding incompetence relative to others). Harmonious passion was found to lead to mastery goals that, in turn, led to deliberate practice that positively predicted performance (as assessed by coaches). Obsessive passion, on the other hand, was positively related to all three types of achievement goals. While performance-approach goals did not predict any variables in the model, performance-avoidance goals negatively predicted performance. Also of interest is the finding that, once again, harmonious passion was positively associated with psychological adjustment while obsessive passion was unrelated to it. This model was replicated in another study involving students who had a passion for studying psychology as their future profession; the study used objective exam scores in a psychology course as a measure of performance (Vallerand et al., 2007, Study 2).

In sum, while harmonious passion fosters a purely adaptive process characterized by improved performance and psychological adjustment, obsessive passion engenders a more mixed achievement process characterized by some adaptive and some maladaptive features. Future research is needed to reproduce these results over longer periods of time.

Passion and relationships

Up to this point our discussion on the role of passion in outcomes has been largely intrapersonal in nature. We wish to conclude this chapter by looking at some interpersonal outcomes that derive from passion. Our conceptualization on passion posits that having an obsessive passion toward an activity should lead to conflict and problems in other life activities, while this should not be the case for harmonious passion. As previously mentioned, results from the Vallerand et al. (2003, Study 1) provided preliminary evidence for this hypothesis by showing that obsessive (but not harmonious) passion for an activity was positively associated with experiencing conflict between activity engagement and other aspects of one's life. Séguin-Lévesque et al. (2003) extended these findings by showing that controlling for the number of hours that people spent engaged in the Internet, obsessive passion for the Internet was positively related to conflict with one's spouse and a decrease in dyadic adjustment, while harmonious passion was unrelated to these variables. A subsequent study with English soccer fans (Vallerand et al., 2008b, Study 3) revealed that having an obsessive passion for being a soccer fan predicted conflict between soccer and the quality of the couple relationship. Conflict, in turn, negatively predicted satisfaction with the relationship. Harmonious passion was unrelated to these variables. Furthermore, individuals who were single were asked to indicate if their passion for soccer was responsible for their being single. Results revealed a strong positive correlation between obsessive passion and this measure, but a negative correlation for harmonious passion.

The above findings reveal that depending on the type of passion for a given activity, one can experience conflict – or not – between that activity and one's relationships outside the passionate activity, thereby affecting the quality of such relationships. One question not addressed by such research is whether one's passion can affect the quality of relationships that one develops in the purview of the passionate activity. As seen previously, research by Fredrickson (2001; Waugh & Fredrickson, 2006), has shown that the experience of situational positive affect is conducive to high quality of relationships. This is so because positive affect facilitates smiles, positive sharing of the activity, connection, and openness toward others, which are all conducive to positive relationships. Because harmonious passion leads one to experience positive affect during engagement in the passionate activity, one would then predict that it should therefore indirectly lead to high-quality relationships within the passionate activity. Conversely, because it is typically unrelated to positive affect and correlated to negative affect, obsessive passion would be expected to negatively affect the quality of relationships that develop within the purview of the passionate activity. As seen earlier, results from a series of studies conducted in a variety of settings, including work and sports, have provided support for these hypotheses (Lafrenière et al., 2008, Study 2; Philippe et al., in press).

Conclusions

Our research (Vallerand et al., 2003, Study 1) reveals that passion pervades human life. Indeed, a vast majority of people are not simply motivated, but are passionate toward at least one activity in their lives. Furthermore, passion also matters with respect to outcomes. In the present chapter, a new conceptualization of passion – namely, the Dualistic Model of Passion – was presented to account for these findings. This model provides us with a better understanding of the psychological forces that lead people to sustain intense engagement in a passionate activity and to experience a variety of outcomes in the process. The model proposes the existence of two types of passion, harmonious and obsessive, which can be differentiated in terms of how the representation of the passionate activity has been internalized into one's identity. It was shown that harmonious passion originates from an autonomous internalization of the activity into one's identity and typically leads to adaptive outcomes. Conversely, obsessive passion emanates from a controlled internalization and generally leads to less adaptive and at times maladaptive outcomes. Research on passion so far has documented the role of passion in a host of subjective and objective outcomes, such as affective experiences, subjective well-being, behavior (persistence and performance), and relationships, and has been applied to a variety of life domains and activities.

In sum, it would appear that the construct of passion seems to aptly describe the phenomenological experiences and processes that most participants go through in their high engagement in the passionate activity. However, in light of the fact that passion research is just beginning, we hasten to underscore that additional research is needed to provide a more comprehensive picture of the determinants and consequences of harmonious and obsessive passion.

Acknowledgement

I would like to thank the numerous colleagues and students who have been involved at one point or another in the present research program on passion. Without their collaboration, such research could not have taken place. This research program was supported by grants from the Fonds Québécois pour la Recherche sur la Société et la Culture (FQRSC) and the Social Sciences

Humanities Research Council of Canada (SSHRC). Additional information on this program of research can be obtained by visiting the following website: www.psycho.uqam.ca/lrcs

Note

1 The original scale (Vallerand et al., 2003) consisted of two 7-item subscales. A slightly revised scale consisting of two 6-item scales is now used. These subscales correlate very highly with their respective original subscale ($r = .80$ and above) and yield the same findings with determinants and outcomes. However, the correlation between the harmonious and obsessive passion subscales is lower than that between the original ones. In addition, we have used a 3-item version (Vallerand et al., 2007) and even a 1-item version (Philippe & Vallerand, 2007) of each subscale with much success.

References

Aron, A., Aron, E. N., & Smollan, D. (1992). Inclusion of other in the self scale and the structure of interpersonal closeness. *Journal of Personality and Social Psychology*, *63*, 596–612.

Carbonneau, N., Vallerand, R. J., Fernet, C., & Guay, F. (2008). The role of passion for teaching in intra and interpersonal outcomes. *Journal of Educational Psychology*, *100*, 977–988.

Castelda, B. A., Mattson, R. E., MacKillop, J. E., Anderson, E. J., Burright, R., & Donovick, P. J. (2007). Psychometric validation of the gambling passion scale (GPS). *International Gambling Studies*, *7*, 173–182.

Davis, R. A. (2001). A cognitive–behavioral model of pathological Internet use. *Computers in Human Behavior*, *17*, 187–195.

Deci, E. L., Eghrari, H., Patrick, B. C., & Leone, D. R. (1994). Facilitating internalization: The self-determination perspective. *Journal of Personality*, *62*, 119–142.

Deci, E. L., & Ryan, R. M. (2000). The "what" and "why" of goal pursuits: Human needs and the self-determination of behavior. *Psychological Inquiry*, *11*, 227–268.

Dorsch, K. D., & Paskevich, D. M. (2007). Stressful experiences among six certification levels of ice hockey officials. *Psychology of Sport and Exercise*, *8*, 585 593.

Elliot, A. J., & Church, M. A. (1997). A hierarchical model of approach and avoidance achievement motivation. *Journal of Personality and Social Psychology*, *72*, 218–232.

Fredrickson, B. L. (2001). The role of positive emotions in positive psychology: The broaden-and-build theory of positive emotions. *American Psychologist*, *56*, 218–226.

Hatfield, E., & Walster, G. W. (1978). *A new look at love.* Reading, MA: Addison-Wesley.

Hodgins, H. S., & Knee, R. (2002). The integrating self and conscious experience. In E. L. Deci & R. M. Ryan (Eds.), *Handbook on self-determination research: Theoretical and applied issues* (pp. 87–100). Rochester, NY: University of Rochester Press.

Lafrenière, M.-A., Jowett, S., Vallerand, R. J., Donahue, E. G., & Lorimer, R. (2008). Passion in sport: On the quality of the coach–player relationship. *Journal of Sport and Exercise Psychology*, *30*, 541–560.

Lafrenière, M.-A., Vallerand, R. J., Donahue, R., & Lavigne, G. L. (2009). On the costs and benefits of gaming: The role of passion. *Cyberpsychology and Behavior*, *12*, 285–290.

Mageau, G. A., & Vallerand, R. J. (2003). The coach–athlete relationship: A motivational model. *Journal of Sports Sciences*, *21*, 883–904.

Mageau, G. A., & Vallerand, R. J. (2007). The moderating effect of passion on the relation between activity engagement and positive affect. *Motivation and Emotion*, *31*, 312–321.

Mageau, G. A., Vallerand, R. J., Charest, J., Salvy, S.-J., Lacaille, N., Bouffard, T., et al. (2009). On the development of harmonious and obsessive passion: The role of autonomy support, activity valuation, and identity processes. *Journal of Personality*, *77*, 601–645.

Mageau, G. A., Vallerand, R. J., Rousseau, F. L., Ratelle, C. F., & Provencher, P. J. (2005). Passion and gambling: Investigating the divergent affective and cognitive consequences of gambling. *Journal of Applied Social Psychology*, *35*, 100–118.

Philippe, F., & Vallerand, R. J. (2007). Prevalence rates of gambling problems in Montreal, Canada: A look at old adults and the role of passion. *Journal of Gambling Studies*, *23*, 275–283.

Philippe, F., Vallerand, R. J., Andrianarisoa, J., & Brunel, P. (2009a). Passion in referees: Examining their affective and cognitive experiences in sport situations. *Journal of Sport & Exercise Psychology*, *31*, 1–21.

Philippe, F., Vallerand, R. J., Houlfort, N., & Lavigne, G. L., & Donahue, E. G. (in press). Passion for an activity and quality of interpersonal relationships: The mediating role of emotions. *Journal of Personality and Social Psychology*.

Philippe, F., Vallerand, R. J., & Lavigne, G. L. (2009b). Passion does make a difference in people's lives: A look at well-being in passionate and non-passionate individuals. *Applied Psychology: Health and Well-Being*, *1*, 3–22.

Ratelle, C. F., Vallerand, R. J., Mageau, G. A., Rousseau, F. L., & Provencher, P. (2004). When passion leads to problematic outcomes: A look at gambling. *Journal of Gambling Studies*, *20*, 105–119.

Rip, B., Fortin, S., & Vallerand, R. J. (2006). The relationship between passion and injury in dance students. *Journal of Dance Medicine & Science*, *10*, 14–20.

Rony, J.-A. (1990). *Les passions* [The passions]. Paris: Presses Universitaires de France.

Rousseau, F. L., & Vallerand, R. J. (2003). Le rôle de la passion dans le bien-être subjectif des aînés [The role of passion in the subjective well-being of the elderly]. *Revue Québécoise de Psychologie*, *24*, 197–211.

Rousseau, F. L., & Vallerand, R. J. (2008). An examination of the relationship between passion and subjective well-being in older adults. *International Journal of Aging and Human Development*, *66*, 195–211.

Rousseau, F. L., Vallerand, R. J., Ratelle, C. F., Mageau, G. A., & Provencher, P. J. (2002). Passion and gambling: On the validation of the Gambling Passion Scale (GPS). *Journal of Gambling Studies*, *18*, 45–66.

Ryan, R. M., & Deci, E. L. (2003). On assimilating identities of the self: A self-determination theory perspective on internalization and integrity within cultures. In M. R. Leary & J. P. Tangney (Eds.), *Handbook of self and identity* (pp. 253–272). New York: Guilford Press.

Séguin-Lévesque, C., Laliberté, M.-L., Pelletier, L. G., Blanchard, C., & Vallerand, R. J. (2003). Harmonious and obsessive passion for the internet: Their associations with the couple's relationships. *Journal of Applied Social Psychology*, *33*, 197–221.

Sheldon, K. M. (2002). The self-concordance model of healthy goal-striving: When personal goals correctly represent the person. In E. L. Deci & R. M. Ryan (Eds.), *Handbook of self-determination research* (pp. 65–86). Rochester, NY: University of Rochester Press.

Simpson, S. (2006). *Dance injury management.* Retrieved November 25, 2008, from http://www.danz.org.nz/Downloads/InjuryMgmt.pdf

Vallerand, R. J. (2008). On the psychology of passion: In search of what makes people's lives most worth living. *Canadian Psychology, 49*, 1–13.

Vallerand, R. J. (2010). On passion for life activities: The dualistic model of passion. In M. P. Zanna (Ed.), *Advances in experimental social psychology* (Vol. 42, pp. 97–193). New York: Academic Press.

Vallerand, R. J., Blanchard, C. M., Mageau, G. A., Koestner, R., Ratelle, C. F., Léonard, M., et al. (2003). Les passions de l'âme: On obsessive and harmonious passion. *Journal of Personality and Social Psychology, 85*, 756–767.

Vallerand, R. J., Donahue, E. G., & Lafrenière, M.-A. K. (in press). Passion in sport. A look at athletes, coaches, and fans. In T. Morris & P. Terry (Eds.), *Sport and exercise psychology: The cutting edge.* Sydney, Australia: Routledge.

Vallerand, R. J., Fortier, M. S., & Guay, F. (1997). Self-determination and persistence in a real-life setting: Toward a motivational model of high school dropout. *Journal of Personality and Social Psychology, 72*, 1161–1176.

Vallerand, R. J., & Houlfort, N. (2003). Passion at work: Toward a new conceptualization. In S. W. Gilliland, D. D. Steiner, & D. P. Skarlicki (Eds.), *Emerging perspectives on values in organizations* (pp. 175–204). Greenwich, CT: Information Age Publishing.

Vallerand, R. J., Mageau, G. A., Elliot, A., Dumais, A., Demers, M.-A., & Rousseau, F. L. (2008a). Passion and performance attainment in sport. *Psychology of Sport & Exercise, 9*, 373–392.

Vallerand, R. J., & Miquelon, P. (2007). Passion for sport in athletes. In D. Lavallée & S. Jowett (Eds.), *Social psychology in sport* (pp. 249–262). Champaign, IL: Human Kinetics.

Vallerand, R. J., Ntoumanis, N., Philippe, F., Lavigne, G. L., Carbonneau, C., Bonneville, A., et al. (2008b). On passion and sports fans: A look at football. *Journal of Sport Sciences, 26*, 1279–1293.

Vallerand, R. J., Rousseau, F. L., Grouzet, F. M. E., Dumais, A., & Grenier, S. (2006). Passion in sport: A look at determinants and affective experiences. *Journal of Sport & Exercise Psychology, 28*, 454–478.

Vallerand, R. J., Salvy, S. J., Mageau, G. A., Elliot, A. J., Denis, P., Grouzet, F. M. E., et al. (2007). On the role of passion in performance. *Journal of Personality, 75*, 505–534.

Wang, C. C., & Chiu, Y. S. (2007). Harmonious passion and obsessive passion in playing online games. *Social Behavior and Personality, 35*, 997–1005.

Wang, C. C., & Yang, H. W. (2006). Passion and dependency in online shopping activities. *Cyberpsychology & Behavior, 10*, 296–298.

Wang, C. K. J., Khoo, A., Liu, W. C., & Divaharan, S. (2008). Passion and intrinsic motivation in digital gaming. *Cyberpsychology & Behavior, 11*, 39–45.

Watson, D., Clark, L. A., & Tellegen, A. (1988). Development and validation of brief measures of positive and negative affect: The PANAS scales. *Journal of Personality and Social Psychology, 54*, 1063–1070.

Waugh, C. E., & Fredrickson, B. L. (2006). Nice to know you: Positive emotions, self–other overlap, and complex understanding in the formation of new relationships. *Journal of Positive Psychology, 1*, 93–106.

Wolfson, S., & Neave, N. (2007). Coping under pressure: Cognitive strategies for maintaining confidence among soccer referees. *Journal of Sport Behavior, 30*, 232–247.

6 Emotion regulation and the social sharing of emotion

Interpersonal and collective processes

Bernard Rimé

Following an emotional episode, the person who experienced it generally talks with others about it (Rimé, 1989; Rimé, Mesquita, Philippot, & Boca, 1991a). The social sharing of emotion has been observed in 80–95% of emotional episodes (Rimé & al., 1991a; Rimé, Noël, & Philippot, 1991b; for reviews, see Rimé, 2005; Rimé, Philippot, Boca, & Mesquita, 1992; Rimé, Finkenauer, Luminet, Zech, & Philippot, 1998). It was evidenced at comparable levels whether people held a university degree or only had an elementary school education, as well as in countries as diverse as some in Asia, North America, and Europe (Rimé, Yogo, & Pennebaker, 1996; Singh-Manoux & Finkenauer, 2001; Yogo & Onoe, 1998). Episodes that involved fear, or anger, or sadness were shared as often as episodes of happiness or of love. However, emotional episodes involving shame and guilt were shared to a somewhat lesser extent (Finkenauer & Rimé, 1998). Laboratory studies confirmed that exposure to an emotion-eliciting condition provokes sharing (Luminet, Bouts, Delie, Manstead, & Rimé, 2000). Generally initiated very soon after experiencing the emotion, sharing is typically a repetitive phenomenon in which more intense emotions are shared more repetitively and for a longer period (Rimé, 2005; Rimé & al., 1998, pp. 163–167).

People's willingness to talk about their emotional experiences suggests that they find some important benefit in it. For positive episodes, some answers to the question of incentive to social sharing exist. Sharing positive episodes reactivates positive emotional feelings, and people are thus led to socially share them further and further. Langston (1994) indeed showed that the sharing of positive emotional episodes involves a process of "capitalization." He demonstrated that expressive displays such as communicating the positive events to others were indeed associated with an enhancement of positive affect far beyond the benefits due to the valence of the positive events themselves. By contrast, sharing negative emotions reactivates negative emotional feelings and memories and should thus be experienced as markedly aversive. It should logically follow that the more an experience is negative, the less it should be shared. Yet, correlations between intensity of negative emotion and extent of sharing are systematically in the opposite direction (for a thorough review, see Rimé et al., 1998, pp. 163–170). Even when it reactivates aversive experiences, sharing is a behavior in which people engage quite willingly. What could be their reward? A widespread belief holds that *merely talking* about an emotional experience would dissolve the emotional impact of this experience and would thus grant emotional recovery. Thus, it is generally thought that people share their emotions because it brings them emotional relief. In line with this belief, recommendations such as "get it off your chest . . ." are often addressed to those who just went through a negative emotional experience. How far does it work?

Before addressing this question, which is at the centre of this chapter, it should be stressed that the interpersonal manifestations just reviewed and the beliefs that are associated to them find their exact parallel at the collective level. Indeed, human beings share emotions not only in person-to-person situations. They also do so in collective contexts. Lay observation of social life reveals collective emotional events such as a victory, a defeat, a loss, or a disaster to elicit collective rituals. The latter involve celebrations or commemorations in which recollecting the event and remembering it together with others is central. As is the case for interpersonal sharing situations, collective rituals quite generally involve the reactivation of the emotions related to the event or episode that is collectively shared. Thus here, again, the question of why people would be willing to reactivate these emotions arises. As far as positive collective emotional episodes are concerned, the capitalization benefits described by Langston (1994) for interpersonal situations are very likely to extend to collective ones. To illustrate, when in 1998 the French national soccer team won the world cup, this became, for an entire nation and for years, a favorite topic of social sharing, supported by innumerable collective recalls in the media or in collective celebrations at later sport events. Though no empirical data tested its impact upon emotional climate, there is little doubt that the memory of this collective triumph largely affected the way French people appraised the condition of their nation in the weeks, months, and even years that followed it. However, in the case of negative collective emotional episodes, communities' and societies' willingness to reexpose their members to it in collective sharing situations is far less obvious. Thus again the question arises of why people would be willing to reactivate these emotions where negative collective episodes are considered. And again, a popular explanation relies upon catharsis: it is commonly believed that collective rituals involving emotional reexposure may "liquidate" the original emotional impact. Is this cathartic view of collective rituals supported?

In this chapter I address this question of the validity of the cathartic view of emotional expression in a social context. In a first step, I consider the case of an interpersonal situation in which an individual shares a negative emotional experience with some target person. Empirical data collected to test the expression-discharge hypothesis are examined. Relying upon the reviewed findings, I then present a model of what expressing emotion in a social context brings and what it does not bring. Next, some tests of this model are described. In a second step, I consider the case of collective rituals in which members are confronted again with a negative emotional episode that affected their community. Here, too, I start by examining what the available evidence reveals about the expression-discharge hypothesis and I then present a model of what reviving emotion in a collective context brings and does not bring. Finally, I describe some tests of this model. I hope to end up demonstrating (1) that what emotional expression in a social context brings and what it does not bring can be clearly established, and (2) that in this regard, the conclusions for interpersonal and collective sharing situations are identical.

Effects of sharing emotion in an interpersonal situation

Testing the expression-discharge hypothesis

The expression-discharge hypothesis was examined in studies in which participants were observed following a definite emotional event (reviewed in Rimé et al, 1998). The research design generally involved assessing (1) the initial intensity of emotions elicited by the episode, (2) the extent of sharing that participants developed after the episode with people around them, and (3) the intensity of emotions elicited when the memory of the episode was activated later. The question was whether a positive correlation occurred between the amount of social sharing after the emotional event and the degree of emotional recovery – or the difference between (1) and (2). Surprisingly, these studies failed to yield such a correlation and thus failed to support the prediction that sharing an emotion would reduce the emotional load.

Following these negative findings, further studies were conducted taking into account *how* people share socially – that is, how they speak when telling others about their emotions and emotional experiences. Pennebaker and Beall (1986), for example, observed that writing about factual aspects of an emotional episode did not affect health variables, whereas writing about emotional aspects did. Experiments involving various types of sharing were thus conducted in order to assess effects of sharing an emotion upon emotional recovery (Zech, 2000; Zech & Rimé, 2005). In three studies, psychology students interviewed relatives about a negative emotional event of their recent past. In a fourth study, participants extensively shared with an experimenter the most upsetting event of their life. In each of these four studies, different sharing conditions were created by instructing participants to emphasize either the factual aspects of the episode or their feelings. Control conditions involved talking about a nonemotional topic. The emotional impact that the shared event still had when reaccessed was assessed through several indices (e.g., emotional intensity of the memory, intensity of bodily sensations when thinking about the event, action tendencies when thinking about the event, challenged basic beliefs) before the sharing interview, immediately following it, and again a couple of days later. In one of the studies, additional assessments were conducted two months later. Contrary to expectations, no effect of sharing type was found on these indices of emotional impact in any of these studies. However, despite these negative findings, when compared to participants in the other conditions, those in the felt emotions condition *consistently* rated the sharing as being more beneficial to them in general (e.g., it was useful), as having relieved their emotions more (e.g., made them feel good), as having helped them more cognitively (e.g., it helped in putting order in themselves), and as being more beneficial interpersonally (e.g., they experienced comforting behaviors from the part of the recipient). Thus, paradoxically, whereas sharing emotional experiences failed to alleviate the load of the emotional memory, participants who shared their emotions found it beneficial compared to the controls.

What benefits did they find in their sharing of an emotion?

Social consequences of sharing an emotion

An answer to this question could be found in data that showed that an interesting interpersonal dynamic develops in sharing situations (Christophe & Rimé, 1997). First, when they rated the intensity of their primary emotions while listening, sharing listeners manifested a remarkable salience of the emotion of interest. This fits data according to which emotional materials exert a fascination in human beings (Rimé, Delfosse, & Corsini, 2005). Second, a clear positive linear relation did indeed occur between the emotional intensity of the episode heard and the intensity of the listeners' emotion. This manifested that hearing an emotional story is emotion-eliciting. Third, responses displayed by sharing listeners varied dramatically as a function of the intensity of the shared episode. For low-intensity episodes, listeners' responses consisted mostly of verbal manifestations. Such responses decreased linearly with increasing intensity of the shared episode. Conversely, the higher the intensity of the episode heard, the more recipients displayed nonverbal behaviors such as touching, body contact, hugging, or kissing. In sum, at increasing levels of emotional intensity, sharing interactions became decreasingly verbal and increasingly nonverbal.

The interpersonal dynamic that develops in the sharing of emotions can thus be sketched as follows. Person A who experienced an emotion feels the need to share this experience and shares it effectively with a Person B. The latter manifests a strong interest for the narrative. This stimulates sharing, and Person A consequently expresses emotions more and more. The enhanced expression arouses emotions in Person B. A reciprocal stimulation of emotion develops in this manner in the dyad, which leads to enhanced empathy and to emotional communion. The empathetic feelings experienced by Person B stimulate a willingness to help and support Person A. If the emotional intensity of the episode shared is high, Person B is likely to reduce his or her verbal communication and to switch to a nonverbal mode, with body contact or touching. Altogether, such a situation is proper to induce an increased liking of B for A. And A, who is the recipient of B's attention, interest, empathy, support, and help, will similarly experience enhanced liking for this sharing target. In sum, the dynamic just sketched manifests that emotion sharing has the potential to bring the sender and the receiver closer to one another. As sharing most often addresses people who already count among intimates (Rimé et al., 1998), it is thus instrumental in maintaining, refreshing, and strengthening important social bonds. Studies of self-disclosure interactions have led to exactly the same conclusions (e.g., Collins & Miller, 1994; Reis & Patrick, 1996).

Thus, targets' responses and the dynamic of sharing interactions obviously favor socio-affective manifestations, with empathy, emotional fusion, feelings of unity, prosocial behavior, social recognition and validation, consolidation of social ties, and social integration. With such socio-affective ingredients, social sharing interactions are well suited to buffer the distress that results from a negative emotional experience. The marked benefits people report after having shared such an experience might well reflect an alleviation of feelings of insecurity, anxiety, and helplessness elicited by this experience. By contrast, cognitive work involving reorganization of motives, reconstruction of schemas, reframing and reappraisal of the event might well be largely absent from sharing situations in which empathy and nonverbal behaviors prevail. In addition, early after an emotion – which is precisely when most sharing takes place – people generally refuse to abandon their frustrated goals, do not consider modifying their hierarchy of motives, stick to their existing schemas, do not want to change their representations, stand by their initial appraisal of the emotional situation, and do not feel ready to reframe it or to change their perspective. Yet completion of such cognitive tasks is essential to emotional recovery. This can explain why sharing an emotion generally fails to bring a sizeable emotional recovery for the shared emotional experience.

Social regulation of the emotional impact of a negative episode: A model

To sum up, people are very eager to share their emotional experiences, and they quite often do so. Contrary to a common assumption, sharing an emotional experience does not bring emotional recovery – in other words, it does not alleviate the impact of the shared emotional experience. Nevertheless, people who have shared an emotion experienced it as beneficial. In order to account for these paradoxical observations, the following concepts are proposed. A negative emotional experience has two distinct consequences. On the one hand, it involves a large number of experiential elements proper to destabilizing the subject. They consist of goal frustration, disconfirmation of expectations, models, and worldviews, loss of symbolic buffers, loss of meaning, and experience of a defeated self. Such elements are the source of a state of *distress* that can take the form of feelings of anxiety, insecurity, help-lessness, estrangement, alienation, loss of self-esteem, loss of self-confidence, and loneliness. On the other hand, *cognitions* resulting from the emotional experience often cause the emotional memory to reaccess the working memory and thus to persist in affecting the person. They then arouse mental rumi-nation, intrusive thoughts and images, a need to talk, and actual sharing. Cognitions of three kinds can provoke such an emotional remanence (Rimé, 2005, 2007): (1) representation of goals that were blocked by the emotion-eliciting situation; (2) expectations, schemas, models, or self- and worldviews that were disconfirmed by the situation; and (3) persistent initial appraisal of the encoded emotional situation – that is, if the person's appraisal of the recalled situation duplicates the initial appraisal of this situation, the same emotion is triggered every time the memory is accessed.

Setting apart these two effects also shows two different aspects in the regu-lation of the emotional impact of a negative episode. On the one hand, in line with developmental theories of attachment (e.g., Ainsworth, 1969), social contacts involving socio-affective manifestations, with empathy, emotional fusion, feelings of unity, prosocial behavior, social recognition and validation, consolidation of social ties, and social integration, are well suited to buffer the *distress* experienced by the person. On the other hand, to eliminate the current impact of a past episode and thus to achieve emotional recovery, emotion regulation should thus turn off each of these various *memory-sustaining cognitions*. This requires completion of all the relevant cognitive tasks: abandonment of one's frustrated goals, reorganization of one's hierarchy of motives, accommodation of one's models and schemas, re-creation of meaning, and assimilation of the event through reframing or reappraisal.

Testing the model

We assume that as it develops in natural conditions, the social sharing of emotion favors the first of these two regulation modes and neglects the second. This would account for the paradoxical fact that sharing an emotion generally failed to reduce the emotional load of the shared episodes while those who shared it experienced the sharing situation as beneficial to them. To test the validity of these assumptions, social sharing situations should be manipulated in a way that allows assessing the effects that are predicted for the two considered regulation modes, respectively. Thus, a sharing situation in which *socio-affective manifestations* would prevail should elicit effects of *social integration*. Conversely, a sharing situation in which *cognitive work* would predominate should result in effects of emotional recovery. Such predictions were tested in two different studies (Nils & Rimé, 2010).

To illustrate, one of the experiments, student volunteers were individually induced into a negative emotional state using a movie clip. Immediately after the film, participants shared their movie experience with a friend of theirs who had come to the lab at the same time. Friends were used as targets, as a number of social sharing studies have shown that sharing very generally addresses friends. Unknown to the participant, the friend was instructed to hold a systematic attitude in the sharing session. Thus, in one condition, the friend had to maintain an empathetic attitude, which corresponded to *socio-affective* responding. In a second condition, the friend had to manifest positive reframing, which corresponded to one modality of *cognitive* responding. In a third, control condition, the friend had to maintain a *neutral* attitude. Dependent variables were measured immediately after the sharing session. Participants had to complete scales assessing emotional, cognitive, and social variables with, respectively, emotional distress, beliefs and worldviews, and loneliness scale. Then, 48 hours later, after reexposure to the film, participants were measured on the same set of scales for a second time. Results showed that movie-related emotional distress was significantly lower in the cognitive condition than in the two other conditions, and this effect was again observed after reexposure to the movie, thus confirming that cognitively oriented sharing brings emotional recovery. In addition, both after sharing and after movie reexposure, beliefs and worldviews that had been challenged by the content of the film (i.e., scenes of human cruelty toward animals) were significantly less dampened in the cognitive than in the two other conditions, thus confirming that cognitively oriented sharing contributes to the reconstruction of assumptions. Finally, both after sharing and after movie reexposure, loneliness scores were much lower in the socio-affective condition than in the two others, thus confirming the interpersonal and social integration benefits of socio-affectively oriented sharing. Altogether, thus, these results were quite consistent with the proposed model.

Effects of reviving emotions in collective rituals

Testing the expression-discharge hypothesis in collective situations

As stated earlier, it is commonly believed that collective rituals involving emotional reexposure can "liquidate" the original emotional impact. Is this cathartic view of collective rituals supported? Empirical observations on collective rituals are extremely scarce. A prototypical case of a social collective situation in which emotions are expressed in a collective context is found in truth commissions. Such commissions take place in countries where major violations of human rights have been perpetrated, such as Northern Ireland, South Africa, Israel–Palestine, Guatemala, Argentine, Chile, Bosnia, Serbia–Kosovo, Haiti, East Timor, Sierra Leone, Rwanda, and El Salvador. In truth commissions, victims are invited to describe publicly, under oath, actions from which they or their relatives had suffered. Similarly, perpetrators describe publicly, under oath, actions as they occurred, in answer to the questions addressed to them. Such situations generally involve strong reactivation of the related emotions and thus offer relevant observations as regards effects of reviving emotions in a collective ritual. Experience with truth commissions in various countries, and in South Africa in particular, has revealed that participation in such tribunals can have both negative and positive emotional consequences for the individuals involved (e.g., Hayner, 2001). As regards negative effects, emotional re-evocation of past dramatic events generally elicited among victims intense emotional reactivation of painful past emotions and eventually unleashed a state of retraumatization. Thus in this domain, too, contrary to widespread views emphasizing the so-called "cathartic" effects of emotional expression in social contexts, no simple emotional "discharge" results from testimony in these tribunals. Here, too, the mere expression of emotions failed to bring emotional recovery. However, at the same time, participating in truth commissions had many positive effects. Survivors often reported having experienced social recognition, pride, relief, and a feeling of completion from having had the opportunity to describe publicly conditions in which they or their relatives had suffered. Thus, as was the case with interpersonal sharing situations, sharing an emotional experience in a collective frame did not reduce the related emotions, but participants manifested important benefits from the sharing process.

A theory of collective rituals: Durkheim (1912)

In his classic work titled *"The elementary forms of religious life,"* Emile Durkheim (1912) formulated concepts proper to making sense of the paradoxical effects of collective rituals. He stressed that collective events such as commemorations, celebrations, feasts, and demonstrations generally involve the presence of the group's symbols (flags, emblems . . .) and of collective expressions (singing, shouting, calling out words or sentences, shared movements, music, and dance) that awaken the latent social dimension of every human being. Particularly central to Durkheim's view was his observation that in such a context individuals' consciousnesses echo one another. Any expression of emotions among participants vividly elicits analogous feelings in people around them, so that a reciprocal stimulation of emotion follows. Such a circular process is particularly propitious to eliciting a state of emotional communion in which participants' salience of their self is lowered and their collective identity is enhanced. They thus end up experiencing unity and similarity. This is how, according to Durkheim, social rituals have the capacity to boost participants' feelings of group belonging and of social integration. By the same token, shared beliefs and collective representations are brought to the foreground, thus consolidating participants' faith in their cultural beliefs and confidence in collective action. As a consequence, participants return to their individual life endowed with feelings of strength, with enhanced trust in life and with feelings of self-confidence.

Durkheim's reasoning leads to the prediction that taking part in a ritual would result in reactivating emotional upset among all participants. Thus, consistently with former observations of truth commissions (e.g., Hayner, 2001) as well as with findings from the study of the social sharing of emotions, participation in such social rituals should have consequences that are at odds with a "cathartic" or discharge view of emotional expression. More specifically, it is predicted that due to strong mutual reactivation in the collective process, negative emotions should be temporarily increased rather than decreased after participation. A second set of consequences considered by Durkheim as resulting from participation in collective rituals regarded social variables. He viewed the emotional communion and fusion elicited by collective rituals as a powerful action lever to stimulate participants' feelings of group belongingness, thus enhancing their social integration. Following the model thus leads to the prediction that after participation in a ritual, participants' perceived societal cohesion and feelings of group belonging should be enhanced.

Testing Durkheim's model

We attempted to test the contrasting predictions from Durkheim investigating participants in the *Gacaca* truth commissions that were set up in the post-genocide Rwanda (Kanyangara, Rimé, Philippot, & Yzerbyt, 2007). In this country, between April and July 1994, it is estimated that some 1,000,000 Tutsis were killed in a genocide. Today, some 130,000 persons accused of participation in the genocide are imprisoned, and more of them die in prisons each year than are judged. To deal with this challenge, a traditional Rwandan community-based conflict resolution system called *Gacaca* was transformed and adapted for judging all those accused of participation in the genocide. We examined whether these Gacaca tribunals exerted an impact on emotions and on social variables. A total of 50 survivors of the 1994 genocide in Rwanda and 50 prisoners accused of being responsible of genocidal acts completed four scales 45 days before and 45 days after their participation in a Gacaca trial. The scales assessed (1) negative emotions presently felt with regard to the genocide, (2) negative stereotypes of the outgroup, and (3) perceived similarity among outgroup members. Based upon Durkheim's (1912) theory, it was predicted that participation in the Gacaca would involve a reactivation of negative emotions in both groups. However, positive consequences were expected for intergroup perception in the form of a reduction of (1) the prejudicial reactions of survivors and prisoners toward each other and (2) the perceived homogeneity of outgroup members.

With the exception of anger that decreased among prisoners and remained stable among survivors, negative emotions (sadness, fear, disgust, anxiety, and shame) were significantly enhanced after participation in the Gacaca, especially among survivors. As for social variables, before Gacaca, survivors were more stereotyped against prisoners than the other way round. However, in line with the model of effects of collective rituals, the negative stereotype toward the other group decreased markedly after the Gacaca, both among survivors and among prisoners. This effect was particularly pronounced for the stereotypes held by survivors toward the prisoners. As regards outgroup homogeneity, research on stereotyping and intergroup relations has demonstrated that one signature of intergroup prejudice is to consider members of the outgroup as being similar to each other (for a collection, see Yzerbyt, Judd, & Corneille, 2004). Building on Durkheim's insights, our hypothesis was that outgroup similarity should decrease after the Gacaca. This is indeed what our results revealed, both in the survivors and the prisoners samples.

Taken together, the patterns of results of both indices of social cohesion are totally in line with Durkheim's hypothesis. The emotionally intense social ritual of the Gacaca increased social cohesion in at least two ways: by lessening the negative stereotypes attributed to the outgroup and by reducing the perceived similarity attached to outgroup members. Thus, at the social-psychological level, the Gacaca would seem to have both significant and positive consequences. In particular, the fact that both negative stereotypes and outgroup similarity perception diminished is evidence of a better psycho-social context, in which prejudice is less likely to be prominent.

To sum up, the above results fully supported the predictions derived from Durkheim's model. They brought out two sets of facts that seemed at first sight to contradict one another: on the one hand, that social sharing of emotions in a collective situation is predictive of enhanced emotional arousal, and, on the other hand, that emotional sharing also predicts positive effects in the form of enhanced social integration.

General conclusion

The theoretical concepts and empirical observations developed in this chapter support the view that the social sharing of emotion, whether in interpersonal situations or in collective rituals, encompasses similar psychosocial ingredients. Neither person-to-person emotional sharing nor collective rituals manifested the capacity to terminate the related emotional experience and to grant affected persons emotional recovery. Both processes necessarily induce the reactivation of the emotional episode upon which they are focused. In the case of negative episodes, such a reactivation inevitably opens upon a temporary rise of negative emotions. However, whether in interpersonal interactions or in collective rituals, an emotional sharing situation quite generally – though not always (for exceptions, see e.g., Pennebaker & Harber, 1993) – involves a process of emotional contagion. Such a process opens up an emotional communion among participants, whether they are intimate social sharing partners or members of a large crowd. Theory and facts converged in showing that such a state of emotional fusion has several major emotional, social, and cognitive consequences, for the group as well as for the individuals involved. These consequences include recognition and validation of the shared suffering, development of prosocial behaviors including social support, and social integration in the form of consolidation of participants' social ties. Such consequences can buffer the destabilizing effects of the shared episode. Still, contrarily to the popular expression-discharge or cathartic view of emotional expression in social situations, these consequences are unlikely to bring emotional recovery. Experiments indeed demonstrated that emotional recovery was obtained only when the emotional sharing markedly involved cognitive work – an ingredient that is often missing from naturally developing sharing situations.

References

Ainsworth, M. D. S. (1969). Object relations, dependency and attachment: A theoretical review of the infant–mother relationship. *Child Development, 40,* 969–1025.

Christophe, V., & Rimé, B. (1997). Exposure to the social sharing of emotion: Emotional impact, listener responses and the secondary social sharing. *European Journal of Social Psychology, 27,* 37–54.

Collins, N. L., & Miller, L. C. (1994). Self-disclosure and liking: A meta-analytic review. *Psychological Bulletin, 116,* 457–475.

Durkheim, F. (1912). *Les formes élémentaires de la vie religieuse* [The elementary forms of religious life]. Paris: Alcan.

Finkenauer, C., & Rimé, B. (1998). Keeping emotional memories secret: Health and subjective well-being when emotions are not shared. *Journal of Health Psychology, 3,* 47–58.

Hayner, P. B. (2001). *Unspeakable truths: Confronting state terror and atrocity.* New York: Routledge.

Kanyangara, P., Rimé, B., Philippot, P., & Yzerbyt, V. (2007). Collective rituals, intergroup perception and emotional climate: Participation in "Gacaca" tribunals and assimilation of the Rwandan genocide. *Journal of Social Issues, 63,* 387–403.

Langston, C. A. (1994). Capitalizing on and coping with daily-life events: Expressive responses to positive events. *Journal of Personality and Social Psychology, 6,* 1112–1125.

Luminet, O., Bouts, P., Delie, F., Manstead, A. S. R., & Rimé, B. (2000). Social sharing of emotion following exposure to a negatively valenced situation. *Cognition and Emotion, 1,* 661–688.

Nils, F., & Rimé, B. (2010). *Beyond the myth of venting: Social sharing modes determine benefits from emotional disclosure.* Manuscript submitted for publication.

Pennebaker, J. W., & Beall, S. (1986). Confronting a traumatic event: Toward an understanding of inhibition and disease. *Journal of Abnormal Psychology, 95,* 274–281.

Pennebaker, J. W., & Harber, K. (1993). A social stage model of collective coping: The Loma Prieta earthquake and Persian Gulf war. *Journal of Social Issues, 49,* 125–145.

Reis, H. T., & Patrick, B. C. (1996). Attachment and intimacy: Component processes. In E. T. Higgins & A. W. Kruglanski (Eds.), *Social psychology: Handbook of basic principles* (pp. 523–563). New York: Guilford Press.

Rimé, B. (1989). Le partage social des émotions [The social sharing of emotions]. In B. Rimé & K. Scherer (Eds.), *Les émotions* (pp. 271–303). Neuchâtel, Switzerland: Delachaux et Niestlé.

Rimé, B. (2005). *Le partage social des émotions* [The social sharing of emotions]. Paris: Presses Universitaires de France.

Rimé, B. (2007). Interpersonal emotion regulation. In J. J. Gross (Ed.), *Handbook of emotion regulation* (pp. 466–485). New York: Guilford Press.

Rimé, B., Delfosse, C., & Corsini, S. (2005). Emotional fascination: Responses elicited by viewing pictures of September 11 attack. *Cognition and Emotion, 19*, 923–932.

Rimé, B., Finkenauer, C., Luminet, O., Zech, E., & Philippot, P. (1998). Social sharing of emotion: New evidence and new questions. In W. Stroebe & M. Hewstone (Eds.), *European review of social psychology* (Vol. 9, pp. 145–189). Chichester, UK: Wiley.

Rimé, B., Mesquita, B., Philippot, P., & Boca, S. (1991a). Beyond the emotional event: Six studies on the social sharing of emotion. *Cognition and Emotion, 5*, 435–465.

Rimé, B., Noël, P., & Philippot, P. (1991b). Episode émotionnel, réminiscences cognitives et réminiscences sociales [Emotional episodes, mental reminiscences, and social reminiscences]. *Cahiers Internationaux de Psychologie Sociale, 11*, 93–104.

Rimé, B., Philippot, P., Boca, S., & Mesquita, B. (1992). Long lasting cognitive and social consequences of emotion: Social sharing and rumination. In W. Stroebe & M. Hewstone (Eds.), *European review of social psychology* (Vol. 3, pp. 225–258). Chichester, UK: Wiley.

Rimé, B., Yogo, M., & Pennebaker, J. W. (1996). [Social sharing of emotion across cultures]. Unpublished raw data.

Singh-Manoux, A., & Finkenauer, C. (2001). Cultural variations in social sharing of emotions: An intercultural perspective on a universal phenomenon. *Journal of Cross-Cultural Psychology, 32*, 647–661.

Yogo, M., & Onoe, K. (1998, August). *The social sharing of emotion among Japanese students*. Poster session presented at ISRE '98, the biannual conference of the International Society for Research on Emotion, Würzburg, Germany.

Yzerbyt, V. Y., Judd, C. M., & Corneille, O. (2004). *The psychology of group perception: Perceived variability, entitativity, and essentialism*. Hove, UK: Psychology Press.

Zech, E. (2000). *The effects of the communication of emotional experiences*. Unpublished doctoral dissertation. University of Louvain, Louvain-la-Neuve, Belgium.

Zech, E., & Rimé, B. (2005). Is talking about an emotional experience helpful? Effects on emotional recovery and perceived benefits. *Clinical Psychology and Psychotherapy, 12*, 270–287.

7 The cultural construction of self and emotion

Implications for well-being

Girishwar Misra

Let a man lift himself by his own self alone; let him not degrade himself because the self alone is the friend of oneself and the self is the enemy of oneself. For one who has conquered his very self by his own self, his very self becomes his friend, but for one who has not conquered his self, his very self will act inimically, as would an actual enemy.

Srimadbhagavadgita (Radhakrishnan, 2002)

Introduction

Recent years have witnessed greater attention to the study of well-being. Such a shift in research focus coincides with an acute awareness about the limits of planet earth, the global environmental crisis, and increasing incidences of hostility and violence in many parts of the world. At the individual level, too, the lack of peace of mind and increased stress and tension are evident. This scenario raises serious questions about wellness of our existence and quality of life. As the citation given above from the *Srimadbhagavadgita* (Radhakrishnan, 2002) – an important ancient Indian text – suggests, the ups and downs in our lives revolve around the self, and everything depends on the way we handle it. In everyday experience, we often notice that the self is critical to navigating through the complex web of life. Taking a cue from these observations, this chapter questions the received notions of self and emotions and examines how they construct and shape well-being and what is the possibility of achieving the state of well-being.

It is argued that while notions of self work as intrinsic sources of emotion and direct the course of appraisals of our linkages with the environment, the self, too, is deeply entrenched in emotions. The emotional engagement transforms the experience of selfhood in significant ways, which may further or interfere with one's well-being. However, the linkages of self and emotions and their implications for well-being may vary in diverse cultural contexts. After examining some of the core assumptions pertaining to these constructs, it is proposed that the indigenous cultural psychology of selfhood plays a critical role in shaping the way self and emotion relate to people's well-being. Being informed by the cultural meanings and practices, the self not only selectively encourages, sustains, or constrains emotional engagements but is also shaped by them. Taking cultural variety into account implies that the notion of well-being has to be expanded to incorporate personal as well as transcendental aspects of selfhood. The notion of selfhood in the indigenous Indian tradition illustrates this point. It is concluded that a more inclusive vision of selfhood is imperative for securing a viable perspective that may furnish a better ground for the future of humanity.

Well-being: A perennial concern

Since antiquity, questions such as "Who am I? What is the good life? Where and how can I find happiness?" have been of great concern for thinkers across the globe. The answers to such perennial questions have been quite varied, because what counts as well-being depends on the way we define who we are and how we feel about that. Such concepts are articulated by cultures in implicit and explicit ways and are sustained with the help of institutions and practices of a given culture. Over two thousand years ago the Buddha realized that suffering (*Dukh*) is an intrinsic part of existence. He also stated that suffering has causes, and those causes can be removed. Even before the Buddha, the Vedic sages treated the pursuit of well-being (*Sukha*) as a reasonable goal of life and aspired to have "a long life with dignity". Similar questions have also been raised by Western thinkers.

In the course of time, modernity has changed the fate of humanity. It has apparently brought humanity to a point when life in the so-called "developed world" has become easier, more comfortable, more disease-free, with more scope for leisure. At the same time, it poses a serious dilemma: Are we happier and do we experience a better state of existence along with prosperity? We are not sure that people are really happier than before. The general life satisfaction (LS) is reported to be greater than average, but unhappiness, too, is present (Diener & Oishi, 2000). The strategy of economic growth has not worked very well (Diener & Seligman, 2005). In fact, certain aspects of economic growth (e.g., pollution, selfishness, breakdown in the community, criminal activities) detract from the more general human well-being. If we consider data about depression, anxiety, and stress, human life at large seems to be in trouble, and people are not well (see Goodwin, 1997; Kessler et al., 2003). The consumer culture, with its emphasis on material goods, is making people more and more vulnerable to temptation, ill-gotten wealth, and a desire for more than is necessary (see Dittmar, 2004; Luthar, 2003). The younger generation in particular is manifesting anger, violence, and other problems of the affective system. In the poor countries the incidence of inequalities, unemployment, malnutrition and disease is present in a significant segment of the population.

We also find that while happiness is certainly the most cherished goal in almost all societies, its meaning varies across cultures (Diener & Oishi, 2000; Veenhoven, 2000). In broad terms people in individualist cultures report higher life satisfaction and happiness and confine happiness to personal achievement. People from collectivist cultures, on the other hand, emphasize relational, communal, and collective aspects of life. In general, there are two main ways of conceptualizing well-being – *hedonic* and *eudaemonic*. The hedonic view emphasizes that well-being refers to the evaluation of life experiences as pleasure and displeasure. Assessed in terms of *subjective well-being* (SWB), it is defined as "a person's evaluative reactions to his or her life – either in terms of life satisfaction (cognitive evaluations) or affect (ongoing emotional reactions)" (Diener & Diener, 1995, p. 653). It includes all judgments about the good and bad aspects of life (Kahneman, Diener, & Schwarz, 1999) that are aimed at maximizing human happiness. SWB is necessary for a good life and good society but is certainly not sufficient for it (Diener, Oishi, & Lucas, 2003). The eudaemonic approach, as Ryff (1989) has noted, implies that living well is not simply a matter of experiencing more pleasure than pain; instead, it involves a striving for perfection and realization of one's potential. Accordingly, Ryff and Keyes (1995) have proposed the notion of psychological well-being in terms of six components – that is, self-acceptance, positive relations with others, autonomy, environmental mastery, purpose in life, and personal growth.

Interestingly, both of the above approaches were developed in the Western cultural context, which respects the value and ideology of liberal individualism. Studies in other parts of the world (e.g., Ng, Ho, Wong, & Smith, 2003; Kitayama, Markus, & Kurokawa, 2000; Sibia, Misra, & Srivastava, 2004; Singh & Misra, 2000; Singhal & Misra, 1994; A. K. Srivastava & Misra, 2003) indicate the significance of harmony in interpersonal relationships, achievement at work, and contentment in life. These features are more salient parts of well-being and happiness. The state of well-being refers to a tranquil state of mind achieved through harmony with other people, society, and nature (Misra, 2005). It lies in the rhythm that characterizes resonance across all life forms and cannot be equated with material prosperity. The evidence does not indicate that the level of happiness or SWB is linearly related to the extent of economic growth (A. K. Srivastava & Misra, 2003). The Indian notions of well-being are less dispositional and more interpersonally distributed. They necessarily entail affective engagement of a relational self in the eco-cultural context. Therefore an examination of the relationship between emotion and the self seems appropriate.

Self and emotions: Separate or mutually constituted?

In psychological scholarship there exists a strong tradition of conceptualizing the self as a cognitive structure. William James (1890/1983) viewed self as "the center of the psychological universe and the lens through which other aspects of the world are perceived". Mead (1934) also considered self-consciousness as "essentially a cognitive rather than an emotional phenomenon" (p. 173). In general, mainstream psychology has opted for a cognitive view of the self (Leary & Tangney, 2003). This position is contested by many social theorists (e.g., Goffman, 1959; Hochschild, 1979; Rosenberg, 1991; Stryker, 2004). Today the study of self clearly follows two disparate lines of research, focusing on cognitive and motivational-emotional aspects, respectively (see Leary, 2007).

The reflexive process involved in the constitution of the self seems to be organized by both cognition and emotion and the sense of self comprises not only self-conceptions but also a set of self-feelings. The onset of internal conversation or "self-talk" usually arises out of interruptions and is certainly mediated by emotions. The self probably has an emotional core that is central to the architecture for self-conception (Gordon, 1989; Scheff, 1990). The fact that self-conscious emotions (e.g., pride, shame, embarrassment) and role-taking emotions involve emotionally reflexive assessments of the identities and actions of self and other (Stryker, 2004) clearly lends support to this concept.

There is another line of inquiry that brings home the point that the self is intimately related to emotions. It is found that memory and self-consciousness are neurologically structured around emotional processes. An emotion-based language seems to be the precursor of higher-order cognitive processes. It has been observed that the emotional relationship in neonates is the foundation of intersubjective awareness and interpersonal bonds with primary caretakers (Stroufe, 1997) and furnishes the necessary foundations for the development of a sense of self. As Damasio (1999) has argued, the biologically based emotional processes are the foundation of cognition, and the self is related to body-based feelings in some fundamental sense. He identifies three layers of self: *proto self*, *core self*, and *autobiographical self*. The proto self consists of the non-conscious dimension of self based on the collection of feelings and neural reactions that an individual experiences at a given moment. The core self is a schematic image based on non-verbal experiences that creates a sense of being. It is derived from the feelings and reactions held in the proto self. The autobiographical self is organized around memories of past experiences facilitated by language and predicated upon preexisting core-self experiences. Thus development of self-consciousness and self-conception is contingent upon emotional processes. In this connection the following remarks of Panksepp (1994) are noteworthy:

> emotional feeling without some type of self referencing seems impossible. I suspect that we will make the most progress in understanding the basic nature of primal forms of consciousness if we start by modifying Descartes' famous epithet: "I think, therefore I am" to "I feel, therefore I am," and then proceed to probe the neural nature of feelings.
>
> (p. 397)

It seems that the structure of self-conceptions is organized around a foundation of emotional self-feelings (Turner, 2000). Also, the cultural models amplify and constrain our emotional experience in significant ways. Emotions are not invariant states triggered and manifested in predetermined ways. Our "feelings," as Rosaldo (1984) succinctly describes, "are not substances to be discovered in our blood but social practices organized by stories that we both enact and tell" (p. 143). The focal, normative, and ideal representations of emotions tend to vary across cultures and are often illustrated within culture regularities.

It has been noted that social context influences emotional experience more in interdependent than in independent cultures (Kitayama, Ishii, Imada, Takamura, & Ramaswamy, 2006; Mesquita, 2001; Misra, 2004a; Shweder & Haidt, 2000). There is a growing body of literature that views emotions as interpersonally distributed phenomena. Self-conceptions and self feelings are both found to be susceptible to interpersonal processes. Emotions emerge as socially emergent phenomena related to roles and mediated by situational expectations and cultural definitions (Averill, 1980; Barrett, 2006; Harre, 1986; Lutz, 1988; Mesquita, 2007; Misra, 2004b). For instance, Kitayama et al. (2000) noted that for the Japanese respondents, there was a higher degree of association between the interpersonally engaged positive emotions and the general positive emotions than between the interpersonally disengaged positive emotions and the general positive emotions. By contrast, for the US respondents there was stronger association between positive emotions and the interpersonally disengaged positive emotions than between the interpersonally engaged positive emotions and the general positive emotions. They also reported that the relationship between positive and negative emotions in the case of the US respondents was largely negative, and in the case of Japanese respondents it was largely positive. The studies also indicate that the basis of life satisfaction judgments, too, varies across cultures (Suh, Diener, Oishi, & Triandis, 1998).

It has also been noted that in the North American context good feelings are conceptualized as the properties of an individual. In the non-Western context emotions are often construed to be much more social and communal, serving as an index of the nature of the attendant social relationship rather than revealing inner states (Lutz, 1988). In the East, people *share* emotions, which are located *between* individuals. In Japan examples of these social emotions include *amae*, or the hopeful anticipation of another's indulgence (Doi, 1973), as well as *ittaikan*, or the feeling of oneness that arises when the person is in a closely knit group (Ng, 2001). The Indian perspective on emotion considers that emotional experience is an emergent experience contingent on joint operation of personal and situational factors (Menon & Shweder, 1994; Shweder & Haidt, 2000). Recently, Misra (2004a) empirically examined the antecedents of emotion experiences in India. He noted that there are multiple pathways through which these emotions are experienced. The antecedents indicate that emotional episodes involve motivational, communicative, and regulatory processes operating within and/or between individuals. It was found that while some of these processes apply or are potentially applicable more generally, others vary considerably across individuals. Emotions seem to perform organizing and motivating functions to facilitate adaptive goal-directed behavior.

It seems that while emotions might be a key organizational force for the constitution of the self, the self is a product of the attunement of self-feelings and socio-cultural expectations for emotional expression. Selfhood, therefore, seems to be constituted from the continuous negotiation of the socio-cultural dynamics of feeling rules and emotion cultures. The experience of emotion, particularly the judgment of significance of some event for one's well-being, is always related to the self. Thus, it is more appropriate to hold the position that self and emotion are mutually constituted in specific cultural contexts.

Culture and self: The variety in selfhood

While the study of the self in mainstream psychology has largely been pre-occupied with delineating its representation as a cognitive structure, people in general always engage with the self in a reflexive manner. It is not only an object of knowledge but also the subject of experience situated in the social context. The reflexive consciousness involved in it, therefore, is not independent of the cultural meanings and practices within which people grow and develop. In general the analysis of self has underlined two aspects of self i.e., agentic and relational or communal. Cultures vary in the degree of emphasis placed on agency and communion (Bakan, 1966; Helgeson & Fritz, 1999; Heelas & Lock, 1981; Kagitcibasi, 1996; Leary & Tangney, 2003).

The cultural scholarship has been showing that many aspects of self are rooted in one's membership in a cultural community and are shaped by the symbolically mediated experiences in it. Studies undertaken in North America and Europe and in Asian countries such as Japan, Korea, China and India have indicated cultural differences in ways of self-construal and understanding, and such differences have implications for various psychological functions (see Baumeister, 1987; Bellah, Madsen, Sullivan, Swidler, & Tipton, 1985; Bhatia, 2005; Chao, 1995; Hermans, 2001; Kitayama, Markus, & Lieberman, 1995; Markus & Kitayama, 1991, 1994; Marsella, DeVos, & Hsu, 1985; Mascolo & Bhatia, 2002; Misra, 2001; Sampson, 1988; Shweder & Bourne, 1984; J. B. P. Sinha & Kanungo, 1997; Triandis, 1989). These studies demonstrate that the autonomous, bounded, and separate notion of self termed as "independent self" found in individualist cultures is not universal. There are also socio-centric and relational notions of the self, which are found in collectivist cultures.

The dichotomous view of self (e.g., independent vs. interdependent), however, does not capture the variety in notions of the self found in totality. In particular, it does not recognize transpersonal/transcendental notions of the self. The Indian notions of the self illustrate this point quite clearly. In particular, it not only situates relationship in the context of other humans, but it also encompasses transcendental or spiritual reality. This aspect has been largely neglected in the study of self. As Cross and Gore have observed,

> given the overwhelming proportion of North Americans who believe in a god or who practice some form of religion, it is puzzling that spirituality has largely been ignored in research on self and identity. Non-Western psychologists and cross-cultural researchers seem to have less reluctance to consider this dimension. To date, Western researchers have paid little attention to this perspective on self.
>
> (Cross & Gore, 2005, p. 557)

The reluctance to consider this aspect of self indicates that culturally informed psychological research is yet to cover much ground (Kitayama, Duffy, & Uchida, 2007). The indigenous Indian perspective on the self, however, goes beyond the dichotomies and presents an alternative model. With this in view, a brief account of the self in the Indian tradition is presented below.

Selfhood in the Indian context: Some observations

Culturally sensitive studies of the self in the Indian context show a number of features that expand the notion of self. They can be briefly summarized as follows:

1. Self–other continuity

Selfhood is conceived to be continuous with others. The individual develops through participation in the unity of all things and demands the pursuit of diverse goals depending on the station in the journey of life. It includes engagement as well as dissociation and detachment. As Roland (1988) explains, Indian selfhood involves familial self as well as spiritual self. Interpersonal behavior depends on the factors of role, place, and relationship. Kakar (1978, 1997) has noted that the basis of social relationships is mutual caring, involvement, and emotional affinity. Recent empirical studies in the Indian context indicate the greater prevalence of social identity (Dhawan, Roseman, Naidu, Thapa, & Rettek, 1995) in self-descriptions. Misra and Giri (1995) observed that interdependent as well as independent kinds of self-construals were present among Indians. In another study R. Srivastava and Misra (1997) reported that independent and interdependent life goals were moderately positively related (see, for a review, Misra, 2001). Mascolo, Misra, and Rapisardi (2004) found that individual and relational concepts of self were present in both Indian and US participants. The cultural differences arose in the specific ways in which the two notions are constructed.

2. Tolerance for dissonance and coexistence of disparate elements

In the Indian perspective reality is always taken to be composed of many elements, and it is the balance among these that becomes crucial. There is a striving to catch hold of the totality and a desire to see continuity in the diverse and contradictory elements, many of them latent or implicit. Multiplicity among the constituents is very common. When dualities are posited, they indicate complementarities (*Ardhanarishwar*). Relationships are often considered complementary, and a person who sees the whole is considered to be the real seer (*Avibhktam vibhaketeshu yah pasyati sa pasyati*).

There are several studies that indicate that in the Indian world view the experience of self involves diverse elements (Marriott, 1976; Ramanujan, 1990; D. Sinha & Tripathi, 1994; Tripathi & Leviatan, 2003). Shweder, Mahapatra, and Miller (1987) have drawn attention to incorporating autonomy, community, and divinity while examining morality. It must be noted that India has been interacting with diverse cultures and has imbibed diverse influences. Taking that into account, J. B. P. Sinha and Pandey (2007) have tried to articulate the construct of the "Indian mindset". They suggest that due to acculturation, Indians have developed a mindset that distinguishes Indians from others. One of the key components of this mindset is tolerance to allow those elements that cannot be integrated to coexist, and maintaining a diversity of values, norms, beliefs, and practices. Indians' high context sensitivity turns this diversity into a competence to shift the mindset in order to respond to various contextual demands.

3. Transcendental self

The indigenous Indian discourses have approached the self from a wide range of positions, ranging from self as illusion (e.g. Buddhism's *Anatta*) to the view of multiple selves. The self-views in India reflected in various schools of thought (e.g., Vedanta, Samkhya, Yoga, Sufism, Jainism, Sikhism) present a multifaceted view of the self. Most of them tend, however, to make a distinction between bodily self (*Ahamkar*) and a higher transcendental self like "*Atman.*" As Desai and Collins (1986) have noted, *Atman* represents the independent and transcendent of temporal change and particulars, while *Ahamkar* represents the inflated sense of personal worth that is a consequence of ignorance of one's true being. This position implies that self is not only body-centered and personal but also transpersonal, shared, and spiritual. In fact, the transcendental self is held as true self and an ideal state of being that is positive and aspired. It goes beyond the empirical self that is socially embedded, context-sensitive, and subject to change. The Atman is a non-material or metaphysical self, as opposed to the material, and empirical self, which is hierarchically lower than the metaphysical self (Bharati, 1985). This aspiration is manifested in the conceptualization of self as an inherently blissful and conscious existence (*Sat Chit Anand*). This approach to the self stands in contrast to the personalized individual self of Western psychology. The Indian view is an example of a potential model of self that offers a more inclusive perspective (see Paranjpe, 1998).

Metaphorically, the individual (*Jiva*) is composed of a multilayered structure with five sheaths. They include the body, the senses, the mind, thinking organ (*Manas*), or ego (*Ahamkara*), and intellect or reflection (*Buddhi*). The real self or *Atman* lies beyond these five sheaths. Owing to ignorance (*Avidya*), *Atman* is often fused with the material elements, and we misidentify ourselves with acquired identities (*Upadhi*) and possessions and develop attachments to them. This idea is reflected in the following verse by Shankaracharya [Adi Shankara, 788–820 CE], a great Vedanta scholar:

> I have a body, but I am not the body:
> I have the senses, but I am not the sense;
> I have a mind, but I am not the mind:
> I have an intellect; but I am not the intellect;
> I am the Eternally Blissful Pure Consciousness.
> — Shankaracharya, *Atma-Shatakam/Nirvana
>   Shatakam* [The Song of the Self]

Thus, to realize the true self and seeking well-being one needs to go beyond the ego (*Ahamkara*) and transcend it. The goal is to expand the empirical self and identify with the higher and more inclusive spiritual self. This has implications for personal as well as social lives, including norms for conducting oneself (*Dharma*). Expanding consciousness by yoga to achieve the state of integral self has been considered as the chief pathway for self-realization (Patañjali, 2003). It embraces mind, body, society, and environment. The Bhagavad Gita states that the process of self-realization involves deconditioning. The deconditioned self is not under the influence of material nature (*prakriti*). The true self is a deeper inner consciousness that identifies the individual with the universe or cosmos. This view proposes a single unity in life, with all entities supposed to share common attributes.

The concern for transcendent or spiritual reality, however, is combined with the web of social life. Thus *dharma* (righteous action), *artha* (wealth), *kama* (pleasure), and *moksha* (spiritual emancipation) are considered equally important goals in life. The primary aspect of dharma is performing the duties that pertain to one's stage in life. Social responsibilities toward the other are mandatory rather than optional. Through devotional practice (*bhakti*), practicing yoga, meditation, and righteous action one's ultimate individual goal is to cultivate the awareness that one's true self is indistinguishable from the transcendental reality (*Brahman*). Thus the journey relates to the spiritual order in the same way as the functions of the self in everyday life are related to fulfilling one's duties in the social order. This necessitates going beyond the dichotomy of independent and interdependent selves and moving towards relational and encompassing models of self-conception.

Roland (1988) argues that the notion of detachment from immediate emotional connection, a theme central to Hindu spirituality, in some sense marks out the spiritual self as a realm of autonomy within the larger Hindu experience of unity. Renunciation in adulthood in the service of spiritual discipline seems to be a step in the loosening of personal attachments and obligations in extended family–communal relationships and a reaching toward personal autonomy in the spiritual sphere (Roland, 1996). Thus in the Indian worldview the themes of autonomy and social interdependence have both been given a significant place (see Collins, 1991; Ramanujam, 1986).

The cosmogenic Indian perspective views a person in context and as organically related to the universe. It essentially subscribes to a biological, organic, and holistic worldview. It envisages an all-encompassing transcendental reality in which man finds the source of his dependent being, the support of life, the security of his well-ordered world. Indians think of humanity more as an instance of a species of living beings than as members of the human race (see Nakamura, 1964).

4. Mind training and self-control

The experience of bliss, happiness, and well-being is contingent on the training of the mind. Equanimity and a state of a balanced mind (*Sthita pragya*) is not hedonic. It is equidistant from both positive and negative affect. This state decreases unwanted attachment to incentives and objects in the external world. Such a state is necessary for remaining healthy, as health lies in the state of being *auto locus* (*Swastha*). Such a person enjoys a harmonious interplay of cognition and affect rather than being subjugated to them. One needs to control the senses rather than being subject to them. Yoga, as defined by its founder, Patañjali, is nothing but regulating the mind and its activities (*Yogaschittavritinirodhah*). At the same time, by placing emphasis on yoking or uniting the self with Self (Universal being), yoga allows people to contribute to the social quality of life (see Patañjali, 2003). The discipline of mind is critical. As the Dalai Lama has beautifully said,

> the systematic training of the mind – the cultivation of happiness, the genuine inner transformation by deliberately selecting and focusing on positive mental states and challenging negative mental states – is possible because of the very structure and function of the brain . . . But the wiring in our brain is not static, not irrevocably fixed. Our brains are also adaptable.
>
> (Dalai Lama & Cutler, 1998, pp. 44–45)

Thus it is evident that the pursuit of happiness and achieving the state of well-being is not a fixed property of a person. It is distributed and shared across persons and situations. As one of the famous ancient Indian social thinkers, Chanakya, says, the source of well-being lies in leading a virtuous life (Dharma) (*Sukhasya mulam dharmah*). Dharma leads to worldly prosperity as well as spiritual growth (*Yatobhyudaya nihshreyas sidhih sa dharmah*). As human beings, we have the power to choose – but we have to make a wise choice and distinguish between the good (*Shreya*) and the merely pleasant (*Preya*). The desire for happiness is the main cause of pain. Desires do not die, and there is no end to the cycle of desires (see Kiran Kumar, 2006). Being more and more attached to them, people become greedy and engage in conflict and violence. True and lasting happiness arises from wisdom, tranquility, and contentment (*Santosha*). Pleasure and pain both are relative. It is the egoistic feeling that leads us to dislike suffering. Well-being requires that we enlarge our consciousness and develop a capacity for enjoying all kinds of experiences, as our empirical life is interspersed with both pleasure and pain. The distributed notion of well-being demands developing socially engaged emotions like empathy, forgiveness, and non violence (*Ahimsa*).

Conclusion

The conclusion can be drawn that well-being is a joint project, embedded in specific cultural settings. Thus various indigenous psychologies have viewed the person or society as the primary reality. Good feelings are configured in different forms. It is through intercultural dialogue that we reach to a thorough understanding of what it means to be and how one can become that. So far, psychology has largely been preoccupied with North American and European perspectives, which underrepresent the modes of being. This chapter makes the culture-specific grounding of the notion of well-being its central focus. Since meanings and concepts are molded by culture, psychology is going to be enriched and become universal if it goes culture-inclusive and opens itself up to ideas from outside the Western tradition, where less individuated alternatives of personhood exist.

It is gratifying that having been culturally bound and blind for a long time, the discipline has moved towards a culturally informed perspective (Gergen, Gulerce, Lock, & Misra, 1996; Marsella, 1998; Nisbett, 2004). In a way it is the revival of an old tradition of scholarship going back to Wundt. Recent years have witnessed a substantial increase in interest in cultural approaches within psychology (see Kim, Yang, & Hwang, 2006; Kitayama & Cohen, 2007; Misra & Mohanty, 2002; Rao & Marwaha, 2005; Valsiner & Rosa, 2007). Culture is increasingly being taken as a moderator or constitutive of psychological processes. Interestingly, this shift coincides with happenings outside the academic world (e.g., increasing immigration, globalization, capital and labor flow, identity politics). Also, instead of viewing culture as a "trait," it is being treated more like a chronic situation or set of situations that determine what kinds of attributes, ways of life, and social practices are possible. In this way, culture becomes an emergent property of individuals interacting with their environments and, hence, an intersubjective, shared, and socially established system of meanings and practices. As a rich network of habits and experiences, culture performs representational as well as performative roles. In these efforts, culture is viewed as a symbolic resource that accumulates and is transmitted across generations.

The actual conditions of life, and what an individual or society makes of those conditions, as well as the way such an individual or society relates to them at the level of perception, thinking, feeling, and action, are important. However, the pursuit of happiness and well-being in hedonistic ways by treating individuals as disconnected social entities would not take us very far. Well-being goes beyond the personal sphere. We need to enlarge the scope of analysis to incorporate the social and transcendental aspects of selfhood in its fold. As Keyes and Haidt (2003) note, people who enjoy well-being or flourish have an enthusiasm for life and are actively and productively engaged with others and in social institutions, in the promotion of human–nature connections, and in social capital (family, friends, community, trust). Well-being promotes a better society, with happy people who are sociable, generous, creative, active, tolerant, healthy, altruistic, and economically productive, and have long life. This requires multidisciplinary effort and the orchestration of resources at different levels (see Royal Society, 2004).

We psychologists are at an exciting moment in history. Our effort to understand self and well-being has potential to transform the understanding of psychology, and of human life in general. However, complete and thorough understanding demands a vision that recognizes the whole range of our being, covering all the layers of existence. As Sri Aurobindo, one of the great Indian thinkers of the twentieth century, has reminded us:

> This bodily appearance is not all;
> The form deceives; the person is a mask;
>
>   . . .
>
> In this investiture of fleshly life
> A soul that is a spark of God survives
> And sometimes it breaks through the sordid screen
> And kindles a fire that makes us half-divine.
> > > > Sri Aurobindo (Ghose, 1954, *Savitri*,
> > > > > Book I, Canto III & II)

Acknowledgments

The encouragement and support received from Ajit Dalal, Sunil D. Gaur, S. K. Kiran Kumar, Matthijs Cornelissen, Pradeep Chakkarath, Madhuri Misra, and Jurgen Straub are gratefully acknowledged.

References

Averill, J. R. (1980). A constructivist view of emotion. In R. Plutchik & H. Kellerman (Eds.), *Emotion: Theory, research and experience: Vol. 1. Theories of emotion* (pp. 305–339). New York: Academic Press

Bakan, D. (1966). *The duality of human existence*. Chicago: Rand McNally.

Barrett, L. F. (2006). Solving the emotion paradox categorization and the experience of emotion. *Personality and Social Psychology Review, 10,* 20–46.

Baumeister, R. F. (1987). How the self became a problem: A psychological review of historical research. *Journal of Personality and Social Psychology, 52,* 163–176.

Bellah, R. N., Madsen, R., Sullivan, W. M., Swidler, A., & Tipton, S. M. (1985). *Habits of the heart: Individualism and commitment in American life*. New York: Harper & Row.

Bharati, A. (1985). The self in Hindu thought and action. In G. Marsella, A. J. DeVos, & F. L. K. Hsu (Eds.), *Culture and self: Asian and Western perspectives* (pp. 185–230). New York: Tavistock.

Bhatia, S. (2005). Critical engagements with culture and self. *Theory and Psychology, 15,* 419–430.

Chao, R. K. (1995). Chinese and European American cultural models of the self reflected in mother's childrearing beliefs. *Ethos, 23,* 328–354.

Collins, A. (1991). From Brahma to a blade of grass: Towards an Indian self-psychology. *Journal of Indian Philosophy, 19,* 143–189.

Cross, S. E., & Gore, J. S. (2005). Cultural models of self. In M. R. Leary & J. P. Tangney (Eds.), *Handbook of self and identity* (pp. 534–564). New York: Guilford Press.

Dalai Lama & Cutler, H. (1998). *The art of happiness*. New York: Riverhead Press.

Damasio, A. R. (1999). *The feeling of what happens: Body and emotion in the making of consciousness*. New York: Harcourt.

Desai, P., & Collins, A. (1986). Selfhood and context: Some Indian solutions. In M. White & S. Pollak (Eds.), *The culture transition* (pp. 261–290). London: Routledge.

Dhawan, N., Roseman, I. J., Naidu, R. K., Thapa, K., & Rettek, S. I. (1995). Self-concepts across two cultures: India and the United States. *Journal of Cross Cultural Psychology, 26,* 606–621.

Diener, E., & Diener, M. (1995). Cross-cultural correlates of life satisfaction and self-esteem. *Journal of Personality and Social Psychology, 68,* 653–663.

Diener, E., & Oishi, S. (2000). Money and happiness: Income and subjective well-being across nations. In E. Diener & E. M. Suh (Eds.), *Culture and subjective well-being* (pp. 185–218). Cambridge, MA: MIT Press.

Diener, E., Oishi, S., & Lucas, R. E. (2003). Personality, culture, and subjective well-being: Emotional and cognitive evaluations of life. *Annual Review of Psychology, 54,* 403–425.

Diener, E., & Seligman, M. E. P. (2005). Beyond money: Toward an economy of well-being. *Psychological Science in the Public Interest, 5,* 1–31.

Dittmar, H. (2004). Are you what you have? Consumer society and our sense of identity. *Psychologist, 17,* 206–210.

Doi, T. (1973). *The anatomy of dependence*. New York: Kodansha International.

Gergen, K. J., Gulerce, A., Lock, A., & Misra, G. (1996). Psychological science in cultural context. *American Psychologist, 51,* 496–503.

Ghose (Sri Aurobindo) (1954). *Savitri*. Pondicherry, India: Sri Aurobindo Ashram.

Goffman, E. (1959). *The presentation of self in everyday life*. New York: Doubleday.

Goodwin, N. R. (1997). Interdisciplinary perspectives on well-being. In F. Ackermann, D. Kiron, N. R. Goodwin, J. M. Harris, & K. Gallaghar (Eds.), *Human well-being and economic goals* (pp. 1–14). Washington, DC: Island Press.

Gordon, S. L. (1989). Institutional and impulsive orientations in selectively appropriating emotions to self. In D. D. Franks & E. D. McCarthy (Eds.), *The sociology of
emotions* (pp. 115–136). Greenwich, CT: JAI Press.

Harre, R. (Ed.). (1986). *Social construction of emotions*. Oxford, UK: Blackwell.

Heelas, P., & Lock, A. (Eds.). (1981). *Indigenous psychologies: The anthropology of the
self*. New York: Academic Press.

Helgeson, V. S., & Fritz, H. L. (1999). Unmitigated agency and unmitigated
communion: Distinctions from agency and communion. *Journal of Research in
Personality, 33*, 131–158.

Hermans, H. J. M. (2001). The dialogical self: Toward a theory of personal and
cultural positioning. *Culture and Psychology, 7*, 243–281.

Hochschild, A. (1979). Emotion work, feeling rules and social structure. *American
Journal of Sociology, 85*, 551–575.

James, W. (1983). *The principles of psychology*. Cambridge, MA: Harvard University
Press. (Original work published 1890.)

Kagitcibasi, C. (1996). *Family and human development across cultures: A view from the
other side*. Mahwah, NJ: Lawrence Erlbaum Associates, Inc.

Kahneman, D., Diener, E., & Schwarz, N. (Eds.). (1999). *Well-being: The foundations
of hedonic psychology*. New York: Russell Sage Foundation.

Kakar, S. (1978). *The inner world: A psycho-analytic study of childhood and society in
India*. New Delhi, India: Oxford University Press.

Kakar, S. (1997). *Culture and psyche*. New Delhi, India: Oxford University Press.

Kessler, R. C., Berglund, P., Demler, O., Jin, R., Koretz, D., Merikangas, K. R.,
et al. (2003). The epidemiology of major depressive disorder results from the
National Co-morbidity Survey Replication (NCS-R). *Journal of American Medical
Association, 289*, 3095–3195.

Keyes, C. L. M., & Haidt, J. (Eds.). (2003). *Flourishing: Positive psychology and the life
well-lived*. Washington, DC: American Psychological Association.

Kim, U., Yang, K., & Hwang, K. K. (Eds.). (2006). *Indigenous and cultural psychology:
Understanding people in context*. New York: Springer SBM Publications.

Kiran Kumar, S. K. (2006). The role of spirituality in attaining well-being: Approach
of Sanatana Dharma. In A. D. Fave (Ed.), *Dimensions of well-being* (pp. 538–551).
Milan: Franco Angeli.

Kitayama, S., & Cohen, D. (Eds.). (2007). *Handbook of cultural psychology*
(pp. 136–174). New York: Guilford Press.

Kitayama, S., Duffy, S., & Uchida, Y. (2007). Self as cultural mode of being. In
S. Kitayama & D. Cohen (Eds.), *Handbook of cultural psychology* (pp. 136–174).
New York: Guilford Press.

Kitayama, S., Ishii, K., Imada, T., Takamura, K., & Ramaswamy, J. (2006). Voluntary
settlement and the spirit of independence: Evidence from Japan's "Northern
Frontier." *Journal of Personality and Social Psychology, 91*, 369–384.

Kitayama, S., Markus, H. R., & Kurokawa, M. (2000). Culture, emotion, and well-
being: Good feelings in Japan and the United States. *Cognition and Emotion, 14*,
93–124.

Kitayama, S., Markus, H. R., & Lieberman, C. (1995). The collective construction
of self-esteem: Implications for culture, self, and emotion. In J. A. Russell &
J. M. Fernandez-Dols (Eds.), *Everyday conceptions of emotion: An introduction to
the psychology, anthropology, and linguistics of emotion* (pp. 523–550). Dordrecht,
The Netherlands: Kluwer Academic.

Leary, M. R. (2007). Motivational and emotional aspects of self. *Annual Review of Psychology, 58*, 317–344.

Leary, M. R., & Tangney, J. P. (2003). The self as an organizing construct in behavioral and social sciences. In M. R. Leary & J. P. Tangney (Eds.), *Handbook of self and identity* (pp. 3–14). New York: Guilford Press.

Luthar, S. S. (2003). A culture of affluence: Psychological cost of material wealth. *Child Development, 74*, 1581–1593.

Lutz, C. A. (1988). *Unnatural emotions: Everyday sentiments on a Micronesian atoll and their challenge to Western theory*. Chicago: University of Chicago Press.

Markus, H. R., & Kitayama, S. (1991). Cultural and the self: Implications for cognition, emotion and motivation. *Psychological Review, 98*, 224–253.

Markus, H. R., & Kitayama, S. (1994). The cultural construction of self and emotion: Implications for social behavior. In S. Kitayama & H. R. Markus (Eds.), *Emotion and culture: Empirical studies of mutual influence* (pp. 89–130). Washington, DC: American Psychological Association.

Marriott, M. (1976). Hindu transactions. In B. Kapferer (Ed.), *Transaction and meaning: Direction in the anthropology of exchange and symbolic behavior* (pp. 109–142). Philadelphia: ISHI Publications.

Marsella, A. J. (1998). Toward a global psychology: Meeting the needs of a changing world. *American Psychologist, 53*, 1282–1291.

Marsella, A., DeVos, G., & Hsu, F. L. K. (1985). Culture and self. In M. H. Bond (Ed.), *The cross-cultural challenge to social psychology* (pp. 266–281). Beverly Hills, CA: Sage.

Mascolo, M. F., & Bhatia, S. (2002). The dynamic construction of culture, self, and social relations. *Psychology and Developing Societies, 14*, 55–92.

Mascolo, M. F., Misra, G., & Rapisardi, C. (2004). Individual and relational conceptions of self in India and the United States. *New Directions for Child and Adolescent Development, Vol. 104. Culture and Developing Selves: Beyond Dichotomization* (pp. 9–26). San Francisco: Jossey-Bass.

Mead, G. H. (1934). *Mind, self and society*. Chicago: University of Chicago Press.

Menon, U., & Shweder, R. A. (1994). Kali's tongue. In S. Kitayama & H. Markus (Eds.), *Emotion and culture: Empirical studies of mutual influence* (pp. 241–284). Washington, DC: American Psychological Association.

Mesquita, B. (2001). Emotions in collectivist and individualist contexts. *Journal of Personality and Social Psychology, 80*, 68–74.

Mesquita, B. (2007). Emotions are culturally situated. *Social Science Information, 46*, 410–415.

Misra, G. (2001). Culture and self: Implications for psychological inquiry. *Journal of Indian Psychology, 19*, 1–20.

Misra, G. (2004a). Culture, self and emotions: The case of antecedents of emotion experiences. *Indian Psychological Abstracts and Reviews, 11*(1), 1–27.

Misra, G. (2004b). Emotion in modern psychology and Indian thought. In K. Joshi & M. Cornelissen (Eds.), *Consciousness, science, society and yoga* (pp. 314–331). New Delhi, India: Centre for Studies in Civilizations.

Misra, G. (2005). From disease to well being: Perspectives from an indigenous tradition. In R. Singh, A. Yadava, & N. R. Sharma (Eds.), *Health psychology* (pp. 281–294). New Delhi, India: Global Vision.

Misra, G., & Giri, R. (1995). Is Indian self predominantly interdependent? *Journal of Indian Psychology, 11*, 15–19.

Misra, G., & Mohanty, A. (Eds.). (2002). *Perspectives on indigenous psychology*. New Delhi, India: Concept.

Nakamura, H. (1964). *Ways of thinking of eastern people: India, China. Tibet and Japan*. Honolulu, HI: The University Press of Hawaii.

Ng, A. K. (2001). *Why Asians are less creative than Westerners*. Singapore: Prentice Hall.

Ng, A. K., Ho, D. Y. F., Wong, S. S., & Smith, I. (2003). In search of the good life: A cultural odyssey in the East and West. *Genetic, Social, and General Psychology Monographs, 129*(4), 317–363.

Nisbett, R. E. (2004). *The geography of thought: How Asians and Westerners think differently . . . and why*. New York: Free Press.

Panksepp, J. (1994). Evolution constructed the potential for subjective experience with the neurodynamics of the mammalian brain. In P. Ekman & R. J. Davidson (Eds.), *The nature of emotion: Fundamental questions* (pp. 396–399). New York: Oxford University Press.

Paranjpe, A. C. (1998). *Self and identity in modern psychology and Indian thought*. New York: Plenum Press.

Patañjali. (2003). *The yoga sutras of Patañjali*, trans. J. H. Woods. New York: Courier Dover.

Radhakrishnan, S. (2002). *The Bhagavad Gita*. New York: HarperCollins.

Ramanujam, B. K. (1986). Social change and personal crisis: A view from an Indian practice. In M. I. White & S. Pollak (Eds.), *The cultural transition: Human experience and social transformation in the third world and Japan* (pp. 65–66). London: Routledge.

Ramanujan, A. K. (1990). Is there an Indian way of thinking? An informal essay. In M. Marriott (Ed.), *India through Hindu categories* (pp. 41–58). New Delhi, India: Sage.

Rao, K. R., & Marwaha, S. B. (Eds.). (2005). *Towards a spiritual psychology: Essays on Indian psychology*. New Delhi, India: Samvad Indian Foundation.

Roland, A. (1988). *In search of self in India and Japan: Towards a cross cultural psychology*. Princeton, NJ: Princeton University Press.

Roland, A. (1996). *Cultural pluralism and psychoanalysis: The Asian and North American experience*. New York: Routledge.

Rosaldo, M. (1984). Toward an anthropology of self and feeling. In R. A. Shweder & R. A. LeVine (Eds.), *Culture theory* (pp. 137–157). New York: Cambridge University Press.

Rosenberg, M. (1991). Self processes and emotional experiences. In J. A. Howard & P. L. Callero (Eds.), *The self society dynamic: Cognition, emotion and action* (pp. 123–142). Cambridge, UK: Cambridge University Press.

Royal Society. (2004). The science of well-being: Integrating neurobiology, psychology and social science. *Philosophical Transactions of the Royal Society B: Biological Sciences, 359*, 1331–1451

Ryff, C. D. (1989). Happiness is everything, or is it? Explorations on the meaning of psychological well-being. *Journal of Personality and Social Psychology, 57*, 1069–1081.

Ryff, C. D., & Keyes, C. L. M. (1995). The structure of psychological well-being revisited. *Journal of Personality and Social Psychology, 69*, 719–727.

Sampson, E. E. (1988). The debate on individualism: Indigenous psychologies of the individual and their role in personal and social functioning. *American Psychologist, 43*, 15–22.

Scheff, T. (1990). *Microsociology: Discourse, emotion and social structure.* Chicago: University of Chicago Press.

Shweder, R. A., & Bourne, F. (1984). Does the concept of the person vary cross-culturally? In R. A. Shweder & R. A. Levine (Eds.), *Culture theory: Essays on mind, self and emotion* (pp. 158–199). New York: Cambridge University Press.

Shweder, R. A., & Haidt, J. (2000). The cultural psychology of emotions: Ancient and new. In M. Lewis & M. Haviland-Jones (Eds.), *Handbook of emotions* (pp. 397–414). New York: Guilford Press.

Shweder, R. A., Mahapatra, M., & Miller, J. C. (1987). Culture and moral development. In J. Kagan & S. Lamb (Eds.), *Emergence of moral concepts in early childhood* (pp. 1–82). Chicago: Chicago University Press.

Sibia, A., Misra, G., & Srivastava, A. K. (2004). Towards understanding emotional intelligence in the Indian context: Perspectives of parents, teachers and children. *Psychological Studies, 49*, 114–123.

Singh, J. K., & Misra, G. (2000). Understanding contentment in everyday life. *Indian Psychological Review, 55*, 113–114.

Singhal, R., & Misra, G. (1994). Achievement goals: A situational-contextual analysis. *International Journal of Intercultural Relations, 18*, 239–258.

Sinha, D., & Tripathi, R. C. (1994). Individualism in a collectivist culture: A case of co-existence of opposites. In U. Kim, H. C. Triandis, C. Kagitcibasi, S. Choi, & G. Yoon (Eds.), *Individualism and collectivism: Theory, method and applications* (pp. 123–136). Thousand Oaks, CA: Sage.

Sinha, J. B. P., & Kanungo, R. N. (1997). Context sensitivity and balancing in organizational behavior. *International Journal of Psychology, 32*, 93–105.

Sinha, J. B. P., & Pandey, A. (2007). Indians' mindsets and the conditions that evoke them. *Psychological Studies, 52*, 1–13.

Srivastava, A. K., & Misra, G. (2003). Going beyond the model of economic man: An indigenous perspective on happiness. *Journal of Indian Psychology, 21*, 12–29.

Srivastava, R., & Misra, G. (1997). *Self construal, control and eastern orientation.* Unpublished manuscript, Department of Psychology, University of Delhi, Delhi, India.

Stroufe, L. A. (1997). *Emotional development: The organization of emotional life in early years.* Cambridge, UK: Cambridge University Press.

Stryker, S. (2004). Integrating emotion into identity theory. *Advances in Group Processes, 23*, 1–23.

Suh, E., Diener, E., Oishi, S., & Triandis, H. C. (1998). The shifting basis of life satisfaction judgments across cultures: Emotions versus norms. *Journal of Personality and Social Psychology, 74*, 482–493.

Triandis, H. C. (1989). The self and social behavior in differing cultural contexts. *Psychological Review, 96*, 506–520.

Tripathi, R. C., & Leviatan, U. (2003). Individualism and collectivism: In search of a product or process. *Culture & Psychology, 9*, 79–88.

Turner, J. H. (2000). *On the origins of human emotions: A sociological inquiry into the evolution of human affect.* Stanford, CA: Stanford University Press.

Valsiner, J., & Rosa, A. (Eds.). (2007). *The Cambridge handbook of sociocultural psychology.* New York: Cambridge University Press.

Veenhoven, R. (2000). Freedom and happiness: A comparative study in forty-four nations in the early 1990s. In E. Diener & E. M. Suh (Eds.), *Culture and subjective well-being* (pp. 257–288). Cambridge, MA: MIT Press.

Section II

Early development

Second
Early development

8 Early childhood development in Southern Africa

Roderick Fulata Zimba

Introduction

My intention in this chapter is to provide an overview of issues critical to early childhood development in Southern Africa. These issues include basic concepts on early childhood development and the role of psychology in promoting children's well-being and optimal early childhood development in the Southern African context. The early childhood development period covered in the chapter is 0–6 years.

Basic concepts on early childhood development as applied in Southern Africa

Basic concepts to be looked at are those of *child development*, *care*, and *protection*.

Child development

Defined in a multidimensional way, Myers (1995) stipulates that child development is "a process of change in which the child learns to handle ever more complex levels of moving, thinking, feeling, and relating to others." To illustrate how this definition is translated into reality in Southern Africa, the material and social contexts of development, the societal goals of development, and the media for development are considered as follows.

Societal goals of child development in a number of communities in the region remain essentially pro-social and group-based. Examples of such goals are respect, obedience, cooperation, hard work, helpfulness, hospitality, honesty, peace, responsibility, and appropriate social decorum (Nxumalo, 1993; Zimba & Otaala, 1993, 1995). The main end point of child development for many adults in the region is human solidarity and oneness, in which persons are other-oriented and feel unfulfilled without others (Chingota, 1998). In this view, persons remain individuals, but in relation to others. Mbiti (1990, p. 106) expresses this form of being as one in which persons say to themselves: "I am, because we are; and since we are, therefore I am." When raising children, care-givers normally foster movement towards this goal by providing interactional environments that are characterized by family warmth, love, encouragement, commitment, responsiveness, concern for the welfare of the children, undivided attention, and social security (Bernard van Leer Foundation, 1994; Evans & Myers, 1994).

Reciprocity plays a significant role as a medium of development. From an early age, children in Southern Africa – as in other parts of Africa – make contributions to the sustenance of their families while being cared for and give their time and energy while being taught (Woodhead, 1996). They acquire functional intellectual capacities by observing adults at work, participating in household and family duties, helping and cooperating with others. For these children the tasks of growing up, work, and learning are interwoven, not separated. Widely applied in the region, the child-to-child approach, which focuses on children's participation in and contribution to health promotion, child stimulation and development, basic education, and nutrition takes advantage of this indigenous strategy of raising children (Aarons, Hawes, & Gayton, 1979; Hawes, 1988).

The unique media used to stimulate development in the region include those of traditional games, song and dance, stories, riddles, proverbs, and rites of passage. It is important to note that development is promoted through purposeful and active face-to-face interaction amongst children and between adults and children (Reynolds, 1989; Zimba & Otaala, 1995). As can be noted, the media demand that the process of development and its goals work in synchrony – that they are group-based and situated in local social settings.

In the mainstream psychology literature, child development is usually conceptualized in the form of developmental stages. Popularized by Jean Piaget and Lawrence Kohlberg, each stage is characterized by abilities, skills, and capacities that children are expected to acquire and exhibit once they have reached it and passed through it. In the 1950s, 1960s, and 1970s many studies were done in Africa in an attempt to validate the universality of Western stage theories of development (Wober, 1975). Among other things, the main thrust of the studies was to demonstrate the manner in which African children acquired and expressed "stage" concepts, abilities, skills, and ways of understanding the world around them (Mwamwenda, 1995; Ohuche & Otaala, 1981; Reynolds, 1989). Notwithstanding the emic and etic debates that took place during this period, the starting point for the majority of the studies was the Western worldview of development and its goals (Cole & Scribner, 1974, 1977; Nsamenang, 2000). The African philosophy of life, epistemology, forms of existence, lived experiences, worldviews, and cultural practices did not essentially provoke the studies. The task for many researchers was to study the development of the African children through the lenses of Western psychological theories of development and methods (Evans, 1970). Currently, this way of studying African children is being reconsidered. The main justification for this is captured by Woodhead: citing

Ingleby (1986) and Burman (1994) and supported by Dawes (1999) and Jenks (1996), Woodhead points out that:

> conventional theories of child development are about culture as well as about children. The child depicted in Psychology textbooks is in two respects, a cultural invention. The process of child development being studied and the theorists' conceptual representation of that process are both strongly shaped by their shared context, in terms of family organization, parental roles, expectations of childhood, economic base, political structures, gender/class differentiation, religious beliefs, life expectancies and the like. It is inappropriate to assume that a concept of development derived from one context can or should be the basis for defining good and poor quality in other contexts.
>
> (Woodhead, 1996, pp. 59–60)

Recognizing this, some researchers and practitioners in the Southern African region now attempt to understand the situation and development of children by employing child–context interaction theories of development. These theories enable workers in the area to "understand how children's development is shaped by their material, social and cultural contexts" (Dawes & Donald, 2000, p. 3). Bronfenbrenner's (1979) ecological framework, Sameroff's (1991) transactional developmental theory, and Aber, Gephart, Brooks-Gunn, and Connell's (1997) developmental epochs idea are examples of such theories. Although this shift represents an important step towards the authentic understanding of the context and process of child development in the region, an appreciation of the unique and indigenous explication of the process needs to be expressed.

To reflect the indigenous African philosophy of life, child development is built on the understanding that in their development, children are moulded and transformed into viable members of particular communities by passing through periods of an unbroken circle of existence. As they do this, children gradually enter into and assume particular forms of personhood, identity, and being. Broadly speaking, these periods are those of conception (encompassing the idea of the unborn as members of families), birth, babyhood, childhood, puberty, adulthood, marriage, and death (as embodied in the concept of the living dead) (Chingota, 1998; Zimba, 2002). The transition from period to period is, in a number of Southern African communities, based on maturation and evolvement. Children's capacities for adequate participation in the life of their communities evolve as they interact with and are directly guided by adult members of these communities.

In the region, rituals, rites of passage, and initiation ceremonies have indigenously been – and in a number of communities still are – used to mark and facilitate the transition from period to period (Chakanza, 1998; Chingota, 1998; Cruz e Silva & Loforte, 1998; Mbiti, 1991; M'Passou, 1998; Nxumalo, 1993; Phiri, 1998; Reynolds, 1989). In Swaziland, for instance, there are rituals and rites pertaining to the burial of the umbilical cord, the introduction of the baby to the world, the protection of the child from thunder, the initiation of the child into Swazi nationality, puberty initiation, boys' regiments, girls' age cohorts, marriage, and funerals and burials (M'Passou, 1998). Communities use rites of passage and other means to facilitate children's development through hands-on participation/activity, formal and informal direct teaching, encouragement, demonstration, observation, exposition, reflection, and mentoring (Mbiti, 1991; Ocitti, 1973; Phiri, 1998).

Childcare

Childcare entails promoting children's optimal survival, growth, and development by meeting their basic needs. These include needs for protection, security, food, health, affection, interaction, stimulation, exploration, and discovery (Myers, 1995), leading to socialization into given cultures. In what unique ways have communities in Southern Africa done and continue to do this? A number of answers to this question have already been given in our discussion of child development. What I wish to highlight here is the contextual conception of who is a child that needs stimulation, nurturance, protection, and psychosocial support.

It appears that communities in the Southern African region are agreed that childhood begins at conception. The child under development during the nine months of pregnancy is considered in a number of communities in the region to be a complete human agent worthy of nurturance, protection, and moral respect. The pregnant mother is expected to be provided with family support to ensure that the unborn child receives the nurturance and protection that he or she deserves.

Notwithstanding this, it should be noted that a large number of pregnant mothers in the region do not receive sufficient material, health, and psychosocial support that the family network is supposed to provide. Poverty and the ravages of the HIV/AIDS pandemic have disabled the family safety net that was to provide adequate support to pregnant mothers (UNICEF, 2008). Moreover, societal disruptions have also contributed to the dis-empowerment of families in the region. As a result of this, we now commonly have not only nuclear and extended families but also single-parent-headed families, child-headed families, grandparent-headed families, and families where parents are not married but cohabiting (Zimba & Zimba, 2004). A number of these family formations lack not only material but also social-cultural and psychosocial resources needed to support pregnant mothers and young children.

The age at which adulthood begins is not clear-cut. According to the 1990 *African Charter on the Rights and Welfare of the Child*, "a child means every human being below the age of 18 years" (Naldi, 1992). This is in line with the 1989 United Nations Convention on the Rights of the Child which stipulates that a child is "every human being below the age of 18 years unless under the law applicable to the child, majority is attained earlier" (Goodwin-Gill &

Cohn, 1994). For many communities in the region, however, puberty (which occurs roughly at about 12–16 years of age) heralds adulthood (Gelfand, 1979; LeVine et al., 1994). For these communities, childcare should cover the period from conception up to 16 years of age. This implies that in the view of a number of Southern Africans, capacities for adult living are expected to be mastered earlier than is the case in other regions of the world. In an integrated manner, these capacities are not limited to biophysical abilities but also extend to the moral, social, relational, and epistemological realms (e.g., Gelfand, 1979).

This discrepancy poses particular conflicts and tensions pertaining to the question of who is the psychosocial and legal agent called a child who requires protection and needs nurturance. Due to this, for instance, cases of child sexual abuse involving persons aged 15 to 16 years become difficult to disentangle if the juridical perspective is relied upon to the exclusion of the indigenous and cultural psycho-social perspective held by some communities. This is also the case when the *African Charter on the Rights and Welfare of the Child* stipulates in its Article 21 that the minimum age of marriage should, by legislation, be set at 18 years of age.

Child protection

The Convention on the Rights of the Child provides a universal framework for child protection. In Africa, the African Charter on the Rights and Welfare of the Child contextualizes the children's rights and recognizes the role of culture in protecting children and in enhancing their development in two main ways. First, in Articles 1 and 21, the Charter urges African nations to discourage and eliminate "harmful social and cultural practices affecting the welfare, dignity, normal growth and development of the child and in particular, those customs and practices discriminatory to the child on the grounds of sex or other status" (Naldi, 1992, p. 191). Second, in Articles 5, 11, and 31 the Charter mandates African nations to ensure the survival, protection, and development of the child, the preservation and strengthening of positive African morals, traditional values, and conventions, and to raise every child in such a way that he or she has responsibilities towards his or her family and society.

The Southern African perspective on children's rights can be illustrated by looking at how children's best interests are conceptualized and catered for in child custody cases and in the functioning of the bride price practice. According to Armstrong (1994), Rwezaura (1994), and Banda (1994), Southern African children's best interests are mainly in the form of basic needs for survival and social needs. The basic needs are those of food, water, shelter, medical care, and clothing. The contemporary social needs are embodied in the children's rights to education.

Armstrong (1994) states that children's best interests are not individual but group-based. In Zimbabwe, for example, the Shona customary law requires that children's best interests be congruent with those of the extended family. This being the case, the obligation to ensure that the children's best interests are respected does not rest with biological parents alone, but implies the entire extended family. As a result, the custody of children in times of peace and in times of dispute is ultimately the responsibility of the extended family.

In times of peace, parents who may not have the material resources to cater for their child's basic and educational needs may ask a relative with more adequate resources to look after the child. A similar situation occurs in the context where urban parents are unable to afford the high cost of accommodation, school fees, and childcare facilities. When this happens, a number of them send their children to their relatives in rural areas, where the children's best interests are expected to be met at a lower cost. In times of turmoil, as is the case in present-day Zimbabwe where the economy has collapsed, these safety nets do not function as optimally as they should.

When parents are in dispute, customary law in most Southern African communities dictates that child custody cases be settled according to either paternal or maternal cultural rights (Armstrong, 1994; Rwezaura, 1994). Under paternal cultural rights, as practiced by the Shona of Zimbabwe (Armstrong, 1994), it is in the best interests of the child to be associated with his or her paternal family, in which familial rather than individual rights are emphasized. Members of the paternal family view and treat the child as "our child". Consequently, custody of the child is given not to a single father but to the paternal family. A Shona mother married under customary law, with all *lobola* (i.e., bride price) obligations met, would understand this from the perspective that the father of her children has paternal rights over the children and give up custody of them.

When persons are married under common law and its documented statuses, child custody cases are handled in such a way that the child's best interests become individualized and spouses are placed on an equal footing. However, persons' worldviews remain important for many in the region, and they take their child custody cases to community local courts, where judgments are informed by customary law (or the living law) and how children are perceived according to this law. Understanding all this at the level of societal conventions produces the insight that children's best interests are conceptualized and catered for in a local and contextualized way by a number of communities in the Southern African region (Dawes, 1999). Attempts to universalize contexts and the sense in which children's best interests are understood and catered for in the region miss this insight (Burman, 1996; Dawes & Cairns, 1998).

It is also important to shift from concepts of custody, access, and guardianship to shared parenting, parental duties, and responsibilities. This shift should benefit from *the child-in-context idea*. The gist of this idea is to relate social-cultural parenting expectations to children's best interests. Parents' duties and responsibilities should be clearly specified when doing this.

The child-in-context idea can also be illustrated by looking at some instances in the region that require child protection. In Namibia, for instance, legislation is needed to regulate male circumcision. Such legislation would protect boys from being subjected to unhygienic circumcision rituals that could make them vulnerable to HIV infection. At a regional and international level, legislation is needed to protect children from inter-country abduction that may be perpetrated for the purpose of child sexual exploitation, prostitution, and pornography (Zimba & Zimba, 2004).

The role of *"situated"* psychology in promoting children's well-being and optimal early childhood development in the Southern African context

The main message of this chapter is that for it to be appropriate to its users, psychology in general and developmental psychology in particular should be *situated* in cosmologies of specific communities and their worldviews. In my view, the following propositions should be regarded as a contribution to developmental psychology from the Southern African communities' conceptions of early childhood development.

First, this chapter demonstrates the wisdom of taking into account unique perceptions of local and contextualized cultural beliefs and practices regarding children's best interests and how these should be catered for. The principle to be underlined here is that conceptions of childhood and child development practices emanate from worldviews and lived experiences of communities: they do not necessarily come from theories of child development (Dawes, 1999; Miller, 2002). A feature of this worth noting is the immersion of the developing children into communities of *linked*, *"bonded"*, *related* and *interdependent* persons whose existence is understood and expressed in a corporate way. Tearing children away from this worldview in order to understand their development at the individual level is inappropriate.

Second, reciprocity as a medium of development is given prominence in the chapter. Application of this principle entails that growing up, work, and learning are interwoven in a social network where young children are enabled to actively participate in their own development and draw upon the fund of their families' and their communities' knowledge, skills, and ways of understanding the social, physical, and metaphysical worlds. Through direct teaching, demonstration, observation, exposition, reflection, and mentoring, families and communities stimulate and promote children's development in a pastoral and corporate way. An important outcome of this process is normally the development, in children, of a sense of community and a spirit of interdependence (Keller & Greenfield, 2000). Southern Africa may have an important contribution to make in a world where the absence of such a sense of community and interdependence amongst people produces anomie, loneliness, and distress.

Conclusion

In this chapter I have discussed a number of early childhood development insights, principles, and propositions on the basis of the Southern African vantage point. In conclusion, I wish the reader to take note of some of these aspects.

With respect to child development, it is essential to take into consideration that child development in Southern Africa goes beyond cognitive and psychosocial aspects of being to encompass a worldview that connects physical reality to social relations, compassion, and spirituality. In this worldview, child development is pro-social, group based, and "other-oriented". Its main goal is that of promoting human solidarity and oneness. This is aimed at realizing the ideal that persons are unfulfilled without others and draw meaning for their lives from being in relation to others. The rallying principle undergirding this states that: "I am because we are." This principle brings into focus an early childhood development regime that fosters love, warmth, and responsiveness.

A rather liberating insight that is based on the *"situated"* principle in psychology is the position that child development practices emanate from the worldviews and lived experiences of communities (Erny, 1973; Sameroff, 1991); they do not necessarily proceed from theories of child development. In the Southern African context, it is important to keep in mind that the worldviews and the lived experiences are dynamic and adapt to adversities in the form of crime, violence, disease, xenophobia, and rampant poverty. The mandate of *"situated"* or contextualized psychology is to help communities to mitigate such adversities.

References

Aarons, A., Hawes, H., & Gayton, J. (1979). *Child-to-child*. London: Macmillan Education.

Aber, J. L., Gephart, M. A., Brooks-Gunn, J., & Connell, J. P. (1997). Development in context: Implications for studying neighborhood effects. In J. Brooks-Gunn, G. J. Duncan, & J. L. Aber (Eds.), *Neighborhood policy: Vol. 1. Context and consequences for children* (pp. 44–61). New York: Russell Sage Foundation.

Armstrong, A. (1994). School and Sadza: Custody and the best interests of the child in Zimbabwe. In P. Alston (Ed.), *The best interests of the child: Reconciling culture and human rights* (pp. 150–190). Oxford, UK: Oxford University Press.

Banda, F. (1994). Custody and the best interests of the child: Another view from Zimbabwe. In P. Alston (Ed.), *The best interests of the child: Reconciling culture and human rights* (pp. 191–201). Oxford, UK: Oxford University Press.

Bernard van Leer Foundation. (1994). *Building on people's strengths: Early childhood in Africa*. The Hague, The Netherlands: Bernard van Leer Foundation.

Bronfenbrenner, U. (1979). *The ecology of human development: Experiments by nature and design*. Cambridge, MA: Harvard University Press.

Burman, E. (1994). *Deconstructing developmental psychology*. London: Routledge & Kegan-Paul.

Burman, E. (1996). Local, global or globalized? Child development and international child rights legislation. *Childhood: A Global Journal of Child Research, 3*, 45–66.

Chakanza, J. C. (1998). Unfinished agenda: Puberty rites and the response of the Roman Catholic Church in Southern Malawi, 1901–1994. In J. L. Cox (Ed.), *Rites of passage in contemporary Africa: Interaction between Christian and African traditional religions* (pp. 157–167). Cardiff, UK: Cardiff Academic Press.

Chingota, F. (1998). A historical account of the attitude of Blantyre Synod of the Church of Central Africa Presbyterian towards initiation rites. In J. L. Cox (Ed.), *Rites of passage in contemporary Africa: Interaction between Christian and African traditional religions* (pp. 146 155). Cardiff, UK: Cardiff Academic Press.

Cole, M., & Scribner, S. (1974). *Culture and thought: A psychological introduction.* New York: Wiley

Cole, M., & Scribner, S. (1977). Developmental theories applied to cross-cultural cognitive research. *Annals of the New York Academy of Sciences, 285*, 366–373.

Cruz e Silva, T., & Loforte, A. (1998). Christianity, African traditional religions and cultural identity in Southern Mozambique. In J. L. Cox (Ed.), *Rites of passage in contemporary Africa: Interaction between Christian and African traditional religions* (pp. 35–45). Cardiff, UK: Cardiff Academic Press.

Dawes, A. (1999, December). *Images of childhood in cultural perspective: Challenges to theory and practice.* Lecture presented to the international interdisciplinary course on children's rights at the Children's Rights Centre, University of Ghent, Belgium.

Dawes, A., & Cairns, E. (1998). The Machel Study: Dilemmas of cultural sensitivity and universal rights of children. *Peace and Conflict: Journal of Peace Psychology, 4*(4), 335–348.

Dawes, A., & Donald, D. (2000). Improving children's chances: Developmental theory and effective interventions in community contexts. In D. Donald, A. Dawes, & J. Louw (Eds.), *Addressing childhood adversity* (pp. 1–25). Cape Town, South Africa: David Philip Publishers.

Erny, P. (1973). *Childhood and cosmos: The social psychology of the black African child.* New York: New Perspectives.

Evans, J. L. (1970). *Children in Africa: A review of psychological research.* New York: Teachers College Press.

Evans, J. L., & Myers, R. G. (1994). Child rearing practices: Creating programs where traditions and modern practices meet. *Coordinators' Notebook: An International Resource for Early Childhood Development, 15*, 1–15.

Gelfand, G. (1979). *Growing up in Shona society: From birth to marriage.* Harare, Zimbabwe: Mambo Press.

Goodwin-Gill, G. S., & Cohn, I. (1994). *Child soldiers: The role of children in armed conflict.* Oxford, UK: Oxford University Press.

Hawes, H. (1988). *Child-to-child: Another path to learning.* Hamburg, Germany: UNESCO Institute for Education.

Ingelby, D. (1986). Development in social context. In M. Richards & P. Light (Eds.), *Children of social worlds.* Cambridge, UK: Polity Press.

Jenks, C. (1996). *Childhood.* London: Routledge.

Keller, H., & Greenfield, P. M. (2000). History and future of development in cross-cultural psychology. *Journal of Cross-cultural Psychology, 31*(1), 52–62.

LeVine, R. A., Dixon, S., LeVine, S., Richman, A., Leiderman, P. H., Keefer, C. H., et al. (1994). *Child care and culture: Lessons from Africa.* Cambridge, UK: Cambridge University Press.

Mbiti, J. S. (1990). *African religions and philosophy* (2nd ed.). Oxford, UK: Heinemann Educational Publishers.

Mbiti, J. S. (1991). *Introduction to African religion* (2nd ed.). Oxford, UK: Heinemann Educational.

Miller, J. G. (2002). Integrating cultural, psychological and biological perspectives in understanding child development. In H. Keller, Y. H. Poortinga, & A. Schölmerich (Eds.), *Between culture and biology: Perspectives on ontogenetic development* (pp. 89–115). Cambridge, UK: Cambridge University Press.

M'Passou, D. (1998). The continuing tension between Christianity and rites of passage in Swaziland. In J. L. Cox (Ed.), *Rites of passage in contemporary Africa: Interaction between Christian and African traditional religions* (pp. 15–33). Cardiff, UK: Cardiff Academic Press.

Mwamwenda, T. S. (1995). *Educational psychology: An African perspective* (2nd ed.). Durban, South Africa: Butterworth.

Myers, R. (1995). *The twelve who survive: Strengthening programmes of early childhood development in the Third World* (2nd ed.). Ypsilanti, MI: High/Scope Press.

Naldi, G. J. (Ed.). (1992). *Documents of the Organization of African Unity*. London: Mansell Publishing.

Nsamenang, A. B. (2000). Issues in indigenous approaches to developmental research in sub-Saharan Africa. *International Society for the Study of Behavioural Development Newsletter, 1*, 1–4.

Nxumalo, A. M. (1993). Indigenous education among the Swazi. *The Swaziland Institute for Educational Research, 13*, 101–109.

Ocitti, J. P. (1973). *African indigenous education as practised by the Acholi of Uganda*. Nairobi, Kenya: East African Literature Bureau.

Ohuche, R. O., & Otaala, B. (Eds.). (1981). *The African child and his environment*. Oxford, UK: Pergamon Press.

Phiri, I. A. (1998). The initiation of *Chewa* women of Malawi: A Presbyterian woman's perspective. In J. L. Cox (Ed.), *Rites of passage in contemporary Africa: Interaction between Christian and African traditional religions* (pp. 129–156). Cardiff, UK: Cardiff Academic Press.

Reynolds, P. (1989). *Childhood in crossroads: Cognition and society in South Africa*. Grand Rapids, MI: Wm. B. Eerdmans.

Rwezaura, B. (1994). The concept of the child's best interests in the changing economic and social context of sub-Saharan Africa. In P. Alston (Ed.), *The best interests of the child: Reconciling culture and human rights* (pp. 82–116). Oxford, UK: Oxford University Press.

Sameroff, A. J. (1991). The social context of development. In M. Woodhead, P. Light, & R. Carr (Eds.), *Becoming a person* (pp. 167–189). London: Routledge/The Open University Press.

UNICEF. (2008). *The state of Africa's children 2008: Child survival*. New York: Author.

Wober, M. (1975). *Psychology in Africa*. London: International African Institute.

Woodhead, M. (1996). *In search of the rainbow: Pathways to quality in large-scale programmes for young disadvantaged children*. The Hague, The Netherlands: Bernard van Leer Foundation.

Zimba, R. F. (2002). Indigenous conceptions of childhood development and social realities in Southern Africa. In H. Keller, Y. H. Poortinga, & A. Schölmerich (Eds.), *Between culture and biology: Perspectives on ontogenetic development* (pp. 89–115). Cambridge, UK: Cambridge University Press.

Zimba, R. F., & Otaala, B. (1993). Child care and development in Uukwaluudhi, Northern Namibia. In K. K. Prah (Ed.), *Social science research priorities for Namibia* (pp. 57–67). Eppindust, Namibia: The University of Namibia and the Council for the Development of Economic and Social Research in Africa.

Zimba, R. F., & Otaala, B. (1995). *The family in transition: A study of child rearing practices and beliefs among the Nama of the Karas and Hardap regions of Namibia.* Windhoek, Namibia: UNICEF and The University of Namibia.

Zimba, R. F., & Zimba, E. (2004). *Review to determine whether current legislations on children in Namibia are in conformity with the Convention on the Rights of the Child.* Windhock, Namibia: UNICEF.

9 Temperance and the strengths of personality

Evidence from a 35-year longitudinal study

Lea Pulkkinen and Tuuli Pitkänen

Virtues and character strengths

Temperance as a virtue

Plato proposed that four core virtues of the ideal Hellenic city – wisdom, courage, justice, and temperance – were anchored in individuals' soul. In the thirteenth century, in Christian theology, three holy virtues – faith, hope, and charity – were combined with the Platonic virtues, resulting in seven cardinal virtues. Other religions also include these virtues, as described by Peterson and Seligman (2004) in their analysis of character strengths and virtues.

The concept of virtue did not enter the terminology of empirical psychology until the emergence of positive psychology at the beginning of this millennium. The concept focuses on the study of positive subjective experiences, positive individual traits, and institutions that enable positive experiences and positive traits (Seligman & Csikszentmihalyi, 2000). One of the goals of positive psychology is to provide a common vocabulary for communication about the good life, as there is vocabulary already available for communication about psychological disorders. Well-being means more than the absence of disease and disorder.

Peterson and Seligman (2004) approached good character in terms of separate strengths. They classified 24 specific strengths under six broad virtues that consistently emerge across history and culture:

1   Wisdom, referring to cognitive strengths; the respective character strengths are creativity, curiosity, open-mindedness, love of learning, and perspective as the product of knowledge and experience.
2   Courage, referring to emotional strengths; the respective character strengths are bravery, persistence, integrity, and vitality.
3   Humanity, referring to interpersonal strengths; love, kindness, and social intelligence are the respective character strengths.
4   Justice, referring to civic strengths; the respective character strengths are citizenship, fairness, and leadership.
5   Temperance, referring to strengths that protect against excess; the

respective character strengths are forgiveness and mercy, humility and modesty, prudence, and self-regulation or self-control.

6   Transcendence, referring to strengths that forge connections to the larger universe and provide meaning; the respective character strengths are the appreciation of beauty and excellence, gratitude, hope (optimism), humor (playfulness), and spirituality (religiousness, sense of purpose).

The character strengths have to meet ten criteria, for instance, fulfilling an individual, being morally valued, and being trait-like in the sense of having a degree of generality across situations and stability across time.

For temperance, character strengths are defined in terms of what a person refrains from doing: forgiveness and mercy protect against hate; humility and modesty protect against arrogance; prudence protects against short-term pleasure with long-term costs and taking undue risks; and self-regulation (self-control) protects against destabilizing emotional extremes. Since temperance strengths are defined by what a person refrains from doing, their absence may be more observable than their presence. It is to be noted, however, that temperance balances or moderates activities and emotions between two extremes rather than suppressing them.

Self-control (self-regulation) as strength for temperance

Self-control (self-regulation) is a character strength that refers to how a person exerts control over his or her own responses (thoughts, emotions, impulses, and performances), so as to pursue goals and live up to standards (ideals, norms, targets, and expectations of other people) (Peterson & Seligman, 2004). The 35-year Jyväskylä Longitudinal Study of Personality and Social Development (JYLS) conducted in Finland by the first author (Pitkänen, 1969; Pulkkinen, 2006) was from the very beginning focused on self-control that allows the analysis of the role of self-control in developmental outcomes. Thus, this study may shed some light on many questions, such as how wide the range is of psychological processes and outcomes related to self-control, listed by Peterson and Seligman (2004) as issues not known about self-control.

The theoretical roots of impulse- or self-control (Pulkkinen, 1986) are found in the following:

1   According to psychoanalytic theory, the ego seeks to reduce the level of tension of the id and to substitute the reality principle for the pleasure principle (Freud, 1949).

2   Roots of self-control are also found in personality theory. Murray (1938) defined impulsion as a general personality trait and scored it as the ratio of impulsion to deliberation.

3   The study of the role of cognitive processes in children's control over motor behavior and speech (Vygotsky, 1962) resulted in a model on how the child achieves self-control (Luria, 1961).

4   The theory of expectancy and value influenced the conception of the subjective values of immediately available versus the temporally delayed payoffs in the delay-of-gratification model.
5   In cognitive-behavioral therapy (Kanfer & Karoly, 1972), self-control refers to a person's attempt to acquire a controlling response in a specific situation.
6   Maccoby (1980) has outlined the characteristics of impulsive children and highlighted the role of the parents in helping the child to achieve self-control over impulses. Kopp (1982, 1987) has described different phases in the development of self-control starting from neurophysiological modulation just after birth and argued that self regulation is a more mature form of control than is self-control, which emerges at about age 2.

In their handbook on self-regulation, Vohs and Baumeister (2004) note that the concepts of self-control and self-regulation have their own histories, but are currently often used interchangeably. The construct of self-regulation has grown from the same sources as the construct of self-control. Additional sources of self-regulation can be found in the following theories:

1   Social learning theory and, particularly, Bandura's (1977) self-efficacy theory.
2   Roots of self-regulation can be found in Heider's (1958) theory on agency motivation, which has been elaborated to cover the idea about humans as the "authors" and active contributors to their behavior (Little, Snyder, & Wehmeyer, 2006).
3   Carver and Scheier (1981) have applied cybernetic theory – especially the feedback loop – to how people monitor their states in relation to goals or other standards. More recently, Carver (2004) has integrated affects into self-regulation theory: affect serves as a signal as to how well or poorly one is doing at achieving one's goals.
4   Roots of self-regulation are seen in the temperament theory of Rothbart and Derryberry (1981), who see temperament as constitutionally based differences in reactivity and self-regulation. Self-regulation serves to modulate reactivity and is operationalized by effortful control defined as "the ability to inhibit a dominant response to perform a subdominant response" (Rothbart & Bates, 1998, p. 137). Empirical research shows that children's ability to regulate their attentiveness is associated with behavior problems through deficits in the regulation of negative emotions, whereas high effortful control is associated with positive emotional, social, and cognitive development (Eisenberg, Smith, Sadovsky, & Spinrad, 2004).
5   Other roots of self-regulation are found in mood management (Morris & Reilly, 1987) and in the development of emotion regulation (Saarni, 1989).

6   Self-regulation has been seen as energy (Baumeister, Heatherton, & Tice, 1994). The self-regulatory strength model involves the idea that individuals have limited and depletable internal resources to inhibit, override, or alter responses that may arise as a result of physiological processes, habit, learning, or the press of the situation (Schmeichel & Baumeister, 2004).

7   Recent studies on the physiological basis of self-control have revealed the important role of executive functioning in many aspects of self-regulatory behavior (Banfield, Wyland, Macrae, Münte, & Heatherton, 2004).

A longitudinal study on self-control

Self-control was defined by Pulkkinen (Pitkänen, 1969) as cognitive control of emotional impulses – which, when introduced, was a novel idea. Emotion regulation theories appeared in the psychological literature later, as presented above. In the 1960s, orientation to positive psychology was also thin or totally lacking. As a researcher of aggression in the 1960s, Pulkkinen became interested in positive, non-aggressive behavior of children. Constructs were lacking for describing this. To understand non-aggressive behaviors, she introduced a two-dimensional impulse control model, which involved the idea that both the expression and the inhibition of impulses can be controlled cognitively (Pitkänen, 1969; Pulkkinen, 1982). Consequently, an uncontrolled expression of anger-related impulses may lead to aggressive behavior, whereas a controlled expression of impulses may result in conciliatory or constructive behavior such as negotiation. Additionally, the inhibition of impulses may also take place in a controlled or uncontrolled way. The controlled inhibition of impulses may appear as deliberate, compliant behavior, and the uncontrolled inhibition of impulses as anxious behavior. Thus, constructive, compliant, and anxious behavior formed the major categories of non-aggressive behavior.

Cross-sectional data with 8-year-old schoolchildren were collected in 1968. Results confirmed the model (Pitkänen, 1969). The study transitioned into the ongoing longitudinal study with the latest data collection at age 50 in 2009 (Pulkkinen, 2009). The major methods were peer nomination and teacher rating in childhood and adolescence, and interview and inventories in adulthood. The intervals of data collection have been 6 to 8 years.

During the course of the study, the impulse control model was modified to encompass the cognitive control of both emotions and behavior, and it was relabeled the model of emotional and behavioral regulation (Pulkkinen, 1995, 2006), along with the emerging study of emotion regulation in psychology in the 1990s. Emotion regulation refers to the redirection, control, and modification of emotional arousal to enable an individual to function adaptively in emotionally arousing situations (Cicchetti, Ganiban, & Barnett, 1991). Emotion regulation and emotion-related behavioral regulation are intimately related (Eisenberg, Fabes, Guthrie, & Reiser, 2002).

The model explicates that both socially active and passive behaviors may be emotionally regulated or dysregulated, and that both low and high control of emotions may manifest in an active or passive way. The concepts of self-control and self-regulation are used here as synonyms. Two dimensions – social activity vs. passivity and low vs. high self-control – define four corners or behavioral strategies as in the original impulse control model: high self-control may emerge in a more active (e.g., constructive) or more passive (e.g., compliant) behavior, and low self-control, respectively, in a more active (e.g., aggressive) or more passive (e.g., anxious) behavior. Hypotheses for the present analyses were that high self-control indicating temperance would be associated with high social and psychological functioning.

2. Empirical evidence on the role of temperance in people's lives

Temperance as an antecedent of adult social and psychological functioning

In the study of the antecedents of psychological functioning in early middle age (42 yrs), adult psychological functioning was not found to be directly linked to childhood temperance, but an indirect link existed via adult career success (Pulkkinen, Feldt, & Kokko, 2006). Psychological functioning was indicated by sense of coherence, trust in life, self-esteem, and psychological well-being. Higher psychological functioning in males was associated with (1) a higher level of career – occupation – defined by the number of years of education and SES, and (2) greater career stability. These two aspects of career success were preceded by adaptive behavior in childhood and adolescence. Adaptive behavior was composed of several aspects of behavior that can be subsumed under the construct of temperance. Regulating negative emotions was assessed in terms of compliance (e.g., is peaceable and patient); prudence and regulation of behavior were assessed in terms constructiveness (e.g., tries to act reasonably in annoying situations, negotiates); and forgiveness (always tries to be friendly to others) and modesty (exaggerates, reversed) were assessed in terms of trustworthiness. These behaviors at ages 8 and 14 formed a latent factor for socially adaptive behavior that explained adult career success and, consequently, positive psychological functioning.

For women, it was only constructiveness that contributed to the level of career and, through it, to positive psychological functioning. The conclusion was that the broad spectrum of character strengths for temperance in males and more specific strengths in females assessed in childhood and early adolescence were antecedents of social and psychological functioning in middle age.

Self-control and criminal behavior

Gottfredson and Hirschi (1990) argued in their general theory of crime that individuals with a high level of self-control would be "substantially less likely at all periods of life to engage in criminal acts" (p. 89). They assumed that low self-control can be identified prior to the age of responsibility for crime, and it tends to persist through life. In the JYLS study, self-control was identified at age 8, while in Finland the age of responsibility for crime is 15, which made it possible to test this assumption for males. For females the number of offenders was too small for any conclusion.

Four groups of male offenders were formed (Pulkkinen, Lyyra, & Kokko, 2009):

1   adolescence-limited offenders, who ended offending by age 21;
2   persistent offenders, who were offending in adolescence and adulthood;
3   adult-onset offenders, whose offending began after age 20; and
4   non-offenders, who had not reported any offences or had not been registered for any crime.

Differences in self-control indicated by aggressiveness and compliance emerged at age 8 and 14, but were shown consistently only between the non-offenders and persistent offenders. Thus, the assumption presented by Gottfredson and Hirschi (1990) was partially confirmed. The only characteristic that differentiated the non-offenders from all offender groups was higher social passivity at age 14 (though not yet at age 8). In adulthood, the non-offenders had higher self-control compared to all offenders, as indicated by lower aggressiveness and neuroticism. The non-offenders also had fewer psychosomatic symptoms than all offenders.

In accordance with Moffitt's (1993) etiological theory of crime, men on the path of persistent offending had displayed more behavioral problems in childhood and early adolescence than men on the paths of non-offending and adolescence-limited offending. Bullying, aggressiveness, and emotional lability showing negative emotionality and weak constraints (difficulty in impulse control) indicated by lower compliance and higher norm-breaking behavior were characteristic of persistent offenders. Still, in adulthood, the persistent offenders were characterized by high impulsivity, disinhibition, risk-taking, and novelty seeking.

The adolescence-limited offenders did not differ from the non-offenders in childhood self-control. Rather, differences were displayed in delayed maturity, as indicated by poorer school success at age 8 but not at age 14, and in higher peer orientation at age 14, which, together with lower anxiety, was associated with onset of the use of alcohol at an earlier age. In adulthood, the offenders who limited their offending to adolescence were controlling their drinking, and they were well established in work and human relationships. The adult-onset offenders, on the other hand, displayed more problem behaviors than the non-offenders at early school age, but not in adolescence, when they were doing well at school. In adulthood, they were more disinhibited and higher in risk-taking than the non-offenders, and they scored higher in alcoholism than the non-offenders.

Well-controlled behavior of the non-offenders resulted in long-term positive consequences in terms of social functioning: the non-offenders had the highest occupational status (most likely a degree), were least likely to have experienced unemployment, and were least likely to be heavy drinkers. Their psychological well-being was better than that of the persistent offenders. The persistent offenders were most likely to display low social and psychological functioning in middle age.

Temperance and lifestyles

The word "temperance" has two meanings in current dictionaries. First, it means moderation, referring to the practice of avoiding excess along with the definition of the virtue of temperance. Second, it means sobriety, referring to abstaining from excess, often from alcohol. Related to the latter meaning, the temperance movement, which grew particularly in the United Kingdom in the early nineteenth century, was aimed at generating temperance in drinking alcoholic beverages. Our third empirical evidence on the role of temperance in human development was focused on a question of whether it was possible to form groups of middle-aged individuals differing in several aspects of temperate behavior, and whether these possible groups would differ in personality and social and psychological functioning.

We chose four indicators of temperance: consumption of alcohol, smoking, adult crime, and weight (body mass index, BMI), and out of a total of 163 women and 187 men, we formed three groups separately for each gender, using data collected in adulthood (from age 27 to age 42).

1   The most temperate group included 42 women and 29 men. The criteria for women and men through adult years were: intoxication (drunkenness) less than once a month, no smoking, and no registered crime after age 20; in addition, for weight, criteria were: BMI < 25 for women and BMI < 30 for men.
2   The middle group (87 women, 118 men) included those between the most temperate and most intemperate groups according to the criteria used.
3   The most intemperate group included 31 women and 41 men. In this group, women met two to four criteria and men three to four criteria out of the following in at least one of the three measurements in adulthood (at age 27, 36, or 42): intoxicated at least once a week, regular smoking, registered for crime after age 20, and BMI > 30.

Because women were, on average, more temperate than men in all criteria, cut-off points had to be compromised. In spite of this, there were more women in the temperate group and, correspondingly, more men in the intemperate group. One-way analysis of variance revealed the bulk of significant group differences in personality, adjustment, and family background between the temperate and intemperate groups for both genders (Table 9.1). Thus, the

Table 9.1 Groups for temperance compared in personality, adjustment, and family background assessed at different ages, and significant differences between the means of the groups; one-way ANOVA and Least Square Deviance test

Variable	Age	Sex	N	Temperate 1	Middle 2	Intemperate 3	F	p =	LSD
Personality									
Constructiveness (TR1)	8	M	184	0.16	0.11	−0.42	4.65	0.011	1, 2 > 3
Compliance (TR1)	8	M	184	0.33	0.11	−0.47	7.02	0.001	1, 2 > 3
Aggression (TR2)	8	M	184	−0.11	−0.18	0.52	7.90	0.001	1, 2 < 3
Constructiveness (TR1)	14	F	163	0.76	0.18	−0.22	11.91	0.000	1 > 2 > 3
		M	184	0.17	−0.17	−0.67	6.54	0.002	1, 2 > 3
Compliance (TR1)	14	F	163	0.56	0.08	0.00	4.56	0.011	1 > 2, 3
		M	184	0.20	−0.14	−0.52	4.51	0.012	1, 2 > 3
Aggression (TR2)	14	F	163	−0.55	−0.29	0.05	6.40	0.002	1, 2 < 3
Disinhibition (SSS)	27	F	144	−0.69	−0.13	0.11	8.46	0.000	1 < 2, 3
		M	143	−0.90	0.47	0.44	20.18	0.000	1 < 2, 3
Psychoticism (EPQ)	27	F	144	−0.37	−0.14	0.37	4.61	0.012	1, 2 < 3
		M	143	−0.37	0.10	0.62	5.91	0.003	1 < 2 < 3
Inhibitory control (KSP)	42	F	118	0.40	−0.19	−0.44	6.55	0.002	1 > 2, 3
		M	115	0.50	0.09	−0.34	3.53	0.032	1 > 3
Benign control (ECQ)	42	F	120	0.34	0.05	−0.36	3.65	0.029	1 > 3
		M	119	0.38	−0.01	−0.54	4.62	0.012	1, 2 > 3
Conscientiousness (B-F)	42/33[a]	F	139	0.52	0.06	−0.29	5.00	0.008	1 > 2, 3
		M	148	0.13	−0.02	−0.52	4.24	0.016	1, 2 > 3
Conformity (KSP)	42	F	118	0.58	−0.03	−0.66	12.61	0.000	1 > 2 > 3
		M	115	0.24	0.07	−0.58	4.46	0.014	1, 2 > 3
Aggression (AQ)	42	F	145	−0.30	0.08	0.39	3.81	0.024	1 < 3
		M	154	−0.39	−0.09	0.39	5.07	0.007	1, 2 < 3
Impulsiveness (KSP)	42	F	118	−0.54	0.07	0.43	9.52	0.000	1 > 2, 3
		M	115	−0.52	0.01	0.64	6.41	0.002	1 < 2 < 3
Adjustment									
School success	8	F	163	0.30	0.02	−0.51	5.99	0.003	1, 2 > 3

Variable	Age	Sex	N	(1)	(2)	(3)	F	p	Comparison
Body Mass Index[b]	8	F	110	14.41	15.03	15.87	7.12	0.001	1 < 2 < 3
School success	14	F	163	1.01	0.37	−0.21	18.83	0.000	1 > 2 > 3
		M	184	0.01	−0.29	−1.01	17.46	0.000	1 < 2 < 3
Body Mass Index[b]	14	F	107	18.20	19.62	20.14	5.34	0.006	1 < 2, 3
		M	104	18.72	18.70	20.43	3.82	0.025	1, 2 < 3
Conduct problems	14	F	152	−2.51	−0.66	1.61	22.91	0.000	1 < 2 < 3
		M	178	−1.07	0.35	2.83	12.76	0.000	1 < 2 < 3
Age of onset of drinking[b]		F	163	17.30	15.16	14.50	16.28	0.000	1 > 2, 3
		M	187	16.67	15.14	14.92	6.46	0.002	1 > 2, 3
Education (years)		F	163	0.52	0.32	−0.33	8.22	0.000	1, 2 > 3
		M	184	0.14	−0.16	−0.68	6.86	0.001	1, 2 > 3
Stable career		F	133	0.31	0.12	−0.78	11.23	0.000	1, 2 > 3
		M	151	0.01	0.22	−0.67	10.86	0.000	1, 2 > 3
Income	43	F	142	−0.03	−0.11	−0.53	4.05	0.020	1, 2 > 3
		M	170	0.08	0.43	−0.57	10.91	0.000	1, 2 > 3
Poor self-rated health	42	F	132	−0.44	0.05	0.55	7.23	0.001	1 < 2 < 3
		M	147	−0.52	0.01	0.24	4.42	0.014	1 < 2 < 3
Eating-related psychosomatic problems	42/36[a]	F	147	−0.40	0.12	0.36	7.13	0.001	1 < 2, 3
		M	162	−0.62	−0.09	0.59	10.40	0.000	1 < 2 < 3
Family background									
Parental heavy drinking		F	163	−0.29	0.04	0.27	3.04	0.051	1 < 3
		M	184	−0.34	−0.06	0.43	5.67	0.004	1, 2 < 3
Mother's smoking		F	163	−0.56	0.15	−0.01	9.68	0.000	1 < 2, 3
Father smokes		F	132	−0.33	0.19	0.35	4.41	0.014	1, 2 < 3
		M	152	−0.50	−0.09	0.24	3.88	0.023	1 < 3
Parental interest in school-work	14	M	184	0.12	0.05	−0.46	3.89	0.022	1, 2 > 3
Parental child-centeredness		F	163	0.34	0.01	−0.32	4.06	0.019	1 > 3
SES of the family of origin	8	F	163	0.015	−0.05	−0.43	3.28	0.040	1, 2 < 3

Note: Variables standardized. ANOVA = analysis of variance. LSD = Least Square Deviance. F = females, M = males. TR1 = teacher rating (see Pulkkinen et al., 2006); TR2 = teacher rating (see Pulkkinen, 1987); SSS = Sensation-Seeking Scale (Zuckerman, 1979); EPQ = Eysenck Personality Questionnaire (Eysenck & Eysenck, 1975); KSP = Karolinska Scales of Personality (Schalling, 1986); ECQ = Emotion Control Questionnaire (Roger & Nesshoever, 1987); B-F = Big Five Inventory (see Rantanen, Metsäpelto, Feldt, Pulkkinen, & Kokko, 2007); AQ = Aggression Questionnaire (see Kokko & Pulkkinen, 2005).

a Missing information at age 42 complemented by previous data.
b Not standardized.

phenomenon was similar for men and women, although there was the gender difference in the absolute level of temperance. The following comparison concerns the temperate and intemperate groups, although the results for the intermediate group are also presented in Table 9.1. The focus of the present analysis is in personality variables, but the means of the groups are also given in Table 9.1 for a few adjustment and background variables. Additional significant group differences are explained in the text.

For differences in personality, it was found that the temperate men and women were higher in teacher-rated self-control, indicated by constructive and compliant behavior in early adolescence (men already at age 8). Consequently, the temperate groups were lower in aggression. In adulthood, both male and female temperates were higher in inhibitory control referring to temperamental characteristics, and in benign control referring to deliberate behavior. The temperate group were also higher in conformity and conscientiousness, which refers to planfulness and carefulness, and less aggressive, impulsive, and disinhibited than the intemperates. In terms of psychoticism, which is a characteristic of antisocial individuals, the temperate groups were lower than the intemperate groups.

For adjustment, it was found that the temperate groups had better school success (females already at age 8) and fewer conduct problems at age 14 than the intemperate groups. The age of onset of drinking was higher in the temperate groups, and from adolescence through adulthood the temperate groups had fewer drinking problems. A risk for drinking problems in adulthood was highly and inversely related to the age of onset of drinking, as shown in another study using the JYLS data (Pitkänen, Lyyra, & Pulkkinen, 2005); furthermore, adolescent drinking was significantly associated with problem drinking in early middle age (Pitkänen, Kokko, Lyyra, & Pulkkinen, 2008). Thus, starting the use of alcohol later (at about 17 yrs compared to about 14.5 yrs among the intemperates) protected the temperates against drinking problems.

Higher BMI at age 14 (for females already at age 8) was more often found in the intemperate than the temperate groups. Both male and female intemperates assessed their health to be poorer at age 42 than the temperates. The intemperates also scored higher in psychosomatic problems related to eating. Conversely, the temperates had more years of education, more stable careers, and higher incomes. Respective differences were in their occupational status, particularly among women. Well-being, self-esteem, and life satisfaction in early middle age were higher among the temperate men than among the intemperate men.

For social background, it was found that the socioeconomic status of the parents did not differentiate between the male groups, but the intemperate women came from a lower social background than did women in the temperate group (Table 9.1). The parents of both intemperate men and intemperate women used alcohol and smoked cigarettes more than did the parents of the temperates. For men's temperance it was important that the parents were interested in their son's school attendance, and that the mother was know-ledgeable about her son's whereabouts (where he was, with whom, and what he was doing). For women's temperance, high parental child-centeredness, including close relationships between father and mother and father and daughter, the mother's sensitivity to the daughter's opinions, and lack of physical punishment were promoting factors. The parents of the temper-ate women were older than those of the intemperate ones, which possibly increased parental maturity and resulted in a more secure family life.

More in the temperate groups were married at age 42 than were those in the intemperate groups, and among the former, there was more cohesion (women) and consensus (men) in the partner relationship. The temperate men ($M = 2.24$) had more children than did the intemperate men (1.26), but among the women there were no group differences ($M = 1.79$ and 1.97, respectively). Thus the intemperate women were as likely as the temperate women to have passed their social inheritance on to their children. With their own children, the temperate men and women were more likely than the intem-perate ones to apply child-centered parenting, which supports the develop-ment of self-control. Thus, the children of the temperate and intemperate parents were exposed to different parenting behavior in addition to different parental modeling of temperate or intemperate behavior.

Conclusions

Empirical studies have confirmed predictions made on the basis of the model of emotional and behavioral regulation concerning the associations between high self-control and successful development. Self-control is one of the core elements of the virtue called temperance. Our results have shown that (1) char-acter strengths for temperance in childhood and adolescence are antecedents of positive social functioning and, in consequence, of psychological function-ing in middle age, (2) self-control in childhood and adolescence protects against a persistent criminal path, and non-offending is associated with posi-tive social and psychological functioning; and (3) individuals characterized by temperate behavior in middle age differ from their intemperate counterparts in personality, home background, and social and psychological functioning.

In the current Western world, strengths of temperance are seldom praised. In fact, just the opposite is often the case: peak experiences are aimed at, people taking high risks are admired, and TV programs on excessive behaviors and experiences are popular. In spite of their higher educational qualification, the occupational status of the temperate men was not higher than that of the intemperate men. Disinhibited and impulsive intemperates had been active and successful in finding occupational positions comparable to those of their temperate counterparts in spite of the difference in edu-cational level. Not infrequently, intemperance is manifested in individuals occupying high social positions causing sensation in media.

Intemperance has become a current issue for the future of the world also due to consumer behavior. As a result, climate change threatens the globe, health problems threaten people, and the unequal distribution of resources between rich and poor countries and people threatens the existence of millions of people. We are approaching a time when a return from heavily individualistic styles of life to the classic virtues – wisdom, courage, justice, and temperance – is needed for the future of the world, both in the upbringing of children and in the self-growth of adults.

Acknowledgments

This chapter is based on a long-term longitudinal project that has been funded by the Academy of Finland since 1986, most recently from grant 127125. The project was a part of the Finnish Centre of Excellence Programme, "Human Development and Its Risk Factors" (grant 44858) in 1997 to 2005.

References

Bandura, A. (1977). Self-efficacy: Toward a unified theory of behavioral change. *Psychological Review, 84*, 191–215.

Banfield, J. F., Wyland, C. L., Macrae, C. N., Münte, T. F., & Heatherton, T. F. (2004). The cognitive neuroscience of self-regulation. In R. F. Baumeister & K. D. Vohs (Eds.), *Handbook of self-regulation: Research, theory, and application* (pp. 62–83). New York: Guilford Press.

Baumeister, R. F., Heatherton, T. F., & Tice, D. M. (1994). *Losing control: How and why people fail at self-regulation.* San Diego, CA: Academic Press.

Carver, C. S. (2004). Self-regulation of action and affect. In R. F. Baumeister & K. D. Vohs (Eds.), *Handbook of self-regulation: Research, theory, and application* (pp. 13–39). New York: Guilford Press.

Carver, C. S., & Scheier, M. F. (1981). *Attention and self-regulation: A control theory approach to human behavior.* New York: Springer-Verlag.

Cicchetti, D., Ganiban, J., & Barnett, D. (1991). Contributions from the study of high-risk populations to understanding the development of emotion regulation. In J. Garber & K. A. Dodge (Eds.), *The development of emotion regulation and dysregulation* (pp. 15–48). Cambridge, UK: Cambridge University Press.

Eisenberg, N., Fabes, R. A., Guthrie, I. K., & Reiser, M. (2002). The role of emotionality and regulation in children's social competence and adjustment. In L. Pulkkinen & A. Caspi (Eds.), *Paths to successful development: Personality in the life course* (pp. 46–70). Cambridge, UK: Cambridge University Press.

Eisenberg, N., Smith, C. L., Sadovsky, A., & Spinrad, T. L. (2004). Effortful control: Relations with emotion regulation, adjustment, and socialization in childhood. In R. F. Baumeister & K. D. Vohs (Eds.), *Handbook of self-regulation: Research, theory, and application* (pp. 259–282). New York: Guilford Press.

Eysenck, H. J., & Eysenck, S. B. G. (1975). *Manual of the Eysenck Personality Questionnaire.* London: University of London Press.

Freud, S. (1949). *An outline of psychoanalysis.* New York: Norton.

Gottfredson, M. R., & Hirschi, T. (1990). *A general theory of crime.* Stanford, CA: Stanford University Press.

Heider, F. (1958). *The psychology of interpersonal relations*. New York: Wiley.

Kanfer, F. H., & Karoly, R. (1972). Self-control: A behavioristic excursion into the lion's den. *Behavior Therapy, 3*, 398–416.

Kokko, K., & Pulkkinen, L. (2005). Stability of aggressive behavior from childhood to middle age in women and men. *Aggressive Behavior, 31*, 485–497.

Kopp, C. B. (1982). Antecedents of self-regulation: A developmental perspective. *Developmental Psychology, 18*, 199–214.

Kopp, C. B. (1987). The growth of self-regulation: Caregivers and children. In N. Eisenberg (Ed.), *Contemporary topics in developmental psychology* (pp. 34–55). New York: Wiley.

Little, T. D., Snyder, C. R., & Wehmeyer, M. (2006). The agentic self: On the nature and origins of personal agency across the life span. In D. K. Mroczck & T. D. Little (Eds.), *Handbook of personality development* (pp. 61–79). Mahwah, NJ: Lawrence Erlbaum Associates, Inc.

Luria, A. R. (1961). *The role of speech in the regulation of normal and abnormal behavior*. New York: Leveright.

Maccoby, E. E. (1980). *Social development: Psychological growth and the parent–child relationship*. New York: Harcourt Brace Jovanovich.

Moffitt, T. E. (1993). "Life-course persistent" and "adolescence-limited" antisocial behavior: A developmental taxonomy. *Psychological Review, 100*, 674–701.

Morris, W., & Reilly, N. (1987). Toward the self-regulation of mood: Theory and research. *Motivation and Emotion, 11*, 215–249.

Murray, H. (1938). *Explorations in personality*. New York: Oxford University Press.

Peterson, C., & Seligman, M. E. P. (2004). *Character strengths and virtues: A handbook and classification*. New York: Oxford University Press.

Pitkanen, L. (1969). *A descriptive model of aggression and nonaggression with applications to children's behaviour* (Jyväskylä Studies in Education, Psychology and Social Research, No. 19). Jyväskylä, Finland: University of Jyväskylä.

Pitkänen, T., Kokko, K., Lyyra, A.-L., & Pulkkinen, L. (2008). A developmental approach to alcohol drinking behavior in adulthood: A follow-up study from age 8 to age 42. *Addiction, 103*(Suppl. 1), 48–68.

Pitkänen, T., Lyyra, A.-L., & Pulkkinen, L. (2005). Age of onset of drinking and the use of alcohol in adulthood: A follow-up study from age 8–42 for females and males. *Addiction, 100*, 652–661.

Pulkkinen, L. (1982). Self-control and continuity from childhood to late adolescence. In P. B. Baltes & O. G. Brim Jr. (Eds.), *Life-span development and behavior* (Vol. 4, pp. 53–105). Orlando, FL: Academic Press.

Pulkkinen, L. (1986). The role of impulse control in the development of antisocial and prosocial behavior. In D. Olweus, J. Block, & M. Radke-Yarrow (Eds.), *Development of antisocial and prosocial behavior: Research, theory, and issues* (pp. 149–206). Orlando, FL: Academic Press.

Pulkkinen, L. (1987). Offensive and defensive aggression in humans: A longitudinal perspective. *Aggressive Behavior, 13*, 197–212.

Pulkkinen, L. (1995). Behavioral precursors to accidents and resulting physical impairment. *Child Development, 66*, 1660–1679.

Pulkkinen, L. (2006). The Jyväskylä Longitudinal Study of Personality and Social Development (JYLS). In L. Pulkkinen, J. Kaprio, & R. J. Rose (Eds.), *Socioemotional development and health from adolescence to adulthood* (pp. 29–55). New York: Cambridge University Press.

Pulkkinen, L. (2009). Personality: A resource or risk for successful development. *Scandinavian Journal of Psychology, 6,* 602–610.

Pulkkinen, L., Feldt, T., & Kokko, K. (2006). Adaptive behavior in childhood as an antecedent of psychological functioning in early middle age: Linkage via career orientation. *Social Indicators Research, 77,* 171–195.

Pulkkinen, L., Lyyra, A.-L., & Kokko, K. (2009). Life success of males on non-offender, adolescence-limited, persistent and adult-onset antisocial pathways: Follow-up from age 8 to 42. *Aggressive Behavior, 35,* 117–135.

Rantanen, J., Metsäpelto, R.-L, Feldt, T., Pulkkinen, L., & Kokko, K. (2007). Long-term stability and change in the Big Five in adulthood. *Scandinavian Journal of Psychology, 48,* 511–518.

Roger, D., & Nesshoever, W. (1987). The construction and preliminary validation of a scale for measuring emotional control. *Personality & Individual Differences, 8,* 527–534.

Rothbart, M., & Bates, J. E. (1998). Temperament. In W. Damon (Series Ed.) & N. Eisenberg (Vol. Ed.), *Handbook of child psychology: Vol. 3. Social, emotional, and personality development* (pp. 105–176). New York: Wiley.

Rothbart, M., & Derryberry, D. (1981). Development of individual differences in temperament. In M. E. Lamb & A. L. Brown (Eds.), *Advances in developmental psychology* (Vol. 1, pp. 37–86). Hillsdale, NJ: Lawrence Erlbaum Associates, Inc.

Saarni, C. (1989). Children's understanding of strategic control of emotional expression in social transactions. In C. Saarni & P. Harris (Eds.), *Children's understanding of emotion* (pp. 181–208). New York: Cambridge University Press.

Schalling, D. (1986). The development of the KSP inventory. In B. af Klinteberg, D. Schalling, & D. Magnusson (Eds.), *Self-report assessment of personality traits* (Reports from the project Individual Development and Adjustment, No. 64, pp. 1–8). Stockholm, Sweden: University of Stockholm, Department of Psychology.

Schmeichel, B. J., & Baumeister, R. F. (2004). Self-regulatory strength. In R. F. Baumeister & K. D. Vohs (Eds.), *Handbook of self-regulation: Research, theory, and application* (pp. 84–98). New York: Guilford Press.

Seligman, M. E. P., & Csikszentmihalyi, M. (2000). Positive psychology: An introduction. *American Psychologist, 55,* 5–14.

Vohs, K. D., & Baumeister, R. F. (2004). Understanding self-regulation: An introduction. In R. F. Baumeister & K. D. Vohs (Eds.), *Handbook of self-regulation: Research, theory, and application* (pp. 1–9). New York: Guilford Press.

Vygotsky, L. S. (1962). *Thought and language.* New York: Wiley.

Zuckerman, M. (1979). *Sensation seeking: Beyond the optimal level of arousal.* Hillsdale, NJ: Lawrence Erlbaum Associates, Inc.

10 A cross-cultural perspective on the development of sharing behavior

Integrating behavioral economics and psychology

Liqi Zhu, Monika Keller,
Michaela Gummerum, and
Masanori Takezawa

A cross-cultural perspective on the development of sharing behavior: Integrating behavioral economics and psychology

Over the last decades, economists have been using the Ultimatum game (UG) and the Dictator game (DG) to measure people's decision-making as reflecting self-interest or norms of altruism. Usually in an Ultimatum game two players are allotted a sum of money. The first player (called the "proposer") offers a portion of the total sum to the second player (called the "responder"). The responder can either accept or reject the proposer's offer. If the responder accepts, s/he receives the amount of the offer, and the proposer receives the remainder. If the responder rejects, then nobody receives anything. The Dictator game differs from the Ultimatum game in that the responder can only accept the proposer's offer. The game is played only once, so the responder cannot reciprocate or punish offers by the proposers. Economists have rarely been interested in developmental questions, while developmental psychologists have long been investigating fair and prosocial behavior in children and adolescents without taking note of the debate in economics. Since the economic games differ from tasks typically used in research on fairness and moral development, connecting these two research traditions seems to be a promising interdisciplinary endeavor to study children's sharing (prosocial) behavior (Gummerum, Keller, Takezawa, & Mata, 2008).

A meta-analysis on the development of prosocial behavior by Eisenberg and Fabes (1998) found significant age differences in the sharing behavior of infants, preschool children, children, and adolescents, with older participants being more prosocial than younger children. However, Damon (1977) showed that distributive justice reasoning was more advanced in hypothetical situations (which is usually true in psychology research) than in real-life sharing situations, but also that children keep more for themselves in a real than in a hypothetical sharing situation. Similarly, a study by Epley and Dunning

(2000) documents that adults overestimate their own future prosocial behavior – that is, they share less than what they predicted they would. Thus, the UG and the DG may serve as good tasks to test children's prosocial behavior when players play with real money and get real payment on the basis of their decision. The two games can be used together to reflect sharing or rational behavior. When a proposer makes a high offer in the UG, this results either from preference of fairness, or from fear of rejection, or both, while in the DG, the high offer of proposers can only arise from fairness. The games are similar to some extent to dilemmas used in studies on the development of moral reasoning, in which a person's own desires conflict with the needs of others and prosocial norms (Eisenberg, 1986; Keller & Edelstein, 1993).

Studies with adults (e.g., Forsythe., Horowitz, Savin, & Sefton, 1994) using the two games have demonstrated that dictators offer on average between 20 and 30% of the original sum to the responder, with the most frequent offers being either zero or half, with few gender differences (see Camerer, 2003, for an overview). A meta-analysis of 37 papers with 75 results from Ultimatum-game experiments found that on average the proposer offers 40% of the pie to the responder (Oosterbeek, Sloof, & Vandekuilen, 2004). Only a few studies have examined developmental trends with both the Dictator game and the Ultimatum game. Also, most studies have been conducted by economists and have not assessed psychological process. Findings from a study by Harbaugh, Krause, and Liday (2003) revealed that children behaved similarly to adults in the DG, while children in Grade 2 offered less in the UG than did the other older groups (4th/5th-, 9th-, and 12th-graders). More recently, Benenson, Pascoe, and Radmore (2007) examined developmental differences with children aged 4, 6, and 9 years. Results demonstrated that older children behaved more altruistically, although the majority of children displayed altruistic behavior even at the youngest age level. Bettinger and Slonim (2006), in a study of children from low-income families, found a similar age effect – namely, that older children were more generous. Murnighan and Saxon (1998) found that in the UG children in Grade 3 offered less than did those in Grade 6. These results were consistent with children's prosocial behavior study in psychology (Eisenberg & Fabes, 1998).

Research has typically focused on individual offers in the UG and the DG. However, defending one's offer in a group situation represents a context that is different from an individual private decision. As Haidt (2001) pointed out, for moral reasoning, persons in a public context may be stimulated and forced to cognitively elaborate their moral convictions in order to convince others. In social psychology, group interaction has been seen as the means by which individual persons exchange information, preferences, attitudes, and norms (Hinsz, Tindale, & Vollrath, 1997). In this process individual group members contribute their own perspectives and values on the situation. Group discussion, therefore, allows individual group members to see whether others make the same choices or arguments or different ones from their own.

When reaching a final agreement, they may either raise or lower individual offers.

Previous studies on group decision making have shown that groups offered less than did individuals in the UG (Bornstein & Yaniv, 1998; Schopler & Insko, 1992). In contrast, Cason and Mui (1997) found that adult dictators tended to offer more in two-person groups than as individuals. Bornstein, Kugler, and Ziegelmeyer (2004) found that groups are more greedy than individuals in the centipede game. As Song, Cadsby, and Morris (2006) point out, the discrepancy between these findings may be better explained if research takes into account the decision-making process in groups. It is important not merely to compare mean differences in individuals' and groups' allocations, because group offers are determined by both the distribution of individual preferences in each group and the group decision-making process. An additional advantage of studying the decisions of groups is that group members' justifications for offers can be assessed by analyzing group discussions. These justifications give insight into how group members construct the game situation and which aspects of this situation they regard as important. Group discussions in the game provide rich material for justifications that cannot usually be captured by distributive justice or (prosocial) moral reasoning research (Gummerum et al., 2008).

In the current study we investigate whether the age differences found in the case of children's and adolescents' allocations in Western cultures will similarly be obtained for Chinese children. Experimental studies with adults have consistently reported cross-cultural variations concerning behavior in economic games (e.g., Hennig-Schmidt, Li, & Yang, 2002; Henrich et al., 2001, 2005). Yet few studies have worked on the developmental trajectory of children in different cultures, and few studies have been conducted with Chinese subjects on how they play economic games, either on an individual or on a group level. Chuaha, Hoffmann, Jones, and Williams (2007) report the results of Ultimatum-game experiments in which Malaysian Chinese and UK subjects played opponents of their own as well as of the other culture. They found the existence of cultural difference in subject behavior in both intra- and international interactions. Hoffmann and Tee (2006) found slightly higher average offers and rejection rates for the non-Chinese subjects, but tests yielded no significant statistics in the study. The authors claimed that these conclusions must be treated as extremely tentative due to the small proportion of non-Chinese subjects and their cultural heterogeneity. Thus, they called for a more explicit examination of Chinese cultural and Ultimatum-game behavior.

The current study is a collaborative study between Chinese and German scholars. In order to have a comparison, we used the same method and procedure as those employed by Takezawa, Gummerum, and Keller (2006) and Gummerum and colleagues (2008). Gummerum and colleagues (2008) reported that individual allocations did not differ by age; they also found that the youngest participants justified offers more frequently by referring to simple distribution principles, while older participants employed more complex reasons to justify deviations from allocation principles. China is traditionally a collectivist society and was recognized as a collectivist culture (Oyserman, Coon, & Kemmelmeier, 2002). We hypothesize that Chinese children may be different from their Western counterparts in terms of their development trajectory and their preference of fairness by offering more than their Western counterparts. In group discussions Chinese children may refer more to group orientations. In this chapter we examine the process by which groups of three peers reach a common allocation decision by starting from the Dictator game. (The discussion process in the UG is more complex and will be analyzed and presented in another paper.)

Method

Participants

Participants in China were students in Grades 3, 6, and 8, recruited from an elementary school and a junior high school in Beijing. Because of the difficulty of getting participants in Grade 11 from senior high schools, we also recruited a group of college freshmen (see Table 10.1), However, the ages of each grade group between the two countries were comparable. Participants in Germany were students in Grades 3, 6, 8, and 11 in an elementary school and a high school in Berlin.

Procedure

The procedure was similar to the one used by Gummerum and colleagues (2008). In their paper, only data on the DG were reported, while in the study both German and Chinese children were requested to play both the Ultimatum game and the Dictator game. During the school day, three same-sex students from the same class were randomly selected and taken into a separate room by a female experimenter. Participants were told that they would

Table 10.1 Participants in China and Germany

Country	Grade	Age	Gender	
			Male	*Female*
China	3	8.5	24	24
	6	11.3	24	24
	8	13.4	24	24
	College freshmen	18.3	27	27
Germany	3	8.7	18	21
	6	11.5	18	27
	8	14.1	15	33
	11	17.7	12	45

play two consecutive games (Dictator game, Ultimatum game) with a different group of three anonymous same-sex and same-grade students. They were told that the other students could be from their own or another school, and that neither group would know with whom they had played the game. Moreover, it was stressed that their decisions would not be revealed to classmates, parents, or teachers by the experimenters. Participants played the Dictator game and the Ultimatum game in a counterbalanced order.

Participants were instructed in the proposer role of the Dictator game and the Ultimatum game. After participants' understanding of the game structure was confirmed, they were asked to privately write down their individual sharing preferences on an answer sheet. Students inserted their answer sheet into an envelope collected by the experimenter. The group was then asked to discuss how much they would like to offer to the other group. Each group had about 10 min to come to a unanimous agreement. If groups had not come to a decision after 10 min, they were prompted by the experimenter to finish the discussion within a few minutes. Discussions were videotaped, and participants were aware of this. The payment was handed to each participant at the end of the session. In both games, there were no real responders: the experimenter accepted any offer in the DG and the UG.

Measures

Dictator game

Students were instructed in the role of the proposer. It was pointed out that they could earn money in this experiment, but that the amount of money they earned would depend on their group decision. German children in Grade 3 were given 20 coins, worth 10 cents each (2 euros in total), those in Grade 6 and 8 received 20 cents each (4 euros in total), and those in Grade 11 were given 30 cents (6 euros in total). Chinese children in Grades 3, 6, and 8 were also given 20 coins, worth RMB 50 cents each (about 1 euro in total); college freshmen received RMB 1 yuan (about 2 euros in total) each.

Participants were told that their group could determine how to allocate the 20 coins between themselves and another anonymous group of three. It was pointed out that offers could range from 0 to 20 coins, in steps of 1 coin. They were told that payment for each group member was the number of coins the group wanted to keep. For example, if a group wanted to keep 10 coins, each group member would receive 10 coins.

Ultimatum game

The instructions were similar to the Dictator game, but the responder could either accept or reject the offer. If the responder accepted the offer, then the money would be allocated according to the proposal; if the offer was rejected, then neither of the two sides would receive anything.

Scoring of justifications in group discussion

A manual was developed for categorizing participants' justifications for offers in the group discussion for the DG. Due to the complexity of the discussions in the UG, we report only the results in the DG in this chapter.

Two types of justifications were differentiated: (1) unconditional preferences and justifications; and (2) conditional attributions and justifications.

1   *Unconditional preferences and justifications*

- *Fairness:* explicit reference to fairness, justice, or democracy without further explanation as to why these concepts are important (e.g., "Because it is fair." . . . "We always want to be fair." . . . "We should split it equally, that would be fair to both sides.").

- *Egoism:* reference to one's own selfish or material desires, without any further explanation (e.g., "Because I wanted to keep the money for myself." . . . "But we want to make more profit." . . . "If you can get profit, why should you give it to others?").

2   *Conditional attributions and justifications*

- *Group:* statements that attribute a social category, trait, or characteristic to the other group, or express concern about how the participant's own group would look in the eyes of others. Participants attribute characteristics to the other group that bring it closer, make it more similar or likeable to their own group, point out the *neediness* of the other group, or they interpret the *anonymity* of the other group in a positive way (e.g., "Look, maybe it's people like us, just like us." . . . "You'd rather share with them more if they are friends than if they are strangers." . . . "We are schoolmates."). Or participants employ attributes or characteristics that make the other group more dissimilar to their own group or create a (psychological) distance between the two groups. Statements in this category include those asserting that the other group does not need the money and those that interpret the anonymity of the other group in a negative way (e.g., "Maybe they are unfair people in the other group." . . . "Maybe they are not likeable, and they don't need the money." . . . "It is no good if I give them a lot of money while they may be someone I dislike." . . . "You don't know who they are: we do not have any relationship with them.").

- *Reciprocity:* statements through which participants put themselves in the position of the other group (role play) or imagine what the other group would do in their position. Group members point out that the other group would reciprocate or would also act in a generous way (e.g., "Imagine they'd give us a lot." . . . "Because one could well imagine that the others would do it, too." . . . "My concern is if we change roles, will we be sad if they give us less?"); or they make statements asserting that the members in the other group would not reciprocate or would act greedily as well (e.g., "I'll tell you why – because the others wouldn't give us anything either." . . . "I don't think they'd give us much either." . . . "If you give to them, they may not give back to you next time.").

- *Hierarchical power:* statements that deal with status differences between the two groups. For example, one group has more power because it can determine the payoff; one group puts in more effort, and so forth. These status differences make the more powerful group responsible for the condition of the less powerful group (e.g., "That means we say how much they get and how much we get: Therefore it is nasty to give only one coin." . . . "Because we bear responsibility for the other group." . . . "Though we have the right to decide, we shouldn't be greedy."). Or the higher-status group is allowed to claim more money because it has more decision power or has invested more effort (e.g., "If I can decide, I will not give them half." . . . "Therefore we have to get money for the work and time we invest in sharing." . . . "If we have the power, why not use it?").

In addition, some justifications were uncodable. These were justifications in which irrelevant explanations for an offer were given (e.g., "Because I like this number.") or in which instructions were repeated. Two independent raters coded discussion transcripts. Discrepancies for codes were discussed to find the best solution.

Results

Individual offers and group offers in the Dictator game

The equal split (10 coins) was the modal offer in all grades and for both cultures. A univariate analysis of variance (ANOVA) revealed that the Chinese children offered marginally significantly more than did the German children, $F(3, 387) = 3.35$, $p = .07$, $\eta^2 = .009$ (see Table 10.2). No significant differences were obtained for grade and Country × Grade interaction. For the group offer, Chinese children ($M = 42.3\%$) offered significantly more than did the German children ($M = 36.5\%$), $F(1, 376) = 14.50$, $p = .00$, $\eta^2 = .04$. A significant main effect for grade was obtained, $F(3, 376) = 3.34$, $p = .02$, $\eta^2 = .03$. There was also a Country × Grade interaction $F(3, 376) = 4.05$, $p = .008$, $\eta^2 = .03$. As indicated in Table 10.2, Chinese children in Grade 3 and 6 offered significantly more than did German children; the difference decreased in Grades 8 and 11.

Individual offers and group offers in the Ultimatum game

Table 10.3 displays the means and standard deviations for individual and group offers in the UG. The equal split was again the typical offer in all

Table 10.2 Individual and group offers in the Dictator game

Country	Grade	Individual offer		Group offer	
		M	SD	M	SD
China	3	42.9	24.5	44.8	24.4
	6	45.8	16.1	45.3	13.5
	8	41.8	15.3	43.1	9.1
	College freshmen	37.8	20.6	36.9	15.9
Germany	3	36.7	23.1	29.6	18.6
	6	40.6	15.6	36.8	12.0
	8	37.9	17.1	42.2	14.2
	11	39.1	16.4	36.1	17.9

Note: In percentages.

Table 10.3 Ultimate game individual and group offers

Country	Grade	Individual		Group	
		M	SD	M	SD
China	3	59.0	22.7	64.7	18.7
	6	53.7	11.3	51.6	3.5
	8	52.1	8.9	51.3	2.8
	College freshmen	49.0	12.4	46.4	10.8
Germany	3	52.8	20.5	55.8	16.8
	6	46.6	8.7	50.0	7.2
	8	51.7	12.9	50.2	9.8
	11	54.6	11.3	55.8	9.6

Note: In percentages.

grades and for both countries. A univariate analysis of variance (ANOVA) showed no main effect for country and grade, but a Country × Grade interaction was obtained, $F(3, 376) = 4.25$, $p = .006$, $\eta^2 = .03$. As indicated in Table 10.3, there was significant difference in Grades 6 and 11. For the group offers, there was no main effect for country, but a main effect of grade and a Country × Grade interaction was obtained: grade: $F(3, 376) = 15.72, p = .00$, $\eta^2 = .11$, and for the interaction, $F(3, 376) = 11.45$, $p = .00$, $\eta^2 = .08$. The difference lies in Grades 3 and 11. Therefore, we find different trajectories for the UG: As they got older, Chinese children were more likely to offer less, while German children's offers showed a U-shape.

Overall, taking both the DG and the UG together, the results showed that generally Chinese elementary school children offered more than did their German counterparts, but the differences gradually disappeared for Chinese and German adolescents.

No significant differences were observed between individual and group offers within either Chinese or German participants, meaning that group discussions neither increased nor decreased individual offers.

Justifications for offers in the group discussion

Table 10.4 shows how often each type of justification was mentioned during the group discussions in each grade. For both Chinese and German children, fairness was used most frequently across age groups, with the exception of the German children in Grade 3, whose most commonly used justification was egoism. Comparing the pattern of children's justifications in the two countries, we found that the major difference was that in Grade 3 German children used more "egoism" while Chinese children were more group-oriented. In Grade 6, German children were more concerned with reciprocity than were their Chinese counterparts, who still used fairness as their dominant strategy. This helped to explain why in the DG Chinese children offered more than did German children. However, more quantitative analysis still needs to be done.

Discussion

In this study, we compared Chinese and German children's and adolescents' individual and group allocations in the Dictator game and the Ultimatum game. Further, we explored the process through which three group members arrived at a common group offer and evaluated which justifications Chinese and German children used for certain allocations in the group discussion, in an effort to understand children's decision-making process. Cross-culturally, the majority of children revealed a fairness orientation by preferring an equal split in both conditions. The average offer was more than those of adults (DG: 20–30%, Camerer, 2003, UG: 40%, Oosterbeek et al., 2004).

Table 10.4 Group discussion

Country	Justification	Grade			
		Third	*Sixth*	*Eighth*	*Eleventh*
China	Fairness	39	43	41	40
	Egoism	22	20	15	10
	Group	34	18	19	23
	Reciprocity	2	3	11	5
	Hierarchical power	3	18	15	19
Germany	Fairness	36	32	38	25
	Egoism	47	15	9	21
	Group	8	18	13	23
	Reciprocity	2	21	18	16
	Hierarchical power	8	14	22	15

Note: Category in percentages.

In psychology, equality has been studied as an important norm for distributing resources. Messick (1993) regards equality as a simple and effective decision rule for situations in which individuals distribute divisible goods. Sharing equally is a simple rule that does not require identifying specific attributes in the other party (e.g., invested effort, need, or deservingness). In that sense, equality can also be seen as a simple, fast, and frugal heuristic in sharing (Gigerenzer, 2007). Messick (1993) notes that this equality heuristic is more likely to be used in situations that are novel, unfamiliar, and ambiguous, such as experimental game situations are. In these situations, equality can be used as a default and a cognitively less demanding decision option that needs no further justification. Thus proposers made higher offers than an economic game theory predicted. The higher offer in the study could also be due to the experiment setting in that three-person groups make the situation feel more public and lead to higher offers. But social desirability influences in this study should be comparable to previous research on children's and adolescents' fair behavior.

Results also showed cultural differences. In the DG, there was a marginally significant difference between Chinese and German children, showing that Chinese children offered more than did German children, which met our hypothesis. Chinese children are more in favor of fairness than are German children, but by Grade 8 (11 years of age) both Chinese and German adolescents had reached the same level of fairness preference. However, in the UG Chinese and German children showed different trajectories. There was an Age × Culture interaction. As they got older, Chinese children were more likely to offer less, while German children's offers showed a U-shape. The results were inconsistent with previous findings in developmental psychology that children's sharing behavior increases as they grow older (Eisenberg & Fabes, 1998). This may be due to the different tasks used. In the case of those studies that also used the DG and the UG to study Western children, differences might also be due to cultural norms concerning sharing in the United States, China, and Germany (Gummerum et al., 2008). Depending on the developmental status of the children (Smetana, 1999) parents and educators use a variety of arguments to communicate social norms of fairness and sharing to children. In China, a collectivist society, parents and teachers tend even more to socialize children into fair and prosocial behavior. This explains the fact that Chinese children offered marginally significantly more than did their German counterparts in the DG, in which only fairness is included, without the fear of the offer being rejected, as in the UG. Collectivism may be more influential for younger than for older children. It is indicated in the results that in both the DG and the UG Chinese elementary school children made higher offers than did adolescents. In their justifications, Chinese children in Grade 3 refer more to "group" than do the German children in the same grade. When Chinese children get older, they tend to be more and more influenced by market economy value and care more about their own interests. But still fairness is the dominant social value that influences all age groups, which is demonstrated not only by their offers but also by their justifications.

The study found no significant difference between individual and group offers: generally, group discussions neither increased nor decreased individual offers. This may be due to the high homogeneity of the group members in the study, who came from same classes and were of the same age and the same gender. The groups were formed by the children themselves, so most of them were group of friends, and friends may share similar values. In our study we found that in many groups across all ages and genders, group members tended to gravitate toward the average. It would be an interesting topic to study heterogeneous groups in the future to see how group offers differ from individual ones. Also, numerous studies in social psychology have demonstrated that majority processes are a default procedure when group members have different opinions in a judgment task (e.g., Hinsz et al., 1997). More analysis needs to be done on the group discussing process. Larger group size study is called for, since interaction in larger compared to smaller groups may foster behavior in line with the majority.

Overall, in this study we have tried to pursue a cross-cultural comparison of sharing behavioral development with a new interdisciplinary connection between experimental economic research and the developmental psychology of fairness. However, there are some methodological limitations that should be addressed in future research, such as group size, group relationship and experimental design (i.e., being videotaped). We didn't recruit even younger children in the study, and we did not address more quantitative analysis of the group negotiation in the chapter. Despite these limitations, we believe that running a cross-cultural study that connects economic game theory and developmental psychology provides an exciting new avenue to the understanding of the universal and culture-dependent development of fair and moral behavior.

Acknowledgment

This study was supported by the Ministry of Science and Technology, and National Natural Science Foundation of China (2010CB8339004; 30970911).

References

Benenson, J. F., Pascoe, J., & Radmore, N. (2007). Children's altruistic behavior in the dictator game. *Evolution and Human Behavior*, *28*, 168–175.

Bettinger, E., & Slonim, R. (2006). Using experimental economics to measure the effects of a natural educational experiment on altruism. *Journal of Public Economics*, *90*, 1625–1648.

Bornstein, G., Kugler, T., & Ziegelmeyer, A. (2004). Individual and group decisions in the centipede game: Are groups more "rational" players? *Journal of Experimental Social Psychology*, *40*, 599–605.

Bornstein, G., & Yaniv, I. (1998). Individual and group behavior in the ultimatum game: Are groups more "rational" players? *Experimental Economics, 1,* 101–108.

Camerer, C. F. (2003). *Behavioral game theory: Experiments in strategic interaction.* Princeton, NJ: Princeton University Press.

Cason, T. N., & Mui, V.-L. (1997). A laboratory study of group polarization in the team dictator game. *The Economic Journal, 107,* 1465–1483.

Chuaha, S., Hoffmann, R., Jones, M., & Williams, G. (2007). Do cultures clash? Evidence from cross-national ultimatum game experiments. *Journal of Economic Behavior & Organization, 64,* 35–48.

Damon, W. (1977). *The social world of the child.* San Francisco: Jossey-Bass.

Eisenberg, N. (1986). *Altruistic emotion, cognition, and behavior.* Hillsdale, NJ: Lawrence Erlbaum Associates, Inc.

Eisenberg, N., & Fabes, R. A. (1998). Prosocial development. In W. Damon (Ed.), *Handbook of child psychology* (Vol. 3, pp. 701–778). New York: Wiley.

Epley, N., & Dunning, D. (2000). Feeling "Holier than thou": Are self-serving assessments produced by errors in self or social prediction? *Journal of Personality and Social Psychology, 79,* 861–875.

Forsythe, R., Horowitz, J. L., Savin, N. E., & Sefton, M. (1994). Fairness in simple bargaining games. *Games and Economic Behavior, 6,* 347–369.

Gigerenzer, G. (2007). *Gut feelings: The intelligence of the unconscious.* New York: Viking Press.

Gummerum, M., Keller, M., Takezawa, M., & Mata, J. (2008). To give or not to give: Children's and adolescents' sharing and moral negotiations in economic decision situations. *Child Development, 79,* 561–576.

Haidt, J. (2001). The emotional dog and its rational tail: A social intuitionist approach to moral judgment. *Psychological Review, 108,* 417–449.

Harbaugh, W. T., Krause, K., & Liday, S. (2003). *Children's bargaining behavior: Differences by age, gender, and height.* Working paper, University of Oregon, USA.

Hennig-Schmidt, H., Li, Z.-Y., & Yang C. (2002). Non-monotone strategies in ultimatum bargaining: First results from a video experiment in the People's Republic of China. *Proceedings of the International Congress of Mathematicians Game Theory and Applications Satellite Conference* (pp. 225–231). Qingdao: Qingdao Publishing House.

Henrich, J., Boyd, R., Bowles, S., Camerer, C., Fehr, E., Gintis, H., et al. (2001). In search of homo economicus: Behavioral experiments in 15 small-scale societies. *American Economic Review, 91*(2), 73–78.

Henrich, J., Boyd, R., Bowles, S., Gintis, H., Fehr, E., Camerer, C., et al. (2005). "Economic man" in cross-cultural perspective: Ethnography and experiments from 15 small-scale societies. *Behavioral and Brain Sciences, 28,* 795–855.

Hinsz, V. B., Tindale, R. S., & Vollrath, D. A. (1997). The emerging conceptualization of groups as information processors. *Psychological Bulletin, 121,* 43–64.

Hoffmann, R., & Tee, J.-Y. (2006). Adolescent–adult interactions and culture in the ultimatum game. *Journal of Economic Psychology, 27,* 98–116.

Keller, M., & Edelstein, W. (1993). The development of a moral self from childhood to adolescence. *Moral Education Forum, 18,* 1–18.

Messick, D. M. (1993). Equality as a decision heuristic. In B. A. Mellers & J. Baron (Eds.), *Psychological perspectives on justice* (pp. 11–31). New York: Cambridge University Press.

Murnighan, J. K., & Saxon M. S. (1998). Ultimatum bargaining by children and adults. *Journal of Economic Psychology*, *19*, 415–445.

Oosterbeek, H., Sloof, R., & Vandekuilen, G. (2004). Cultural differences in ultimatum game experiments: Evidence from a meta-analysis. *Experimental Economics*, *7*, 171–188.

Oyserman, D., Coon, H. M., & Kemmelmeier, M. (2002). Rethinking individualism and collectivism. *Psychological Bulletin*, *128*(1), 3–72.

Schopler, J., & Insko, C. (1992). The discontinuity effect in interpersonal and inter-group relations: Generality and mediation. *European Review of Social Psychology*, *3*, 121–151.

Smetana, J. G. (1999). The role of parents in moral development: A social domain analysis. *Journal of Moral Education*, *28*, 311–321.

Song, F., Cadsby, C. B., & Morris, T. (2006). Other-regarding behavior and behavioral forecasts: Females versus males as individuals and group representatives. *International Journal of Conflict Management*, *15*, 340–363.

Takezawa, M., Gummerum, M., & Keller, M. (2006). A social world for the rational tail of the emotional dog: Roles of moral reasoning in group decision making. *Journal of Economic Psychology*, *27*, 117–139.

11 Developmental science

An Africentric perspective

A. Bame Nsamenang

Introduction

Global age openness to the statement by UNESCO that "All cultures can contribute scientific knowledge of universal value" (UNESCO, 1999, p. 1) has motivated my introduction of an emergent Africentric developmental science perspective into the powerful international narrative on developmental psychology.

Globalization challenges African scholars to draw on understandings of human ontogenesis and individuation at local levels and on the contextually embedded cultural theories and practices that follow on from them to identify and insert Africentric concepts and principles into a disciplinary landscape that has long denigrated such knowledge. This chapter endeavors to contribute to this prospect by depicting in broad strokes the African developmental environment and drawing an emergent developmental science perspective within Africa's theory of the universe. It is anchored in the theoretical concepts of biological embedding and interactive contextualism. I highlight indigenous African developmental precepts, practices, and principles as productive ideas and methodological caveats for innovative theorization and instrumentation to enrich and extend the frontiers of developmental science beyond the constraints imposed by Euro-Western epistemologies and grids, within the purview of the wisdom of looking "for alternatives to the traditional views, not so that those views may necessarily be displaced, but so that we may come to wider, fuller understanding of man *qua* man [sic] . . . even if we learn that a certain view is worthless, we have learned something important" (Wright, 1984, p. xiv).

Africa's developmental environment

Africa is a significant world region, at least in land mass – the out-of-Africa-theory origin of modern humans, reproductive ideologies, and precious resources. Africa's 53 states resulted from arbitrary Balkanization by imperial Europe in its scramble for the continent's rich resources. The "scramble" created an African paradox pertaining to Africa's inability or failure to "garner the means to provide for its next generations in spite of its rich material and human resources, which have thus far been drained by and for foreign interests" (Pence & Nsamenang, 2008). It may seem accurate to characterize Africa as a "continent sitting on top of infectious diseases, strangled by corruption and tribal vengeance, and populated by people with mouths and hands open to receive international aid" (Diawara, 1998). Amazingly, however, even rights advocates and benevolent donors have failed to analyze why Africa should persist in abject poverty while its enormous resources visibly serve Western interests instead of alleviating poverty and enhancing scholarship in the dark continent.

The African world is distinct in peculiar ideas, practices, and issues that contrast with those of a group of cultures loosely referred to as Western (Serpell, 1992), which are not homogeneous but provide the referential grids of developmental science. Reagan (2000) counsels against using visible but superficial differences to prevent understanding of the subtle commonalities that unite Africa's peoples and historic experiences. "Africa ... is one cultural river with numerous tributaries characterized by specific responses to history and the environment" (Asante & Asante, 1990). Thus, while Diop (1960) posits Africa's "cultural unity," Maquet (1972) points to "a certain common quality" emerging from the "common political and social institutions with only slight variations" (Nkwi, 1983, p. 102) that stems from similar patterns of ecological and cultural adaptations to slavery, colonialism, population movements, and the raging localization–globalization schisms.

Compared to other cultural regions, Africa holds pronatalist reproductive ideologies and positive attitudes to childcare, although colonial and post-colonial abrasive forces have eroded much of Africa's indigenous reproductive ideas and practices. Indeed, Africa is heir to three significant heritages that have blended into a restive cultural braid of Eastern and Western legacies, superimposed on a deeply resilient Africanity [indigenous Africa]. In consequence, African parents and caregivivers "have been caught up in the web of cultural transition where there are no longer clearly defined values and moral codes of behavior that should be instilled in children and young people" (Cohen, 2001, p. 6). As images of the human condition from the different heritages "coexist uneasily, confront, and/or collide with" one another (Nsamenang, 1992a, p. 124), they offer Africa as a rich terrain for inventive theory development and pioneering methodologies.

Biological embedding and interactive contextualism

The process of early experience becoming solidified to influence health and development over the lifespan is known as *biological embedding* (Hertzman, 1999). Human ontogenesis is a context-sensitive phenomenon (Nsamenang, 2009) that always unfolds in a specific cultural context whose features vary. "The interaction that occurs between individual characteristics (genetic and physiologic) and experiences and exposures drawn from the environment is basic to the development of the child" (Irwin, Siddiqi, & Hertzman, 2007, p. 19). "Culture, as social heritage and cultural tools, is a determinative complement of genotype that shapes human psychosocial differentiation in the direction of a given people's cultural meaning systems" (Nsamenang, 2008a, p. 73). The child is impacted upon by and in turn impacts the caregiving and social environment (Grieve, 1992, pp. 5.6–5.21). Contextual theories "share a common awareness of behavior and development as interactive elements in a fluid and changing interplay" (Pence, 1988) of environmental and social factors in specific cultural contexts or communities of practice.

Contextualism calls for approaches that "always contextualize our study findings, our policies, our programs in the socio-historical and cultural contexts from which they arise" (Hoskyn, Moore, Neufeld, LeMare, & Stooke, 2007) instead of persisting with those that address a nonexistent, universal child (Pence & Hix-Small, 2007). It requires awareness that the universal human need to thrive and become an integrated member of one's own society is socialized and canalized in the world's diverse cultures into different endpoints of development (Nsamenang, 2008a). Through biological embedding and interactive contextualism, children construct knowledge through their own efforts and actions in and on their world (e.g., Piaget, 1952). Interactionism orbits on the developmental agency of the child and the interdependence between individuals and the societies in which they are developing, which extends to cyberspace and the virtual environment. Peers are a significant developmental space but theorists and interveners have not yet fully noticed and explored the value of child-to-child templates (Pence & Nsamenang, 2008).

"Agency" refers to social processes or situations wherein the infant, child, or youth is an initiating or willful force that drives experience and further learning and development (Schwartzman, 2005). Human newborns are "agentic" in that they are genetically wired to emit biological signals such as cries and facial prompts that invite culturally appropriate nurturance. If we could see children as social actors who are "better together" "as participants in cultural communities" (Rogoff, 2003, p. 3), we would appreciate and wish to explore the value of fostering "the organization of childhood such that children can acquire physical, intellectual, and practical education through their own initiatives" (Nsamenang & Lamb, 1995, p. 622). Such an approach would permit and dispose children themselves to learn to reflect upon their life circumstances, "so that they can gradually begin to take greater responsibility in creating communities different from the ones they inherited" (Hart, 2001, cited in Morales, 2007).

A developmental science perspective emerging from Africa's theory of the universe

An African theory of the universe is holistic; it visualizes the environment, cosmology, and the human condition as conceptually inseparable (Nsamenang et al., 2008). This is consistent with a viewpoint in applied developmental science "that social life and intraindividual processes are bound and it makes little sense to conceptually pull them apart for study" (Granger, 2005, p. xxxviii). Therefore, the person/setting and proximal/distal contexts are best understood as a dynamic system with a developmental path. Such a conceptualization directs attention more clearly on the relationships among levels of the system rather than on discrete features of any particular level or facet of the system.

In intermeshing spirituality and the human condition, the African theory imputes a sacred value on childbearing and childrearing (Nsamenang, 1992a). It also sanctions and positions procreation and childrearing within family life. The family, constituted by a mature man and woman in marriage and their extended kin (Nsamenang, 1996), is the acceptable procreative institution and the hub of childcare and relational values. As a result, the germinal processes of individuation, self-definition, and the evolving sense of selfhood begin with socio-affective premises in families. Early learning within the family determines how children view the self, enter into and handle the interpersonal field, and engage with the world. For most people, the most enduring lessons in interpersonal connectedness and self-definition occur in the family (Nsamenang, 2008b). Children acquire a sense of "belonging" within their own culture, which may nevertheless allow them to accept and co-exist with individuals of other belief systems and cultures (Brooker, 2008, p. 22). Legal identity is thus "established from birth, whereas personal, social and cultural identity grows and changes" (Woodhead, 2008, p. 4) with the circumstances that instantiate an individual's developmental trajectory.

African kinship "is the nucleus from which social networks ramify, moral behavior is initiated and prosocial values, productive skills and the mother tongue are learned. The family is central to all this, because it ensures the supply and maintenance of new members without whom the society would fail in its generative role" (Nsamenang et al., 2008, pp. 55–56). Zimba (2002, p. 94), for example, reviewed evidence of the "indigenous network of support" reserved for newborns and their mothers in the southern Africa region. In both West and East Africa, there is a "deep and comforting sense of tradition and community" that sustains newborns (Nsamenang, 1992b, p. 427), who are seen and handled as "precious treasure[s] . . . nurtured, and enjoyed by the whole family" (Harkness & Super, 1992, p. 446).

Every culture has "a framework for understanding the ways that parents think about their children, their families and themselves, and the mostly implicit choices that parents make about how to rear the next generation" (Harkness et al., 2001, p. 12). An Africentric vision of childcare and education is framed in recognition of a cyclic life cycle trajectory in three phases – two metaphysical periods of selfhood and a social or existential selfhood. Social ontogenesis is initiated when the human offspring begins to steadily take on a social selfhood in an existing human community, even from conception, while the dying person is at the verge of taking on an ancestral/spiritual selfhood on transition into the world of the *living-dead* at his or her biological death (Mbiti, 1990). A universal but mostly inferred recognition of the metaphysical phases of the human life cycle is evident in the intentions and connotations of funeral rites and the signification of the wide variety of memorabilia people in all cultures hold of their *loving dead* (Nsamenang, 2005a) decades, even centuries, after they died. As one of the world's most visited monuments, the Veteran Memorial in Washington DC exemplifies this point. Although the metaphysical facets of the life cycle are matters of intimate concern for many people, developmental science excludes them from its focal content. For instance, people in all cultures loathe death because most can never be actually ready for it or come to terms with imagining the "emptiness" that would follow their death and what would await them in the afterlife, if they believed in one. Some people can be seen deploying more time and resources into anticipating their afterlife than to ensuring the welfare of the living. To the extent that Africans cognize the personal implications of the metaphysical phases of the human life cycle, such concerns constitute an essential component of their psychosocial being and functioning and stand in the face of "science" to develop a capacity to operationalize the metaphysical phases of human selfhood and the tools to measure their dimensions (Nsamenang & Lo-oh, 2009).

Social selfhood, the anchor content of Euro-Western developmental psychology, is the experiential self that the African worldview partitions into seven ontogenetic stages: the neonatal period, social priming, social apprenticeship, social entrée, social internment, adulthood, old age/death (see Nsamenang, 1992a, 2005b), which are added to the ancestral and spiritual selfhoods to give a total of nine distinct phases of the human life cycle. Each period is marked by distinctive developmental tasks, defined within the framework of the culture's conception of child, family, and their welfare. An essential task that traverses all developmental stages is responsibility training, which begins from an early age. Africans cherish and invest in "responsible intelligence" (Nsamenang, 2006) not because they fail to socialize cognition as an end in itself but because instead they foster "applied cognition" as it enhances social services and the satisfaction of human needs. Africans invest in responsible intelligence because responsibility subsumes cognition; they are aware that it is possible for some people to be cognitively alert but quite irresponsible in an analogous manner that a child could be "mature" in chronological age but inept in abilities.

Phases of the life cycle are best understood as social constructs (e.g., Jenks, 1982). African developmental rites of naming, marriage, death, and so on typically extend and facilitate the transition of the identity of individuals by assimilating them into meaningful social roles and relationships (Pence & Nsamenang, 2008). Some of Africa's indigenous institutions that have formalized transition rites, include the *poro* (for boys) and the *sande* (for girls) in Liberia (Gormuyor, 1992), the voodoo convents in Benin (Hounkpè, 2008), and the *bogwera* (for boys) and the *bojale* (for girls) in Botswana

(Shumba & Seeco, 2007). Africentric patterns of socialization and education, especially during the early phases of life, differ in remarkable ways from the Eurocentric mode, perhaps because in their patterns of childcare, sub-Saharan Africans follow "different moral and practical considerations" from those espoused by Western child development experts (LeVine, 2004, p. 163). In addition, while Euro-Western cultures privilege adults with childcare and teaching (Nsamenang, 2009), African cultures separate childcare skills from the life period of parenthood and situate childcare training as a familial commitment for children to learn as part of their share of family duties (Weisner, 1987).

African pedagogies diverge from Eurocentric instrumental agendas of "certainties and predetermined outcomes" (Urban, 2006, p. 1), as they construct and "use" children as "social agents" (Nsamenang, in press) in their own "becoming" (Erny, 1968). The African construction recognizes a maturation process in human offspring in the sense that children are not seen "as a set of organisms to be molded into a pattern of behavior specified in advance as educational outcomes, but as newcomers to a community of practice, for whom the desirable outcome of a period of apprenticeship is that they would appropriate the system of meanings that informs the community's practices" (Serpell, 2008, p. 74). Siblings and peers are "certified" partners in the apprenticeship of appropriating and generating developmental knowledge (Nsamenang et al., 2008). In Africa's community-based childcare patterns, "better together" (Nsamenang, 2004a; Rogoff, 2003; Singer & de Haan, 2007) in the school of life (Moumouni, 1968, p. 29) wherein *"people develop as participants in cultural communities"* (Rogoff, 2003, p. 3) is a basic principle. The apprenticeship system engages children's "agency" in their own developmental learning. In this light, Africa's centuries-old version of children's agency could illumine fussy ongoing efforts to figure out how best to actualize the "citizenship" of young people and their participation in the world in which they live, as enshrined in the United Nations Convention on the Rights of the Child (UNCRC). African parents and caregivers may be unaware of the developmental theories and principles held by the so-called child development experts, but their socialization and education of children is "guided by 'their own' notions of development, desirable child states, and caregiving" as they "apply some unwritten, as yet unexplored, criteria to assess the extent to which children are thriving" (Nsamenang, 1992a, p. 149). The engagement of children's agency transforms the peer culture into an important space for psychosocial differentiation and identity formation.

The process of individuation in children – that is, the process of developing a sense of self or who one is – is a matter of connecting, or "resisting" from connecting, a personal identity to a changing social identity, which is a function of a child's ontogenetic group affiliations. By fostering children's close identification with the group, traditional social values in many African cultures can be seen to partially align with Erikson's (1968) focus on social development. The image of individuation and identity development in African cultures is that of "polycropping," not monoculture: in other words, it emphasizes the shared and social, rather than the unique and individual, aspects of identity (Nsamenang, 2008b). While Vygotsky (1978) is embraced in the West for his theory of development of self through social processes, in some way traditional African cultures transcend Vygotsky by sensitizing children from an early age to seeking out others from whom to extract intelligences (Nsamenang, 2006) and with whom to sharpen the self-concept, particularly within peer cultures, such that children "gain significance from and through their relationships with others" (Ellis, 1978, p. 6). In one specific instance of self-definition, Zimba (2002) described the South African Zulu as nurturing, "*umuntu umuntu ngabantu*," which literally means, "a person is only a person with other people."

African peer cultures not only allow for free-spirited play settings, but also more importantly, permit self-education, generative learning, and peer mentoring in extensive child-to-child interactions and interstimulation (Nsamenang, 2004a; Nsamenang & Lamb, 1995). The peer culture is a developmental space whose features especially children's creation of "playthings" from local materials and planning of their own activities – rouses and reinforces their cognitive and creative abilities as well as prosocial values and life skills (Segall, Dasen, Berry, & Poortinga, 1999). As a developmental theory, social ontogenesis (Nsamenang, 1992a, 2004a), which posits significant learning occurring within the peer culture, goes beyond Vygotsky's theoretical space of adult mediation of children's learning within zones of proximal development (ZPD), in that the mediators of learning are not adults but peer mentors and older or more forceful peers. The peer culture fosters children's development of intelligences and social skills more through the children's self-generated activities in the style of interactive-extractive learning espoused by Piaget (1952) than through the prodding of parents, teachers, or practitioners. While sharing adult spaces and taking advantage of the spaces adults make for them, African "children create and maintain cultural environments which are appropriate for them. They develop social practices and networks of relations in specific social spaces" (Rabain-Jamin, 2003, p. 3). "In rehearsing and enacting adult roles, children later use the peer culture to readdress and resolve the problems, confusions, and uncertainties raised in their interactions with adults" (Nsamenang & Lamb, 1995, pp. 623–624). The African peer culture thus extends and brings into children's experiences and discourses familial issues and societal processes that are foundational to identity formation and self-development. The peer culture enables a significant portion of African children to literally "emerge" by themselves out of the circumstances of their lives, rather than being "raised" by parents, teachers or interveners in the conventional sense of "bringing up" children (Nsamenang, 2004b, pp. 42–43).

The theory of developmental learning (Nsamenang et al., 2008) explains why African children are responsible and productive as they learn or teach themselves their curricular content of domestic tasks, prosocial values, and dutiful roles. It is perhaps in this sense that Hort (2007) and Reagan (2000) interpreted the purpose of education as improving and enhancing the interests of one's own group. This viewpoint faults current systems of education in Africa, beginning with ECD programs, wherein children imbibe purportedly *universal knowledge* and skills, which systematically distance and alienate them from the stark realities of their own cultures and life circumstances. Graduates of Africa's education systems who are "slim on local wisdom and situated intelligences" (Nsamenang, 2005b, p. 279) can hardly understand their circumstances, much less improve their living conditions.

Developmental principles and techniques of African pedagogies

Africa's theory of the universe posits a life cycle human ontogenesis in phases with milestones that are social and cultural markers. Its holistic outlook fuses metaphysical and physical forces with the conditions of *being* human into a frame of reference that differs from that which informs contemporary Western developmental science. As such, it channels psychosocial differentiation and individuation of connectedness to others from an early age. This encourages a relational developmental trajectory that "differs in theoretical focus from the more individualistic accounts proposed by Freud, Erikson and Piaget" (Serpell, 1994, p. 18).

Cultures vary in the endstates of development that they cherish and seek and the visions and strategies by which they strive to achieve them. The child is a *seed*, nursed into a seedling and cultivated into fruition in a sociological garden in which roles are shared amongst multi-age "gardeners" of mixed abilities. Development and learning can be enhanced through processes of nurturing, socialization, education, cultivation, and mentoring not only by parents, teachers and practitioners, but also by peer mentors in the activity settings and processes of peer cultures. Indigenous Africans might never have considered articulating their developmental theories, but by reflecting garden metaphors, those theories signify a genetic potentiality for self-generation and self-education. Aware of a directive maturation process in children, Africans do not invest in the "incompleteness" of children but begin responsibility training from an early age. Unborn children are perceived as "buds of hope and expectation" (Zimba, 2002), and newborns are seen as gradually "becoming" (Erny, 1968) socialized agents of the culture, as they are progressively inducted into the canonical ways of the culture from early in life.

The educational ideas and pedagogy that follow from an African theory permit core cultural and developmental learning more in participatory spaces of the family and peer culture than in instructive processes with adult mediators (Nsamenang, 2004b). Although socialization and education in African family traditions are not organized to acquire encyclopedic intelligence, parents engage children's agency by sensitizing them from an early age to seek out peer groups from whom to "extract" competencies and to figure out and feel their way into the world beyond the family and neighborhood, but with "attentive parental cautions that leave a lasting imprint, such as: 'venture into the world, but be a good child' " (Nsamenang, 2009).

African participative pedagogies engender tacit cultural practices and techniques that are inaccessible to conventional research methods and instruments. For instance, much African developmental knowledge is embedded in nonverbal acts like gaze, touch, and spatial use of cues and gestures as well as in maxims, proverbs, folklores, and oral traditions not easily translatable into scientific jargon or other languages, except at the cost of impairment to their essence or distortion of their full meaning (Ojiaku, 1974). Current assessment tools cannot effectively capture the developmental meaning of these knowledge sources and techniques, such as silence, non-response to children's queries, cultural practices and peer culture processes, all of which are suffused not only with tacit teaching and learning but also with reflective cognitive stimulation. For example, African parents or peer mentors do not routinely provide direct answers to children's questions. A typical response to an inquisitive child is often a terse rhetorical "Don't you see?" In practical terms, this translates into: "I expect you to watch, understand, and learn from what I do and know. It is not for me to teach or 'instruct' you."

Conclusion

Africa offers many "opportunities for learning and development, which simply do not exist in the West and therefore are not considered by the predominant theories" (Curran, 1984).

1   "Africa's numerous political and socio-economic units provide many examples of political and social engineering for students of under-developed world societies" (Cummings, 1986, p. 1).
2   The African child is a member of a larger social network than the extant developmental literature contains, ranging from 4.7 siblings per family with the Nso ethnic community in Cameroon (Nsamenang, 1992a) to 7.0 siblings in some West African families (Ware, 1983).
3   The African child performs "a much wider range of economically productive and maintenance activities" than is the case in most cultures (Nsamenang, 2001, p. 7298).
4   The African pattern of childcare differs from the Eurocentric, which has supplied the grids of the "science." Indeed, a Gusii infant study in Kenya provided evidence that "alternative patterns of care based on different moral and practical considerations can constitute normal patterns of development that had not been imagined in developmental theories" (LeVine, 2004, p. 163).
5   Indigenous African pedagogies permit children to learn in participatory processes at home, in the community, in peer cultures, and in other activity settings through "work–play" processes, with little or no explicit didactic support. The peer culture is central to supporting

African children's developmental learning, even in school, but it remains a largely uncharted developmental space.

6   Africa's integrative theory of the universe inspires "a holistic and integrated way of looking at the family and the universe ... to make a paradigm shift in the way we see" children and their development away from Western concepts that devalue and outdate indigenous cultures (Callaghan, 1998, p. 32).

7   Finally, Africa's complex mélange from three significant heritages has been little contemplated or theorized about in developmental research. "No existing theory fittingly explains it and no antecedent evolutionary template exactly corresponds to its" triple-strand cultural braid (Nsamenang, 2005b, p. 276). Thus, Africa is a goldmine for theoretical innovation and creative methodologies that could extend developmental science beyond dominant Euro-Western molds.

"For every child the processes of development, socialization and acculturation proceed hand-in-hand within the child's own social and physical environments" (Hinde & Stevenson-Hinde, 1990, p. 63), such that social context is, at a variety of levels, intrinsic to the developmental process (Richards, 1986). Interactive contextualism presses for research, policy, and intervention that "represent the particular context that determines why the project is there, what it is doing, and how it is doing it" (Smale, 1998). Contemporary African dynamics are the product of a triple-strand inheritance that exudes the concocted developmental trajectories of Africanity and those of Islamic-Arabic heritage and the Christian-scientific West. The Euro-Western developmental trajectory is being proselytized by powerful interest groups and the development community, including the United Nations organizations and the Bretton Woods Institutions, as a universal one, a state of the field that pathologizes the African.

Globalization obliges "research that interrogates policy (instead of informing it)" and that dissuades the "construction of *a* knowledge which is exclusive of many other knowledges" (Urban, 2006). "Humanity deserves a unified science to which Africa's contribution could be a sociogenic lifecycle theory and the social ethos" and the responsible intelligences it engenders (Nsamenang, 2007).

References

Asante, M. K., & Asante, K. W. (Eds.). (1990). *African culture: The rhythms of unity*. Trenton, NJ: Africa World Press.

Brooker, L. (2008). *Supporting transitions in the early years*. Maidenhead, UK: McGraw-Hill/Open University Press.

Callaghan, L. (1998). Building on an African worldview. *Early Childhood Matters, 89*, 30–33.

Cohen, R. N. (2001). Foreword. In A. Njenga & M. Kabiru (Eds.), *In the web of cultural transition: A tracer study of children in Embu District of Kenya* (pp. 5–7). The Hague: Bernard van Leer Foundation.

Cummings, R. J. (1986). Africa between ages. *Africa Studies Review, 29*(2), 1–26.

Curran, H. V. (1984). Introduction. In H. V. Curran (Ed.), *Nigerian children: Developmental perspectives.* London: Routledge & Kegan Paul.

Diawara, M. (1998). Toward a regional imagery in Africa. In F. Jameson & M. Miyoshi (Eds.), *The cultures of globalization* (pp. 103–124). Durham, NC: Duke University Press.

Diop, C. A. (1960). *L'Universe culturelle de l'Afrique Noire* [The Black African cultural world]. Paris: Presence Africaine.

Ellis, J. (1978). *West African families in Great Britain.* London: Routledge.

Erikson, E. (1968). *Childhood and society.* Harmondsworth: Penguin.

Erny, P. (1968). *L'enfant dans la pensee traditionnelle d'Afrique Noire* [The child in traditional African social thought]. Paris: Le Livre Africain.

Gormuyor, J. N. (1992). Early childhood education in Liberia. In G. A. Woodwill, J. Bernhard, & L. Prochner (Eds.), *International handbook of childhood education* (pp. 337–341). New York: Garland.

Granger, R. C. (2005). Foreword. In C. B. Fischer & R. M. Lerner (Eds.), *Encyclopedia of applied developmental science* (pp. xxxvii–xxxviii). Thousand Oaks, CA: Sage.

Grieve, K. W. (1992). *Play based assessment of the cognitive abilities of young children.* Unpublished doctoral thesis, Unisa, Pretoria, South Africa.

Harkness, S., & Super, C. M. (1992). Shared childcare in East Africa: Sociological origins and developmental consequences. In M. E. Lamb et al. (Eds.), *Day care in context: Socio-cultural perspectives* (pp. 441–459). Hillsdale, NJ: Lawrence Erlbaum, Associates, Inc.

Harkness, S., Super, C. M., Axia, V., Eliasz, A., Palacios, J., & Welles-Nystrom, B. (2001). Cultural pathways to successful parenting. *ISSBD Newsletter 1*(38), 9–13.

Hart, R. (2001). *Children's participation: The theory and practice of involving young citizens in community development and environmental care.* Barcelona: UNICEF and P.A.U. Education.

Hertzman, C. (1999). The biological embedding of early experience and its effects on health in adulthood. *Annals of the New York Academy of Science, 896,* 85–95.

Hinde, R. A., & Stevenson-Hinde, J. (1990). Attachment: Biological, cultural and individual desiderata. *Human Development, 33*(1), 62–72.

Hort, E. (2007). *Why and how the African child is miseducated in the western educational system.* Retrieved January 8, 2010, from http://horte.over-blog.fr/categorie-10101808.html

Hoskyn, M., Moore, D., Neufeld, P., LeMare, L., & Stooke, R. (2007). Letters from the editors. *Child Development, Health & Education, 1*(1), i–iii.

Hounkpè, A. D. G. (2008). Education in voodoo convents in Benin. In P. R. Dasen & A. Akkari (Eds.), *Educational theories and practices from the majority world* (pp. 306–325). New Delhi, India: Sage.

Irwin, L. G., Siddiqi, A., & Hertzman, C. (2007). *Early child development: A powerful equalizer – Final report.* Vancouver, BC: Canada: Human Early Learning Partnership (HELP).

Jenks, C. (Ed.). (1982). *The sociology of childhood: Essential readings.* London: Batsford.

LeVine, R. A. (2004). Challenging expert knowledge: Findings from an African study of infant care and development. In U. P Gielen & J. Roopnarine (Eds.), *Childhood and adolescence: Cross-cultural perspectives and applications* (pp. 149–165). Westport, CT: Praeger.

Maquet, J. (1972). *Africanity*. New York: Oxford University Press.

Mbiti, J. S. (1990). *African religions and philosophy*. Oxford, UK: Heinemann Educational.

Morales, J. M. (2007). Review of R. Hart (2001): *Children's participation: The theory and practice of involving young citizens in community development and environmental care*. Barcelona, Spain: UNICEF and P.A.U. Education. Retrieved March 17, 2008, from http://thunder1.cudenver.edu/cye/review.pl?n=227

Moumouni, A. (1968). *Education in Africa*. New York: Praeger.

Nkwi, P. N. (1983). Traditional diplomacy, trade and warfare in the 19th century Western Grassfields. *Science and Technology Review*, *1*, 101–116.

Nsamenang, A. B. (1992a). *Human development in cultural context: A third world perspective*. Newbury Park, CA: Sage.

Nsamenang, A. B. (1992b). Early childhood care and education in Cameroon. In M. E. Lamb et al. (Eds.), *Day care in context: Socio-cultural perspectives* (pp. 419–439). Hillsdale, NJ: Lawrence Erlbaum, Associates, Inc.

Nsamenang, A. B. (1996). Cultural organization of human development within the family context. In S. Carr & J. Schumaker (Eds.), *Psychology and developing societies*. Westport, CT: Greenwood.

Nsamenang, A. B. (2001). Indigenous view on human development: A West African perspective. In N. J. Smelser & P. B. Baltes (Eds.-in-Chief), *International encyclopedia of the social and behavioral sciences* (pp. 7297–7299). London: Elsevier.

Nsamenang, A. B. (2004a). *Cultures of human development and education: Challenge to growing up African*. New York: Nova.

Nsamenang, A. B. (2004b). *The teaching–learning transaction*. Bamenda, Cameroon: HDRC Publication.

Nsamenang, A. B. (2005a). African culture, human ontogenesis within. In C. Fisher & R. Lerner (Eds.), *Encyclopedia of applied developmental science* (pp. 58–61). Thousand Oaks, CA: Sage.

Nsamenang, A. B. (2005b). Educational development and knowledge flow: Local and global forces in human development in Africa. *Higher Education Policy*, *18*, 275–288.

Nsamenang, A. B. (2006). Human ontogenesis: An indigenous African view on development and intelligence. *International Journal of Psychology*, *41*, 293–297.

Nsamenang, A. B. (2007). A critical peek at early childhood care and education in Africa. *Child Health and Education*, *1*(1), 14–26.

Nsamenang, A. B. (2008a). Editorial: Culture and human development. *International Journal of Psychology*, *43*(2), 73–77.

Nsamenang, A. B. (2008b). Constructing cultural identity in families. In L. Brooker & M. Woodhead (Eds.), *Social inclusion and respect for diversity: Developing positive identities*. Milton Keynes, UK: The Open University.

Nsamenang, A. B. (2009). Cultures of early childhood care and education. In M. Fleer, M. Hedegaard, & J. Tudge (Eds.), *World Yearbook of Education 2009: Childhood studies and the impact of globalization: Policies and practices at global and local levels* (pp. 23–45). New York: Routledge.

Nsamenang, A. B. (in press). The culturalization of developmental trajectories: A perspective on African childhoods and adolescences. In L. Arnett Jensen (Ed.),

Bridging cultural and developmental psychology: New syntheses in theory, research, and policy. New York: Oxford University Press.

Nsamenang, A. B., Fai, P. J., Ngoran, G. N., Ngeh, M. M. Y., Forsuh, F. W., Adzemye, E. W., et al. (2008). Ethnotheories of developmental learning in the Western Grassfields of Cameroon. In P. R. Dasen & A. Akkari (Eds.), *Educational theories and practices from the majority world* (pp. 49–70). New Delhi, India: Sage.

Nsamenang, A. B., & Lamb, M. E. (1995). The force of beliefs: How the parental values of the Nso of Northwest Cameroon shape children's progress towards adult models. *Journal of Applied Developmental Psychology, 16*(4), 613–627.

Nsamenang, A. B., & Lo-oh, J. L. (2009). Afrique Noire. In M. H. Bornstein (Ed.), *Handbook of cultural developmental science* (pp. 383–407). New York: Psychology Press.

Ojiaku, M. O. (1974). Traditional African social thought and Western scholarship. *Presence Africaine, 90*(2), 204–205.

Pence, A. R. (1988). *Ecological research with children and families: From concepts to methodology*. New York: Teachers College Press.

Pence, A. R., & Hix-Small, H. (2007). Global children in the shadow of the global child. *International Journal of Educational Policy, Research and Practice, 8*(1), 83–100.

Pence, A. R., & Nsamenang, A. B. (2008). *Respecting diversity in an age of globalization: A case for early childhood development in sub-Saharan Africa*. Bernard van Leer Foundation Working Paper, No. 51. The Hague: Bernard van Leer Foundation.

Piaget, J. (1952). *The origins of intelligence in children*. New York: International Universities Press.

Rabain-Jamin, J. (2003). *Implications of sibling caregiving for sibling relations and teaching interactions in two cultures*. Unpublished manuscript.

Reagan, T. (2000). *Non-Western educational traditions: Alternative approaches to educational thought and practice* (2nd edition). Mahwah, NJ: Lawrence Erlbaum Associates, Inc.

Richards, M. (1986). Introduction. In M. Richards & P. Light (Eds.), *Children's social worlds* (pp. 1–25). Cambridge, MA: Harvard University Press.

Rogoff, B. (2003). *The cultural nature of human development*. Oxford, UK: Oxford University Press.

Schwartzman, J. (2005). *Working paper 4: Promoting the agency of young people*. Richmond, VA: CCF.

Segall, M. H., Dasen, P. R., Berry, J. W., & Poortinga, Y. H. (1999). *Human behavior in global perspective*. Boston: Allyn & Bacon.

Serpell, R. (1992, April). *Afrocentrism: What contribution to science of developmental psychology*. Paper presented at the First ISSBD Africa Region Workshop on Child Development and National Development in Africa, Yaounde, Cameroon.

Serpell, R. (1994). An African social ontogeny: Review of A. Bame Nsamenang (1992): Human development in cultural context. *Cross-Cultural Psychology Bulletin, 28*(1), 17–21.

Serpell, R. (2008). Participatory appropriation and the cultivation of nurturance: A case study of African primary school health science curriculum development. In P. R. Dasen & A. Akkari (Eds.), *Educational theories and practices from the majority world* (pp. 71–97). New Delhi, India: Sage.

Shumba, A., & Seeco, E. G. (2007). Botswana. In J. J. Arnett (Ed.), *International encyclopedia of adolescence* (pp. 87–99). New York: Routledge.

Singer, E., & de Haan, D. (2007). *The social lives of young children*. Amsterdam: B.V. Uitgenvetij.

Smale, J. (1998). Culturally appropriate approaches in ECD. *Early Childhood Matters*, *89*, 3–5.

UNESCO (1999). *UNESCO World Conference on Science Declaration on Science and the Use of Scientific Knowledge*. Retrieved April 24, 2003, from http://www.unesco.org

Urban, M. (2006, November). *Strategies for change: Reflections from a systematic, comparative research project*. Paper presented to the early childhood care and education policy seminar on A Decade of Reflection from the Introduction of the Childcare Regulations 1996 Through to Today.

Vygotsky, L. (1978). *Mind in society: The development of higher psychological processes*. Cambridge, MA: Cambridge University Press.

Ware, H. (1983). Male and female life cycles. In C. Oppong (Ed.), *Male and female in West Africa* (pp. 6–31). London: Allen & Unwin.

Weisner, T. S. (1987). Socialization for parenthood in sibling caretaking. In J. B. Lancaster, J. Altman, A. S. Rossi, & L. R. Sherrod (Eds.), *Parenting across the lifespan: Biosocial dimensions* societies (pp. 237–270). Hawthorne, NY: Aldine de Gruyter.

Woodhead, M. (2008). Identity at birth – and identity in development? In M. Woodhead & L. Brooker (Eds.), *Early childhood in focus 3: Developing positive identities, diversity and young children*. Milton Keynes, UK: The Open University.

Wright, R. A. (1984). Preface. In R. A. Wright (Ed.), *African philosophy* (1st edition). Lanham, MD: University Press of America.

Zimba, R. F. (2002). Indigenous conceptions of childhood development and social realities in southern Africa. In H. Keller, Y. P. Poortinga, & A. Scholmerish (Eds.), *Between cultures and biology: Perspectives on ontogenetic development* (pp. 89–115). Cambridge, UK: Cambridge University Press.

Section III
Culture and ethnicity

12 Doing a psychology of the Chinese people

Discoveries for the world from one end of the Silk Road

Michael Harris Bond

Marco Polo (1254–1324) was the intrepid Venetian traveler to the East whose skill, enterprise, and fascination with the cultures he encountered along the great Silk Road brought him to the Court of Kublai Khan first in 1266, and again in 1274, bearing gifts from the newly elected Pope Gregory. An engaging storyteller and skilled diplomat, Polo served the Khan with distinction for the next 17 years. The Polo family returned to Venice in 1295, creating a sensation with their stories of the exotic East. Marco recorded the history of his travels and his dealings with the Great Khan and his fellow countrymen in his magnum opus, *Il Milione*. He is my hero, my inspiration, and my guide in "the realms of gold," as Keats termed the world of the beckoning unknown.

Like Marco Polo, I am another foreigner made welcome by the Chinese, having spent my last 34 years in one of the "Dragon Court's" contemporary out-stations, Hong Kong, exploring social psychological ground. My hope, like Marco's, has been to pass the map test given by the Great Khan by extending the ambit of the known – in my case, by bringing Chinese culture and its manifestations into international psychological discourse. What do I think we have found?

In this cultural collaboration, my Chinese colleagues and I have provided evidence for at least four constructs that might otherwise have remained uncharted: ethnic affirmation to questionnaires, the value dimension of morality versus reputation, relationship harmony and its maintenance, and the five dimensions constituting social axioms. As an emergent from these discoveries, my theorizing about social behavior has been broadened to include an over-arching cultural component. In the course of mapping these conceptual outposts, perhaps I have been personally transformed by the cultural leavening of confronting an alien cultural reality and working with its cultural representatives in academia. I attempt to describe these discoveries and developments in what follows, hoping "to show its vibration, its color, its form; and through its movement, its form, and its color, reveal the substance of its truth – disclose its inspiring secret" (Conrad, 1897/2007).

The *mise-en-scene*

I arrived in Hong Kong on 10 August 1974, a wife and 18-month-old daughter in tow. We had spent the three previous years in Takarazuka, Japan, where I worked as a Research Associate at Kwansei Gakuin University and as an English teacher at Reiseikan Gakuin. There, as now in Hong Kong, I felt totally unprepared for the life and academic role I was about to undertake. Fortunately we had those three prior years of full cultural immersion in a very foreign cultural environment to temper us, and the Chinese University provided a supportive living environment. My colleagues respected my training in psychology, and, based on my Japanese experience, they had confidence in my resilience and adaptability.

Nonetheless, I had much to learn. There were new courses for me to teach, a different kind of student to work with, a complicated administrative system to figure out, office procedures to master, and substantiation (a new British term meaning "tenure") to pass a mere two and a half years later. That meant papers to publish, based in part on work initiated in Hong Kong. Where could one find "subjects," as experimental participants were then called? Was there any financial support for research projects? How could I and my three colleagues in the psychology section (we were not yet an academic department!) find lab space? Could our teaching assistants be used as research assistants, interfacing for us with local Cantonese-speaking participants? How could data, once collected, be analyzed?

More importantly, whatever was I going to study? I had not planned my graduate education, with Chinese culture as a target of understanding, as a puzzle box to be intellectually essayed. In fact, I had received no training in culture, except what little I had previously picked up in Japan. There, I had read what I could of Japanese anthropology, history, sociology, and psychology and had even mastered a little of the daunting Japanese language. But I knew nothing about Chinese culture and its Hong Kong variant, currently under British administration. How was I going to identify researchable topics that would eventually be published, enabling me to stay on in a setting I was coming to appreciate? Such was my dilemma after my first year of teaching in 1975: what was I going to study?

Initial research in Hong Kong

My answer was to repeat my past – to study what I had been studying in Japan: topics I had some knowledge base to pursue, the methodology to handle, and the available resources to examine. These included a close look at the minutiae of gazing, the impact of expecting to compete with a stranger on perceptions of his or her character, and the structure of personality descriptions. Doing such work, combined with writing up prior research done in Japan, helped justify the substantiation of my employment at the Chinese University. This labor sufficed for present purposes in the life of a young academic raising a family and adapting to a foreign land. But, where were the Chinese, their culture, and its reflections in their psychological responses?

Harbingers of surprise

Even from these early forays into Chinese culture, my participants were beginning to speak to my opening mind through the language of the measures I used. They spoke of surprises, of something distinctive: those anticipating competition against others were rating those others more positively, not negatively, as I had expected (Bond, 1979a); the Chinese dimension of conscientiousness was infused with a Western descriptor for the supposedly unrelated dimension of intellect (Bond, 1979b). I was observing the life surrounding me and noticing strangenesses that provoked my thinking (Bond, 1994).

Into this puzzling vortex came Kuo-Shu Yang, the doyen of Chinese social-personality psychologists, in 1979, as the Head of our psychology section. We began an ongoing conversation that continues today about Chineseness and how best to represent its psychological manifestations fully and validly. He was my sounding board, often informing me that I had not yet "quite" understood the phenomenon of interest – face, for example. These discussions provoked and prodded me to try to get the experiments I was conducting culturally "right." Fortunately, the Emperor was patient and this Marco eager to learn.

The yield from the new Silk Road

What follows is my attempt to select and briefly describe the notable outputs from the ongoing conversation that I have spent the last 34 years in Hong Kong enjoying. I have selected four. These conversations were with the "subjects of the realm" through the opaque lens of the various measures my colleagues and I concocted for the purpose of decoding Chinese psychological reality so as to test our hypotheses about that reality. These hypotheses, or sometimes simply intuitions or curiosities, had been developed out of conversations held in the *lingua franca* of English with my bilingual colleagues, playing the role of the Great Khan to this Marco Polo.

Ethnic affirmation

In an early collaboration with Yang, we gave our participants a questionnaire that offered them 20 paired choices between a Western and a Chinese attitude for their endorsement. We were concerned about the consequences of safari research, in which researchers brought their favorite instruments to a foreign setting where English was often used as the language of instruction. So these researchers would often side-step the hassle of translating their instruments into the local language and administer them instead in English. What were the consequences of forcing respondents from one cultural heritage to respond in the language of a different cultural tradition?

We assumed – as do the "cultural primers" of today (e.g., Oyserman & Lee, 2008) – that our respondents' foreign language of English would elicit by learned association those attitudes, values, beliefs, and norms believed to characterize that foreign group in contrast to their own group, the Hong Kong Chinese. To our surprise, we found the opposite: when our Hong Kong Chinese respondents completed the English version of the questionnaire, they affirmed Chinese attitudes more strongly than Western attitudes. In another intriguing aside, they affirmed their Chineseness some-what more strongly when they were instructed by Western than by Chinese experimenters.

So at least one aspect of one's Chineseness, cultural attitudes, was negoti-able: it varied depending on the language of the questionnaire, the experi-menter's ethnicity, the language of instruction used, and – it turned out under closer examination – the content of the attitude item itself. This early discovery provoked a series of studies examining a host of factors that might influence whether a bicultural respondent would evince ethnic affirmation or cross-cultural accommodation (e.g., Bond, 1983)

These studies remained confined to the sidelines of the intercultural and cross-cultural literature until the phenomenon of cultural priming hit the mainstream of social psychology in the mid-1990s (e.g., Higgins, 1996). Now there is a host of studies attempting to limn the parameters of this phenomenon. For me, however, the detection of shifts in ethnic identification as a function of language change in bilinguals constitutes one of my early collaborative discoveries along the Silk Road. Had the Great Khan's patience been rewarded?

Chinese values?

Hofstede (1980) finished his monumental *Culture's Consequences* by inviting scholars from different intellectual–philosophical traditions to contribute their cultural insights to scholarship about values. In our conversations during his visits to Hong Kong in the early 1980s we had mused about whether there were distinctive Chinese values. Furthermore, would his four-dimensional structure of values be recovered if a Chinese value survey were to be developed and sent around the globe for data collection and analysis. Musing metaphorically about this fantasized value survey, I wondered how the artifacts sourced by Marco Polo during his travels in China might reson-ate in the sensibilities of the Italians of his birthplace and the other foreigners who bordered on the Silk Road and beyond.

The results surpassed expectations: data from 22 national cultures were analyzed at the ecological level (Chinese Culture Connection, 1987), just as Hofstede and I had earlier done with data from the Rokeach Value Survey (RVS) in 10 such cultures (Ng et al., 1982). It yielded four dimensions, just as

Hofstede's earlier work had done (Hofstede, 1980). However, simple correlations of the resultant country scores with Hofstede's revealed that one of the four dimensions from each survey, the Western and the Chinese, was distinct.

This distinctive Chinese dimension was named, "Confucian work dynamism" in part because it positioned countries in ways that corresponded to their levels of economic growth over the last 25 years. So, this new discovery from the far end of the Silk Road not only defined new value space, it was also meaningful as a predictor of one economic phenomenon that the original Hofstede dimensions could not redict (see Bond, 2007, for elaboration of this discovery process).

Struggling with individuals

This is all fine and well, but where were the individuals in this process of using national averages as input in the ecological-level analyses? How were we to get to the psychological level with this data set? How were we to find the individual-level factor structure of these values, so that scores on these value factors could be calculated for each respondent and then compared across individuals to ascertain their nomological networks? As a psychologist, I knew what I wanted, but not how to get there.

Fortunately, I was blessed by having a colleague in our new department who was, and remains, a dynamo of creativity and statistical insight. Kwok Leung and I wrestled with this problem, eventually producing a solution (Leung & Bond, 1989) that I eagerly applied to this multicultural data set of more than 2,200 individuals (Bond, 1988). Again – and just as had happened at the national level of analysis – this individual level of analysis revealed a dimension of valuing that was not available from an analysis of its predecessor, the Rokeach Value Survey. This value dimension, Reputation versus Morality, ordered the typical persons from our constituent countries differently than the four dimensions extracted from the RVS. Again, out of conversation with another Great Khan, this Marco Polo had sourced and transported something new from the Eastern end of the Silk Road for the Westerners at the other end of its long reach to contemplate.

Relationship harmony and harmonizing relationships

Anyone who becomes familiar with writing about Chinese social life soon comes to appreciate the emphasis constantly being accorded relationships and their representations – *guan shi*, face and favor, harmony, and the archetypal *wu lun*, the five cardinal relationships of Confucian social ideology. Psychologists have slowly and carefully picked up this intellectual gauntlet, translating these general notions about what is crucially important in Chinese social living into measurable, testable concepts. Many take as their manifesto Ho's (1998) trumpet call for a sub-discipline called "relationshipology," whereby the relationship itself would become the unit of culturally driven, scientific attention. Western individualism, with its focus on the separate person, would yield to Chinese collectivism, with its focus on the relationships, dyadic, group, and beyond, within which separate individuals are embedded. As the Great Khan chided Marco, "Why do you speak to me of stones? It is only the arch that matters to me" (Calvino, 1974, p. 82).

Relationships and their importance have recently become a topic of considerable interest to Western psychologists (Reis, Collins, & Berscheid, 2000). This exploration has developed partly in response to the growing evidence that social support is crucial to individual well-being, termed "life, liberty and the pursuit of happiness" in the American Declaration of Independence (see, e.g., Pierce, Sarason, & Sarason, 1996). Relationships had emerged as a matter of some importance in empirical work done in Chinese cultures by Bond, Leung, and Wan (1982) on maintenance concerns in resource allocation and on avoidance of relationship disintegration in procedural justice (Leung, 1987).

The explicit focus on relationship itself emerged with Kwan, Bond, and Singelis's (1997) study of achieved relationship harmony as a factor influencing life satisfaction cross-culturally. Lun and Bond (2006) later examined the level of relationship harmony achieved in long-term task groups, assessing the consequences of a group's harmony in its members' relations for successful group functioning. That work followed Cheung's confirmation that their indigenously identified personality dimension of interpersonal relatedness could be identified in Western culture as a factor distinct from the established Big Five (see Cheung, Cheung, Leung, Ward, & Leong, 2003). McAuley, Bond, and Kashima (2002) selected dyadic relationships themselves as the unit of analysis and compared their dimensionality cross-culturally, moving the discipline into the social psychology of dyads as a context-shaping individual behavior. We have recently been exploring how relationships at risk through a member's harmful actions towards a partner are repaired or dissolved: the intention to maintain the relationship plays a crucial role in this drama (Lun & Bond, 2008). Out of this research activity, relationships have thus come to be a recognized topic of interest for Chinese psychology, a topic sustained by the indigenous Chinese foregrounding of relationship as fundamental to human social life.

Social axioms

As we struggled to figure out how to analyze multicultural sets of values, Kwok Leung and I mused about why we were spending so much intellectual energy with the values construct. Yes, values and differences in value were the defining criterion for culture and differences across cultural groups since Kluckhohn's seminal work in the 1950s and 1960s (e.g., Kluckhohn & Strodtbeck, 1961). Hofstede's (1980) later empirical work had super-glued that presumption into place for cross-culturalists.

But was there more, and would this "more," whatever it might be, prove a better predictor of social behavior? After all, differences in observed social behavior were and remain what drives cross-cultural curiosity. Appropriately, Triandis (1977) had entitled one of his earliest intellectual forays, "interpersonal behavior." Describing then understanding how people do what they do – their customs as cultural groups and their idiosyncrasies as individuals – was our job (Bond, 2005), from which the "American revolution" of social cognition and its more amenable measures had distracted us (Sampson, 1981).

We recalled that Hofstede (1980) had prefaced his book on values with a quote from Pascal, which he translated as, "There are truths on one side of the Pyrenees that are falsehoods on the other." Ironically, this was a quote about truths, not values, expectancies about the world, not goals to be pursued. Accordingly, we began by planning a cross-cultural study pitting values against expectancies in predicting the behaviors of our current interest – styles of conflict resolution and resource allocation (Bond, Leung, & Schwartz, 1992). The outcome of this study confirmed our intuition that truths were another way into culture and into the differences in behavior of persons from different cultural groups.

Over the next decade, we developed the concept of social axioms, recently defined as:

> generalized beliefs about people, social groups, social institutions, the physical environment, or the spiritual world as well as about categories of events and phenomena in the social world. These generalized beliefs are encoded in the form of an assertion about the relationship between two entities or concepts.
>
> (Leung & Bond, 2008, p. 200)

We started our search for axioms in daily use by mining the heritages of Hong Kong Chinese culture, and then Venezuelan culture, assisted by our colleague, Sharon de Carrasquel. From the outset, our concern was to represent people's lives-as-lived in our assessment of the beliefs they used in negotiating their lives, so focus groups, media productions, ancient classics of received wisdom, and so forth were culled for possible use. To ensure cultural representativeness in our work, German, Japanese, and American psychologists collected data from their culture carriers (Leung et al., 2002).

What emerged from this study was a pan-cultural, five-factor model of beliefs about the world, subsequently confirmed in a 40-culture study (Leung & Bond, 2004). People everywhere, it seems, develop a position over time on these five central issues characterizing their individual worldview (Koltko-Rivera, 2004). Subsequent research revealed that their profile on social axioms was distinguishable from the personality as measured by available tests like the Big Five and the Chinese Personality Assessment Inventory (CPAI) and was different from their values profile, but it could be combined with either or both of these established constructs and their measures to improve our ability to predict their social behavior (see Bond, 2009, for a recent summary). The axioms construct has now entered the arena of psychological constructs and is widely used by psychologists to explore phenomena of local interest in their own cultural traditions (Leung & Bond, 2009). We are currently refining the measures of the axiom dimensions, so that we and they can continue to test their respondents' reality with greater prospect of success.

Conversing in the context of discovery

I am one of many nodes through which Chinese psychology is being disseminated into our world (see Bond, 2010, for the most recent compilation). My contributions to this enterprise have emerged out of conversations with its culture carriers, many of whom did not realize that they were doing social science with a social psychologist trying to map out foreign territory. Others, my colleagues and collaborators, knew full well what we were attempting and joined the colloquy with a spirit of scientific enthusiasm. What I judge as the most productive of those conversations with fellow professionals I have described or cited above.

Some of these conversations continue to this day, and their longevity is worthy of comment. How have we sustained them, and why? As for why, I believe that we each and all "choose knowledge over politics," to quote Lucinda Williams, in a suggestive line from her album, *West*. Although we each respect Chinese culture, its wealth and legacy, we are each focused on understanding how it manifests itself in the lives of its members, the contemporary Chinese. We are not unbridled cultural chauvinists and discipline our enthusiasm with the dictates and strictures of the scientific method. We let the data, carefully analyzed and scrupulously considered, lead us. We want to understand, not to win; our desire to understand continues, undiminished, as does our desire to communicate that understanding: the etymology of the word, "conversation," involves a turning together, and in our case this togetherness has been an intercultural journey conducted in a variety of English designed not to interfere with the discovery process. I have become ever more vigilant about ensuring that our conversations are unfettered by language concerns, and I have learned to speak less and to ground our discussions more. Of course, we eventually have the data produced by our measures to focus and discipline our meanderings. No co-authored production ever proceeds without mutual challenges about meaning, consultation about possible alternatives, and agreement that we have done our level best to communicate a joint vision (for an elaboration on this process, see Bond, Fu, & Pasa, 2001).

Marco responds to the Khan's challenge about bridges being defined by the arch, noting that, "Without stones, there is no arch." Each party to our collaborations brings the stones of his or her talents into the construction process. I have been blessed in my work with well-trained behavioral scientists:

knowledgeable about the topics we are keen to explore, methodologically acute, and statistically sophisticated. They are conscientious, trustworthy, generous and good humored, virtues that make it easier for us to sustain a relationship over their inevitable challenges. We appreciate one another's distinctive cultural backgrounds and are both willing and able to discuss this potentially sensitive issue that provides so much fodder for our creativity as cross-cultural psychologists (Bond, 1997). These "stones" enable the arches to span the divide between individuals; they help to give us a richer, truer future for Chinese psychology, for a universal psychology that must include Chinese psychological reality.

References

Bond, M. H. (1979a). Winning either way: The effect of anticipating a competitive interaction on person perception. *Personality and Social Psychology Bulletin, 5*, 316–319.

Bond, M. H. (1979b). Dimensions used in perceiving peers: Cross-cultural comparisons of Hong Kong, Japanese, American, and Filipino university students. *International Journal of Psychology, 14*, 47–56.

Bond, M. H. (1983). How language variation affects inter-cultural differentiation of values by Hong Kong bilinguals. *Journal of Language and Social Psychology, 2*, 57–66.

Bond, M. H. (1988). Finding universal dimensions of individual variation in multi-cultural studies of value. *Journal of Personality and Social Psychology, 55*, 1009–1015.

Bond, M. H. (1994). Continuing encounters with Hong Kong. In W. J. Lonner & R. Malpass (Eds.), *Readings in psychology and culture* (pp. 41–46). Needham Heights, MA: Allyn & Bacon.

Bond, M. H. (1997). Preface: The psychology of working at the interface of cultures. In M. H. Bond (Ed.), *Working at the interface of cultures: 18 lives in social science* (pp. xi–xix). London: Routledge.

Bond, M. H. (2005). A cultural-psychological model for explaining differences in social behavior: Positioning the belief construct. In R. M. Sorrentino, D. Cohen, J. M. Olsen, & M. P. Zanna (Eds.), *Culture and social behavior* (Vol. 10, pp. 31–48). Mahwah, NJ: Lawrence Erlbaum Associates, Inc.

Bond, M. H. (2007). Fashioning a new psychology of the Chinese people: Insights from developments in cross-cultural psychology. In S. J. Kulich & M. H. Prosser (Eds.), *Intercultural research, Vol. 1. Intercultural perspectives on Chinese communication* (pp. 233–251). Shanghai, China: Shanghai Foreign Language Education Press.

Bond, M. H. (2009). Believing in beliefs: A scientific but personal quest. In K. Leung & M. H. Bond (Eds.), *Psychological aspects of social axioms: Understanding global belief systems* (pp. 319–341). New York: Springer.

Bond, M. H. (Ed.) (2010). *The Oxford handbook of Chinese psychology*. New York: Oxford University Press.

Bond, M. H., Fu, P. P., & Pasa, S. F. (2001). A declaration of independence for editing a new international journal of cross cultural management? *International Journal of Cross Cultural Management, 1*, 24–30.

Bond, M. H., Leung, K., & Schwartz, S. H. (1992). Explaining choices in procedural and distributive justice across cultures. *International Journal of Psychology, 27,* 211–225.

Bond, M. H., Leung, K., & Wan, K. C. (1982). How does cultural collectivism operate? The impact of task and maintenance contributions on reward allocations. *Journal of Cross-Cultural Psychology, 13,* 186–200.

Calvino, I. (1974). *Invisible cities,* trans. W. Weaver. Orlando, FL: Harcourt.

Cheung, F. M., Cheung, S. F., Leung, K., Ward, C., & Leong, F. (2003). The English version of the Chinese Personality Assessment Inventory. *Journal of Cross-Cultural Psychology, 34,* 433–452.

Chinese Culture Connection (1987). Chinese values and the search for culture-free dimensions of culture. *Journal of Cross-Cultural Psychology, 18,* 143–164.

Conrad, J. (2007). *The nigger of the Narcissus.* Harmondsworth, UK: Penguin. (Originally published 1897.)

Higgins, E. T. (1996). Knowledge activation: Accessibility, applicability, and salience. In E. T. Higgins & A. W. Kruglanski (Eds.), *Social psychology: Handbook of basic principles* (pp. 133–168). New York: Guilford Press.

Ho, D. Y. F. (1998). Interpersonal relationships and relationship dominance: An analysis based on methodological relationism. *Asian Journal of Social Psychology, 1,* 1–16.

Hofstede, G. (1980). *Culture's consequences.* Thousand Oaks, CA: Sage.

Kluckhohn, F. R., & Strodtbeck, F. L. (1961). *Variations in value orientation.* Westport, CT: Greenwood.

Koltko-Rivera, M. E. (2004). The psychology of worldviews. *Review of General Psychology, 8,* 3–58.

Kwan, V. S. Y., Bond, M. H., & Singelis, T. M. (1997). Pancultural explanations for life satisfaction: Adding relationship harmony to self-esteem. *Journal of Personality and Social Psychology, 73,* 1038–1051.

Leung, K. (1987). Some determinants of reactions to procedural models for conflict resolution: A cross-national study. *Journal of Personality and Social Psychology, 53,* 898–908.

Leung, K., & Bond, M. H. (1989). On the empirical identification of dimensions for cross-cultural comparisons. *Journal of Cross-Cultural Psychology, 20,* 133–152.

Leung, K., & Bond, M. H. (2004). Social axioms: A model for social beliefs in multicultural perspective. *Advances in experimental social psychology* (Vol. 36, pp. 119–197). San Diego, CA: Elsevier Academic Press.

Leung, K., & Bond, M. H. (2008). Psycho-logic and eco-logic: Insights from social axiom dimensions. In F. van de Vijver, D. van Hemert, & Y. P. Poortinga (Eds.), *Individuals and cultures in multilevel analysis* (pp. 199–221). Mahwah, NJ: Lawrence Erlbaum Associates, Inc.

Leung, K., & Bond, M. H. (Eds.). (2009). *Psychological aspects of social axioms: Understanding global belief systems.* New York: Springer.

Leung, K., Bond, M. H., de Carrasquel, S. H., Muñoz, C., Hernández, M., Murakami, F., et al. (2002). Social axioms: The search for universal dimensions of general beliefs about how the world functions. *Journal of Cross-Cultural Psychology, 33,* 286–302.

Lun, V. M.-C., & Bond, M. H. (2006). Achieving relationship harmony in groups and its consequence for group performance. *Asian Journal of Social Psychology, 9,* 195–202.

Lun, V. M.-C., & Bond, M. H. (2008). *Responding to aversive interpersonal experience in a friendship: Norm violation, attributions and behavioral responses*. Unpublished manuscript, Victoria University of Wellington, New Zealand.

McAuley, P., Bond, M. H., & Kashima, E. (2002). Towards defining situations objectively: A culture-level analysis of role dyads in Hong Kong and Australia. *Journal of Cross-Cultural Psychology, 33*, 363–380.

Ng, S. H., Akhtar-Hoosain, A. B. M., Ball, P., Bond, M. H., Hayashi, K., Lim, S. P., et al. (1982). Values in nine countries. In R. Rath, H. S. Asthana, D. Sinha, & J. B. H. Sinha (Eds.), *Diversity and unity in cross-cultural psychology* (pp. 195–206). Lisse, Netherlands: Swets & Zeitlinger.

Oyserman, D., & Lee, S. (2008). Does culture influence what and how we think? Effects of priming individualism and collectivism. *Psychological Bulletin, 134*, 311–342.

Pierce, G. R., Sarason, B. R., & Sarason, I. G. (Eds.). (1996). *Handbook of social support and the family*. New York: Plenum.

Reis, H. T., Collins, W. A., & Berscheid, E. (2000). The relationship context of human behavior and development. *Psychological Bulletin, 126*, 844–872.

Sampson, E. E. (1981). Cognitive psychology as ideology. *American Psychologist, 36*, 730–733.

Triandis, H. C. (1977). *Interpersonal behavior*. Monterey, CA: Brooks/Cole.

13 Culture of conflict

Evolvement, institutionalization, and consequences

Daniel Bar-Tal

Conflicts are inherent in every intergroup relation, but special attention is directed to interethnic intractable conflicts that first of all have a determinative effect on the well-being of the societies involved but often also influence the security and welfare of other nations as well. These conflicts last for a long time because the real disagreements over goals and interests are fueled by the socio-psychological repertoire that is well grounded in the culture of the engaged societies – that is, in longstanding, violent, and vicious intractable conflicts, societies evolve a culture of conflict that has a tremendous influence on the way these conflicts are managed, because it provides important foundations for their continuation and it thwarts their peaceful resolution. Conflicts in the Middle East, Sri Lanka, Kashmir, or Northern Ireland provide good examples of this type of conflict. This chapter describes the features of the intractable conflict and the evolution of the culture of conflict, its nature, and its consequences.

Intractable conflicts

Features of intractable conflicts

The following seven features have been proposed as characteristic of intractable interethnic conflicts (Bar-Tal, 1998a, 2007a; Kriesberg, 1993, 1998):

1   *They are total.* Intractable conflicts are perceived as being about essential and basic goals, needs, and/or values that are regarded as indispensable for the society's existence and/or survival.
2   *They are perceived as irresolvable.* Society's members involved in intractable conflict do not perceive a possibility of resolving the conflict peacefully.
3   *Intractable conflicts are violent.* Intractable conflicts involve physical violence in which members of society – soldiers and civilians – are wounded and killed in wars, small-scale military engagements, or terrorist attacks.
4   *Intractable conflicts are perceived as being of a zero sum nature.* Intractable

conflicts are all-out conflicts, without willingness to compromise and with inflexible adherence to all the original goals.

5   *They are central.* Intractable conflicts occupy a central place in the lives of the individual society's members and of society as a whole. Members of the society are constantly and continuously involved with the conflict.

6   *They demand extensive investment.* Parties engaged in an intractable conflict make vast material (i.e., military, technological, and economic) and psychological investments in order to cope successfully with the situation.

7   *They are protracted.* Intractable conflicts persist for a long time – for at least a generation – which means that at least one generation has not known a different reality.

In sum, some of the essential features of intractable conflict described above are purely psychological, such as viewing it as being existential, irresolvable, and of a zero sum nature. Other features are associated with different realms of experience. All of the features may evolve with time, and each of them has its own pace of development. If all of them appear, the state of intractability begins, in which each characteristic adds to this chronic reality. But it is only when all the seven features emerge in their extreme form that intractable conflicts appear in their most extreme nature. Generally, intractable conflicts differ in terms of the intensity of each of the seven features. Moreover, intractable conflicts fluctuate: they may deescalate and then escalate again. Thus, the seven features are of changing intensity over time (see also Coleman, 2003).

Challenges of intractable conflicts

The described characteristics of intractable conflicts clearly imply that these conflicts inflict severe negative experiences, such as threat, stress, pain, exhaustion, grief, traumas, misery, hardship, and cost, both in human and material terms (see, e.g., Cairns, 1996; de Jong, 2002; Robben & Suarez, 2000). Also, during intractable conflicts collective life is marked by continuous confrontation that requires mobilization and sacrifice on the part of members of society. This situation is chronic, as it persists for a long time. Thus, members must adapt to the conditions in both their individual and their collective lives (see, e.g., Hobfoll & deVries, 1995; Shalev, Yehuda, & McFarlane, 2000). I would like to suggest that from a psychological perspective, this adaptation requires meeting three basic challenges.

First, it is necessary to satisfy needs that remain deprived during intractable conflicts – like, for example, psychological needs of knowing, mastery, safety, positive identity, and so on (Burton, 1990; Staub, 2003; Tajfel, 1982). Second, it is necessary to learn to cope with the stress, fears, and other negative psychological phenomena that accompany intractable conflict situations. Third, adaptation requires development of psychological conditions that will be conducive to successfully withstanding the rival group – that is, to attempts to win the conflict or, at least, not to lose it.

To meet the above challenges, societies in conflict develop socio-psychological repertoires that include shared beliefs, attitudes, motivations, and emotions.[1] This eventually turns into societal psychological infra-structure, which means that the shared repertoire is crystallized into a well-organized system of societal beliefs,[2] attitudes, and emotions and penetrates into institutions and channels of the society. As this socio-psychological infrastructure plays a determinative role in intractable conflict, I now describe and analyze it with special reference to its functional roles in meeting the challenges presented above.

Socio-psychological infrastructure in intractable conflicts

A basic premise of this chapter is that the central socio-psychological infrastructure in intractable conflict consists of three elements – collective memories, ethos of conflicts, and collective emotional orientation – which are mutually interrelated.

Collective memory

Collective memory is made up of societal beliefs that present the history of the conflict to society's members (Cairns & Roe, 2003; Connerton, 1989; Halbwachs, 1992; Wertsch, 2002). This narrative develops over time, and the societal beliefs describe the conflict's beginning and its course, providing a coherent and meaningful picture (Devine-Wright, 2003). In terms of particular contents, the societal beliefs of collective memory of intractable conflict touch on at least four important themes in terms of the perception of the conflict and its management. First, they justify the outbreak of the conflict and the course of its development. Second, they present a positive image of the in-group (e.g., Baumeister & Gastings, 1997). Third, they delegitimize the opponent (Bar-Tal, 1990; Oren & Bar-Tal, 2007). Fourth, they present their own society as the victim of the opposing one (Bar-Tal, 2003). This view is formed over a long period of violence as a result of the society's sufferings and losses and is sometimes even viewed as "chosen trauma" (Bar-Tal, 2003; Mack, 1990; Volkan, 1997).

It follows that opposing groups in a conflict will often entertain contra-dictory and selective historical collective memories of the same events. By selectively including, or excluding, certain historical events and processes from the collective memory, a group characterizes itself and its historical experiences in unique and exclusive ways (Baumeister & Gastings, 1997; Irwin-Zarecka, 1994). Such a narrative is, by definition, unique, distinctive, and exclusive. It tells the particular story of the group's past and reflects a group's self-description and characterization. In short, the narrative of collective memories relating to an intractable conflict provides a black-and-white picture that enables a parsimonious, fast, unequivocal, and simple understanding of the history of the conflict.

Ethos of conflict

In addition to the narrative of collective memory, societies also evolve a narrative about the present – this is called an ethos. I have defined ethos in previous work as *the configuration of shared central societal beliefs that provide a particular dominant orientation to a society at present and for the future* (Bar-Tal, 2000). Ethos supplies the epistemic basis for the hegemonic social consciousness of the society and serves as one of the foundations of societal life. It binds the members of a society together, connects between the present and the goals and aspirations that impel them toward the future, and gives meaning to societal life (see, e.g., McClosky & Zaller, 1984, who analyze beliefs about democracy and capitalism in the US ethos).

I would like to suggest that in prolonged intractable conflict societies develop a particular ethos – an ethos of conflict – which gives a general orientation and direction and provides a clear picture of the conflict, its goals, conditions, and requirements, and images of their own society and that of the rivals (Bar-Tal, 2000).

In earlier work I proposed that the challenges of intractable conflict lead to the development of eight themes of societal beliefs that comprise the ethos of conflict (Bar-Tal, 1998a, 2000).[3] They include: *Societal beliefs about the justness of the society's own goals*, which first of all outline the goals in the conflict, indicate their crucial importance, and provide explanations and rationales for them. Every society has goals, and they have to be perceived as justified by the members of the society because otherwise the latter will not act collectively to achieve them. But in situations of intractable conflict the justification and rationale play a crucial motivating role because of the sacrifices demanded from the collective, including the sacrifice of life. In addition, the societal beliefs negate and delegitimize the goals of the other group. These societal beliefs motivate the members of the society to struggle and fight for these goals and help them to endure and bear the sacrifices, losses, stress, and costs of the intractable conflict.

Societal beliefs about security refer to the importance of personal safety and national survival and outline the conditions for their achievement. In the context of intractable conflict, beliefs about the maintenance of security in its widest terms – including military mobilization, volunteerism, and heroism – are of special importance. These beliefs are essential when the intractable conflict involves violence in the form of acts of hostility and wars and poses a threat to the life of individuals, collective existence, economic well-being, and even to central values.

Societal beliefs of positive collective self-image concern the ethnocentric tendency to attribute positive traits, values, and behavior to one's own society. In times of intractable conflict, characteristics related to courage, heroism, and endurance on the one hand, and those related to humaneness, morality, fairness, trustworthiness, and progress on the other are propagated with special intensity. The enemy is presented in stark contrast, allowing for a clear differentiation between the two parties (Sande, Goethals, Ferrari, & Worth, 1989). Moreover, these beliefs supply moral strength and a sense of superiority.

Societal beliefs of victimization concern self-presentation as a victim, especially in the context of the intractable conflict (Mack, 1990; Volkan, 1997). The focus of these beliefs is on the unjust harm, evil deeds, and atrocities perpetrated by the adversary. They provide the moral incentive to seek justice and oppose the opponent, as well as to mobilize moral, political, and material support on the part of the international community.

Societal beliefs of delegitimizing the opponent concern beliefs that deny the adversary's humanity (Bar-Tal & Teichman, 2005; Holt & Silverstein, 1989; Rieber, 1991). Through dehumanization, extreme negative trait characterization, outcasting, and the use of negative political labels and negative group comparisons a society places the opponent "into extreme negative social categories which are excluded from human groups that are considered as acting within limits of acceptable norms and/or values" (see Bar-Tal, 1989, p. 170; Bar-Tal, 1990). These beliefs explain the causes of the conflict's outbreak, its continuation, and the violence of the opponent. They also justify one's own hostile acts against the rival group.

Societal beliefs of patriotism generate attachment to the country and society by promoting loyalty, love, care, and sacrifice (Bar-Tal & Staub, 1997; Somerville, 1981). Patriotic beliefs increase social cohesiveness and dedication and serve an important function for mobilizing the society's members to active participation in the conflict and the endurance of hardship and difficulties, to the point of sacrificing their lives for the society.

Societal beliefs of unity refer to the importance of ignoring internal conflicts and disagreements during intractable conflict in order to unite the forces in the face of the external threat. These beliefs strengthen the society from within, develop a consensus and a sense of belonging, increase solidarity, and allow society's forces and energy to be directed toward coping with the enemy.

Finally, *societal beliefs of peace* refer to peace as the ultimate desire of the society. They present peace as an ultimate goal of the society, and its members as peace-loving. Such beliefs have the role of inspiring hope and optimism. They strengthen positive self-image and positive self-presentation to the outside world.

In addition to societal beliefs, the socio-psychological infrastructure includes a collective emotional orientation.

Collective emotional orientation

Societies may develop characteristic collective emotional orientations, with an emphasis on one or on a number of particular emotions (Barbalet, 1998;

Bar-Tal, 2001; Kemper, 1990; Mackie & Smith, 2002). Societies involved in intractable conflict, I would argue, tend to be dominated by a number of collective emotional orientations (see also, e.g., Halperin, 2008; Petersen, 2002; Scheff, 1994). The most notable of these is the collective orientation of fear, but they may, in addition, be dominated by hatred and anger, as well as by guilt or pride.

Functions

I would like to suggest that the above socio-psychological infrastructure (i.e., collective memory, ethos of conflict, and collective emotional orientations) fulfills important functions, on both the individual and collective levels, for societies involved in intractable conflicts, especially during their climactic and irreconcilable phase. In general, it helps them to meet the challenges that intractable conflict poses: It helps to satisfy unfulfilled needs, facilitates coping with stress, and is functional in withstanding the enemy.

First, the socio-psychological infrastructure – especially the societal beliefs of collective memory and of ethos of conflict – fulfills the epistemic function of illuminating the conflict situation. The situation of intractable conflict is extremely threatening and is accompanied by stress, vulnerability, uncertainty, and fear. In view of such ambiguity and unpredictability, individuals must satisfy the need for a comprehensive understanding of the conflict, which provides a coherent and predictable picture of the situation (e.g., Burton, 1990). The collective memory and ethos of conflict fulfill these demands, providing information and explanations about the conflict. These societal beliefs explain the nature of the conflict to group members: Why did the conflict erupt? What was the course of the conflict? Why does it still continue, and why can it not be resolved peacefully? What is the enemy's responsibility for and contribution to the conflict? How did the in-group act in the conflict? What are "our" goals in the conflict? Why are they existential? What are the challenges facing society? And so on.

Furthermore, the societal beliefs of collective memory and ethos of conflict are functional for coping with stress created by the conditions of intractable conflict. Successful coping with stress often involves making sense of and finding meaning in the stressful conditions within existing schemes and the existing worldview, or an integration between events and the existing worldview (Antonovsky, 1987; Frankl, 1963; Janoff-Bulman, 1992; Taylor, 1983). The societal beliefs of collective memory and ethos of conflict provide such meaning and allow "sense-making." Moreover, certain contents, such as well-defined goals, positive self collective view, recognition of being a victim, and seeing difficult conditions as a challenge to be overcome with patriotism and in unity, are especially functional for coping with stress. The societal beliefs of collective memory and ethos of conflict include these contents and are therefore highly functional for coping with the stressful conditions of intractable conflict.

Second, in its moral function, the socio-psychological infrastructure serves to justify the acts of the in-group toward the enemy, including violence and destruction (see, e.g., Apter, 1997; Jost & Major, 2001). It lends justification for group members to carry out misdeeds, perform intentional harm, and institutionalize aggression toward the enemy. This is an important function that resolves feelings of dissonance, guilt, and shame for group members. Human beings do not usually willingly harm other humans. The sanctity of life is perhaps the most sacred value in modern societies. Killing or even hurting other human beings is considered the most serious violation of the moral code. However, in intractable conflict groups hurt each other most grievously, even resorting to atrocities, ethnic cleansing, and genocide. The psychological repertoire allows this violence. It justifies and legitimizes the most immoral acts and allows the attribution of one's own immoral behavior to external situational factors.

Third, the socio-psychological infrastructure creates a sense of differentiation and superiority (Sidanius & Pratto, 1999). It sharpens intergroup differences because it describes the opponent in delegitimizing terms and at the same time glorifies and praises its own society and presents it as a sole victim of the conflict. Since societies involved in intractable conflict view their own goals as justified and perceive themselves in a positive light, they attribute all responsibility for the outbreak of the conflict and its continuation to the opponent. The repertoire focuses on the violence, atrocities, cruelty, lack of concern for human life, and viciousness of the other side. It describes the other side as inhuman and immoral and the conflict as intransigent, irrational, far-reaching, and irreconcilable, and this view precludes any peaceful solution. These beliefs stand in contrast to the societal beliefs about positive collective self-image, which portray the in-group in positive terms. Being accompanied by strong emotions, this differentiation allows a needed positive self-collective esteem and also feelings of superiority, which are of special importance in the situation of intractable conflict, when both sides engage in violence, often performing immoral acts (Sandole, 1999).

Fourth, the socio-psychological infrastructure prepares the society to be ready for threatening and violent acts of the enemy, as well as for difficult life conditions. The narratives of collective memory and ethos and the collective emotional orientations tune the society into information that signals potential harm and continuing violent confrontations, allowing psychological preparations for the lasting conflict and immunization against negative experiences. The society is attentive and sensitive to cues about threats so no sudden surprises can arise. In this sense the psychological repertoire also allows economic predictability, which is one of the basic conditions for coping successfully with stress (e.g., Antonovsky, 1987; Lazarus & Folkman, 1984). This is so because human beings need to live in a world the future of which can, to some extent, be predicted, and they have to have a feeling of mastery over their fate. Moreover, unpredictable events, especially when harmful, may give rise to negative psychological reactions. Given, however, that some degree of unpredictability is unavoidable, people prefer to be surprised positively. In this way, expectations of negative events prevent disappointments. Themes such as the opponent's delegitimization, a sense of one's own victimhood and insecurity, as well as fear, hatred, and anger, all serve as a basis for these expectations, for perceptual turning to and preparation for the challenges of conflict.

Fifth, the socio-psychological infrastructure has the function of motivating solidarity, mobilization, and action (Bar-Tal & Staub, 1997). Coser (1956) pointed out that conflict with another group heightens the morale within the group and "leads to mobilization of the energies of group members and hence to increased cohesion of the group" (p. 95). The ethos of conflict implies a threat to the society's well-being and even to its survival. It raises the security needs as a core value and indicates a situation of emergency that requires joining the societal forces. Solidarity and unity are crucial for muting the threat. Moreover, by justifying the goals of the conflict and focusing on delegitimization and on the intransigence and violence of the opponent, as well as on self-victimhood, fear, hatred, and anger, the repertoire implies the necessity to exert all the efforts and resources of the group in the struggle against the enemy. It plays a central role in stirring up patriotism, which leads to readiness for various sacrifices in order to defend the group and the country and avenge acts of past violence by the enemy. In addition, it reminds group members of past violent acts by the rival and indicates that these acts could recur. The implication is that society's members should mobilize and be united in view of the threat, and perhaps should even carry out violent acts to prevent possible harm. This function is therefore crucial for the challenge of withstanding the enemy.

Last, but not least, the described narratives of collective memory and ethos fulfill the unique role of contributing to the formation, maintenance, and strengthening of a social identity that reflects the lasting conditions and experiences of intractable conflict. Intractable conflicts have a major effect on the nature, contents and functioning of social identity (Ashmore, Jussim, & Wilder, 2001; Cash, 1996; Ross, 2001; Worchel, 1999). First, in times of intractable conflict society's members tend to increase their sense of identification with the society in order to fulfill their need for belonging and security. Second, in times of intractable conflict social identity lends strength to society's members as their sense of common fate and belonging increases. Third, enhanced social identity provides the basis for the unity, solidarity, and coordination needed to cope with the conditions of the conflict. Strong social identity is one of the forces that facilitate society's members' mobilization for the conflict, with a readiness to make sacrifices – even extreme ones.

Furthermore, in the context of intractable conflict, the evolved socio-psychological infrastructure (especially its societal beliefs of collective memory and ethos), which dominates the society throughout the years of the conflict, eventually shapes the nature of social identity: that is, societal beliefs of ethos of conflict and collective memory offer contents par excellence that imbue social identity with meaning (Barthel, 1996; Cairns, Lewis, Mumcu, & Waddell, 1998; Gillis, 1994; Oren, Bar-Tal, & David, 2004). These are expressed in language, societal ceremonies, symbols, myths, commemorations, holidays, canonic texts, and so on. They are part of the evolved culture of conflict, as described below. In fact, strong identification with a society involved in intractable conflict is related to an acceptance of major shared beliefs (e.g., societal beliefs of ethos and collective memory). As a result, when social identity is dominated by meanings that provide ethos of conflict and collective memory, this supports the continuation of the conflict (Liu & Hilton, 2005). Such a social identity forms the epistemic ground for the antagonistic views of the other society that lead to intractable conflict (Oren et al., 2004).

Evolvement of culture of conflict

It is proposed that on the basis of the socio-psychological infrastructure societies involved in intractable conflict form a stable view of the violence, while the continuous stream of negative information and experiences validate and reinforce it. This negative repertoire is thus individually stored, frozen, and continuously accessible. Since most of the members of a society in intractable conflict are involved with it (actively or passively, directly or indirectly), this repertoire is often widely shared and spreads within the societal institutions and channels of communication.

In view of these processes, it is suggested that societies that live under prolonged experiences of intractable conflict with the dominant socio-psychological infrastructure evolve a *culture of conflict*, which develops when societies saliently integrate into their culture tangible and intangible symbols that are created to communicate a particular meaning about the prolonged and continuous experiences of living in the context of conflict (Geertz, 1993; Ross, 1998). Symbols of conflict become hegemonic elements in the culture of societies involved in intractable conflict: They provide a dominant meaning about the present reality, about the past, and about future goals, and they serve as guides for practice.

In societies with a culture of conflict, the socio-psychological infrastructure as described above is not only widely shared but also appears to be dominant in public discourse via societal channels of mass communication. Moreover, it is often used for justification and explanation of decisions, policies, and courses of action taken by the leaders. It is also expressed in institutional ceremonies, commemorations, memorials, and so on. In addition, socio-psychological infrastructure is expressed in cultural products such as literary books, TV programs, films, theatre, visual arts, monuments, and so on. It becomes a society's cultural repertoire, relaying societal views and shaping society's members' beliefs, attitudes, and emotions. Through these channels it can be widely disseminated and can reach every sector of the society. Finally, the socio-psychological infrastructure appears in school textbooks, is used by teachers and by schools, and appears prominently even in higher education. This element is of special importance because the beliefs presented in the educational textbooks reach all of the younger generation.

Characteristics of the culture of conflict

Culture of conflict has the following characteristics. First, it is suggested that the general themes of the culture of conflict, as reflected in the collective memory and ethos of conflict, are universal. The eight themes described, which are part of the ethos of conflict and appear in the narrative of collective memory of the conflict, serve as an organizing framework to view the past, present, and future. Second, each society has particular contents that fill out the general themes with narratives that concern all its specific symbols, including experiences, history, conditions, events, individuals, myths, and so on (see, e.g., Bar-Tal, 2007b). Third, the culture of conflict evolves through a long process that takes years and even decades. It takes time to construct the symbols and institutionalize them via processes of dissemination and socialization until they become dominant parts of the culture that is shared by at least the majority of society's members. Fourth, the specific symbols of the culture of conflict (e.g., sacrifice) are expressed through different content (e.g., stories about heroes, old myths, aspirations, prescriptions, stories about events). This means that the same symbols appear and reappear in different narratives. Fifth, the contents of the culture of conflict are expressed through different societal modes and channels, such as books, ceremonies, art, films, speeches, monuments. That is, various institutions and channels take an active part in the dissemination of the contents among society's members and their socialization. Finally, the culture of conflict changes dynamically in accordance with prolonged experiences that the society and its members go through and the changing context in which they live. The changes are usually gradual, because a culture does not change overnight. It is possible that in societies involved in intractable conflict an alternative culture with symbols propagating peace will slowly emerge.

Nature of the culture of conflict

A culture of conflict is characterized by a supply of information, symbols, and knowledge that confirm and validate its hegemonic themes. It leads to selective, biased, distorted information processing by society's members, which perpetuates and eternalizes its hegemonic themes and symbols. Thus these themes and symbols are consolidated, and they persevere and endure even in the face of contradictory information.

In addition, the culture evolves societal mechanisms to maintain and preserve its hegemonic themes and symbols. Among the societal mechanisms that are used to control and maintain the culture of conflict are, among others: the continuous dissemination of information that supports the dominant repertoire; governmental censorship of information; dissemination of disinformation; the use of punishment against providers of alternative information; the control of mass media; the delegitimization of alternative information and its sources; the closure of archives; and the encouraging and rewarding of cultural products supporting the socio-psychological repertoire of conflict. Though these mechanisms are mostly used by the formal institutions of the society, individuals may also practice many of them informally by developing self-censorship, for instance, or through using sanctions against the other society's members, groups, or organizations who provide information negating the socio-psychological repertoire of conflict.

Effects of the culture of conflict

Because of its nature and characteristics, a culture of conflict may have a number of effects on the society in which it evolves: First, issues related to the conflict are given major status and weight in decision making; in other words, themes of culture of conflict are central in public debates and agendas, policy-making, and courses of action. They are hegemonic in the public repertoire and have great influence on individual and collective decision making as, for example, in selecting leaders, voting in elections, legislation, division of the national budget, and even ruling in the courts. Second, problems and issues that direct attention away from the conflict are set aside. This means that societies in conflict are completely concentrated on the conflict and neglect various other problems that plague them. They pass over such issues because they want to avoid redirection of major goals, polarization, loss of energies, and financial resources. Third, a culture of conflict leads to the emergence of the powerful and influential military stratum in the society. This process is unavoidable, as the military carries the major burden in the struggle with the rival, which requires mobilization and sacrifices. It is glorified and presented as a model of patriotism. As a result, the military echelon not only gains high prestige and status but also has a great influence on policy making and decision making. Fourth, a culture of conflict crystallizes the traditional gender roles and the gap between them. Since males, who constitute most of the fighters, take a major role in the conflict, they are also rewarded for this participation and their sacrifices by gaining rewards, glorification, and stature. Fifth, a culture of conflict eventually leads to a deterioration of moral standards and a disregard for human rights and codes of international behavior. Societies engaged in conflict with the repertoire of the culture of conflict become accustomed to mistreating the rival population, and this process penetrates into the norms, values, beliefs and attitudes of the societies and the culture. For example, the massive delegitimization of the rival frequently leads to atrocities and other immoral behaviors, including genocide, without feelings of guilt or shame. It becomes a major justification for the violations of the moral standards. In addition, the prolonged conflict diminishes sensitivity to breaches of moral values and desensitizes the moral constraints of the societies. This means that eventually such immoral behavior is not only performed toward the rival but also reaches the intra-societal system, because society's members generalize their behaviors and go over the boundaries to carry the immoral acts also toward their peers and their own institutions. All this leads to the weakening of democratic principles. Societies that engage for a long time in intractable conflict have great difficulty in maintaining democratic values and principles because the essence of the conflict demands their transgression. For example, maintaining security often requires the violation of human rights principles. As a result, a culture of conflict often leads to a penetration of illegality into the society.

Conclusions

It was proposed that a culture of conflict that evolves in times of intractable conflict serves as a major factor for the continuation of the conflict and as a barrier to resolving it – in fact, this is part of the vicious cycle of the intractable conflict. Considering that this process involves the two parties in the conflict simultaneously, it is obvious how such a vicious cycle of violence operates. As the conflict evolves, so each of the opponents develops a culture of conflict, which initially fulfills important functional roles on both the individual and collective levels. With time, however, this culture comes to serve as the major motivating, justifying, and rationalizing factor of the conflict.

Such vicious cycles of intractable conflict are detrimental to the well-being of both the individuals and the societies involved, while also posing a danger to the world. Since, as we have seen, the culture of conflict plays an important role in these cycles, it is of vital necessity to change it, if we want to change the relations between the rival groups, by advancing a peace process and stopping the violence. This is a crucial challenge in view of the behavioral consequences of culture of conflict in situations of intractable conflict, leading to violence, loss of human life, ethnic cleansing, and even genocide.

A culture of conflict has to change, and in its place there is need to evolve a culture of peace (Bar-Tal, 2008). This is a very long, complex, and difficult process. But as a conflict begins in the human mind, so its ending also has to be initiated in the human mind. To change a culture of conflict requires, first of all, the emergence of a belief that continuation of the intractable conflict harms societal goals and needs and that the conflict causes unbearable losses, suffering, and hardship. Also there has to emerge the view that the violent conflict violates moral norms and international codes and an idea of the need to resolve the conflict peacefully. This process of change usually begins with a minority who promote these ideas and struggle to legitimize and institutionalize them. This minority is often subjected to delegitimization and even persecution by members of their own group. Sometimes the minorities win, persuade the majority, and bring the desired peace, prosperity, and benevolence to a suffering society. This process of changing the culture of conflict lasts for years. But striving toward peace should not be a dream or a wish, but a continuous struggle to mobilize peace supporters and achieve the signing of a peace agreement and eventually to the development of a culture of peace.

As the assassinated Prime Minister of Israel Yitzhak Rabin, who was the architect of such a process, said when he received the Nobel Peace Prize in Oslo for this achievement:

> "We will pursue the course of peace with determination and fortitude.
> We will not let up.
> We will not give in.
> Peace will triumph over all our enemies, because the alternative is grim
> for us all.
> And we will prevail.
> We will prevail because we regard the building of peace as a great
> blessing for us, and for our children after us."

This message should be propagated and remembered!

Notes

1 This idea is based on conceptual and empirical literature, which suggests that successful coping with threatening and stressful conditions requires construction of a meaningful world view (e.g., Antonovsky, 1987; Frankl, 1963; Janoff-Bulman, 1992; Taylor, 1983).
2 Societal beliefs are cognitions shared by members of a society on topics and issues that are of special concern for their society and contribute to their sense of uniqueness (Bar-Tal, 2000).
3 The proposed eight themes of the ethos were found in the public opinion of the Israeli Jewish society between 1967 and 2000 and served as their organizing scheme (Oren, 2005). They were also found to be central motif in Israeli school textbooks (Bar-Tal, 1998a, 1998b). They have recently been extensively analyzed as providing a foundation for the culture of conflict in Israeli society (Bar-Tal, 2007b).

References

Antonovsky, A. (1987). *Unraveling the mystery of health: How people manage stress and stay well*. San Francisco: Jossey-Bass.

Apter, D. E. (Ed.). (1997). *Legitimization of violence*. New York: New York University Press.

Ashmore, R. D., Jussim, L., & Wilder, D. (Eds.). (2001). *Social identity, intergroup conflict, and conflict reduction*. Oxford, UK: Oxford University Press.

Barbalet, J. M. (1998). *Emotion, social theory, and social structure: A macrosociological approach*. Cambridge, UK: Cambridge University Press.

Bar-Tal, D. (1989). Delegitimization: The extreme case of stereotyping and prejudice. In D. Bar-Tal, C. F. Graumann, A. W. Kruglanski, & W. Stroebe (Eds.), *Stereotyping and prejudice: Changing conceptions* (pp. 169–182). New York: Springer-Verlag.

Bar-Tal, D. (1990). Causes and consequences of delegitimization: Models of conflict and ethnocentrism. *Journal of Social Issues, 46*(1), 65–81.

Bar-Tal, D. (1998a). Societal beliefs in times of intractable conflict: The Israeli case. *International Journal of Conflict Management, 9*, 22–50.

Bar-Tal, D. (1998b). The rocky road towards peace: Societal beliefs functional to intractable conflict in Israeli school textbooks. *Journal of Peace Research, 35*, 723–742.

Bar-Tal, D. (2000). *Shared beliefs in a society: Social psychological analysis.* Thousand Oaks, CA: Sage.

Bar-Tal, D. (2001). Why does fear override hope in societies engulfed by intractable conflict, as it does in the Israeli society? *Political Psychology, 22*, 601–627.

Bar-Tal, D. (2003). Collective memory of physical violence: Its contribution to the culture of violence. In E. Cairns & M. D. Roe (Eds.), *The role of memory in ethnic conflict* (pp. 77–93). Houndmills, UK: Palgrave Macmillan.

Bar-Tal, D. (2007a). Sociopsychological foundations of intractable conflicts. *American Behavioral Scientist, 50*, 1430–1453.

Bar-Tal, D. (2007b). *Living with the conflict: Socio-psychological analysis of the Israeli-Jewish society.* Jerusalem: Carmel. (In Hebrew.)

Bar-Tal, D. (2008). Reconciliation as a foundation of culture of peace. In J. de Rivera (Ed.), *Handbook on building cultures for peace* (pp. 363–377). New York: Springer.

Bar-Tal, D., & Staub, E. (Eds.). (1997). *Patriotism in the life of individuals and nations.* Chicago: Nelson-Hall.

Bar-Tal, D., & Teichman, Y. (2005). *Stereotypes and prejudice in conflict: Representation of Arabs in Israeli Jewish society.* Cambridge, UK: Cambridge University Press.

Barthel, D. (1996). *Historic preservation: Collective memory and historical identity.* New Brunswick, NJ: Rutgers University Press.

Baumeister, R. F., & Gastings, S. (1997). Distortions of collective memory: How groups flatter and deceive themselves. In J. W. Pennebaker, D. Paez, & B. Rimé (Eds.), *Collective memory of political events: Social psychological perspectives* (pp. 277–293). Mahwah, NJ: Lawrence Erlbaum Associates, Inc.

Burton, J. W. (Ed.). (1990). *Conflict: Human needs theory.* New York: St. Martin's Press.

Cairns, E. (1996). *Children in political violence.* Oxford, UK: Blackwell.

Cairns, E., Lewis, C. A., Mumcu, O., & Waddell, N. (1998). Memories of recent ethnic conflict and their relationship to social identity. *Peace and Conflict: Journal of Peace Psychology, 4*, 13–22.

Cairns, E., & Roe, M. D. (Ed.). (2003). *The role of memory in ethnic conflict.* New York: Palgrave Macmillan.

Cash, J. D. (1996). *Identity, ideology and conflict.* Cambridge, UK: Cambridge University Press.

Coleman, P. T. (2003). Characteristics of protracted, intractable conflict: Towards the development of a metaframework: I. *Peace and Conflict: Journal of Peace Psychology, 9*(1), 1–37.

Connerton, P. (1989). *How societies remember.* New York: Cambridge University Press.

Coser, L. A. (1956). *The functions of social conflict.* New York: Free Press.

de Jong, J. (Ed.). (2002). *Trauma, war, and violence: Public mental health in socio-cultural context.* New York: Kluwer Academic/Plenum Publishers.

Devine-Wright, P. (2003). A theoretical overview of memory and conflict. In E. Cairns & M. D. Roe (Eds.), The *role of memory in ethnic conflict* (pp. 9–33). New York: Palgrave Macmillan.

Frankl, V. E. (1963). *Man's search for meaning*. New York: Washington Square Press.

Geertz, C. (1993). *The interpretation of cultures: Selected essays*. London: Fontana Press.

Gillis, J. (1994). Memory and identity: The history of a relationship. In J. Gillis (Ed.), *Commemorations: The politics of national identity*. Princeton, NJ: Princeton University Press.

Halbwachs, M. (1992). *On collective memory*. Chicago: University of Chicago Press.

Halperin, E. (2008). Group-based hatred in intractable conflict in Israel. *Journal of Conflict Resolution, 52*, 713–736.

Hobfoll, S. E., & deVries, M. W. (Eds.). (1995). *Extreme stress and communities: Impact and intervention*. New York: Kluwer Academic/Plenum Publishers.

Holt, R. R., & Silverstein, B. (1989). On the psychology of enemy images: Introduction and overview. *Journal of Social Issues, 45*(2), 1–11.

Irwin-Zarecka, I. (1994). *Frames of remembrance: The dynamics of collective memory*. New Brunswick, NJ: Transaction.

Janoff-Bulman, R. (1992). *Shattered assumptions: Towards a new psychology of trauma*. New York: The Free Press.

Jost, J. T., & Major, B. (Eds.). (2001). *The psychology of legitimacy: Emerging perspectives on ideology, justice, and intergroup relations*. New York: Cambridge University Press.

Kemper, T. D. (Ed.). (1990). *Research agendas in the sociology of emotions*. Albany, NY: State University of New York Press.

Kriesberg, L. (1993). Intractable conflict. *Peace Review, 5*, 417–421.

Kriesberg, L. (1998). Intractable conflicts. In E. Weiner (Ed.), *The handbook of interethnic coexistence* (pp. 332–342). New York: Continuum.

Lazarus, R. S., & Folkman, S. (1984). *Stress, appraisal, and coping*. New York: Springer.

Liu, J. H., & Hilton, D. J. (2005). How the past weighs on the present: Social representations of history and their role in identity politics. *British Journal of Social Psychology, 44*, 537–556.

Mack, J. E. (1990). The psychodynamics of victimization among national groups in conflict. In V. D. Volkan, D. A. Julius, & J. V. Montville (Eds.), *The psychodynamics of international relationships* (pp. 119–129). Lexington, MA: Lexington Books.

Mackie, D. M., & Smith, E. R. (Eds.). (2002), *From prejudice to intergroup emotions: Differentiated reactions to social groups*. Philadelphia, PA: Psychology Press.

McClosky, H., & Zaller, J. (1984). *The American ethos: Public attitudes toward capitalism and democracy*. Cambridge, MA: Harvard University Press.

Oren, N. (2005). *The Israeli ethos of the Arab–Israeli conflict 1967–2000: The effects of major events*. Dissertation submitted to Tel Aviv University, Tel Aviv, Israel.

Oren, N., & Bar-Tal, D. (2007). The detrimental dynamics of delegitimization in intractable conflicts: The Israeli–Palestinian case. *International Journal of Intercultural Relations, 31*, 111–126.

Oren, N., Bar-Tal, D., & David, O. (2004). Conflict, identity and ethos; The Israeli–Palestinian case. In Y.-T. Lee, C. R. McCauley, F. M. Moghaddam, & S. Worchel (Eds.), *Psychology of ethnic and cultural conflict* (pp. 133–154). Westport, CT: Praeger.

Petersen, R. G. (2002). *Understanding ethnic violence: Fear, hatred, and resentment in twentieth-century Eastern Europe*. Cambridge, UK: Cambridge University Press.

Rieber, R. W. (Ed.). (1991). *The psychology of war and peace: The image of the enemy*. New York: Plenum Press.

Robben, A., & Suarez, O. M. M. (Eds.). (2000). *Cultures under siege: Collective violence and trauma*. New York: Cambridge University Press.

Ross, M. H. (1998). The cultural dynamics of ethnic conflict. In D. Jacquin, A. Oros, & M. Verweij (Eds.), *Culture in world politics* (pp. 156–186). Houndmills, UK: Macmillan.

Ross, M. H. (2001). Psychocultural interpretations and dramas: Identity dynamics in ethnic conflict. *Political Psychology, 22*, 157–198.

Sande, G. N., Goethals, G. R., Ferrari, L., & Worth, L. T. (1989). Value-guided attributions: Maintaining the moral self-image and the diabolical enemy-image. *Journal of Social Issues, 45*(2), 91–118.

Sandole, D. (1999). *Capturing the complexity of conflict: Dealing with violent ethnic conflicts of the post-cold war era*. London: Pinter/Continuum.

Scheff, T. J. (1994). *Bloody revenge: Emotions, nationalism, and war*. Boulder, CO: Westview Press.

Shalev, A. Y., Yehuda, R., & McFarlane, A. C. (Eds.). (2000). *International handbook of human response to trauma*. Dordrecht, Netherlands: Kluwer Academic.

Sidanius, J., & Pratto, F. (1999). *Social dominance*. New York: Cambridge University Press.

Somerville, J. (1981). Patriotism and war. *Ethics, 91*, 568–578.

Staub, E. (2003). *The psychology of good and evil: The roots of benefiting and harming other*. New York: Cambridge University Press.

Tajfel, H. (1982). *Social identity and intergroup relations*. Cambridge, UK: Cambridge University Press; Paris: Maison des Sciences de l'Homme.

Taylor, S. E. (1983). Adjustment to threatening events: A theory of cognitive adaptation. *American Psychologist, 38*, 1161–1173.

Volkan, V. (1997). *Blood lines: From ethnic pride to ethnic terrorism*. New York: Farrar, Straus & Giroux.

Wertsch, J. V. (2002). *Voices of collective remembering*. Cambridge, UK: Cambridge University Press.

Worchel, S. (1999). *Written in blood: Ethnic identity and the struggle for human harmony*. New York: Worth.

14 Cultural psychology of globalization

Chi-yue Chiu and Shirley Y. Y. Cheng

Introduction

Recent theoretical advances in (cross-)cultural psychology have deepened our understanding of how culture influences behaviors (see Chiu & Hong, 2006, 2007; Lehman, Chiu, & Schaller, 2004). However, not much attention has been given to individuals' psychological responses to the cultural impacts of globalization. To make up this gap, in this chapter we present a recipe for a cultural psychology of globalization.

The ingredients: Globalization, culture, and psychology

Globalization

There are many different definitions of globalization. A widely accepted one refers to globalization as the "acceleration and intensification of economic interaction among the people, companies, and governments of different nations" (Carnegie Endowment for International Peace, 2007). In this chapter we will use this definition as the working definition of globalization.

Globalization involves the spread of the global economy to regional economies around the world. On the one hand, multinational corporations' investments in a developing country bring jobs and income to the country and provide training for local workers and managers. As globalization proceeds, previously isolated economies are integrated into the world economy via international trade and investment. The most globalized developing countries (e.g., China) have benefited from this process and enjoyed high GNP per capita growth. On the other hand, most developing countries that have not participated actively in globalization face negative income growth rates. As a result, there is a widening gap between the richest and poorest countries (Alderson & Nielsen, 2002).

With the rapid growth of global linkages and global consciousness, social life is organized on a global scale. As Robertson (1992) has noted, globalization involves "the compression of the world and the intensification of consciousness of the world as a whole" (p. 8). The rapid speed of air transportation and the instantaneous electronic transfer of information and capital have led to what Anthony Giddens (1985) refers to as the experiential compression of time and space. A postmodern global culture is often characterized as one "of virtuality in the global flows which transcend time and space" (Castells, 1998, p. 350). The constraints that have delimited different knowledge traditions to a confined space have disintegrated. Consequently, contemporary travelers are no longer surprised at the co-existence of different cultural traditions in the same space.

Culture

Like globalization, the term culture has many different meanings (Chiu & Hong, 2006). In this chapter we define culture as a loose network of ideas and practices produced and reproduced by a collection of interconnected individuals to coordinate their goal-oriented activities under a set of physical and human-made constraints and opportunities (Chiu & Chen, 2004). Three defining features in this definition of culture are: (1) sharedness (but not diffuse sharedness), (2) historicity, and (3) externalization. Culture is partially shared, and it has a history. A set of ideas that is shared but does not have a history is like a fad, a set of ideas that has a history but is not widely shared is like the family tradition of a small family, and a set of ideas that lacks sharedness and historicity is like a set of personal beliefs. According to this definition, a culture does not have to be a national culture: it can be a political culture, a religious culture, an organizational culture, a consumer culture, and so on.

Culture is like the memory of the society (Kluckhohn, 1954). For culture to be an effective device for coordination, members of the society must share *and* expect others to share at least some important parts of the collective memory (Mead, 1934/1962). Also, the collective memory of a cultural tradition (e.g., Christianity) is externalized in (1) institutions (e.g., the Church), cultural legends and myths (the miracles), scriptures (the Holy Bible), customs (Midnight Mass on Christmas Eve), rituals (baptism), cultural narratives (Acts of the Apostles), (2) the icons of the culture (the Crucifix), and (3) external memory devices (e.g., pictograms, books, audiotapes, videotapes, CDs, DVDs, or the Internet). Thus it is possible to gain some insights into a culture by analyzing the ideas encoded in its institutions, customs, and rituals, as well as the contents of cultural discourses and narratives (e.g., Menon, Morris, Chiu, & Hong, 1999). It is also possible to study the way the activation of cultural representations in the presence of various cultural icons and symbols influences emotions, thoughts, and behaviors (e.g., Hong, Benet-Martinez, Chiu, & Morris, 2003; Hong, Chiu, & Kung, 1997; Hong, Morris, Chiu, & Benet-Martinez, 2000; Sui, Zhu, & Chiu, 2007). We can also learn something about a culture by examining its intersubjective cultural representations (e.g., Wan, Chiu, Peng, & Tam, 2007a; Wan et al., 2007b).

People are not passive recipients of culture. Instead, they debate what their culture is and negotiate ownership of it (Hong, Wan, No, & Chiu, 2007). Culture setters and brokers are particularly active in this negotiation process, particularly when their societies undergo rapid change and when their heritage culture meets the global culture in the same space (e.g., Wang, 2005).

Psychology

Mental representations of culture

People with some direct or indirect experiences with a certain culture will develop a cognitive representation of it (see Chiu & Hong, 2007). Individuals with extensive direct experiences with a culture tend to develop elaborate cognitive representations of it that are backed up with rich experiential information. In contrast, individuals who have cursory or indirect experiences with a culture tend to develop only stereotypic representations (Chiu, 2007). Upon seeing an iconic symbol of the culture, people will retrieve from memory their cognitive representation of the culture. For instance, among Americans, subsequent to viewing an American cultural cue, their awareness of American values is enhanced (e.g., freedom, individuality). Similarly, for Chinese, after viewing a Chinese cue, they spontaneously think of Chinese values (e.g., obedience) (Fu, Chiu, Morris, & Young, 2007a; Hong et al., 1997). Once a cultural representation has been activated, it influences subsequent information processing strategies (Sui et al., 2007), inferential practices (Hong et al., 1997, 2003), and interaction styles (Wong & Hong, 2005) – the individual tends to think and act in ways expected from the activated culture.

When the iconic symbols of two cultures are present in the environment, as is often the case in globalized space, the cognitive representations of both cultures will be activated (Chiu, Mallorie, Keh, & Law, 2009). For example, a Starbucks coffee shop in the Imperial Museum in Beijing, China, may call up the cognitive representations of both American and Chinese culture: Starbucks coffee activates the perceiver's representation of American culture, while the Forbidden City calls up a cognitive representation of Chinese culture (Chiu & Cheng, 2007).

When two cultural representations are activated simultaneously, perceivers will use "culture" as a schema to organize their attention, perception, and other cognitive processes. As a result, the perceivers' attention is drawn to the defining characteristics of the two cultures. On the one hand, this enhances the awareness of cultural differences; on the other hand, it enhances the perceived entitativity of cultures (the perception of cultures as real entities). These processes are less likely to occur when only one cultural representation is activated, even when that representation is one of a foreign culture (Chiu et al., 2009).

Motivation and culture

Culture is of (the) people, for (the) people, and by (the) people (Chiu & Hong, 2006). People often recruit culture to satisfy a variety of social and psychological needs under certain given constraints and opportunities. One such need is the need for epistemic security – the feeling that there is a firm answer for important issues in life. Culture provides a means to satisfy the need for epistemic security because it offers time-honored and widely accepted solutions to problems. Supporting this idea, research has shown that within a country, people who have a higher need for firm answers are more likely to appropriate cultural ideas to interpret the meanings of social events (Chiu, Morris, Hong, & Menon, 2000) and manage interpersonal conflicts (Fu et al., 2007b).

Culture is also recruited to manage existential anxiety. There is considerable evidence that when reminded of their mortality, people experience existential anxiety. To manage this, they would adhere to and defend their cultural worldview. They do so because a cultural worldview confers a sense of symbolic immortality: when the self is seen as a part of an imperishable culture, the self seems immortal (Greenberg, Porteus, Simon, & Pyszczynski, 1995).

Mixing the ingredients

The three ingredients can be mixed in several ways to create different research programs. For example, researchers can study how local cultures respond to the infusion of global culture. Do local communities accept or reject it? If global culture is granted admission to a local community, are local and global cultural practices integrated in the same domain of life, or are they separated into different life domains? What factors may affect the relative likelihood of each mode of response? How may local cultures' responses to globalization transform local culture, creating transient and/or permanent changes in the local communities?

Researchers may also mix psychology and globalization to create an individual psychology of globalization, examining the identity and health implications of cultural contacts. Some important research topics in this category include, among others, negotiation and construction of a multicultural identity (Hong et al., 2007; Wan et al., 2007b), cultural shock (Ward, Bochner, & Furnham, 2001), and acculturation stress (Chao, Chen, Roisman, & Hong, 2007). Given the space we have, we cannot delve into these topics; we will discuss instead one under-investigated topic: psychological reactions to the cultural implications of globalization.

When the iconic symbols of local and global cultures are seen together in a globalized environment, "culture" will become a salient mental category for organizing perceptions; people will attend to the differences between local and foreign cultures, become sensitive to the cultural implications of the infusion of foreign cultures, and have hot or cool reactions to foreign cultures.

Hot reactions

Hot reactions are emotional, reflexive responses evoked by perceived threats to the integrity of one's heritage cultural identity. These reactions often lead to xenophobic, exclusionary behaviors. People on the receiving end of global culture are often concerned that globalization will ultimately lead to homogenization of cultures via *global hegemony*. At first glance, the global hegemony project is destined to succeed. Western nations, representatives of global culture, are generally perceived to be more economically advanced than non-Western nations. Developing countries that aspire to become an industrialized nation may treat Western economic powers as reference nations not only in the domain of economic development, but also in the realm of cultural restructuring. Global culture has been characterized as new, modern, scientific, and result-oriented. It privileges consumerism, individualism, competition, and efficiency (Pilkington & Johnson, 2003). These values may be seen as values that separate advanced societies from economically backward traditional economies. Thus, global culture may become a reference culture for some developing countries that seek to emulate Western economic powers by embracing global values. In consequence, global culture exerts its hegemonic influence on some local cultures via voluntary submission to global culture (van Strien, 1997).

Furthermore, globalization has brought rapid changes in consumption patterns and in the spread of global "brand-name" goods. An expanding consumerist culture, with its attending global marketing strategies such as global advertising, tends to exploit similar basic material desires and create similar lifestyles (Parameswaran, 2002).

Fear of global culture's hegemonic influence on local culture often takes the form of contamination anxiety—the worry that global culture will contaminate local culture (Pickowicz, 1991). Such fear of contamination was responsible for the closing of the Starbucks coffee shop in the Imperial Palace Museum in Beijing. In January 2007, Chenggang Rui, Director and Anchor of *BizChina*, the prime-time daily business show on CCTV International, led an online campaign to have the Starbucks coffee shop removed from Beijing's Forbidden City (the Palace Museum). In his online article, Rui (2007) maintained that:

> The Forbidden City is a symbol of China's cultural heritage. Starbucks is a symbol of lower middle class culture in the west. We need to embrace the world, but we also need to preserve our cultural identity. There is a fine line between globalization and *contamination*. . . . But please don't interpret this as an act of nationalism. It is just about we Chinese people respecting ourselves. I actually like drinking Starbucks coffee. I am just against having one in the Forbidden City.

This article had attracted more than half a million readers and had inspired more than 2,700 comments, most of which were written in Chinese and were sympathetic to Rui's cause. In July 2007, Starbucks closed its coffee shop in the Forbidden City.

Attacking the contaminants is not the only kind of hot response to contamination anxiety; another hot response is quarantinization—the isolation of the erosive effects of the global culture in selected life domains so that these effects can be prevented from spreading to other life domains, particularly those that are central to the definition of a local culture. Lal (2000) draws a distinction between the material and the cosmological beliefs in a culture. Material beliefs pertain to ways of making a living or beliefs about the material world, particularly the economy. By contrast, cosmological beliefs define the purpose and meaning of life and an individual's relationship to others. Lal believes that although the material beliefs in global culture will gain popularity as a country is integrated into the global market, cosmological beliefs in local cultures are relatively resistant to the influence of globalization.

Consistent with this hypothesis, Inglehart and Baker (2000) found, on the basis of detailed analyses of longitudinal survey data from 65 societies, that economic development is accompanied by an increased adherence to values that emphasize secularism, rationality, and self-expression, which may reflect an increased reliance on science, instrumental rationality, and individualism for guiding economic activities. However, the broad knowledge traditions (e.g., Protestantism, Confucianism) that define personhood and sociality in a society are resistant to the erosive effects of globalization.

In a related study, Fu and Chiu (2007) reported that although modernization and Westernization often arrive in one package, Hong Kong Chinese distinguish between modernization and Westernization, with modernization involving the acquisition of specific skills and competencies that have fueled the economic development in the West, and Westernization involving the adoption of Western social-moral values. The Hong Kong Chinese welcome the arrival of modern, instrumental values (e.g., power and creativity) more than they do Western moral values (e.g., individuality and uniqueness). The strategy of quarantinization shelters the core moral values in Chinese culture from the erosive effects of globalization, resulting in the differential rates of cultural change in different life domains (Cheung et al., 2006).

Cool reactions

In contrast to hot responses, cool responses are reflective mental processes that facilitate the use of ideas from foreign cultures as a means to further one's valued goals. Individuals view the newly arrived foreign cultures as intellectual resources that complement their own heritage for achieving valued goals. Individuals with multicultural experiences can flexibly switch their cultural frames in response to the changing cultural demands in the environment: they retrieve culturally appropriate interpretive frames and behavioral scripts depending on whether they interact with a member of the in-group or out-group culture (Chiu & Hong, 2005). They are willing to appropriate ideas from foreign cultures to generate creative solutions to a problem (Leung & Chiu, in press). Indeed, creative synthesis of ideas from diverse cultures has led to product innovations in local and global markets. One example is Starbucks Coffee Singapore's introduction of a range of handcrafted snow-skin mooncakes – *Caramel Macchiato*, *Cranberry Hibiscus*, and *Orange Citron* – to the market. In the company's news release, Belinda Wong, Managing Director of Starbucks Coffee Singapore, states that these new, innovative mooncakes will make a delicious complement to their customers' favorite coffee, as well as great gift for friends and family in the Chinese Mid-Autumn Festival. She considers Starbucks mooncakes a business innovation created by combining a sip of the American Starbucks coffee culture with a bite of the Chinese custom of celebrating the Mid-Autumn Festival with a traditional sweet delight.

Individuals who display cool responses may also be aware of globalization's hegemonic influence on local culture. However, these individuals are able to maintain their heritage's cultural identity while at the same time appropriating intellectual resources from foreign cultures to attain their valued goals. The success of Stephen Chow's film *Kung Fu Hustle* in US cinemas provides a good illustration of such cool reactions. Stephen Chow is a Hong Kong filmmaker whose recent film *Kung Fu Hustle* is one of the three Chinese films that have made over 1 billion US dollars in the box office (the other two are *Crouching Tiger, Hidden Dragon*, and *Hero*). When making *Kung Fu Hustle*, Chow was not shy in appropriating elements from the popular cultures of Hong Kong and the United States to compose a collage of images familiar to viewers of Hong Kong action films and Hollywood movies. As Chow (2005) put it,

> I love Hollywood movies – I grew up on them, I love them, and I use a lot of elements of them in my films. Clips, whole routines, *the Roadrunner* in the new film, floods of blood from *The Shining* – so many perfect images. I want to take them and incorporate them, and more than just imitation, I want to demonstrate how important those films were to me, how much I love them. And I think that my willingness to incorporate so many western elements in my films will, in a way, humanize these films for American audiences.

To Stephen Chow, appropriating elements of foreign cultures to advance a personal project is both an artful and a tactful matter. For example, behind the success of *Kung Fu Hustle* hides a story of a previously vibrant local industry's bitter struggle for survival in the face of global competition. At the time when the movie was planned, with the unrivalled popularity of Hollywood movies in Mainland China, Hong Kong, and Taiwan (following the overwhelming success of *Titanic*), Hong Kong's film industry was in a very bad shape: new productions had dropped from 200 new films in 1993 to 52 in 2006. To survive the keen competition from large-budget Hollywood productions, the Hong Kong film industry had to go global. Against this backdrop, Stephen Chow made a conscious decision: He would make a Hong Kong movie for global audiences and finance it with US capital – *Kung Fu Hustle* was 95% financed by Columbia (Sony). Aside from incorporating many elements of American popular culture in the film to cater for the taste of US audiences, he was willing to comply with the production norms in Hollywood, investing heavily in the development of the storyboard. Chow's deliberation may remind some readers of the Self-Strengthening Movement that took place in China in the late nineteenth century, when China faced the threat of foreign imperialism. A slogan in the Movement was "to combat the foreigners by learning from their strengths."

Activation of hot and cool responses

There is experimental evidence that the simultaneous activation of two cultures (e.g., Starbucks coffee in China's Imperial Palace Museum) increases the likelihood of both hot and cool responses (Chiu & Cheng, 2007), possibly because the simultaneous activation of two cultures increases the centrality of culture as an organizing category for processing information. As a result, perceivers become highly aware of the cultural significance of the stimuli (e.g., the presence of a Starbucks coffee shop) in the environment. This in turn increases the likelihood of reacting to the cultural implications of globalization. For instance, individuals become more receptive to ideas from foreign cultures and more creative after viewing symbols both from their own culture *and* a foreign culture. However, viewing symbols either of one's own culture or a foreign culture alone has no creative benefits (Leung & Chiu, in press). Likewise, viewing icons of one's own and a foreign culture increases the defensive reactions when the individual perceives a threat to their heritage culture, but viewing icons of either one's own or a foreign culture does not have this effect (Torelli, Chiu, Tam, Au, & Keh, 2010).

Not much is known about what induces people to display hot or cool responses toward the cultural effects of globalization. Two determining factors seem to be the need for firm answers (or closed-mindedness) and existential anxiety. As mentioned, the need for firm answers drives individuals to become culturocentric: they rely on their inherited cultural perspective to guide their judgments and do not consider alternative cultural perspectives (Chiu et al., 2000; Fu et al., 2007b). Indeed, although exposure to multiple cultures is associated with more cool responses (greater receptiveness to ideas from foreign cultures and higher creativity), for those who crave firm answers and hence are not open-minded, exposure to multiple cultures brings a higher risk of mental freezing (un-cool responses) – these individuals become less receptive to ideas from the foreign culture (Leung &

Chiu, 2008) and less creative (Leung & Chiu, 2008; Klafehn, Banerjee, & Chiu, 2008).

Experimental evidence also shows that under the influence of the salience of mortality, simultaneous activation of cultures should incite hot, exclusionary reactions. Specifically, results from these studies indicate that when people are reminded of their mortality *and* when two cultural representations are activated simultaneously, people are particularly likely to resent and resist any actions that can undermine the viability of their own cherished cultural worldview. In one study (Torelli et al., 2010), the participants were European American undergraduates who identified strongly with American culture. To manipulate mortality salience, half of the participants were asked to describe the emotions that the thought of their own death arouses in them (mortality salience condition), and the remaining ones were asked to describe the emotions aroused by the thought of having dental work done (control condition). To activate the representation of Chinese culture, all participants evaluated products imported from China and with Chinese brand names. Half of the participants evaluated products that are icons of American culture (e.g., jeans, breakfast cereals, trainers). Thus, for these participants, representations of both Chinese and American cultures were cognitively salient (two-culture condition). The remaining participants evaluated products that are not American cultural icons. For these participants, only the Chinese cultural representation was salient (one-culture condition).

Following the manipulations, the participants studied a business case that described Nike's (an iconic American brand) out-of-the-box marketing plan to strengthen its presence in the Middle East. The key strategies in the marketing plan included adopting a new brand name using the Arabic word for "sportsmanship," eliminating the "Swoosh" mark from the product, selecting well-known local soccer players (a popular sport in the Middle East) as endorsers, having the endorsers wear traditional Islamic attire and a pair of "Sportsmanship" running shoes, and using a new slogan, "Dress modestly, the Islamic spirit" in the new brand's advertisements. All these strategies could be seen as ones that could undermine the Americanness of Nike.

As expected, compared to the participants in the other three conditions, participants in the two-culture mortality-salient condition reacted most negatively to the marketing plan: They believed most strongly that the plan would fail, the consumers in the Middle East would dislike the new brand name, the news of the plan would bring down Nike's stock price in the New York Stock Exchange, and Nike's market share in the United States would decrease.

This result highlights the importance of existential anxiety in eliciting hot reactions. Even when both cultural representations were salient, the participants displayed exclusionary reactions only when they also experienced existential anxiety. Similarly, when individuals experience existential anxiety, exposing them to foreign cultures lowers their likelihood of displaying cool responses – that is, they reduce their receptiveness to ideas from foreign cultures (Leung & Chiu, in press).

Bringing it to the table

We have discussed how individuals may respond to the cultural impact of globalization. We began with a discussion of the possible cultural impact of globalization and the basic cognitive and motivational principles that mediate some cultural processes. Based on these principles, we then described the hot and cool responses to the cultural impacts of globalization and argued that simultaneous activation of two cultural representations increases the likelihood of both cool and hot responses and that existential anxiety and a need for firm answers increase the likelihood of hot responses and decreases that of cool responses.

The importance of bringing these issues to the table cannot be overstated. The globalizing space in many parts of the world is richly ornamented with symbols of multiple cultures. If our results are valid, people's social perceptions and reactions will become increasingly more culturally motivated. On the one hand, as globalization proceeds, individuals are exposed to many novel ideas from other cultures. Thus, if people from different nation-states and cultural backgrounds can freely exchange their ideas and practices and appreciate those of others, globalization can be a profoundly enriching process that opens minds to new experiences and leads to greater creativity (Appiah, 2006).

On the other hand, increased cultural contact also exposes people to conflicting beliefs and values, some of which may fall in the rejection zone of traditional cultures. This may increase the need for firm answers. If individuals manage their epistemic insecurity by resorting to hot, exclusionary practices, intercultural conflicts may take on cultural significance and turn into a clash of civilizations, violent conflicts between cultures may emerge and escalate into wars and terrorist attacks. When people are constantly reminded of the wasted lives in these calamities, rising existential fear may spur even more hot responses, creating a vicious circle.

Thus, how individuals manage their reactions to the cultural impact of globalization is a research topic that requires urgent research attention. It is important to identify the controlling stimuli of the hot responses, to know their downstream cognitive and motivational consequences, and to understand how individuals' self-regulatory competence may moderate these hot responses. Furthermore, hot responses seem to be highly contagious. In the Starbucks coffee incident, a provocative message on the Internet could incite widespread protestation against the coffee chain within a short period of time. It is important to know how hot responses become contagious in a human group, and what can be done to stop the spread of the infection.

It is equally important to identify the controlling factors of the cool responses. If globalization can be an enriching process and mere exposure to foreign cultures does not always lead to creative benefits, research should inform us what is needed to make multicultural experience an empowering and constructive self-transformational experience.

The disciplinary perspective we take here is social-psychological. However, we believe that a cross-disciplinary perspective is required to answer the above questions. For example, we need to understand how the self-regulatory system works in multicultural contexts. This is where personality psychology, cultural psychology, and social cognitive neuroscience can contribute. We also need to situate intercultural contacts in their historical and political contexts. This is where humanists and social scientists can contribute. We believe that concerted effort from a multidisciplinary research team will deliver a holistic answer to our global problems.

References

Alderson, A. S., & Nielsen, F. (2002). Globalization and the great U-turn: Income inequality trends in 16 OECD countries. *American Journal of Sociology, 107*, 1244–1299.

Appiah, K. A. (2006). *Cosmopolitanism: Ethics in a world of strangers*. New York: Norton.

Carnegie Endowment for International Peace (2007). *Culture and globalization*. Retrieved April 28, 2007, from http://www.globalization101.org/issue/culture

Castells, M. (1998). *End of millennium*. Oxford: Blackwell.

Chao, M. M., Chen, J., Roisman, G., & Hong, Y.-y. (2007). Essentializing race: Implications for bicultural individuals' cognition and physiological reactivity. *Psychological Science, 18*, 341–348.

Cheung, T. S., Chan, H. M., Chan, K. M., King, A. Y. C., Chiu, C.-y., & Yang, C. F. (2006). How Confucian are contemporary Chinese? Construction of an ideal type and its application to three Chinese communities. *European Journal of East Asian Studies, 5*, 157–180.

Chiu, C.-y. (2007). How can Asian social psychology succeed globally? *Asian Journal of Social Psychology, 10*, 41–44.

Chiu, C.-y., & Chen, J. (2004). Symbols and interactions: Application of the CCC model to culture, language, and social identity. In S.-h. Ng, C. Candlin, & C.-y. Chiu (Eds.), *Language matters: Communication, culture, and social identity* (pp. 155–182). Hong Kong: City University of Hong Kong Press.

Chiu, C.-y., & Cheng, S. Y.-y. (2007). Toward a social psychology of culture and globalization: Some social cognitive consequences of activating two cultures simultaneously. *Social and Personality Psychology Compass, 1*, 84–100.

Chiu, C.-y., & Hong, Y. (2005). Cultural competence: Dynamic processes. In A. Elliot & C. S. Dweck (Eds.), *Handbook of motivation and competence* (pp. 489–505). New York: Guilford Press.

Chiu, C.-y., & Hong, Y. (2006). *The social psychology of culture*. New York: Psychology Press.

Chiu, C.-y., & Hong, Y.-y. (2007). Cultural processes: Basic principles. In E. T. Higgins & A. E. Kruglanski (Eds.), *Social psychology: Handbook of basic principles* (pp. 785–809). New York: Guilford Press.

Chiu, C.-y., Mallorie, L., Keh, H.-T., & Law, W. (2009). Perceptions of culture in multicultural space: Joint presentation of images from two cultures increases ingroup attribution of culture-typical characteristics. *Journal of Cross-Cultural Psychology*, *40*, 282–300.

Chiu, C.-y., Morris, M., Hong, Y., & Menon, T. (2000). Motivated cultural cognition: The impact of implicit cultural theories on dispositional attribution varies as a function of need for closure. *Journal of Personality and Social Psychology*, *78*, 247–259.

Chow, S. (2005). *It's Stephen Chow's time*. Retrieved June 29, 2007, from http://filmfreakcentral.net/notes/schowinterview.htm

Fu, H.-y., & Chiu, C.-y. (2007). Local culture's responses to globalization: Exemplary persons and their attendant values. *Journal of Cross-Cultural Psychology*, *38*, 636–653.

Fu, H.-y., Chiu, C.-y., Morris, M. W., & Young, M. (2007a). Spontaneous inferences from cultural cues: Varying responses of cultural insiders and outsiders. *Journal of Cross-Cultural Psychology*, *38*, 58–75.

Fu, H.-y., Morris, M. W., Lee, S.-l. Chao, M.-c., Chiu, C.-y., & Hong, Y.-y. (2007b). Epistemic motives and cultural conformity: Need for closure, culture, and context as determinants of conflict judgments. *Journal of Personality and Social Psychology*, *92*, 191–207.

Giddens, A. (1985). *The nation state and violence*. Cambridge, MA: Polity Press.

Greenberg, J., Porteus, J., Simon, L., & Pyszczynski, T. (1995). Evidence of a terror management function of cultural icons: The effects of mortality salience on the inappropriate use of cherished cultural symbols. *Personality and Social Psychology Bulletin*, *21*, 1221–1228.

Hong, Y., Benet-Martinez, V., Chiu, C.-y., & Morris, M. W. (2003). Boundaries of cultural influence: Construct activation as a mechanism for cultural differences in social perception. *Journal of Cross-Cultural Psychology*, *34*, 453–464.

Hong, Y., Chiu, C-y., & Kung, M. (1997). Bringing culture out in front: Effects of cultural meaning system activation on social cognition. In K. Leung, Y. Kashima, U. Kim, & S. Yamaguchi (Eds.), *Progress in Asian social psychology* (Vol. 1, pp. 139–150). Singapore: Wiley.

Hong, Y., Morris, M., Chiu, C-y., & Benet-Martinez, V. (2000). Multicultural minds: A dynamic constructivist approach to culture and cognition. *American Psychologist*, *55*, 709–720.

Hong, Y.-y., Wan, C., No, S., & Chiu, C.-y. (2007). Multicultural identities. In S. Kitayama & D. Cohen (Eds.), *Handbook of cultural psychology*. New York: Guilford Press.

Inglehart, R., & Baker, W. E. (2000). Modernization, cultural change, and the persistence of traditional values. *American Sociological Review*, *65*, 19–51.

Klafehn, J., Banerjee, P., & Chiu, C.-y. (2008). Navigating cultures: A model of metacognitive intercultural intelligence. In S. Ang & L. Van Dyne (Eds.), *Handbook of cultural intelligence*. Armonk, NY: M. E. Sharpe.

Kluckhohn, K. (1954). Culture and behavior. In G. Lindzey (Ed.), *Handbook of social psychology* (Vol. 2, pp. 921–976). Cambridge, MA: Addison-Wesley.

Lal, D. (2000). Does modernization require westernization? *The Independent Review*, *5*, 5–24.

Lehman, D., Chiu, C.-y., & Schaller, M. (2004). Culture and psychology. *Annual Review of Psychology*, *55*, 689–714.

Leung, A. K.-y., & Chiu, C.-y. (2008). Interactive effects of multicultural experiences and openness to experience on creativity. *Creativity Research Journal, 20*, 376–382.

Leung, A. K.-y., & Chiu, C.-y. (in press). Multicultural experiences, idea receptiveness, and creativity. *Journal of Cross-Cultural Psychology*.

Mead, G. H. (1934). *Mind, self, and society: From the standpoint of a social behaviorist*. Chicago, IL: University of Chicago Press, 1962.

Menon, T., Morris, M., Chiu, C.-y., & Hong, Y. (1999). Culture and the construal of agency: Attribution to individual versus group dispositions. *Journal of Personality and Social Psychology, 76*, 701–717.

Parameswaran, R. (2002). Local culture in global media: Excavating colonial and material discourses in *National Geographic: Communication Theory, 12*, 287–315.

Pickowicz, P. G. (1991). The theme of spiritual pollution in Chinese films of the 1930s. *Modern China, 17*, 38–75.

Pilkington, H., & Johnson, R. (2003). Relations of identity and power in global/local context. *Cultural Studies, 6*, 259–283.

Robertson, R. (1992). *Globalization: Social theory and global culture*. London: Sage.

Rui, C. (2007). *Why Starbucks needs to get out of the Forbidden City?* Retrieved April 28, 2007, from http://blog.sina.com.cn/u/4adabe27010008yg

Sui, J., Zhu, Y., & Chiu, C.-y. (2007). Bicultural mind, self-construal, and recognition memory: Cultural priming effects on self- and mother-reference effect. *Journal of Experimental Social Psychology, 43*, 818–824.

Torelli, C.-J., Chiu, C.-y., Tam, K.-p., Au, K. C., & Keh, H. T. (2010). *Psychological reactions to foreign cultures in globalized economy: Effects of simultaneous activation of cultures*. Unpublished manuscript.

van Strien, P. J. (1997). The American "colonization" of northwest European social psychology after World War II. *Journal of the History of the Behavioral Sciences, 33*, 349–363.

Wan, C., Chiu, C.-y., Peng, S., & Tam, K.-p. (2007a). Measuring cultures through intersubjective norms: Implications for predicting relative identification with two or more cultures. *Journal of Cross-Cultural Psychology, 38*, 213–226.

Wan, C., Chiu, C.-y., Tam, K.-p., Lee, S.-l., Lau, I. Y.-m., & Peng, S.-q. (2007b). Perceived cultural importance and actual self-importance of values in cultural identification. *Journal of Personality and Social Psychology, 92*, 337–354.

Wang, J. (2005). Bourgeois bohemians in China? Neo-tribes and the urban imaginary. *China Quarterly, 83*, 532–548.

Ward, C., Bochner, S., & Furnham, A. (2001). *Psychology of culture shock*. London: Routledge.

Wong, R. Y., & Hong, Y. (2005). Dynamic influences of culture on cooperation in the prisoner's dilemma. *Psychological Science, 16*, 429–434.

15 "Race", racism, and knowledge production in South African psychology

Implications for dealing with racism in contemporary South Africa

Norman Duncan

Scrutiny of the pervasive racism of South African psychology has constituted the focus of several publications in South Africa in recent years (Van Ommen, 2008). It is therefore perhaps not all that surprising that one is increasingly discerning a discourse in psychology circles that this focus is becoming somewhat overdone and "tired". As an aside, this discourse is not too different from an increasingly strident discourse in broader South African society, which, very crudely articulated, states: "Apartheid is dead. Racism is therefore no longer a significant problem in South Africa."

While it might appear that the attention currently given to the study of racism in South African psychology may perhaps be disproportionate when compared to the attention afforded other critical social problems currently experienced there, I want to argue here that sustained and focused attention to the study of racism in South African psychology and South Africa more generally is, in fact, necessary. It is necessary quite simply because of the extent to which racism still dominates the social landscape in South Africa. Moreover, it is necessary in view of the genesis and particular historical trajectory of this discipline and profession.

Indeed, I want to argue that it is perhaps partly because of South African psychology's genesis and the embedded "traces" or memories of its early history that the discipline has shown itself to be so manifestly ill-equipped to deal with the various manifestations of racism that currently blemish the South African social and political landscape.

Here I want to draw attention to a series of incidents that have outraged many South Africans over the last few years.

In *August 2000* the white owner of a construction company, Mr Pieter Odendaal, tied one of his workers to the back of his truck and dragged him for more than five kilometres along a road. The worker, a black man, died of the injuries he sustained as a result of this brutal assault (BBC News, 2000).

In *January 2004* another white construction company owner, together with three of his employees, tied a black former employee, Nelson Shisane, to a tree and brutally assaulted him. It is alleged that Shisane was subsequently thrown alive into a lion enclosure a few kilometres from where he was assaulted. Police reported that when they later searched the enclosure, they found "only a skull, scraps of bone and strips of clothing" identified as belonging to Shisane (Govender & Rondganger, 2004, n.p.). When Shisane's murderers appeared in court, they were confronted by a group of demonstrators venting their anger by shouting slogans such as, "We are tired of the boers [farmers/whites]", "Fed up with killer-boers", and "Kill the farmer, kill the boer". These slogans created an outcry in various circles because they were deemed profoundly racist (Govender & Rondganger, 2004).

In *December 2001* a group of four white schoolboys, all from affluent families and attending prestigious historically white schools in Pretoria, were arrested for wantonly kicking a homeless man to death (Pretoria News, 2008).

In *January 2008* an 18-year-old white youth, Johan Nel, went on an ostensibly senseless shooting rampage in Skierlik, an informal settlement inhabited primarily by people of colour in the North West province of South Africa. In this shooting spree he reportedly killed three adults and a toddler and wounded nine other people (South African Broadcasting Corporation, 2008).

In *February 2008* South Africa was treated to a shocking video recording of four young white University of the Free State students laughing raucously as they duped five middle-aged black cleaners into various demeaning activities, including eating what looked like dog food. The food was allegedly spiked with the urine of one of the students (Associated Press, 2008).

In *April 2008*, while South Africa was still trying to digest and come to terms with this crude and cruel expression of racism at the University of the Free State, a range of other racist incidents were reported at the University of Johannesburg. These included incidents of black students being beaten up by fellow white students in a bar on the university campus (University World News, 2008).

Then in *May 2008*, South Africa was rocked by a series of brutal xenophobic attacks against foreigners. These attacks led to the death of 56 people and the displacement of approximately 30,000 foreign nationals, all of them people of colour (Reuters, 2008).

In the face of this seemingly unrelenting exhibition of racist degeneracy and abuse, South African psychologists have unfortunately been disconcertingly mute, silent/silenced in attempts to make sense of, and respond to, these events, at least in the public domain. This silence has been all the more resounding in a context in which various educationists, sociologists, and political scientists have attempted to bring their disciplinary knowledge to bear in an effort to decipher or make sense of these horrendous events (see, for example, Jansen, 2008).

This characteristic – though no less disconcerting for all that – silence on the part of South African psychology in respect of the problem of racism also extends, of course, to the less mediatized and sensational ways in which racism continues to impact on South African society, such as the ongoing racialized patterns of social power and poverty, as well as the rigid racialized patterns of social interaction that still characterize this country (Duncan, 2005).

The question that we could pose ourselves here is: Why is it that South African psychologists have been rendered so mute in the public arena and so unresponsive – or perhaps indifferent – to a problem about which we should have something to say? There is, of course, a range of factors that could be seen to contribute to this silence. These include, as indicated earlier, other pressing social issues that also require attention, such as the HIV/AIDS pandemic currently ravaging Southern Africa, the high levels of unemployment and crime characterizing the country, as well as the high levels of interpersonal violence that appear to have become endemic to South African society (Stevens, 2009). Another important factor is organized psychology's ever-growing enthralment with private practice, to the exclusion of nearly everything else (cf. Painter & Terre Blanche, 2004) and, hence, its disinclination to deal with the "messier" public and ostensibly more intractable aspects of the current South African social reality.

As important as these factors may be, in this chapter I want to focus on another factor that is, to my mind, critical if one is to make sense of the response of South African psychology to the racism endemic in South African society – namely, its peculiar historical relationship with issues of "race" and racism. More specifically, I want to focus on the manner in which South African psychology has historically constructed "race" and how this, in turn, has influenced the articulation of the ideology of racism in South Africa. I want to argue that it is this that has served as a key impediment to South African psychology engaging more meaningfully with racism and its consequences. Simultaneously, it is this, too, that makes necessary an ongoing and critical focus on the historical impact of "race" and racism on South African psychology. As an aside, it has to be noted that the many other problems afflicting South African society that I have just referred to (e.g., HIV/AIDS, violence, and crime) are all over-determined by "race" politics. This, of course, further underlines the need for South African psychology to continue to focus on issues of "race" and racism.

South African psychology

For the purposes of this chapter, I outline the history of South African psychology's responses to issues of "race" and racism in terms of four broad temporal categories:

1   the 1920s to the end of the 1940s,
2   the 1950s and 1960s,
3   the 1970s and 1980s, and, then
4   the 1990s and beyond.

Here it should be noted that this section is largely based on research conducted in collaboration with a colleague (Duncan & Bowman, 2009).

Before embarking on the history of South African psychology's responses to "race" and racism in South Africa it might be appropriate to first define the term *racism*. For the purposes of this chapter, racism is defined as:

> An ideology through which the domination or marginalisation of certain racialised groups by another racialised group or groups is enacted and legitimated. It is a set of ideas and discursive and material practices aimed at (re)producing and justifying systematic inequalities between racialised groups.
>
> (based on the definition formulated in Duncan, van Niekerk, de la Rey, & Seedat, 2001, p. 2)

Thus, the chapter departs from the assumptions (1) that racism is a social and systemic phenomenon; (2) that it is inextricably linked to power, and (3) that it is perpetuated by means of a multiplicity of interactional practices and institutions, including scientific and professional ones.

1920s to 1940s: Psychology and the otherization of blacks

Psychological research, training, and teaching in South Africa from the 1920s to the 1940s were largely confined to the psychology and cognate departments at the universities of Pretoria, Rhodes, Stellenbosch, and the Witwatersrand (Louw & Foster, 1991). Unsurprisingly – given the international context in which South African psychology emerged (see Howitt & Owusu-Bempah, 1994; Painter & Terre Blanche, 2004) – available commentaries suggest that from their inception, these departments exhibited a near-obsession with the study and measurement of "race". This is despite the fact that since its introduction into the social sciences, the notion of the existence of biologically and psychologically distinct human "races" had consistently been refuted and had been recognized as central to the perpetuation of racism (racism is, after all, based on the valorization of the notion of human "races").

To a certain extent, the foundations of this fixation on "race" were laid just prior to the 1920s, with the research of the South African psychologist, Charles Templeton Loram (1917). Beginning in the second decade of the twentieth century, Loram had administered a series of intelligence tests to Asian, White, and African schoolchildren in an effort to establish the extent of racial difference in childhood intelligence. Based on his fundamentally specious research, he argued that African children were, as he put it, "much less efficient" and "much slower in their thinking" than the other children tested (in Louw & Foster, 1991, p. 62).

It has been argued that Loram's research had set the tone not only for South African psychology's initial preoccupation with "race", but also for its apparent obsession with the construction of "racial" difference, so as to confirm the "superiority" of the white "race" in relation to all other "races"[1] in South Africa (Duncan & Bowman, 2009). Consequently, in the 1920s M. L. Fick (1929), on the basis of further research in this field, argued that only a small percentage of African children could achieve the median scores attained by white children on a selection of intelligence tests. Much similar – and logically flawed – research saw the light of day subsequently, including the research of J. A. J. van Rensburg (in Dubow, 1995), who held that African children's performance on certain learning tasks was significantly inferior to that of white children. Moreover, van Rensburg claimed that this difference in performance increased with age.

Many South African psychologists of the time relentlessly pursued intelligence testing and research amongst various racialized groups because such testing and research, so it was argued, were key to enhancing education and occupational policies in South Africa (Rich, 1990). Of course, there is no denying that such testing and research were also critically linked to attempts to provide "scientific" evidence of the existence of "races" and so-called "racial" differences associated with fixed psychological attributes. Furthermore, such testing and research were also centrally linked to narratives of "racial" superiority and inferiority.

Indeed, the South African psychologists Louw and Foster (1991) maintain that research of the nature conducted and proposed by the likes of Loram and Fick was not aimed simply to enhance educational policies; it also provided "scientific" legitimization of the widespread belief among whites at the time of their natural – indeed, God-ordained – "superiority" and the putative "inferiority" of people of colour. Very importantly too, as Chisholm (in Dubow, 1995, p. 235) incisively observes, this type of research also played the crucial role of identifying socially and economically marginalized whites, so as to organize their fuller inclusion into the "white body politic", in an effort to ensure the fortification of an increasingly racially stratified South Africa. And, indeed, in the main, the racial intelligence research on whites at the time played an important social surveillance and regulatory function, aimed at identifying and controlling those whites whose functioning and positions in society would compromise the narrative of white superiority.

Of course, the research and views of early white psychologists such as Fick, van Rensburg, and their kind did not go completely uncontested. As elsewhere in the world at the time (see Benjamin, 1997; Dubow, 1995; Zuckerman, 1990), these views and research provoked various drawn-out debates over whether assumed racial differences between human groups in fact existed and, if they did exist, whether they were a consequence of hereditary or of environmental factors. On the one hand, those such as Fick (1929) and Robbertse (1967) argued, of course, that racial differences did indeed exist and, furthermore, that people of colour were intellectually "inferior" to whites because of genetic differences. On the other hand, psychologists like MacCrone (1937), Malherbe (in Rich, 1990), and Biesheuvel (1972) held that studies such as those conducted by van Rensburg, Fick, and Loram did not provide sufficient evidence of innate differences between blacks and whites.

Nonetheless, in the final analysis it was South African psychology's commitment to the inscription of a racial hierarchy of power and privileges in South African society that prevailed, as amply illustrated by the rationale for the establishment of the Carnegie commission of enquiry into the "poor white" problem. In 1927, the South African psychologist, E. G. Malherbe was approached by the President of the Carnegie Corporation, F. P. Kepple, to identify the most pressing social problem in South Africa. The corporation would then make the necessary funds available to allow for research on the problem (Cooper, Nicholas, Seedat, & Statman, 1990). Malherbe without hesitation identified the "poor white" problem as the most pressing social problem in South Africa (Malherbe, 1981). More specifically, the problem, as he saw it, was that South Africa at the time had more than 100,000 so-called "poor whites" and that they were "becoming a menace to the self-preservation and prestige of *our White people, living as we do* in the midst of the native [black] population which outnumbers *us* 5 to 1" (Malherbe, 1981, p. 119, emphasis added). Malherbe's identification of the "poor white" problem as the most pressing problem in South Africa at the time is telling, given that it was essentially blacks who bore the brunt of the burden of poverty at the time, largely due to being dispossessed of their land by the then government (Fleisch, 1993; Louw, 1986).

In the event, the Carnegie Corporation made substantial funding available for research on this problem (Cooper et al., 1990; Louw, 1986). Through his identification of the "poor white" problem as the most significant social problem of the day, Malherbe, in the words of Dubow (1995, p. 171), signalled that white (as opposed to black) poverty was "both anomalous and unacceptable". Furthermore, Malherbe and the other psychologists who contributed to the Carnegie Commission, through their identification of the "poor white" problem as the most critical problem of the day, as reported in an earlier publication,

> Laid the foundations for the ideological trajectory of psychology as a discipline that apparently would not have any qualms about privileging the concerns and needs of whites over those of blacks; i.e. a discipline that would not have any qualms in advancing the fundamentally racist social order in which it was located.
>
> (Duncan, Stevens, & Bowman, 2004, p. 366)

By way of concluding this section, it should be observed that while between the 1920s and 1940s South African psychology was a relatively small discipline, it was represented by a very influential coterie of white (largely male) psychologists. Important to note is that this cohort of psychologists not only defined the discipline's agenda during this formative period in its history, but also provided critical support to the government of the day's aspirations for the establishment of an institutionalized system of racial separatism.

In the main, the agenda that large sectors of South African psychology seemed to pursue with single-mindedness was the development of a psychology of "race" differences and constructions of an inferiorized black Other. That the research and policies that resulted from this agenda were to be harnessed for the scientific justification of formal apartheid and apartheid policies at a later stage obviously speaks volumes about the role played by South African psychology in the development of institutionalized racism there during the early decades of the twentieth century.

As Vaughan (1991, p. 8) observes, disciplines like psychology "Played an important part in constructing the . . . ["raced" Other] as an object of know ledge, and elaborated . . . systems and practices which have been seen as intrinsic to the operation of [oppressive] power."

1950s and 1960s: The otherization of blacks continued

While research aimed at developing a theory of racial differences continued well into the 1940s, as early as the 1930s a pioneer South African social psychologist, I. D. MacCrone (in Rich, 1990), argued that it was becoming increasingly important for South African psychology to start focusing on the study of inter-racial problems and relationships within the cultural and psychosocial contexts of their genesis rather than obsessing about "race" differences. It is widely acknowledged that MacCrone's research on inter-group relations significantly shifted the focus of South African research away from its earlier misguided efforts at establishing a theory of "racial" differ-ence (Bowman, Duncan, & Swart, 2008; Painter & Terre Blanche, 2004). Moreover, the focus pioneered by MacCrone received a significant boost in the 1950s with the visit to South Africa by the American proponents of inter-group psychology, Thomas Pettigrew and Gordon Allport (Bowman et al., 2008).

Here it should be noted that the gradual renunciation on the part of South African psychology of the discipline's obsessive preoccupation with establish-ing the existence of racial differences and the "inferiority" of some racialized groups on the basis of these purported differences may, in part, have been due to the realization in South Africa and elsewhere in the world that finding proof for the existence of a relationship between putative biological "races" and various psychological attributes was a futile exercise. Furthermore, it has to be remembered that following the excesses of various fascist regimes in Europe and colonial governments in Africa, Asia, and Central and South America, the scientific community, internationally, became increasingly wary of, or averse to, notions of "race" and racial differences (Dubow, 1995; Duncan, 1994).

Following the visit by Pettigrew and Allport, as well as various internal developments in South African psychology (see Louw & Foster, 1991), the 1960s saw the emergence of several South African studies on "race" relations. Specifically, Pettigrew's research on authoritarianism and prejudice stimulated a range of cognate South African psychological research, most notably by van den Berghe (cited in Louw & Foster, 1991) and Morsbach and Morsbach (cited in Louw & Foster, 1991). Additionally, a number of studies on ethnocentrism and "racial" identification or misidentification in children also saw the light of day during this period.

Revealingly, however, during this period psychological research related to "racial" prejudice and authoritarianism appeared to focus on the latter as *individual*, rather than *group* or *systemic* attributes or aberrations. Very importantly, too, many South African psychologists, largely through the way in which they articulated their research, seemed in many instances to continue to reinforce the notion of the existence of fundamentally different "races" (Duncan, 1994).

During this period, in response to the needs of apartheid capital, South African psychology appeared to turn its endeavours in relation to research on "race" and racism increasingly to the industrial labour arena. This was particularly apparent in the work of the National Institute for Personnel Research (NIPR) (Painter & Terre Blanche, 2004). A study by Terre Blanche and Seedat (2001) of the research conducted by the Institute between 1946 and 1984 produced several revealing findings. First, according to this study, research undertaken by the NIPR during the period under consideration seems to have revived the "racial differences" thesis developed by South African psychology during the 1920s to 1940s. Second, researchers within the NIPR appeared to be fixated on uncovering processes through which said racial differences could be harnessed to optimize the exploitation of black workers, so as to better serve the interests of apartheid capital. Of course, this research agenda was clearly predicated on the assumption that blacks were not only different, but were a less-than-human other. Through their research, the NIPR and significant sections of South African psychology, Hussein Bulhan (1993, p. 3) argues, contributed significantly during this period to a construction of blacks that not only objectified and negativized them, but also served as a means of justifying their subjugation and exploitation by the white minority.

1970s and 1980s: Scientific neutrality and silence

Patently eschewing a critical focus on the institutional causes and consequences of racialization processes and racism, during the 1970s, South African psychology preferred to focus its attention on "racial" identification or misidentification in children.

Furthermore, instead of a critical engagement with institutionalized racism, psychology in South Africa remained silent about the damaging effects of the phenomenon. Moreover, when it was confronted with the manifestly pernicious psychosocial effects of apartheid racism, it typically defended itself by appealing to notions of scientific neutrality (Cooper et al., 1990; Durrheim & Mokeki, 1997). Appeals for South African psychologists to maintain a scientific neutrality in the face of the excesses of the apartheid order were championed by some of the most widely published and respected South African psychologists of the time (see, for example, Biesheuvel, 1987; Cooper et al., 1990). Obviously, through its ostensible neutrality and its indifference to the impact of "race" theory and institutionalized racism on the psychosocial well-being of South Africans, South African psychology continued its complicity with the apartheid state – albeit largely through omission rather than commission – during the 1970s and 1980s (Duncan, 2001; Painter & Terre Blanche, 2004).

1990s and beyond: Glimmers of a psychology of liberation?

The South African psychologist Garth Stevens (2003) has undertaken a critical review of trends in the construction of "race" and the examination of racism in South African psychology from the 1990s onwards. In this review he found, like Durrheim and Mokeki (1997) before him, that from the 1990s on South African psychology appeared to be more open to the possibility of studying the impact of racism on South African society. However, where South African psychology was willing to engage with the problem of racism, it did so primarily through research on "race" attitudes, stereotypes, and racism scales. Tellingly, too, Stevens (2003) found that the said research (as had been the case earlier in the history of South African psychology) was generally conducted in a manner that reflected an uncritical acceptance of "racialized" categories and "race" differences (cf. Painter & Terre Blanche, 2004).

More encouragingly, however, Stevens (2003) also found that during this period, South African psychological research and publications were increasingly focusing on providing critical evaluations of the history of psychology and its relevance as a discipline. This critical orientation was often expressed in the form of research and publications on the social relevance of psychology from a material and historical perspective. Moreover, he found that during the 1990s South African psychology was increasingly turning its attention to the study of experiences of blacks. Previously, the tendency in South African psychology had largely been to conduct studies *on* blacks as research subjects rather than as social agents who had something meaningful to say about racism.

However, despite the emergence of these progressive features, during the 1990s South African psychology appeared by and large impervious to the need to address issues of racialized patterns of poverty and marginalization, as Stevens (2003) notes. Indeed, we note a perceptible return currently to a more conservative psychology – one that is preoccupied by "first-world" research agendas (such as for example, the increasing focus on neuropsychology and professional concerns) and less inclined to engage with issues that will improve the lived reality of the poor and marginalized in South Africa, the majority of whom are black (cf. Painter & Terre Blanche, 2004).

Moreover, we can also observe the increasing re-inscription of "race" in South African psychology. Whereas ten years ago only the most conservative of academics in South African psychology persisted in using "race" as an unquestioned entity, today we observe in mainstream psychology publications a strong resurgence of "race" as a primary and unquestioned group descriptor across all sectors of the South African psychology community.

A synthesis

There can be no denying South African psychology's complicity with the racism so endemic to the country's society through the way it has traditionally engaged with issues of "race" and racism. Indeed, as illustrated, at various points in its history South African psychology was a key role-player in the development and refinement of racist state policies – from its prioritization of the study of "race" differences, to its reification of racial categories, to its patent neglect of the study of racism and its deleterious impact on the lives of South Africans.

Various factors have contributed to this state of affairs. In view of space constraints, I will here briefly explore only two of these factors, both of them linked to the history of South African psychology.

The first of these is related to the demographics of South African psychology. For much of South African psychology's history, people of colour were significantly under-represented in the discipline and profession. Indeed, as Seedat (1990) observes, psychology in pre-1990s South Africa was almost exclusively served by white researchers and practitioners, who determined the scope, agenda, and methods of the discipline largely in the service of the interests of the white minority. Specifically, until ten years ago people of colour constituted a mere 10% of all registered psychologists in South Africa (Duncan, 2001).

In the second place, in South Africa there has always been a general reticence to deal with the pervasive racism that characterizes the country. Elsewhere it has been argued that this unwillingness to deal with the racism endemic to our society may be influenced by a socio-psychological need to deny or obliterate memories of the atrocities that litter South Africa's past and present (Duncan, 2005). More specifically, it is argued that this widespread amnesia may perhaps reflect an a posteriori attempt to mitigate the full horror and barbarism of the pre-1994 racist apartheid policies and practices and the substantive contributions of some psychologists to the production and maintenance of earlier forms of institutionalized racism. Clearly, if the impression could be created that racism is no longer a problem in contemporary South Africa, then it would be reasonable to infer, by extension, that the racism of the pre-1994 period was not as horrendous and enduring in its impact as history unequivocally suggests. Thus, perhaps many South Africans' and more specifically South African psychologists' unwillingness to deal with current instances and processes of racism may be linked to an inability to acknowledge and deal with their individual and collective pasts (cf. Derrida, 2004). More pessimistically, perhaps the discipline's inability to deal with issues of "race" and racism could also be linked to its beginnings as a science committed to an agenda of otherization and the advancement of the most powerful sectors of society.

However, as noted, this may be too pessimistic a view. We need not be held captive by our past. Nonetheless, in order to transcend our past, it is imperative that we first acknowledge this past and then work with it and beyond it.

This effectively brings me back to my introductory remarks. I want to argue that *more*, rather than less, research on the impact of racism on South African society is required. And a good starting point would be, as just indicated, to acknowledge, come to terms with, and counter the effects that psychology has historically produced in relation to extant constructions of "race" and the elaboration of the ideology of racism. As part of this endeavour, it will be necessary for South African psychology to acknowledge how it has historically helped to shape "forms of consciousness and unconsciousness, which [were] closely related to the maintenance . . . of . . . systems of power [and which were] . . . also closely related to what it [meant] to be a person" (Eagleton, in Vaughan, 1991, p. 3).

In this way, we might be able to deal with the ongoing manifestations of racism, such as those cited at the beginning of this chapter, in South African society.

Note

1 In the old political order the South Africa population was divided into four so-called races – namely, whites, Indians (i.e., people of Indian origin), Africans (i.e., so-called autochthonous groups), and "coloureds" (i.e., people of "mixed race").

References

Associated Press. (2008, February 27). *Black staff duped in S. African university* [Video]. Retrieved July 17, 2008, from http://www.msnbc.msn.com/id/23378050
BBC News (2000). SA worker dragged to death. *BBC News*. Retrieved March 10, 2008, from http://news.bbc.co.uk/1/hi/world/africa/900978.stm
Benjamin, L. (1997). *A history of psychology: Original sources and contemporary research*. New York: McGraw-Hill.
Biesheuvel, S. (1972). An examination of Jensen's theory of educability, heritability and population differences. *Psychologia Africana, 14*, 87–94.
Biesheuvel, S. (1987). Psychology: Science and politics. Theoretical developments and applications in a plural society. *South African Journal of Psychology, 17*(1), 1–8.
Bowman, B., Duncan, N., & Swart, T. M. (2008). Social psychology in South Africa: Towards a critical history. In C. Van Ommen & D. Painter (Eds.), *Interiors: A history of psychology in South Africa* (pp. 324–357). Pretoria: UNISA Press.

Bulhan, H. A. (1993). Imperialism in the studies of the psyche: A critique of African psychological research. In L. J. Nicholas (Ed.), *Psychology and oppression: Critiques and proposals* (pp. 1–34). Johannesburg: Skotaville.

Cooper, S., Nicholas, L., Seedat, M., & Statman, J. (1990). Psychology and apartheid: The struggle for psychology in South Africa. In L. Nicholas & S. Cooper (Eds.), *Psychology and apartheid* (pp. 1–21). Johannesburg: Madiba/Vision.

Derrida, J. (2004). *Versöhnung, ubuntu, pardon*: Quel genre? [*Versöhnung, ubuntu, pardon*: Which type?]. In B. Cassin, O. Cayla, & P. J. Slazar (Eds.), *Vérité, réconciliation, réparation* [Truth, reconciliation and reparation] (pp. 111–158). Paris: Seuil.

Dubow, S. (1995). *Illicit union: Scientific racism in modern South Africa*. Cambridge, UK: Cambridge University Press.

Duncan, N. (1994). *Discourses on racism*. Unpublished doctoral thesis. University of the Western Cape, Bellville, South Africa.

Duncan, N. (2001). Dislodging the subtexts: An analysis of a corpus of articles on racism produced by South African psychologists. In N. Duncan, A. van Niekerk, C. de la Rey, & M. Seedat (Eds.), *"Race", racism, knowledge production and psychology in South Africa* (pp. 125–152). New York: Nova Science.

Duncan, N. (2005, October). *"Race", racism and the university*. Inaugural lecture presented at the University of the Witwatersrand, Johannesburg, South Africa.

Duncan, N., & Bowman, B. (2009). Liberating South African psychology: The legacy of racism and the pursuit of representative knowledge production. In M. Montero & C. Sonn (Eds.), *Psychology of liberation* (pp. 93–114). New York: Springer.

Duncan, N., Stevens, G., & Bowman, B. (2004). South African psychology and racism: Historical determinants and future prospects. In D. Hook (Ed.), *Critical psychology* (pp. 360–388). Lansdowne: UCT Press.

Duncan, N., van Niekerk, A., de la Rey, C., & Seedat, M. (Eds.). (2001). "Race", racism, knowledge production and psychology in South Africa. Introduction. In N. Duncan, A. van Niekerk, C. de la Rey, & M. Seedat (Eds.), *"Race", racism, knowledge production and psychology in South Africa* (pp. 1–6). New York: Nova Science.

Durrheim, K., & Mokeki, S. (1997). Race and relevance: A content analysis of the South African Journal of Psychology. *South African Journal of Psychology*, *37*(4), 206–213.

Fick, M. (1929). Intelligence test results of poor White, Native (Zulu), Coloured and Indian school children and the educational and social implications. *South African Journal of Science*, *26*, 910.

Fleisch, B. (1993, April). *American influences on the development of social and educational research in South Africa, 1929 to 1943*. Paper presented at the Annual Meeting of the American Educational Research Association, Atlanta, GA, USA.

Govender, P., & Rondganger, L. (2004). Racism roars in lion death case. *Independent Online*. Retrieved July 17, 2008, from http://www.iol.co.za/index.php?click_id=&art_id=vn2004 0218041238901 C244778&set_id=1

Howitt, D., & Owusu-Bempah, J. (1994). *The racism of psychology: Time for change*. New York: Harvester Wheatsheaf.

Jansen, J. (2008, July). *Bearing whiteness: A pedagogy of compassion in a time of troubles*. Fifth Annual Han Brenninkmeijer Memorial Lecture, Johannesburg, South Africa.

Loram, C. (1917). *The education of the South African native*. New York: Longmans & Green.

Louw, J. (1986). *This is Thy work: A contextual history of applied psychology and labour in South Africa.* Doctoral thesis, University of Amsterdam, The Netherlands.

Louw, J., & Foster, D. (1991). Historical perspective: Psychology and group relations in South Africa. In D. Foster & J. Louw-Potgieter (Eds.), *Social psychology in South Africa* (pp. 57–92). Johannesburg: Lexicon.

MacCrone, I. D. (1937). The problem of race differences. *South African Journal of Science, 33,* 92–107.

Malherbe, E. G. (1981). *Never a dull moment.* Cape Town: Howard Timmins.

Painter, D., & Terre Blanche, M. (2004). *Critical psychology in South Africa.* Retrieved July 17, 2008, from http://www.criticalmethods.org/collab/critpsy.htm

Pretoria News (2008). Justice seems tipped for Waterkloof four. *Pretoria News.* Retrieved July 17, 2008, from http://www.pretorianews.co.za/index.php?fSectionId= 665&fArticleId=vn20080503084609847C863026

Reuters (2008, May 27). *South African xenophobic violence under control.* Creamer Media. Retrieved July 17, 2008, from http://www.polity.org.za/print_version.php?a_id=134188.

Rich, P. B. (1990). Race, science, and the legitimization of white supremacy in South Africa 1902–1940. *International Journal of African Historical Studies, 23*(4), 665–686.

Robbertse, P. M. (1967). Rasseverskille en die Sielkunde [Race differences and psychology]. *PIRSA Monographs, 72,* 1–11.

Seedat, M. (1990). Programmes, trends, and silences in South African psychology: 1983–1988. In L. J. Nicholas & S. Cooper (Eds.), *Psychology and apartheid* (pp. 22–50). Johannesburg: Vision.

South African Broadcasting Corporation (2008, July 14). Skierlik murder case to go to high court. *SABC News.* Retrieved July 17, 2008, from http://www.news24.com/News24v2/components/generic

Stevens, G. (2003). Academic representations of "race" and racism in psychology: Knowledge production, historical context and dialectics in transitional South Africa. *International Journal of Intercultural Relations, 27*(2), 189–207.

Stevens, G. (2009). Violent crime and human development in South Africa. In J. Watt, C. Cockcroft, & N. Duncan (Eds.), *Developmental psychology* (pp. 514–538). Wetton: UCT Press.

Terre Blanche, M., & Seedat, M. (2001). Martian landscapes: The social construction of race and gender at South Africa's National Institute for Personnel Research, 1946–1984. In N. Duncan, A. van Niekerk, C. de la Rey, & M. Seedat (Eds.), *"Race", racism, knowledge production and psychology in South Africa* (pp. 61–82). New York: Nova Science.

University World News (2008, April 27). University to probe racism claims. *University World News.* Retrieved July 17, 2008, from http:www.universityworldnews.com/article.php?story=20080425111908561

Van Ommen, C. (2008). Writing the histories of South Africa Psychology. In C. Van Ommen & D. Painter (Eds.), *Interiors: A history of psychology in South Africa* (pp. 25–62). Pretoria: UNISA Press.

Vaughan, M. (1991). *Curing their ills: Colonial power and African illness.* New York: Polity Press.

Zuckerman, M. (1990). Some dubious premises in research and theory on racial differences. *American Psychologist, 45,* 1297–1303.

16 The research and practice of work and organizational psychology in Brazil

Challenges and perspectives for the new millennium

Maria Cristina Ferreira

Organizational and work psychology has made a great deal of progress over the last decades in different parts of the world and has contributed substantially to a better understanding of the world of work and the improvement of society, organizations, and individuals. One aspect that stands out when consulting the literature is the current lack of consensus in the terminology used to describe this subject.

In the United States and Canada, this discipline is usually called industrial/organizational psychology (Campbell, 2002). In Europe, some designate it as industrial, work, and organizational psychology (Anderson, Herriot, & Hodgkinson, 2001), others as work psychology (Furnham, 2004), and still others as work and organizational psychology (Peiró & Munduate, 1994; Schaper, 2004). In Brazil (Zanelli, Borges-Andrade, & Bastos, 2004), the most commonly used expression is work and organizational psychology (WOP). Nevertheless, these definitions tend to concentrate around one central theme, which is the mutual influences established between the individual and organizations, within the context of the world of work.

Originally, industrial/organizational psychology was a typically American discipline. The demands of the First and Second World Wars were responsible for the initial focus on the selection, placement, and training of large contingents of personnel in a short time, based on the tools and theories in the tradition of individual difference psychology and the measurement of human abilities (Ilgen, 2000).

At the present time, the Society of Industrial and Organizational Psychology (SIOP), a division of the American Psychological Association (APA), recognizes that the field of industrial/organizational psychology covers three different disciplines: personnel psychology, which is dedicated to selection, training, and personnel development; organizational psychology, which is focused on individual, group, and organizational phenomena in the social context of work; and human factors psychology, which is aimed at the analysis of the impact of equipment and tasks on individual performance (Campbell, 2002).

In Brazil, Zanelli and Bastos (2004) consider that WOP can be divided into three different areas: work psychology, focused on the work organization and its effects on the quality of the worker's life and health; personnel management, concerned with the selection, assessment, and development of the organizational members; and organizational psychology, interested in the analysis of micro- and macro-organizational phenomena and their interaction.

The purpose of this chapter is to assess the present situation of work and organizational psychology in Brazil. A brief presentation of the sociopolitical and economic Brazilian scenario in which the subject developed is followed by a description of university education in Brazil, data on the profession, and, finally, a five-year analysis of the development of scientific investigation in the area. In conclusion, it focuses on the challenges and future perspectives in this field of study within the Brazilian context.

The sociopolitical and economic Brazilian context

Located in South America, Brazil is a continent-sized country (more than 8 million km^2). Its population of around 184 million inhabitants is concentrated in urban centres in the south-eastern region of the country. The official language is Portuguese. Brazil is a Federal Republic, with a presidential government; it is composed of 26 states and the capital, Brasília.

The Brazilian economy evolved from an agrarian structure into an industrialized one at the end of the nineteenth century. Throughout the first half of the twentieth century, it was stable and was characterized by solid and sustainable growth (Martins, 2001). In the 1950s, industrial production superseded agricultural production, and this continues to the present day (Chiochetta, Hatakeyama, & Leite, 2004). One of the milestones of this period was the Consolidation of Labour Law (CLT), which was proclaimed in 1943 and continues to be in force even today. It regulates labour relations in Brazil by recognizing the rights of workers in relation to holidays, thirteenth month's salary,[1] and pensions, among others.

At the beginning of the 1960s, the country was marked by political upheavals that culminated in a military coup; the military dictatorship that followed lasted from 1964 to 1985, after which a president was again chosen by popular vote. The initial period of the dictatorship was characterized by an economic recession and efforts by the military to contain the high levels of inflation. Following this, the country went through a period of industrial expansion, which created jobs for unqualified workers and was known as the "Brazilian miracle" (Kinzo, 2001). This period was again followed, towards the end of the military government, by a time of high inflation rates and economic stagnation, with an increase in unemployment rate and a tightening of salaries, a stagnation that continued to accompany the succeeding democratic governments. Between 1986 and 1994, the country went through a long period of instability, four changes of currency, and six economic stabilization plans, of which only the last – the Plano Real – proved to be successful

(Kinzo, 2001). Through the latter the government was able to finally bring inflation under control, and the Brazilian economy began to pick up once again. This period brought the promulgation of the New 1988 Constitution, which promoted important advances in labour rights and in the welfare standards of workers.

From the beginning of the 1990s, the globalization of the world economy, the increase in competition among organizations and countries, the growth in technological innovations, the increase in the level of demands made by the clients, and the drop in interest rates would create repercussions in Brazil, too. The country saw the opening of the Brazilian market to imports, the entry of foreign capital into the industrial sector, and the implanting of new industries that caused substantial alterations to the labour relations and to the requirements in workers' profiles.

As a result of the need to adjust to the constant changes in the market, Brazilian organizations therefore went through a significant restructuring in production, working processes, and management models (Farina & Neves, 2007). For the workers, such changes meant an increase in work load and in their responsibilities, a need for a greater variety of skills, the execution of activities not previously performed, and greater control and supervision of their activities. In addition to this, the level of demands of companies in relation to qualifications rose considerably, leading to a progressive exclusion from the work market of workers with low education and skills (DIEESE, 2001). These practices were also responsible for the gradual loss of permanent employment, a growth in the rate of unemployment, and greater flexibility in labour relations. In summary, the contingent of workers entering the informal work market has become ever greater.

At present, Brazil has a solid economy, which is growing at a moderate rate; the unemployment rate has fallen; inflation is under control; exports have been increasing, as has the Brazilian gross national product. With all this, the country continues to live under huge economic and social inequalities, even though more recent analysis has pointed to a reduction in these inequalities (Ramos, 2007). One of the challenges is, however, to deal with the real drop in workers' salaries, the accelerated increase in the informal work sector, and the negative consequences of the changes in the work organization on the health and well-being of workers (Scopinho, 2002). This is the scenario that Brazilian WO (work and organizational) psychologists face at the beginning of the twenty-first century.

The training in work and organizational psychology in Brazil

Psychology began to spread in Brazil as early as the nineteenth century, particularly in the medical institutions (Antunes, 2007). In this period, psychological themes already appear in doctoral theses defended in medical courses and in books written by doctors, even though psychology had not yet been recognized as an academic subject or a profession (Motta, 2005).

In the early decades of the twentieth century, psychology began to be taught in educational courses for elementary-school teachers, and the first experimental psychological laboratories were created in educational and medical institutions in the cities of Rio de Janeiro and Sao Paulo (Pessotti, 1988). During the 1930s, psychology became a compulsory subject in the curricula of a number of undergraduate courses, such as philosophy, education, and the social sciences (Pereira & Pereira Neto, 2003). During this period, education in psychology was marked by the presence of various visiting foreign professors who gave courses and organized laboratories and by a strong influence from experimental North American psychology, as well as from its French counterpart (Pessotti, 1988).

The first Brazilian university undergraduate courses specifically in psychology were established at the end of the 1950s (Gomes, 2003). Nevertheless, it was only in 1962 that the Federal Education Council established the minimum curriculum for psychology courses, requiring a certain number of basic and professional subjects, a minimum number of internship hours, and a duration of five years. It was at the discretion of each institution to decide what other subjects should be offered.

Throughout the following decades, psychology courses proliferated quickly throughout the country. From a total of 3 in 1962, these increased to 40 by 1974; 73 by 1984; and 111 by 1996 (Gomes, 2003). At present, the number of undergraduate courses in psychology available in Brazil is around 240. Such courses are offered by government (where the courses are free) and private (where the courses have to be paid for) institutions; the majority of them are concentrated in the south-eastern region of the country, the most economically developed region.

Such courses gradually become more and more concerned with the training of professional psychologists (Pessotti, 1988), which led to an absence of education in scientific research in these courses (Gomes, 2003). On the other hand, they favoured a more generalist education – that is, they emphasized a more open range of subjects, to prepare students for the great variety of fields in applied psychology. Due to this, the offer of subjects more directly related to WOP became very limited (Zanelli, 1995). Furthermore, compulsory internships may be carried out in every applied field of psychology, leading to insufficient acquisition of experience during WOP internships (Gomide, 1988). Consequently, undergraduate courses in psychology in Brazil were assessed by professional psychologists as inadequate for the preparation for a good professional practice (Gomide, 1988).

However, with the development of national curriculum directives by the National Council of Education in 2004, changes were implemented in psychology undergraduate courses. Contrary to the minimum curriculum that had for so long been in force in psychology courses, the new directives offer greater autonomy to the institutions in organizing their own curricula. In this way, they require only a set of skills and competencies to be developed during the course, together with a number of hours of internship. The aim is to provide the student with an education that covers professional activities, research, and teaching in psychology. They also stipulate that the aspects to be emphasized throughout the course should be in tune with the characteristics of each institution, although they emphasize the need for the student to have a more generalized education.

Once they have completed the undergraduate course in psychology, students become legally qualified to be professional psychologists. They may work in any field of psychology, including that of WOP, since under Brazilian legislation it is not necessary to hold a graduate degree to be a professional psychologist. However, as the training received at undergraduate level is very general, the majority of professionals look for graduate courses in order to become better prepared to carry out the profession of WO psychologist.

Graduate courses in Brazil are divided into specialization courses, master's degrees, and doctorates. The specialization courses are mainly chosen by those who want to work as psychologists inside organizations. Such courses last, in general, eighteen months and have marked technical characteristics. Those that arouse the greatest interest are focused on human resources or personnel management.

The master's courses and doctorates are, on the other hand, more appropriate for those who want to dedicate themselves to research and teaching in psychology. Such courses appeared in the country at the end of the 1960s and the beginning of the 1970s and have expanded rapidly during the subsequent decades (Gomes, 2003). In 1998, there were 29 graduate programmes in psychology, of which 10 (34%) had research projects associated with WOP. In 2006, the number of programmes had risen to 54, of which 21 (38%) presented projects in WOP, which represents a slow growth in the interest of Brazilian researchers in this field. Those courses have contributed considerably to the dissemination in Brazil of scientific research in psychology in general and in WOP in particular (Gomes, 2003).

The professional practice of psychology in Brazil

The first applications of psychology in the workplace began in the 1920s, with an acceleration through the 1930s and 1940s, accompanying Brazilian industrial expansion and the consequent demand for the application of scientific principles as a way to rationalize the productive process. During this time, some institutions were created to carry out research and the selection of individuals for a variety of professions (Antunes, 2007; Motta, 2005). Such activities were performed by professionals from different areas, who were prepared specifically to carry out such functions, through general courses offered in institutions or through university courses where the curriculum covered topics in psychology.

In 1962, when there were only 15 practising psychologists in Brazil, the profession of psychologist was officially regulated. In 1971 the Federal Council for Psychology was created, with the mission of guiding and supervising an adequate level of performance in the profession. From then on, activities inherent to psychology – including those specific to WOP – were carried out only by those people who had graduated from recently created university psychology courses. By 1972, the country had 5,835 psychologists; by the end of 2007, the total number of psychologists in practice had reached 141,219, spread throughout the country.

In 1988, the Federal Council for Psychology published the first large survey into professional psychology in Brazil (Conselho Federal de Psicologia, 1988). The data showed that the number of psychologists in professional practice at that time was around 58,277, of whom 75% were in only three states – Sao Paulo, Rio de Janeiro, and Minas Gerais (Rosas, Rosas, & Xavier, 1988). Female psychologists represented around 80% of the total, and around 85% of these professionals were between the ages of 22 and 39. These data lead to the conclusion that at that time psychology was typically a young and female profession (Rosas et al., 1988).

Of the 2,042 who participated in this survey and had a professional practice, 23% declared that they had started in the WOP area as their first job – that is, soon after having graduated from their undergraduate course in psychology. The reasons given for this were primarily personal achievement (52%) and salary (30%) (Bastos, 1988). However, 30% of these professionals later abandoned this field; the reason given by more than half (51%) was to go to work as clinical psychologists.

At the time of the survey, 24% of psychologists were in the WOP field. Motives responsible for this, according to Bastos (1988), were factors not associated with the nature of the work itself (such as salary, for example), which caused a high index of dissatisfaction with the job (about 30%). Consequently, a reasonable number (20%) of these professionals expressed their desire to change to another field of applied psychology, which is perfectly understandable if one considers the fact that many of them were there in the first place only because of the financial attractions it offered (Borges-Andrade, 1988).

As for the activities that these psychologists performed, the five cited most frequently were selection, application of tests, recruiting, personnel follow-up, and training. The five least cited were consulting, psycho-diagnosis, professional orientation, supervision of academic internees, and situational diagnosis. However, between the first job and the activities performed at the time of the research, the percentage of more technical activities (recruiting, selection, and training) tended to diminish while the percentage of management, planning, and consulting activities was increasing (Carvalho, 1988).

The most recent survey carried out among Brazilian psychologists was in 2004, involving 1,673 interviewees (IBOPE, 2004). Of this total, 17% worked in the WOP field, in contrast to the 55% who worked in the field of clinical psychology. The WO psychologists worked mainly in companies and government institutions, within the human resources department or with responsibility for technical functions in other departments. From the total of respondents,

42% had no complementary education with their undergraduate course, and another 49% had carried out only some sort of specialization course.

Summing up, studies carried out in Brazil about the activities of psychologists show that the proportion who choose the WOP field has remained stable over the last years, at about 20%. The area has stayed in second place in terms of preference for psychologists, as the professional aim of the great majority is clinical psychology. In general, psychologists have been performing only the most operational functions in organizations. However, there are some signs that this situation is changing, as some professionals have been requested to perform more complex tasks that go beyond the traditional limits of the area (Zanelli, 2002).

Scientific research in work and organizational psychology in Brazil

The expansion of graduate programmes and the promotion of national and international events by scientific societies in Brazil, together with the increase in the number of journals published in the area, has contributed to a great impetus in scientific research in WOP. The role of the graduate programmes has revealed itself in the increasing number of scientific projects, dissertations, and theses concerning various issues in WOP.

National and international congresses in psychology are another indicator of the development of WOP in Brazil. One of the most traditional scientific congresses in psychology is promoted by the Brazilian Psychological Society, which was founded in 1971. Since its foundation, it has been holding annual scientific meetings, where WO researchers have had the opportunity to present their work.

The first scientific Brazilian society specifically dedicated to WOP is the Brazilian Work and Organizational Psychology Association, which was founded in 2001. Its main purpose is to expand and consolidate this area in Brazil, and currently it has about 300 associates. At the first Congress of the society, held in 2004, 174 works were presented, distributed among symposia, oral presentations, and panels; by 2006, this number had already risen to 302, and by 2008 to 357.

Scientific research in WOP in Brazil has been published mainly in Brazilian psychology and business journals. More recently, Brazilian researchers could also count on the *Work and Organizational Psychology Journal*, the only Brazilian journal specializing in the field of WOP.

For the purposes of presenting a recent profile of Brazilian scientific research in WOP, a survey was conducted of the articles published over the last five years (2003 to 2007) in two main business journals (*Journal of Business Management* and *Journal of Contemporary Management*) and two main psychology journals (*Psychology: Theory and Research* and *Psychology: Reflection and Critics*). The *Work and Organizational Psychology Journal* was also consulted.

All the articles published in these five journals during the assigned period were examined. Out of this total, all those that focused on the study of relationships between the individual, work, and organizations were selected for later analysis. However, those that were related to WOP but whose authors were not affiliated to universities or Brazilian research centres were excluded, as were studies that had been carried out with foreign samples.

A total of 91 volumes, containing 948 articles, were examined, and among these, 182 (19%) were related to WOP. As expected, the larger percentage of articles about WOP (90%) were found in the only Brazilian journal dedicated to the field, followed by the two business journals (29 and 20%, respectively) and, lastly, by the two psychology journals, with a few articles (5%) on the subject. These data demonstrate that the *Work and Organizational Psychology Journal* has come to fill an important gap in the WOP area in Brazil.

Proceeding with the analysis of such material, a thematic classification of the 182 articles included in the database was performed, using a system of nine categories. The criteria for choosing these were that they were not too extensive yet could still encompass the multiplicity of themes that may be included in the WOP field. The most frequent categories were management, leadership, and power (17%), organizational behaviour (16%), and organizational learning (15%). The intermediate categories were consumer behaviour (13%), organizational processes, structures, and politics (13%), the individual and her/his work (10%), and health and quality of life in organizations (8%). The least frequent were work motivation (4%) and a varied category that included topics such as ergonomics and personnel recruitment and selection (also 4%).

Following the analysis, the articles were classified in accordance with the nature of the study. This showed that the largest majority (85%) was empirical, involving data collection and analysis aimed at carrying out studies of some phenomenon or proving hypotheses and theoretical models. The other 15% were theoretical articles characterized by reviews or critiques of concepts, models, and theories. Among these theoretical articles, a few studies proposing new theoretical models were also found.

Those articles classified as empirical were then analysed on the basis of the type of sample, instrument, and data analysis used. Concerning the sample type, the largest number were surveys conducted in various organizations (39%), followed by surveys carried out in single organizations (25%) and case studies involving a descriptive and in-depth analysis of various phenomena (22%). The minority were related to investigations supported by documental consultation (3%) and to researches carried out in the form of surveys on the population as a whole, such as with students, consumers, and so on (1%).

Regarding the type of data collection instruments, the largest number of empirical studies analysed used scales or questionnaires (59%) or interviews (31%). Far fewer worked with secondary data (7%) or observations (3%). Finally, concerning the type of data analysis, the most frequent ones were quantitative analyses using inferential complex statistics (37%) and qualitative analyses (33%), and the least frequent were quantitative techniques using descriptive statistics (11%), inferential simple statistics (10%), and structural equation modelling (9%). In synthesis, the recent Brazilian WOP scientific research is mainly characterized by empirical studies, conducted through surveys, with samples from different organizations and through the use of quantitative data-analysis techniques, which is consistent with the tendency observed in international journals of the area.

Conclusions

The social and economic changes over the last decades have brought about considerable changes in the world of work and the organizations in Brazil, with direct repercussions on the work force, the management models, and organizational structures. Such changes have implied significant modifications in the fields of training, professional practice, and scientific research in WOP in Brazil.

With regard to the undergraduate training of WO psychologists, university courses have been characterized by a huge gap between theory and practice, which impairs students' acquisition of the necessary competencies for an adequate professional performance; consequently, they seek graduate courses to complement their education. However, this situation has shown signs of improvement, as a result of recent reforms in the curricula of psychology courses. The challenges for the near future are, therefore, to implement these changes, in order to have Brazilian psychologists better prepared to face the challenges of the world of work and organizations in this millennium.

Concerning graduate training, there are currently few people with doctorates in WOP, although the number has been progressively increasing. The challenges for the future are, then, to increase the number, since such a growth will, in the medium term, most probably be reflected in the training of future psychologists and in professional practice in WOP. First, educational institutions will then be able to count on professors who are better prepared to teach the specific subjects associated with WOP. Second, as some of those with master's degrees and doctorates enter the work market, especially government institutions, they will be able to perform not only technical activities but also scientific research and reflective criticism of knowledge, qualities developed mainly in the master's and doctorate programmes.

Concerning the practice of WOP in Brazil, a change can be seen in the primarily technical functions carried out in the past, which had been restricted mainly to personnel selection, training, and development. The challenge is, then, to try to extend more and more the traditional limits of the profession, toward a more diversified performance. This will involve the use of multidisciplinary teams to develop managerial activities, strategic planning, and the formulation of policies, as well as the expansion of the work into many different sectors, such as government, service, union, and third-sector organizations.

It is imperative, therefore, that WO psychologists become ever more aware of the social role that they can play and that they prepare themselves adequately to face the new challenges of the workplace. In other words, the expansion of the profession should be toward a professional practice based on an integrated view of the individual, work, and organization. This can contribute to an improvement in the health, well-being, and quality of life of the members of organizations, consequently providing relevant services to society as a whole.

With regard to scientific research, we have seen that Brazilian studies have covered a great variety of topics and are aligned with the recent international research in WOP. Themes such as organizational culture and climate, work-related stress, and learning within the organizations, which have long been studied by North American and European researchers, are also of interest to Brazilian researchers. However, other themes in the international WOP research agenda are still almost absent from Brazilian investigations. The challenge is, then, to expand Brazilian research and incorporate themes such as the impact on workers' health and well-being of new forms of working contract (part-time work, short-term contracts, and contracts by project). Other examples include studies into the perspective of positive organizational psychology, which have, since the beginning of the decade, been increasingly the focus of international research.

On the other hand, Brazilian WOP studies on the basis of original proposals are still scarce – many constitute merely replications of relationships investigated earlier in foreign studies. In addition, these studies do not always apply to the Brazilian reality. The challenges that face national researchers are, then, to develop more original theoretical or empirical studies, even if these are derived from theories and constructs consolidated abroad.

Furthermore, it is imperative to build an ethno-psychological knowledge base specifically associated to the Brazilian reality. The influence of the richness and diversification of Brazilian culture on different organizational processes and behaviours has so far been approached in only a few studies, although such cultural aspects are constantly invoked as an explanation for certain results. Empirical verification of such statements is urgently needed, and it may contribute to the progressive building of a true Brazilian theoretical and practical knowledge base.

It is worth mentioning also that few Brazilian studies in WOP are focused on the development of new technologies on a scientific basis, a tendency seen not only in Brazil but also in the international context. This is surprising, if one considers that WOP is a truly applied science. A reversal of this situation is, therefore, another challenge for this millennium: Brazilian investigators should make efforts to develop new technologies in WOP, in order to provide psychologists with the instruments, strategies, and intervention models necessary to place their professional practice on a stronger basis.

In summary, Brazilian WOP has made considerable progress in the last few decades and strides towards its true consolidation as a scientific field of inquiry, training, and professional application. Some roads still need to be crossed to enable this area in our country to answer to the social and professional demands of Brazilian organizations, as well as in the international scientific scenario, within this twenty-first century.

Note

1 The thirteenth salary is an extra month's salary payable annually in December to all registered employees of companies in Brazil. If the employee has worked for the full year, it is paid in full, otherwise it is pro rata at 1/12 of the respective monthly salary for each month worked.

References

Anderson, N., Herriot, P., & Hodgkinson, G. P. (2001). The practitioner researcher divide in industrial, work and organizational (IWO) psychology: Where are we now, and where do we go from here? *Journal of Occupational and Organizational Psychology*, 74, 391–411.

Antunes, M. A. M. A. (2007). *A psicologia no Brasil: Leitura histórica sobre sua constituição* [Brazilian psychology: A history of its formation] (5th edition). São Paulo: Educ.

Bastos, A. V. (1988). Áreas de atuação: Em questão o nosso modelo de profissional [Fields of practice: Our professional model under debate]. In Conselho Federal de Psicologia (Ed.), *Quem é o psicólogo brasileiro?*) [Who is the Brazilian psychologist?] (pp. 163 193). São Paulo: EDICON.

Borges-Andrade, J. E. (1988). A avaliação do exercício profissional [Assessment of professional practice]. In Conselho Federal de Psicologia (Ed.), *Quem é o psicólogo brasileiro?* [Who is the Brazilian psychologist?] (pp. 252–272). São Paulo: EDICON.

Campbell, W. J. (2002). Consideration of consulting/organizational educational principles as they relate to the practice of industrial-organizational psychology and The Society for Industrial and Organizational Psychology's education and training guidelines. *Consulting Psychology Journal: Practice and Research, 54*, 261 274.

Carvalho, A. A. (1988). Atuação psicológica: Uma análise das atividades desempenhadas pelos psicólogos [Psychological practice: An analysis of the activities performed by psychologists]. In Conselho Federal de Psicologia (Ed.), *Quem é o psicólogo brasileiro?* [Who is the Brazilian psychologist?] (pp. 217–235). São Paulo: EDICON.

Chiochetta, J. C., Hatakeyama, K., & Leite, M. L. (2004). *Evolução histórica da indústria brasileira: Desafios, oportunidades e formas de gestão* [Historical evolution of Brazilian industry: Challenges, opportunities, and management models]. In Congresso Brasileiro do Ensino de Engenharia-COBENGE2004 [Brazilian Congress of Engineering Teaching]. Brasília: COBENGE. Retrieved June 28, 2008, from http://www.pg.cefetpr.br/ppgep/Ebook/ARTIGOS/17.pdf

Conselho Federal de Psicologia (1988). *Quem é o psicólogo brasileiro?* [Who is the Brazilian psychologist?]. São Paulo: EDICON.

DIEESE – Departamento Intersindical de Estatística e Estudos Sócio-Econômicos (2001). *Mercado de trabalho no Brasil* [The work market in Brasil]. São Paulo: Author. Retrieved June 28, 2008, from http://www.dieese.org.br/esp/mercadodetrabalho.pdf

Farina, A. S., & Neves, T. F. S. (2007). Formas de lidar com o desemprego: Possibilidades e limites de um projeto de atuação em psicologia social do trabalho [Ways of coping with unemployment: Possibilities and limits of a project concerning the social psychology of work]. *Cadernos de Psicologia Social do Trabalho, 10,* 21–36.

Furnham, A. (2004). The future (and past) of work psychology and organizational behaviour: A personal view. *Management Revue, 15,* 420–436.

Gomes, W. B. (2003). *Pesquisa e prática em psicologia no Brasil* [Research and practice in Brazilian psychology]. Retrieved June 28, 2008, from http://www.ufrgs.br/mudeupsi/ppnb.htm

Gomide, P. I. C. (1988). A formação acadêmica: Onde residem suas deficiências? [Academic training: Where is it deficient?]. In Conselho Federal de Psicologia (Ed.), *Quem é o psicólogo brasileiro?* [Who is the Brazilian psychologist?] (pp. 69–85). São Paulo: EDICON.

IBOPE Opinião (2004). *Pesquisa de opinião com psicólogos inscritos no Conselho Federal de Psicologia* [Opinion survey with psychologists enrolled in Federal Council of Psychologists]. Retrieved June 28, 2008, from http://www.po.org.br/pol/export/sites/default/pol/publicacoesDocumentos/Pesquisa_IBOPE.pdf

Ilgen, D. R. (2000). Industrial and organizational psychology: Theories and methods of study. In A. E. Kazdin (Ed.), *Encyclopedia of psychology* (Vol. 4, pp. 255–258). New York: APA.

Kinzo, M. D. (2001). A democratização brasileira [The Brazilian democratization]. *São Paulo em Perspectiva, 15,* 3–12.

Martins, M. A. C. (2001). *Regimes constitucionais, crescimento e estagnação na economia brasileira: 1947–1999* [Constitutional regime, growth, and stagnation in the Brazilian economy: 1947–1999]. Brasília: Universidade de Brasília. Retrieved June 28, 2008, from http://www.aeconomiadobrasil.com.br/artigo.php?artigo=87

Motta, J. M. C. (2005). *A psicologia e o mundo do trabalho no Brasil: Relações, história e memória* [Psychology and the world of work in Brazil: Relationships, history, and memory]. São Paulo: Ágora.

Peiró, J. M., & Munduate, L. (1994). Work and organisational psychology in Spain. *Applied Psychology: An International Review, 43,* 231–274.

Pereira, F. M., & Pereira Neto, A. (2003). O psicólogo no Brasil: Notas sobre seu processo de profissionalização [The psychologist in Brazil: Notes on his professionalization]. *Psicologia em Estudo, 8,* 19–27.

Pessotti, I. (1988). Notas para uma história da psicologia brasileira [Notes on the history of Brazilian psychology]. In Conselho Federal de Psicologia (Ed.), *Quem é o psicólogo brasileiro?* [Who is the Brazilian psychologist?] (pp. 17–31). São Paulo: EDICON.

Ramos, L. (2007). A desigualdade de rendimentos do trabalho no período pós-real: O papel da escolaridade e do desemprego [The inequality in employment salary during the post-real period: The role of unemployment and schooling]. *Economia Aplicada, 11,* 281–301.

Rosas, P., Rosas, A., & Xavier, I. B. (1988). Quantos e quem somos [How many and who are we?]. In Conselho Federal de Psicologia (Ed.), *Quem é o psicólogo brasileiro?* [Who is the Brazilian psychologist?] (pp. 32–48). São Paulo: EDICON.

Schaper, N. (2004). Theoretical substantiation of human resource management from the perspective of work and organisational psychology. *Management Revue, 15,* 192–200.

Scopinho, R. A. (2002). Privatização, reestruturação e mudanças nas condições de trabalho: O caso do setor de energia elétrica [Privatization, restructuring, and changes in working conditions: The case of the power sector]. *Cadernos de Psicologia Social e do Trabalho*, 5, 19–36.

Zanelli, J. C. (1995). Formação e atuação do psicólogo organizacional: Uma revisão de literatura [The training and practice of the organizational psychologist: A literature review]. *Temas em Psicologia*, 1, 95–107.

Zanelli, J. C. (2002). *O psicólogo nas organizações de trabalho* [The psychologist in working organizations]. Porto Alegre: Artmed.

Zanelli, J. C., & Bastos, A. V. (2004). Inserção profissional do psicólogo em organizações e no trabalho [Professional practice of psychologist in work and organizations]. In J. C. Zanelli, J. E. Borges-Andrade, & A. V. Bastos (Eds.), *Psicologia, organizações e trabalho no Brasil* [Work, organizations, and psychology in Brazil] (pp. 466 491). São Paulo: Artmed.

Zanelli, J. C., Borges-Andrade, J. E., & Bastos, A. V. (2004). *Psicologia, organizações e trabalho no Brasil* [Work, organizations, and psychology in Brazil]. São Paulo: Artmed.

17 Paternalistic leadership in the Chinese contexts

A full-cycle indigenous approach

Bor-Shiuan Cheng and Yi-Cheng Lin

Introduction

As globalization has fostered the concept of multiculturalism, the relationship between culture and organizational behavior has become increasingly valued. However, intense debates on how to approach the relationship between culture and organizational behavior have restricted research progress in this field. For example, some scholars claim that research should be based on the results of existing studies – that is, tailored to the findings of the research, which is mainly done in North America, and applied to different cultural contexts in order to develop theories of generalized organizational behavior (Whetten, 2009). Others think that theories with rich cultural meanings can only be constructed by examining the indigenous culture, with the aim of studying local cultural characteristics and their relationship to organizational behavior (Barney & Zhang, 2009). The former is called an ethnic approach or outsider's view, and the latter the endemic approach, or insider's view. For organizational studies, most of the research over the past two decades has generally been based on the ethnic approach to intercultural comparisons. Only limited research has been done on the basis of the endemic approach. Therefore, our current knowledge and insights regarding organizational behavior in different cultural contexts appear somewhat limited (Gelfand, Erez, & Aycan, 2007). The same conclusion can also be applied to the Chinese research community, where most of the researchers use mainstream theories developed in North America rather than probing into unique organizational behavior in a Chinese context (H. Y. Cheng, 2007; Huang, 2007).

Why do current researchers in the Chinese societies tend to adapt existing theories but ignore the indigenous organizational behavior in certain cultural contexts? Although most researchers are trained in North America at institutions that publish articles in the Western journals or outlets and the cross-cultural approach is easy to follow, the most important reason is a lack of methodological guidance about how to develop a Chinese theory of organizational behavior (Cheng, Wang, & Huang, 2009).

The purpose of this study is to use our experience in Chinese indigenous organizational behavior studies in the past 15 years to demonstrate the research methodology and to inspire more organizational studies to be conducted in a Chinese cultural context. We chose a study of paternalistic leadership as an example to describe how indigenous organizational behavior is explored; then, the research logic – a full-cycle indigenous research approach – is explained; finally, the implication of the approach on Chinese organizational behavior in the global age is discussed.

Paternalistic leadership: A brief review

Leadership has long been a critical research subject in organizational behavior studies, most of which were conducted in North America (Yukl, 1998). Before the 1980s, scholars suggested that research results in North America could be generalized to other regions with different cultures. They followed the nomothetic approach, which considers universal leadership a quality that is not influenced by culture, region, or nation (House, Wright, & Aditya, 1997). However, after the 1980s, the idea of universal leadership was challenged by many practitioners and researchers (Chemers, 1993; Cox, 1993). They suggested that leadership might be universal in terms of a kind of social process but that the content of leadership was affected by the culture. Different cultures would lead to different contents, styles, and effectiveness of leadership (Chemers, 1993; Hofstede, 1980). In most situations, leadership styles may not reveal leaders' personal will but will reflect the culture and tradition of the societies they are in (Hofstede, 1980, 1994). Moreover, the effectiveness of leadership would also be influenced by local social context (Farh & Cheng, 2000).

Cultural psychologists have found Chinese culture, with its characteristics of collectivism and "higher power distance," very different from North American or Anglo-Saxon cultures (Hofstede, 1980). Moreover, the performance of the Asian economy controlled by the Chinese (including Hong Kong, Singapore, Taiwan, many Southeast Asian nations, and China) is outstanding. Managerial philosophy and practices in Chinese firms and organizations have therefore become quite interesting to many researchers (Cheng, 1995a; Redding, 1990; Whitley, 1992). These researchers, though not guided by any particular research trend, adopted an indigenous approach in exploring leadership in Chinese family businesses (CFBs) in Hong Kong, Indonesia, Singapore, and Taiwan (Cheng, 1995a; Redding, 1990) and suggested that top leaders in Chinese enterprises revealed significant and definite characteristics that could be called a paternalistic leadership style. They referred to this leadership style as being similar to the patriarchal style. The leaders have specific and strong authority, but consideration for their subordinates and moral leadership are also involved (Cheng, 1995a; Farh & Cheng, 2000; Westwood & Chan, 1992). The leadership style was found not only in CFBs, but also in non-CFB organizations and governmental institutions in Asian countries (Pye, 1981, 1985).

With the introduction of the paternalistic leadership concept, issues related to paternalistic leadership have become more and more valued by Chinese and Western leadership researchers. Farh and Cheng (2000) generalized the related studies on Chinese business leadership conducted by Silin (1976), Redding (1990), Westwood (1997), and Cheng (1995a), and then analyzed the historical and cultural foundations of paternalistic leadership. Based on the assumption that Chinese leadership is embedded in the cultural traditions of Confucianism and Legalism, they further suggested that it involves three critical elements: authoritarian, benevolent, and moral leadership. They also developed a conceptual framework of leader behavior and subordinate responses to elaborate the relationship between paternalistic leadership and subordinates' responses of reverence, obedience, gratitude, and identification. In addition to past studies on a dual model of paternalistic leadership and the framework of the tripartite model, Cheng, Chou, and Farh (2000) developed a measurement tool of paternalistic leadership that validated its constructs and made further exploration on related issues possible. The researchers launched a series of quantitative studies that not only studied the effectiveness of paternalistic leadership by exploring the relationships between the leadership characteristics of benevolence, authoritarianism, moral leadership, and the subordinate response, but also investigated possible mediating and moderating effects between paternalistic leadership and subordinate effectiveness.

Proposal of the concept

The Chinese researcher who first targeted Chinese indigenous leadership studies without applying a Western leadership model was B. S. Cheng, who studied familism and leadership (Cheng, 1991). His idea was based on his personal experiences in a Chinese family enterprise, as well as Silin's (1976) case study on a large-scale Taiwanese firm, Weber's (1968) analysis of domination in human society, and Hamilton's (1990) sharp observations on the patriarchal authority in Chinese society.

At the end of the 1980s, in order to investigate the leadership in a patriarchal system, Cheng (1995a) explored the leadership of Taiwanese CEOs and managers of family enterprises through case-study research, participant observation, and a clinician approach. His findings concerning Chinese supervisors' leadership dimension were similar to Silin's (1976) and Redding's (1990) observations. Moreover, between 1993 and 1994, he interviewed 18 heads of private enterprises and 24 high-ranking supervisors in Taiwan, confirmed that paternalistic leadership prevailed in Taiwanese firms, and then named the style paternalistic leadership. The value of Cheng's study is that with the use of dyadic relationships as units of analysis, a detailed quantitative description of leadership behavior and subordinate response is provided, as well as a dual model of paternalistic leadership (Farh & Cheng, 2000).

In short, Cheng proposed the concept of paternalistic leadership and a dynamic relationship between leaders and subordinate response; he also introduced a dual model including benevolence and authoritarianism to allow us to understand the content of paternalistic leadership. Cheng did not investigate moral leadership in related studies; however, by studying his research carefully (Cheng, 1995a, 1996), it can be found that moral leadership was present in benevolent leadership, and benevolent leadership also included integrity and modeling. The reason for this is that in Chinese society, benevolence shown by the upper level would tend to be treated as morality by the lower level. Thus, it is difficult to separate moral leadership from benevolence in Cheng's studies.

Establishing the tripartite model

After synthesizing Silin's (1976) on-site observations of the leader of a large-scale enterprise in Taiwan, Redding's (1990) interview and study on the leadership of CFBs, Westwood's (1997) theoretical analysis of Chinese corporate leadership in Southeast Asia, and Cheng's (1995a, 1995b, 2005) observations, interviews, and analysis of the leaders of several private Taiwanese enterprises, Farh and Cheng (2000) proposed the tripartite model of paternalistic leadership, which suggests that paternalistic leadership contains three critical elements: authoritarian leadership, benevolent leadership, and moral leadership. Authoritarianism in leadership was found to be similar to authoritarianism as defined by Cheng (1995a, 1996), meaning that leaders emphasized that their authority could not be challenged, and subordinates were strictly controlled and required to obey totally. Benevolent leadership was found to be related to benevolence as proposed by Cheng (1995a), indicating that leaders had individualized, complete, and long-term care for subordinates' welfare. As to moral leadership, leaders must show higher personal integrity to win subordinates' respect; in particular, modeling and being just (not abusing power to gain private profits) were the most significant traits.

Farh and Cheng (2000) defined paternalistic leadership as: "a father-like leadership style in which clear and strong authority is combined with concern, considerateness, and elements of moral leadership" (Farh & Cheng, 2000, p. 94). They proposed that the tripartite model of paternalistic leadership was based on complementary roles and interaction between leaders and subordinates; then they constructed the initial model of paternalistic leadership and subordinates' psychological responses. Farh and Cheng indicated that with regard to moral leadership, subordinates would follow the leaders and identify with them; with regard to authoritarian leadership, subordinates would express reverence and obedience; as to benevolent leadership, subordinates would be grateful and wish to repay their leaders with loyalty. The cultural foundation of this framework is based on the assumption of the in-depth influence of the *zun-zun* (respect for superiors) principle or "higher power distance" in Chinese culture on leadership. The tripartite model of paternalistic leadership is shown in Figure 17.1.

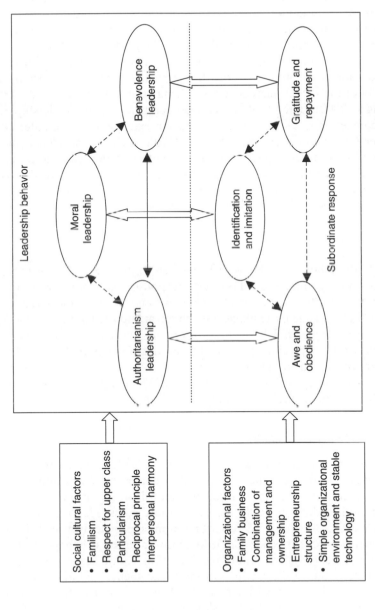

Figure 17.1 Tripartite model of paternalistic leadership. Adapted from J. L. Farh & B. S. Cheng, A cultural analysis of paternalistic leadership in Chinese organizations. In A. S. Tsui & J. T. Li (Eds), *Management and organizations in China* (London: Macmillan, 2000), pp. 94–127.

Measurement development

According to the theory of concept evolution, a proposed new concept should be examined through legitimation, which means that researchers not only have to explain the definition and the importance of the new concept to the academic community or to researchers, but they should also propose feasible research methods and use quantitative techniques to illustrate that the concept can be applied to the real world (Thagard, 1992). Therefore, it is critical to construct a measurement of paternalistic leadership with reliability and validity in order to verify the tripartite model of paternalistic leadership and the related factors. Thus, Cheng et al. (2000) extended Farh and Cheng's (2000) analysis of the concept of paternalistic leadership to investigate benevolent, moral, and authoritarian leadership within paternalistic leadership. They modified Cheng's (1996) dual (benevolence and authoritarianism) model questionnaire of paternalistic leadership and added moral leadership items to establish a new scale to measure the tripartite model of paternalistic leadership. The new scale revealed satisfying reliability and validity from samples of Taiwanese corporations and educational institutions. It led to a series of empirical studies of paternalistic leadership, such as:

1   What is the relationship between benevolent, moral, and authoritarian leadership styles and the subordinate response? Are there interaction effects between the three leadership elements and the outcome variables?
2   What effect does the psychological mechanism and mediating process of paternalistic leadership have on subordinate effectiveness? Compared with previous leadership models such as transformational leadership, what are the incremental validity and effects of paternalistic leadership?
3   What is the external validity of paternalistic leadership? What contextual factors moderate the effect of paternalistic leadership?

Validation on the tripartite model

According to the tripartite model of paternalistic leadership, authoritarian leadership would lead to a higher level of subordinates' reverence and obedience; benevolent leadership would result in subordinates' gratitude and wish to repay; moral leadership would increase subordinates' identification and imitation. After investigating 543 subordinates in 60 private firms in Taiwan, the researchers found that benevolent leadership led to the strongest effect on gratitude, repayment, identification, and imitation; moral leadership led to the greatest effect on obedience. In addition, benevolence and authoritarian leadership revealed a positive interaction effect on subordinate response; moral and authoritarian leadership showed a negative interaction effect. There was no interaction effect between benevolent and moral leadership (Cheng, Chou, Huang, Wu, & Farh, 2004). The positive interaction effect of benevolence and authoritarian leadership showed that this kind of leadership was better than leadership styles with a high level of benevolence and a low level of authoritarianism, a high level of authoritarianism and a low level of benevolence, and low levels of both benevolence and authoritarianism. In terms of the negative interaction effect of moral and authoritarian leadership on subordinate response it was found that the effect of strongly moral and authoritarian leadership was not necessarily better than that of a strongly moral but less authoritarian one. The results can be understood from traditional Chinese political reality. When officers with integrity and justice use authoritarianism to govern people, they punish those violating the laws severely, regardless of the reasons and relationship. Thus, the lower level or subordinates regard them as indifferent, and the interpersonal distance between subordinates and leaders is increased (Pye, 1985).

In addition, the study sampled 248 dyads in 57 firms in Beijing and also showed that benevolent, moral, and authoritarian leadership had a positive effect on subordinate response (Cheng, Chou, Huang, Farh, & Peng, 2003). In terms of subordinates' attitudes, moral leadership had the greatest influence. As to the interactive effect of benevolent, moral, and authoritarian leadership, two aspects were consistent with the sample in Taiwan: there was a positive interactive effect between benevolence and authoritarian leadership and a negative interactive effect between moral and authoritarian leadership.

The above two studies only partly validated the tripartite model of paternalistic leadership and did not investigate the validity of a general model. To validate an overall model, Farh, Cheng, Chou, and Chu (2006) used 292 employees as participants and adopted structural equation modeling (SEM) to examine the fitness of the tripartite model (Figure 17.2) in private firms in Suzhou, China. They found that the fitness index was over the criterion and most of the paths in the tripartite model were validated in the SEM. Authoritarian leadership revealed indirect and negative effects on supervision satisfaction and organizational commitment that resulted from reverence and fear; authoritarian leadership also revealed weak, indirect, and positive effects on obedience caused by fear. The influence of moral leadership on obedience, supervision satisfaction, and organizational commitment came about through identification and imitation. Finally, the positive effect of benevolent leadership on obedience was mediated by gratitude and the wish to repay; moreover, benevolent leadership also had indirect and positive effects on supervision satisfaction and organizational commitment; the effects were mediated by gratitude, identification, and imitation.

The research result not only confirmed past research findings with regard to paternalistic leadership and its effectiveness, but it also examined further the overall model of the tripartite model of paternalistic leadership. The researchers found that the three elements of paternalistic leadership would influence subordinates' work attitude through reverence and fear, gratitude and the wish to repay, as well as identification and imitation.

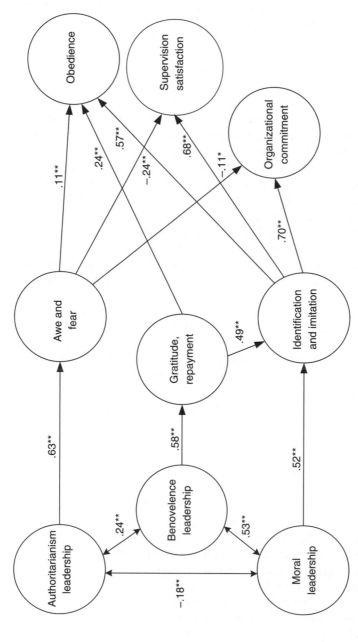

Figure 17.2 Validation on the tripartite model of paternalistic leadership (*p < .05; **p < .01; unimportant paths were omitted in the figure). Adapted from J. L. Farh, B. S. Cheng, L. F. Chou, & X. P. Chu, Authority and benevolence: Employees' response to paternalistic leadership in China. In A. S. Tsui, Y. Bian, & L. Cheng (Eds.), *China's domestic private firms: Multidisciplinary perspectives on management and performance* (Armonk, NY: M. E. Sharpe, 2006), pp. 230–260.

Comparison with transformational leadership

In the theory of conceptual evolution, a new concept must be unique and able to elaborate aspects that could not be explained by previous concepts. Thus, to compare the model of paternalistic leadership with previous leadership concepts, it is necessary to use transformational leadership to clarify the unique effect of paternalistic leadership.

Cheng and his colleagues conducted studies regarding the unique effect of paternalistic leadership in industrial and educational organizations in Taiwan and China. The research results showed that after controlling for transformational leadership in firms in Taiwan and China, paternalistic leadership still revealed significant and unique effects on the subordinate responses and attitudes. With regard to gratitude and the wish to repay, sacrifice for supervisor, supervision satisfaction, and organizational commitment, the unique effects of paternalistic leadership were stronger than for transformational leadership; as to identification and imitation, as well as subordinates' job satisfaction, the unique effect of transformational leadership was more significant; in terms of obedience, the influences of paternalistic leadership and transformational leadership were the same (Cheng et al., 2004). In a study on educational institutions in Taiwan, after controlling for transformational leadership, paternalistic leadership revealed unique and significant effects on the quality of supervisor–subordinate relationships and subordinate performance (Cheng, Shieh, & Chou, 2002b).

Moderators of paternalistic leadership and outcomes

Many leadership researchers emphasize that there is no single leadership style that can be applied to all scenarios in the same cultural context (Lord, Brown, Harvey, & Hall, 2001). Thus, the effects of paternalistic leadership in Chinese organizations could be different because of different contextual factors. Contextual factors in past studies have included subordinates' authority orientation, subordinates' dependence on the leaders, and the leaders' competence.

In terms of *subordinates' authority orientation*, Cheng et al. (2004) reviewed past studies and found that the modernization of Chinese society has had a significant impact on the foundations of the orientation of Chinese authority. Today, obedience to authority is not necessarily the shared value of all Chinese; different attitudes of subordinates' obedience to authority might be a critical moderator between organizational behavior and outcomes (Farh, Earley, & Lin, 1997; Farh, Leung, & Law, 1998). Researchers concluded that for subordinates with different authority orientations, paternalistic leadership affected the subordinate response in different ways. If subordinates were less orientated toward authority, they were less likely to accept authoritarian leadership, or the influence of authoritarian leadership might be less. As the functions of moral and benevolent leadership are similar to traditional society, the moderating effect of authority orientation might not be that significant. Based on this conclusion, researchers conducted an empirical study to test the hypothesis with the help of participants from Taiwan and China, respectively. The results showed that the moderating effect of subordinates' authority orientation in paternalistic leadership effectiveness was in accordance with the hypothesis.

As to *subordinates' dependence*, Hamilton (1990) suggested that Chinese leaders' authority was based on subordinates' dependence. Thus, subordinates' dependence on supervisors might moderate the effect on outcomes of paternalistic leadership (Cheng, 1995a). Subordinates who are strongly dependent on leaders accept very authoritarian leaders and do the work assigned by supervisors; subordinates with strong need for independence, on the contrary, prefer to finish the work by themselves and don't want leaders' interference. Therefore, for subordinates with a low level of dependence, highly authoritarian leaders would usually reduce the subordinates' effectiveness, whereas less authoritarian leaders may increase subordinates' work effectiveness and satisfaction. The hypotheses were also supported by data from Taiwan and China. When subordinates relied more on supervisors, the effect of authoritarian leadership on subordinates' supervision satisfaction, loyalty towards supervisors, and job performance are found to be stronger (Chou, Cheng, & Jen, 2005).

With regard to *leaders' competence*, Farh and Cheng (2000) argued that the effect of paternalistic leadership could be moderated by leaders' competence. In other words, authoritarian leadership methods by a competent supervisor tended to be accepted by subordinates. As to benevolent leadership, researchers concluded that if supervisors were more competent, then the influence of benevolent leadership on subordinate effectiveness was more significant. With regard to moral leadership, if supervisors showed more moral leadership, then the effects of supervisors' talents on effectiveness would be relatively insignificant. Leaders' competence revealed a positive moderating effect on authoritarian leadership, benevolent leadership, and subordinate effectiveness, but a negative mediating effect on moral leadership and subordinate effectiveness (Chou et al., 2005).

In summary, as a concept of Chinese indigenous organizational behavior, paternalistic leadership has been valued by many researchers, and many rich empirical studies can be found (Cheng, Farh, & Chou, 2006; Pellegrini & Scandura, 2008). Based on our review of the literature on paternalistic leadership in the Chinese context, we find that paternalistic leadership prevails in the greater China region, and Chinese, Taiwanese, and overseas Chinese employees still place a high value on it. The results of empirical studies provide evidence of construct and internal and external validity for the tripartite model of paternalistic leadership.

A full-cycle indigenous research approach

As a new area of leadership research, paternalistic leadership has drawn more and more attention, though some important issues, such as how to conduct paternalistic leadership research and related methodology, are often neglected. Therefore, we introduce the approach to be applied further to the paternalistic leadership studies. We consider it a feasible way to study Chinese indigenous organizational behavior.

Taking a series of studies of paternalistic leadership as examples, some researchers first conducted observation studies and cultural analyses and then proposed an initial model to develop instruments for empirical validation. They gradually modified the theoretical model to make it more precise. The method is obviously different from traditional organizational behavior studies. In most studies, theory-building and theory-testing were separated, and researchers have different views and positions (Chatman & Flynn, 2005).

According to the experience acquired through the paternalistic leadership studies and the suggestions of a few organizational scientists, such as Chatman and Flynn (2005), we propose a full-cycle indigenous research approach to study Chinese indigenous organizational behavior. The essence of the research cycle upon the phenomenon is first introduced, followed, subsequently, by both inductive and deductive methods; researchers then further deepen the research framework and concept by constructing a theoretical model with construct and internal and external validity. Moreover, we suggest that only one researcher or one research team rather than several different research groups should conduct the entire research process. Thus, researchers can fully understand the model and possibly find a precise and sophisticated theory that complies with Chinese organizational behavior in reality. In the following, the processes of the full-cycle indigenous research approach are discussed further. The process is shown in Figure 17.3.

Phase 1: From personal experience to concept construction

The inspiration for the concept of paternalistic leadership came when Cheng was a human resources and organizational consultant for an owner in a shoe factory in Taiwan. Cheng systematically observed the leadership style of the CEO. He found that what he had learned in the factory over the course of four years did not match the idea of current Western leadership theory; instead, it showed characteristics of Chinese familism and met Weber's concept of traditional domination. Cheng proposed a conceptual framework involving familism, interpersonal values, and leadership, indicating that paternalistic authority and the relation (or *guanxi*) differences are two critical cultural values that influence Chinese leadership (Cheng, 1991).

As Cialdini (1980) suggested, systematic personal observation and experience tend to contribute to future theoretical insights and breakthrough. With the consulting experience in the shoe factory, Cheng changed "believing

1. Personal experience
   • Consulting experience in a shoe factory (Cheng, 1991, 1992)

   Developing the initial concept

2. Field observation
   • Clinician observation on CEO of a family business enterprise (Cheng, 1995a)
   • Multiple cases studies on large-scale family business enterprises (Cheng, 1995b)

   Confirming the prevalence of the phenomenon

3. Cultural analysis and instrument development
   • Cultural analysis and literature review (Farh & Cheng, 2000)
   • Instrument development (Cheng, Chou, & Farh, 2000)

   Establishing a theoretical framework and developing measurements

4. Validating the internal and external logic relation of the theories
   • Validation of the tripartite model (Cheng, Chou, Huang, Wu, & Farh, 2004; Farh, Cheng, Chou, & Chu, 2006)
   • Comparison with transformational leadership (Cheng, Shieh, & Chou, 2002b)
   • Mediating mechanisms (Farh, Cheng, Chou, & Chu, 2006; Wu, Hsu, & Cheng, 2002)
   • Moderating factors (Chou, Cheng, & Jen, 2005)

   Strengthening the internal and external validity of the theories (cause/effect and the boundary)

5. Theory refinement and application
   • Generalizability study in different organizations, regions, and nations (Chou, Cheng, & Jiang, 2008; Cheng, Chou, Huang, Farh, & Peng, 2003; Cheng, Huang, & Chou, 2002a)
   • Educational training
   • Action research

   Strengthening the generalizability and solidity of the theories

Figure 17.3 A full-cycle indigenous research approach to paternalistic leadership.

is seeing" into "seeing is believing" and acquired a different perspective on leadership. Moreover, he also found that this kind of leadership was critical in Chinese organizations and significantly affected behavior in organizations (Cheng, 2007). However, he still could not fully discover the uniqueness of this kind of leadership. What was the prevalence in Chinese organizations? What were the basic concepts and research framework? He conducted two qualitative case studies to search for the answers.

Phase 2: From on-site observation to verification of prevalence

In order to further grasp the characteristics of paternalistic leadership, Cheng used a clinical ethnography approach to select as participants a CEO in a medium-sized firm in Taiwan and his subordinates. He found that paternalistic leadership included at least two factors: authoritarianism and benevolence. These two elements of leadership were totally different from researchers' claims in Western leadership studies (Cheng, 1995a). In order to investigate the prevalence of leadership in firms in Taiwan, he further interviewed 42 managers and upper-level supervisors of large-scale enterprises in Taiwan and collected the necessary documents and data for empirical validation. The results confirmed that this kind of leadership did generally exist in different Taiwanese firms (Cheng, 1995b, 2005). In a study of organizational behavior, using a qualitative case study tends to be one of the necessary phases in the construction of theories (Eisenhardt & Graebner, 2007). After proving the uniqueness and prevalence of paternalistic leadership, Cheng and the research team started to consider how to define this type of leadership. They also conducted cultural and literature analyses in order to investigate the relationship between the leadership and Chinese culture, as well as the existing literature on this issue.

*Phase 3: From cultural analysis to development of
theoretical framework*

In order to study the relationship between paternalistic leadership and traditional Chinese culture values, Cheng and his colleagues conducted precise cultural and literature analyses, examining the function of Confucianism and Legalism in traditional Chinese culture in the construction of paternalistic leadership. Critical research results, such as the research findings of Silin (1976), Redding (1990), Westwood (1997), and Cheng (1995a), were reviewed. Subsequently, they worked on an operational definition of paternalistic leadership, extracted moral leadership from benevolent leadership, and proposed an initial theory framework of the tripartite model (see Figure 17.1) as the basis of empirical study (Farh & Cheng, 2000). They then developed a questionnaire of paternalistic leadership and testified to its validity and reliability (Cheng et al., 2000).

*Phase 4: From examining internal and external logic relation to
validating the internal validity of the theory (including the
cause-and-effect relationship and the theoretical boundary)*

In order to check the validity of the tripartite model of paternalistic leadership, the researchers observed the main effects, interaction effects, and contextual boundaries of authoritarian, benevolent, and moral leadership on effectiveness by using questionnaires and scenario design. In addition, they investigated mediating effects of paternalistic leadership on subordinates' and organizational effectiveness and looked for a significant mediating effect caused by subordinates' psychological responses; they also studied the quality of leader–subordinate relations. Finally, they also compared the predictive effect of paternalistic leadership and transformational leadership on outcomes. The results showed that paternalistic leadership was unique and different from transformational leadership in terms of constructions and effects. As to the main effects of authoritarian, benevolent, and moral leadership, the researchers found that the influence on objective performance of authoritarian leadership was positive and significant, and the influence of benevolent and moral leadership on subordinates' attitude effectiveness was more significant. In addition, subordinates' psychological reactions and the quality of leader–subordinate relations could mediate the relationship between paternalistic leadership and outcomes (Niu, Wang & Cheng, 2009; Cheng et al., 2002b; Wu, Hsu, & Cheng, 2002). Moreover, subordinates' dependence and authority orientation, as well as the leader's competence, could moderate the relationship and outcomes (Chou et al., 2005). These empirical studies demonstrated the internal validity and boundaries of the tripartite model of paternalistic leadership.

Phase 5: Theory refinement to strengthen evidence of the theory

Having confirmed the internal validity and boundaries of the theoretical model, the researchers continued to probe into the generalization of the tripartite model in different organizations, regions, and nations. Since the concept of paternalistic leadership was based on Chinese culture and higher power distance, the researchers examined the generalizability of the model in different organizations located in different regions and nations (Chou, Cheng, & Jiang, 2008) to validate the cultural boundary of the model and its generalizability. Furthermore, researchers applied the tripartite model to organizational fields and examined practical applications of paternalistic leadership by field studies such as educational training or action research to see whether paternalistic leadership is useful and whether it would lead to similar results as in the basic studies. If the answer was positive, then the researchers could re-confirm the results of the basic study, and apply it to the organization to solve actual problems. If the answer was negative, then the researchers could return to the previous phase and review the characteristics of various organizations or contexts to understand what had caused the possible results. In conclusion, through Phase 5, they could recognize the on-site application of paternalistic leadership and further strengthen the solidity and generalizability of the theory.

Implications for Chinese organizational behavior studies

In Figure 17.3, studies about paternalistic leadership are reviewed. Although it was simple, it clearly elaborated upon the practice of the full-cycle indigenous research approach. The method is highly consistent with Cialdini's (2001) and Chatman and Flynn's (2005) approach.

Cialdini (2001) suggested that an ideal research process in social psychology should involve participant observation, theoretical construction, and theoretical validation in order to increase internal and external validity. Based on Cialdini's (2001) suggestions, Chatman and Flynn's (2005) proposed the concept of a full-cycle organizational research method, suggesting that in order to further understand individual and group behavior in organizations, researchers should conduct the following: (1) use participant observations to discover interesting organizational phenomena, (2) construct a cause-and-effect theoretical framework of the phenomena, (3) examine empirical validation on the cause-and-effect relationship of the theory, and (4) conduct further participant observations to strengthen the application quality of the theory. Furthermore, different studies should be related, and the researchers should think over and validate all the research processes repetitively in order to construct inspiring and precise theoretical models.

Although Chatman and Flynn proposed the above views, they did not emphasize cultural and historical knowledge and high levels of cultural sensitivity as the basis of theorization about the causes of observed phenomena. Thus, we will use the research on paternalistic leadership as an example to further analyze the advantages of adopting a full-cycle research approach on Chinese indigenous organizational behavior studies. The approach has the advantages of participant observation and experimental study, as well as characteristics of qualitative studies that may possibly lead to a theoretical concept matching the local context. By repetitively working through the whole cycle, researchers can develop an inspiring indigenous model.

First of all, since there is no perfect study (McGrath, 1982), it is better to conduct a series of studies and use multiple methods rather than a single study; obviously, the full-cycle research approach matches this requirement. In the initial stages, researchers can enter the research field and learn surprising or contradictory concepts from real phenomena. Additionally, they can approach Chinese organizations and make significant breakthroughs; subsequently, cultural analyses help researchers to clarify the phenomena or concepts and the complicated relations among Chinese culture, history, and system and further develop the theoretical framework matching the local context. As to well-controlled experimental studies or questionnaire surveys, the validity of the theory can be examined to order to decide whether to modify the theory or model. Finally, on-site application studies not only validate the external validity of the theory and its practical significance, but also further expand and modify the theory.

Second, a single individual or a group instead of the whole research community should follow the full-cycle research approach. The reason is that one researcher or one team can judge more precisely and decide whether to enter the next phase or return to the previous one. Thus, a single researcher or a team should go through the whole theoretical and practical cycle based on the phenomena observed and the theory constructed, instead of only extracting certain aspects and focusing on certain types of studies (Chatman & Flynn, 2005). In this way, a bridge between the practicability of organizational behavior and academic study can be built. The practices can be more precise and the theory can be more practical. This is therefore also one of the reasons why many prominent organizational researchers pursue only a few critical issues in their lives.

Finally, it might take several years to conduct a full-cycle research study or finish the research cycle. Therefore, researchers need more academic persistence; otherwise, research findings cannot be effectively accumulated. In this situation, it is necessary to build a research team – through members' cooperation, exchange, and support a full research process can be accomplished in a shorter time. Moreover, research findings can be published in individual papers or integrated into one book, which should facilitate the complete and immediate communication of the research findings. We call for indigenous scholars to go through the full research cycle and build new theories with indigenous cultural origins in the global age.

Conclusions

This chapter elaborates upon the construction, development, and current research situation of paternalistic leadership that has emerged from Asia and is a new area for leadership research. It then discusses the methodological issues of theoretical construction and model validation of paternalistic leadership, suggesting the advantages of taking a full-cycle research approach in studying Chinese indigenous organizational behavior. Since a full-cycle research study involves participant observation, cultural analysis, model construction, theoretical validation, and on-site application, it can effectively enhance the solidity, precision, and practicability of the theory and meet cultural values.

We also suggest that although it takes time and energy to conduct a full research study, this method facilitates the creation and accumulation of knowledge. Therefore, it should be encouraged that indigenous organizational behavior studies be conducted by taking this approach and, for better results, to go through the whole process with a single researcher or a team. Having the persistence for continuous development is necessary. We hope that our review encourages other researchers to take the full-cycle indigenous research approach to studying Chinese organizational behavior and help the field to reach maturity by considering both theory and practice in precise and useful terms to subsequently promote the quality of the work and lives of one-fifth of the population of the world.

References

Barney, J. B., & Zhang, S. (2009). The future of Chinese management research: A theory of Chinese management versus a Chinese theory of management. *Management and Organization Review*, 5(1), 15–28.

Chatman, J. A., & Flynn, F. J. (2005). Full-cycle micro-organizational behavior research. *Organization Science*, 16(4), 434–447.

Chemers, M. M. (1993). An integrative theory of leadership. In M. Chemers & R. Ayman (Eds.), *Leadership theory and research: Perspectives and directions*. New York: Academic Press.

Cheng, B. S. (1991). Familism and leadership. In C. F. Yang & H. Kao (Eds.), *Chinese and mind* (pp. 366–407). Taipei: Yuanliu. (In Chinese.)

Cheng, B. S. (1992). Paternalism and leadership style. In K. S. Yang (Ed.), *Proceedings of conference on Chinese psychology and behavior*. Taipei: Academia Sinica.

Cheng, B. S. (1995a). Paternalistic authority and leadership: A case study of a Taiwan CEO. *Bulletin of the Institute of Ethnology Academia Sinica, 79,* 119–173. (In Chinese.)

Cheng, B. S. (1995b). *Paternalism and leadership: Empirical studies on Taiwanese private enterprises*. Technical Report for National Science Council, Taiwan. (In Chinese.)

Cheng, B. S. (1996). *Paternalistic authority and leader behavior*. Technical Report for National Science Council, Taiwan. (In Chinese.)

Cheng, B. S. (2005). *Leadership in Chinese organizations: Theory and reality*. Taipei: Laureate. (In Chinese.)

Cheng, B. S. (2007). Clinical approach in organization: Interests and models. *Applied Psychology Research, 33,* 101–125. (In Chinese.)

Cheng, B. S., Chou, L. F., & Farh, J. L. (2000). A triad model of paternalistic leadership: The constructs and management. *Indigenous Psychological Research in Chinese Societies, 14,* 3–64. (In Chinese.)

Cheng, B. S., Chou, L. F., Huang, M. P., Farh, J. L., & Peng, S. (2003). A triad model of paternalistic leadership: Evidence from business organizations in Mainland China. *Indigenous Psychological Research in Chinese Societies, 20,* 209–250. (In Chinese.)

Cheng, B. S., Chou, L. F., Huang, M. P., Wu, T. Y., & Farh, J. L. (2004). Paternalistic leadership and subordinate responses: Establishing a leadership model in Chinese organizations. *Asian Journal of Social Psychology, 7*(1), 89–117.

Cheng, B. S., Farh, J. L., & Chou, L. F. (2006). *Paternalistic leadership: Model and evidence*. Taipei: Hwatai. (In Chinese.)

Cheng, B. S., Huang, M. P., & Chou, L. F. (2002a). Paternalistic leadership and its effectiveness: Evidence from Chinese organizational teams. *Journal of Psychology in Chinese Societies, 3*(1), 85–112. (In Chinese.)

Cheng, B. S., Shieh, P. Y., & Chou, L. F. (2002b). The principal's leadership, leader–member exchange quality, and the teacher's extra-role behavior: The effects of transformational and paternalistic leadership. *Indigenous Psychological Research in Chinese Societies, 17,* 105–161. (In Chinese.)

Cheng, B. S., Wang, A. C., & Huang, M. P. (2009). The road more popular versus the road less traveled: An "insider's" perspective of advancing Chinese management research. *Management and Organization Review, 5*(1), 91–105.

Cheng, H. Y. (2007). Research on intragroup conflict management in Taiwan. In B. S. Cheng, D. Y. Jiang, & H. Y. Cheng (Eds.), *Organizational behavior studies in Taiwan* (2nd edition, pp. 340–375). Taipei: Hwatai. (In Chinese.)

Chou, L. F., Cheng, B. S., & Jen, C. K. (2005). *The contingent model of paternalistic leadership: Subordinate dependence and leader competence*. Paper presented at the annual meeting of the Academy of Management, Hawaii, USA.

Chou, L. F., Cheng, B. S., & Jiang, D. Y. (2008). *Paternalistic leadership: A generalization study under globalization*. Proceedings of workshop on Taiwan, China, and the regionalization of global production networks. Taipei: National Taiwan University.

Cialdini, R. B. (1980). Full-cycle social psychology. In L. Bickman (Ed.), *Applied social psychology annual* (Vol. 1, pp. 21–47). Beverly Hills, CA: Sage.

Cialdini, R. B. (2001). Systematic opportunism: An approach to the study of tactical social influence. In J. P. Forgas & K. D. Williams (Eds.), *Social influence: Direct and indirect processes* (pp. 25–39). Philadelphia, PA: Psychology Press.

Cox, T. J. (1993). *Cultural diversity in organizations: Theory, research and practice.* San Francisco: Berrett-Koehler.

Eisenhardt, K. M., & Graebner, M. E. (2007). Theory building from cases: Opportunities and challenges. *Academy of Management Journal, 50*(1), 25–32.

Farh, J. L., & Cheng, B. S. (2000). A cultural analysis of paternalistic leadership in Chinese organizations. In A. S. Tsui & J. T. Li (Eds.), *Management and organizations in China* (pp. 84–127). London: Macmillan.

Farh, J. L., Cheng, B. S., Chou, L. F., & Chu, X. P. (2006). Authority and benevolence: Employees' response to paternalistic leadership in China. In A. S. Tsui, Y. Bian, & L. Cheng (Eds.), *China's domestic private firms: Multidisciplinary perspectives on management and performance* (pp. 230–260). Armonk, NY: M. E. Sharpe.

Farh, J. L., Earley, P. C., & Lin, S. C. (1997). Impetus for action: A cultural analysis of justice and organizational citizenship behavior in Chinese society. *Administrative Science Quarterly, 42*, 421–444.

Farh, J. L., Leung, F., & Law, K. (1998). On the cross-cultural validity of Holland's model of vocational choices in Hong Kong. *Journal of Vocational Behavior, 52*, 425–440.

Gelfand, M. J., Erez, M., & Aycan, Z. (2007). Cross-cultural organizational behavior. In S. T. Fiske, A. E. Kasdin, & D. L. Schacter (Eds.), *Annual Review of Psychology*, (Vol. 58, pp. 479–514). Palo Alto, CA: Annual Reviews.

Hamilton, G. G. (1990). Patriarchy, patrimonialism, and filial piety: A comparison of China and Western Europe. *British Journal of Sociology, 41*(1), 77–104.

Hofstede, G. H. (1980). *Culture's consequences: International differences in work-related values.* Beverly Hills, CA: Sage.

Hofstede, G. H. (1994). Cultural constraints in management theories. *International Review of Strategic Management, 5*, 27–48.

House, R. J., Wright, N. S., & Aditya, R. N. (1997). Cross-cultural research on organizational leadership: A critical analysis and a proposed theory. In P. C. Earley & M. Erez (Eds.), *New perspectives on international industrial/organizational psychology* (pp. 535–625). San Francisco: New Lexington Press.

Huang, M. P. (2007). Research on leadership in Taiwan. In B. S. Cheng, D. Y. Jiang, & H. Y. Cheng (Eds.), *Organizational behavior studies in Taiwan* (2nd edition, pp. 248–279). Taipei: Hwatai. (In Chinese.)

Lord, R. G., Brown, D. J., Harvey, J. L., & Hall, R. J. (2001). Contextual constraints on prototype generation and their multilevel consequences for leadership perceptions. *Leadership Quarterly, 12*(3), 311–338.

McGrath, J. E. (1982). Dilemmatic: The study of research choices and dilemmas. In J. E. McGrath, J. Martin, & R. Kulka (Eds.), *Judgement calls in research.* Beverly Hills, CA: Sage.

Niu, C. P., Wang, A. C., & Cheng, B. S. (2009). Effectiveness of a moral and benevolent leader: Probing the interactions of the dimensions of paternalistic leadership. *Asian Journal of Social Psychology, 12*(1), 32–39.

Pellegrini, E. K., & Scandura, T. A. (2008). Paternalistic leadership: A review and agenda for future research. *Journal of Management, 34*(3), 566–593.

Pye, L. W. (1981). *Dynamics of Chinese politics*. Cambridge, MA: Oelgeschlager, Gunn, & Hain.

Pye, L. W. (1985). *Asia power and politics*. Cambridge, MA: Harvard University Press.

Redding, S. G. (1990). *The spirit of Chinese capitalism*. New York: Walter de Gruyter.

Silin, R. H. (1976). *Leadership and value: The organization of large-scale Taiwan enterprises*. Cambridge, MA: Harvard University Press.

Thagard, P. (1992). *Conceptual revolutions*. Princeton, NJ: Princeton University Press.

Weber, M. (1968). *Economy and society*, trans. G. Roth & C. Wittich. Berkeley, CA: University of California Press.

Westwood, R. I. (1997). Harmony and patriarchy: The cultural basis for paternalistic leadership among the overseas Chinese. *Organization Studies, 18*(3), 445–480.

Westwood, R. I., & Chan, A. (1992). Headship and leadership. In R. I. Westwood (Ed.), *Organizational behaviour: A Southeast Asian perspective*. Hong Kong: Longman Group.

Whetten, D. A. (2009). An examination of the interface between context and theory applied to the study of Chinese organizations. *Management and Organization Review, 5*(1), 29–55.

Whitley, R. (1992). *Business system in East Asia firms, markets, and societies*. London: Sage.

Wu, T. Y., Hsu, W. L., & Cheng, B. S. (2002). Expressing or suppressing anger: Subordinates' anger responses to supervisors' authoritarian behaviors in a Taiwan enterprise. *Indigenous Psychological Research in Chinese Societies, 18*, 3–49. (In Chinese.)

Yukl, G. (1998). *Leadership in organizations*. Englewood Cliffs, NJ: Prentice Hall.

Section IV

Conceptual issues in psychology

18 Psychology and behavior analysis

The nature of the controversy

Ruben Ardila

Introduction

Psychology, during the greater part of its development as an area of knowledge, has concentrated on the study of the "soul," of the "mind," and later, of "behavior." The discussions about the nature of psychology have been broad and all-embracing and have been centered on its subject matter, on the most appropriate methodology to research it, on the problem of the universality vs. contextualism of psychological laws, and recently on the science–profession relationship. These have been the "dilemmas" of psychology (Ardila, 2007).

From the first thinkers who reflected on subject matters that we call psychological, including the non-European cultures, then Greece, and later on European philosophy, the possibility has always been debated of constructing an objective, contrastable psychology, with knowledge that did not depend on subjective points of view but had, rather, empirical referents. This took form in the nineteenth century with the proposal of Wilhelm Wundt of a psychology that used experimental science methods to study the mind. This had been preceded by the ideas of the British empiricists, of Bekhterev in Russia and his objective psychology, and other efforts in many countries. It was a search for a psychology that would be part of the natural sciences.

We could conclude that the development of psychology in the last centuries has been the search for objectivity, contrastability, valid and reliable knowledge, affirmations based on evidence. What distinguishes psychology from other ways of reflecting about mind and behavior is precisely this: objectivity, the possibility of replicating findings, of putting hypotheses to test, of altering theories, and, in general, of using the methodology of science for the study of phenomena that have traditionally been called psychological.

How is "subjective" turned into "objective"? How does one go from speculations about the soul and mind to the study of behavior, feelings, perception, cognition, and social relationships from an objective perspective? In other words, how can that which is apparently "subjective" by nature be converted into "objective"? This was the challenge that faced psychology's pioneers in the nineteenth and twentieth centuries.

Wundt, Ebbinghaus, Krüger, Selz, Pavlov, Bekhterev, Thorndike, Watson, Lashley, Piéron, Skinner, Bartlett, Bandura all pursued a long complex road to make the psychology of their respective times objective and contrastable, based on evidence. The behaviorist revolution, the cognitive revolution, the role of the neurosciences, experimental social psychology, the study of the human being from conception to death (life cycle), research on individual and personality differences, the origin of psychological processes in non-human species, the great relevance of motivation, the relationships between cultures, weltanschauung (worldviews), the utilization of novel information technology and computers, mathematical models of behavior – all these milestones marked very important developments on the road to make psychology more objective, more based on the model of the natural sciences.

Nevertheless, a one-way vision of the development of psychology does not do justice to this discipline. Simultaneously with previous advances in the direction of objectivity, there were other psychologists who tried to make psychology more "holistic," more intuitive, social, human, and less a natural science like biology or physics, and to draw it closer to the humanities and the new social sciences. This movement toward what are called "soft sciences" – as opposed to the "hard sciences" – was also very influential in the study of language, in the role of culture, in the concern for values, and in the appraisal of scientific and quantitative methodology. All the constructionist and post-modernist approaches are in that direction. We might say that psychology was emphasizing the "rigor" and not the "vigor," and these movements decided to emphasize the "vigor" without worrying too much about the "rigor."

Today psychology is a varied and heterogeneous science, with many scientific discoveries, many theories, reliable and valid facts, and great emphasis on objectivity, contrastability, and evidence-based procedures. But at the same time there are psychologists interested in speculations, in non-scientific methods, in intuition – more in understanding phenomena than in describing or explaining them. Psychology is a quite varied and wide discipline, which is its strength but at the same time its weakness. This is psychology at the beginning of the twenty-first century.

Behavior analysis

Behavior analysis is located in the perspective of maximum "rigor." It comes from all the intents to make psychology a natural and objective science. Behavior analysis owes a great deal to Loeb, Sechenov, Pavlov, Darwin, Watson, Thorndike, Hull, Tolman, and, especially, Skinner.

Watson's critiques of the introspective psychology of his time led him to insist on the necessity of a science of behavior that would not need consciousness at all, just as consciousness is not needed by physics or chemistry. This new psychology, which owed much to Darwin, was called "behaviorism." Today it has become clear that behaviorism is the philosophy that underlies behavior analysis. Therefore (according to Skinner, 1974) we have to distinguish between:

- A philosophy of science, which is behaviorism.
- A science of behavior, which is behavior analysis.
- A set of applications for the whole spectrum of human life and societal issues called applied behavior analysis.

That philosophy of science is established in pragmatism, in Mach's inductivism, and in later developments. Radical behaviorism (Skinner) differs from methodological behaviorism, which, in its emphasis on inductivism and pragmatism, is the conceptual frame of reference of the majority of experimental psychologists. Radical behaviorism rejects the dualism between the inner and the outer world. Behavior analysis deals with one world and the behavior to be found in that one world (see Zuriff, 1985).

Such a philosophy of science deals with matters like determinism and free will, the status of scientific laws, ethics and morals, social responsibility, methodological inductivism – in short, an important series of philosophical issues, some classic and others recent.

Pragmatism, one of the conceptual foundations of radical behaviorism, is a philosophical position holding that the truth value of a theory or proposition is to be found in its practical consequences. It is the philosophy proposed by Charles Peirce (1839–1914) and by William James (1842–1910). Pragmatism influenced Ernst Mach (1838–1916), who applied such philosophy to the science of mechanics. Science, according to Mach, has to do with experience and especially with making sense of our experience. Science originated in the need for people to communicate efficiently and economically with one another. The inductivism of Mach had a great influence on Skinner – unlike positivism, either in its classic (Comte) or in its later version (logical positivism, Vienna circle). Behaviorism and positivism are very far from each other, in contrast to what is commonly believed (see Smith, 1986).

Scientific explanation, in line with Mach, with pragmatism, and with radical behaviorism, consists in describing events in terms that are familiar; it has nothing to do with revealing some hidden reality beyond our experience. Science deals with the task of making sense out of our experience.

This philosophy has been the frame of reference for a science of behavior. A large quantity of scientific research, data, theories, discoveries, and applications have flowed from that science, which is called behavior analysis. Many experiments in operant conditioning, behavioral neuroscience, behavioral pharmacology, and experimental social psychology have formed the foundation of this science. Behavior analysis has been institutionalized and has acquired an identity with professional societies on the subject, the main one being the Association for Behavior Analysis (ABA). Professional identity has been consolidated with specialized journals, the first and most important ones being *Journal of the Experimental Analysis of Behavior* (JEAB, founded in 1958), *Journal of Applied Behavior Analysis* (JABA, founded in 1968), and *The Behavior Analyst* (TBA, founded in 1978). There are other very important associations and other very important journals, but these are the pioneers and continue to give identity to the area of behavior analysis.

Psychology and behavior analysis

Behavior analysis was born within psychology and in great part continues as part of it. Nonetheless, other disciplines – like pharmacology, the neurosciences, education, and even anthropology (in the work of Marvin Harris and others) – also use methods of behavior analysis.

Although psychology as well as behavior analysis give priority to experimental methods, they are not always akin to each other. Psychology generally uses group experimental design, while behavior analysis places more importance on single-case experimental design. In Table 18.1 we can see a comparison between the methodology of experimental psychology and the methodology of behavior analysis.

In addition to the methodological divergences and convergences between them, the focal questions are:

1   Is behavior analysis a part of psychology?
2   Is it the same as psychology?
3   Is it a discipline that is independent from psychology?

From the answer we give to these queries, the controversy between psychology and behavior analysis is inferred.

Psychologists as well as behavior analysts seek to find laws of behavior and start with behavior as their initial data. It is possible that cognitive psychologists make assumptions about internal causes, mind, psyche, or another

Table 18.1 Methodologies of behavior analysis and experimental psychology

Dimension	Behavior analysis	Experimental psychology
1. Number of participants	Few	Many
2. Research design	Within-subjects	Between-subjects
3. Data collection	Direct, repeated measures of behavior	Various methods, often indirect and unrepeated measures of behavior
4. Data analysis	Graphic	Statistical
5. Approach to variable data	Consider the variability as imposed; isolate and control the responsible extraneous variables	Consider the variability as intrinsic; use statistics to detect the effects of the independent variable despite the variability

entity. Not so with the behavior analysts. But the similarity is considerable. As Baum (2005) points out:

> most experimental psychologists seem to be methodological behaviorists. They claim to study something inside – mind, memory, attitudes, personality, and so on – by making inferences about the internal world from external behavior, such as performance on stimulation tasks, puzzles, paper-and-pencil tests, or questionnaires. Such experimental psychologists have no methods to study the inner world, however, they study outer behavior with objective methods. The only difference between this approach and methodological behaviorism is that the psychologists make the inferences about the inner world whereas the behaviorists would not.
>
> (pp. 31–32)

The distinction between methodological behaviorism and radical behaviorism is that the first is based on "realism" and the second adds "pragmatism" to its conceptualization.

Conceptual controversies

For traditional psychology, the study of private events was very relevant; this is not the case with behavior analysis. Public events are those that can be reported by more than one person, while the private events – sensations, feelings, thoughts – correspond to only one person. We cannot know what another person thinks in a given moment, if it is not expressed verbally. These thoughts are private events.

For radical behaviorism the only difference between private and public events is the number of persons who can report them. They are the same kind of events and hold the same properties. "The world under the skin" is not a definitive limit. It only deals with privileged access to some phenomena (thoughts, feelings). We know these events through behavior. Public and private events are both natural events. Verbal behavior is a natural event: To say "I feel happy to see you" is a natural event, and the same with walking, writing, or planning the future.

For Kant's philosophy the main difficulty for psychology becoming a science was that psychological phenomena occur in time and not in space, and for something to be part of science it should occur in time and in space. (See a contemporary analysis of this issue in Tolman, 2004, especially pp. 176–182.)

In behavior analysis, on the other hand, private events should be observable in principle; they must be locatable in time and space, although they might not be observable in practice. Aggressive behavior is observed, intelligent behavior is described. We note that some persons spend more time in the company of other people than alone, and we say "they are" aggressive, or intelligent, or sociable. These behaviors occur in time and in space, and as such psychology as the science of behavior is not vulnerable to Kant's and his philosophy's attacks on the criteria for psychology to be a (natural) science. Psychology as a science of behavior (events occurring in time and space), as opposed to psychology as a study of the mind (events occurring only in time) represents an important advance in research of its subject matter.

Cognitivism

During the first half of the twentieth century, behavior analysis was considered "the mainstream" of psychology. Research works, models, theories, training programs were influenced by behaviorism as a philosophy and by behavior analysis as a laboratory science. This predominance was challenged by cognitivism, which had its beginnings in the early 1960s and has risen to prominence in psychology since then.

Today cognitivism – and not behaviorism – is considered to be the dominant paradigm in psychology. It has been stated that behaviorism is "dead" and that twenty-first-century psychology is predominantly cognitivist.

This is not entirely true. In the first place, it is not accurate to say that behaviorism had been the dominant approach in psychology until the 1960s. In fact, during that period other models, such as Gestalt psychology, humanistic/existential psychology, psychoanalysis, structuralism, were also influential. Behaviorism was not the only model, and it certainly cannot be said that it was predominant at a worldwide level: it only predominated in some centers of great development in scientific psychological research. Alternatively, it is also not true to say that behaviorism has "passed away." At the present time, behavior analysis is active in basic and applied research, in novel technological developments, and in conceptual and philosophical analysis of great depth, at the world level (see Ardila, 2006a). Behavior analysis continues to hold a place of great importance in psychology, as well as in other disciplines, such as education, anthropology, pharmacology, the neurosciences, political science, and even philosophy.

However, it is important to make clear that in the last few decades cognitivism has been considered as the alternative to behaviorism. The role of internal variables, thinking processes, language, purpose, computer models, memory, have become central in psychological research. At the beginning, the so-called cognitive revolution "existed more in contrast with behaviorism than as a school of thought in its own right" (Wispé & Thompson, 1976, p. 346).

George A. Miller, with his book entitled *Psychology: The Science of Mental Life* (1962), and Neisser, with his *Cognitive Psychology* (1967), were landmarks in the establishment of the cognitive revolution. (For a contemporary analysis of those developments, see Mandler, 2007.)

It is important to define some basic concepts of cognitive psychology and related areas:

> *Cognitive psychology* is the branch of psychology that studies higher mental processes, including perceiving, reasoning, thinking, language,

memory, mainly through inferences from behavior. Cognitive psychology considers that behavior is mediated and cannot be understood by stimulus–response chains.

Cognitive science is a broader term and includes work in cognitive psychology, artificial intelligence (AI), psycholinguistics, philosophy of mind, epistemology, and other disciplines interested in human thought processes.

Cognitive neuroscience is based on the new brain-imaging technologies such as positron emission tomography (PET), functional magnetic resonance imaging (fMRI), superconducting quantum interference device (SQUID), and so on.

The modeling of psychological processes by computer has been very relevant in the development of cognitive approaches. The study of artificial intelligence (AI) by psychologists and physical scientists has aided the understanding of perception, memory, thinking processes, problem solving, scientific creativity, and many other traditional psychological topics. AI aims to produce programs that simulate human intelligence.

There are strong and weak versions of AI: The strong AI version says that all mental processes can be simulated computationally. The weak version views the brain as a digital computer. The Turing Test is designed to determine in what situation a computer program might be said to be intelligent. The test isolates an individual in a room, connected either to a computer or to another person. If the person in the room cannot tell if he/she is talking to the computer or to the other person, then the program on the machine should be seen as intelligent.

Computer modeling of psychological processes has advanced considerably. But objections to cognitivism and to the computer metaphor have also advanced at the same rate. Philosophers argue that cognitivism is failing because the computer metaphor is wrong, and also because cognitivism is not mental enough. On the other hand, some AI researchers argue that the emphasis on representation and symbolic thought is largely irrelevant to the development of truly intelligent systems. Many psychologists state that to say that the brain (the "source" of behavior) works as a symbol-manipulating device (as a computer) is not a useful way for understanding human behavior. As Fodor (2000) has said, "the mind doesn't work that way."

Cognitivism should explain how psychology, defined as "the science that investigates the representation and processing of information by complex systems" (Holyoak, 1999, p. xxxix, in *The MIT Encyclopedia of Cognitive Sciences*) is able to explain all behavior, human and not human, motor, motivated behavior, emotional, adaptive or not adaptive behavior – a task that cognitive psychology should share with behavior analysis if it is going to go farther than the computer metaphor.

Behaviorology

At the end of the 1980s a movement was formed to create a new academic discipline, different from psychology and derived from the experimental analysis of behavior; this discipline was called behaviorology. It represented the culmination of efforts to ensure that radical behaviorism had its own place in the academic world, independent of psychology.

This new science sought to use the concepts of experimental analysis of behavior and its most recent developments in order to understand and solve problems in the traditional fields of psychology, sociology, education, anthropology, evolutionary biology, and the neurosciences. Its aim was to study behavior in a wide perspective, with the strictest, most valid and most reliable methods of the natural science.

This discipline gave rise to an organization founded in 1987 initially called The International Behaviorology Association (TIBA); later, its name was changed to International Society for Behaviorology (ISB). It published a bulletin with the name *Selections* and two journals, *Behaviorology* (which began in 1993) and *The International Behaviorologist*. It organized annual conventions around 20 March – the day of B. F. Skinner's birthday. The first convention took place in 1989. The most recent was in 2008.

Behaviorology is defined as the science that studies the variables that are responsible for the changes in the behavior of organisms throughout their lives. It is interested in the behavior of all living organisms, but is has centered its research and conceptualizations especially on the task of providing scientific answers to questions that are as old as Homo sapiens: Why do people do the things they do? What are the causes of behavior, including our own behavior? How can we recognize these causes, with the idea of helping us to behave more effectively (in the care of children, in education, in daily life, at work, in recreation and leisure time, in art, in academic activities, and in science)?

Behaviorology begins in a formal mode with Skinner's book *The Behavior of Organisms* (1938). This book presents the way of investigating the phenomena of behavior from a new perspective, which is different from the "mentalism" that had characterized a great part of psychology throughout history.

Behaviorology is a natural science. It is the midpoint level of analysis among other sciences of life and culture. The sciences with special importance in behaviorology are those that are based on the causal mode of selection as their explicative frame of reference. The theory of evolution (Darwin and the later developments) has been very relevant, as have the works on selection by followers of Skinner, the research on verbal behavior, and even on cultural design.

Behaviorology has had a certain level of development, in the sense of fomenting research programs, training programs, books, research journals, conventions, and in general a disciplinary context of its own. Nevertheless, it has not been able to become an autonomous science, separate from psychology. On the other hand, traditional behavior analysis, which has been less radical in its conceptualization, has gone further in the definition of its field of research work. Behavior analysis has its best expression in the Association for Behavior Analysis (ABA), while behaviorology has it in the International Society for Behaviorology (ISB). Both associations are dedicated to the advancement of behavior analysis as a science, as a technology, and as a form of improving human life, understanding the way organisms act, and constructing a better society.

A different discipline from psychology?

The underlying issue in the postulation of behaviorology as a discipline with its own field of study is whether it is necessary to come up with a scientific discipline that is different from psychology and that is defined as a natural science the backbone of which is the behavior of organisms; one that is not interested in the "mind," nor in the traditional speculations of psychology, with a solid evolutionary neo-Darwinist base, with monistic not dualistic explanations, with its own area of professional training, research programs, philosophy of science, and practical applications. In a way, calling behaviorology a separate science would be a recognition that the research program of psychology as a science is not able to free itself from speculations, mentalism, dualism, nor the ideological prejudices that it has come up against throughout its development.

The advantages and disadvantages of a behaviorology separate from psychology can be pointed out in the following way:

A *Advantages*
1   The possibility of a natural science of behavior. Despite the efforts of many psychologists over more than 130 years, present-day psychology continues to be extremely diverse, with contradictory theories, lack of integration, many speculations, and profound internal divisions. A different science, behaviorology, could start from the beginning and avoid the historical errors that psychology has committed.
2   To possess its own academic space (a department of behaviorology) would be very useful for the development of the area, and it would not have to depend on a department of psychology, nor of any other discipline.
3   That new discipline would not only use scientifically proven psychological knowledge, but also knowledge gained by other sciences: evolutionary biology, neurosciences, genetics, sociology, anthropology, linguistics, and so on. It would not be exclusively psychological.

B *Disadvantages*
1   The separation would lead to the isolation of behaviorology as a discipline.

2   By separating behaviorology from psychology, it is clear that psychology would turn even more speculative than it is at present (according to what some authors think).

3   Psychology has contributed issues and study topic areas to behavior analysis that would surely have not been researched had behavior analysis not been within psychology. As an example of these topics, we can mention abnormal behavior and psychotherapy, which gave birth to its behavioral version, behavior therapy. In turn, experimental analysis provided objectivity, reliability, and scientificity to psychology. This relationship of mutual support between psychology and behavior analysis would probably disappear if behaviorology were to free itself completely from psychology.

The cross-fertilization between psychology and behavior analysis has been fruitful in both ways. Even though many psychologists look reluctantly at behavior analysis and vice versa, it is possible that the independence of behavior analysis from psychology (in the formation of a new science of behaviorology) would be more negative than positive for both disciplines. It is a fact that knowledge is becoming increasingly more specialized, that the areas of work have specific objectives, specific methodologies, theories, laboratory findings, and their own conceptualizations. Psychology is a truly heterogeneous and diverse science. Behavior analysis is much less diversified, although there also exist several "behaviorisms" (see Pérez-Acosta, Guerrero, & López López, 2002). This growth could be considered positive and is an example of the complexity of the scientific study of behavior, both human and non-human.

Conclusions

The development of psychology as a discipline has been the search for objectivity, for working within the framework of science, for finding laws that are accurate, reliable, and, preferably, universal. It has had the purpose of studying "mind," "human nature," or "behavior," according to how psychology has defined it over time. This process of turning into objective what has apparently been subjective has had many ups and downs and has generated different approaches, methodologies, viewpoints, schools, systems, and so forth.

The study of psychology as a science has had difficulties associated with its complex subject matter, its methodology, the formulation of laws, the search for a balance between universality and context. Moreover, human beings are very close to the object of psychological study, and this has made it difficult for us to distance ourselves and to research psychological phenomena without getting involved with them.

One of the ways of conducting research in psychology has been the approach initially called experimental analysis of behavior, and later behavior analysis – the research and conceptualization based on the framework of natural sciences, evolution, and the most meticulous methodology. This field of knowledge could be considered as a branch of psychology, or as psychology as a whole, or as a scientific discipline different from psychology.

After occupying a central role, at the core of psychology, behavior analysis yields this place to cognitivism. The cognitive revolution was analogous to what had come before the behavioral revolution and attempted to surmount and replace it. Psychology, at the dawn of the twenty-first century, is cognitive-oriented, and behavior analysis is no longer at the center of the psychological discipline. Behavior analysis, in its turn, has been trying to become an autonomous science, and this has had its peak with behaviorology.

The amount of research, theorizations, and applications of psychology allow us to talk about tendencies of convergence, not only about divergence. Let us consider that a unified psychology is possible, as the most mature and advanced disciplines that have achieved a consensus on a unifying paradigm are. I have suggested an experimental synthesis of behavior as a unifying paradigm for psychology, with a behavior analysis base (Ardila, 2006b). We have more areas of convergence in psychology, more tacit and explicit agreements, than divergences and conflicts. And even though there is still a long path ahead, it is possible and desirable to consider a unified psychology in the near future.

In this new phase, psychology and behavior analysis will join their efforts and will probably overcome the traditional controversy that has existed between them.

References

Ardila, R. (2006a). Behavior analysis in an international context. In A. C. Brock (Ed.), *Internationalizing the history of psychology* (pp. 112–132). New York: New York University Press.

Ardila, R. (2006b). The experimental synthesis of behaviour. *International Journal of Psychology, 41*, 462–467.

Ardila, R. (2007). The nature of psychology: The great dilemmas. *American Psychologist, 62*, 906–912.

Baum, W. M. (2005). *Understanding behaviorism* (revised edition). Malden, MA: Blackwell.

Fodor, J. (2000). *The mind doesn't work that way*. Cambridge, MA: MIT Press.

Holyoak, K. J. (1999). Psychology. In R. A. Wilson & F. C. Keil (Eds.), *The MIT encyclopedia of the cognitive sciences* (pp. xxxix–xlix). Cambridge, MA: MIT Press.

Mandler, G. (2007). *A history of modern experimental psychology*. Cambridge, MA: MIT Press.

Miller, G. A. (1962). *Psychology: The science of mental life*. New York: Harper & Row.

Neisser, U. (1967). *Cognitive psychology*. New York: Appleton-Century-Crofts.

Pérez-Acosta, A. M., Guerrero, F., & López López, W. (2002). Siete conductismos contemporáneos. Una síntesis verbal y gráfica [Seven contemporary behaviorisms: A verbal and graphic synthesis]. *International Journal of Psychology and Psychological Therapy, 2*, 103–113.

Skinner, B. F. (1938). *The behavior of organisms*. New York: Appleton-Century-Crofts.

Skinner, B. F. (1974). *About behaviorism*. New York: Knopf.

Smith, L. D. (1986). *Behaviorism and logical positivism*. Stanford, CA: Stanford University Press.

Tolman, C. W. (2004). Philosophical doubts about psychology as a natural science. In C. D. Green, M. Shore, & T. Teo (Eds.), *The transformation of psychology: Influences of 19th-century philosophy, technology and natural science* (pp. 175–193). Washington, DC: American Psychological Association.

Wispé, L. G., & Thompson, J. N. (1976). The war between the words: Biological versus social evolution and some related issues. *American Psychologist, 31*, 341–347.

Zuriff, G. (1985). *Behaviorism: A conceptual reconstruction*. New York: Columbia University Press.

19 Social interactions

Conceptual reflections and an experimental approach

Emilio Ribes-Iñesta

Social behavior has been an elusive theoretical issue for psychology. Theoretical approaches to social behavior have been inspired either by sociological, political, economic, and folk sources (Abelson et al., 1968; Thibaut & Kelley, 1959), or by extensions of cognitive models to account for the interactions between individuals within a group (Bandura, 1977, 1986; Secord & Backman, 1974). Both sources of interpretation have promoted reductionistic explanations, stressing social interactions as mental intersubjective relationships or as the mental mirroring of social institutional ideas and values by individuals' cognition and action.

Naturalistic formulations of social behavior, on the other hand, have been stimulated by the study of animal species-specific behavior (Scott, 1958; Thorpe, 1956; Wilson, 1975) and by the extrapolation of concepts and experimental preparations originated in the study of animal learning and motivation (Miller & Dollard, 1941; Mowrer, 1960; Skinner, 1962). These formulations share a common limitation: to conceive social behavior in terms of the interaction of two or more individual organisms, regardless of the functional environment in which the interaction takes place. The social nature of behavior is identified as a necessary outcome of inter-individual interactions within groups. According to this view, the processes accounting for social interactions are the same as those that take place during individual behavior regarding objects and events. Social contingencies are thought to consist of one-way or two-way stimulus and response relations between at least two individual organisms.

In both approaches, "more than one" has been the critical criterion to identify behavior as social. The assumption of a social medium or environment is made according to the number of participating individuals. I have elsewhere argued against this logic to identify social behavior (Ribes, 2001; Ribes, Rangel, & López, 2008). It is logical to assume that social interactions demand at least the relation between two individuals, and that group-life is a necessary condition for the development of inter-individual interactions. However, it does not necessarily follow that these are by themselves sufficient conditions for social behavior to take place. A source of confusion is to name human and animal groups under the same term, "society." Human societies are radically different from so-called animal societies and groups. Human groups and individuals, while coexisting and living together, are regulated and adjust themselves to conventions. These conventions depend on the specific roles of individuals within a systematic division of labor. The different settings in which this division of labor takes place constitute social institutions, which circumscribe the roles of groups of individuals. Labor division in human societies is based on a delayed exchange of the produced or stocked goods and services, in contrast to immediate consumption or satisfaction prevailing in situation-bound interactions typical of animal groups.

Insect societies, as an example of complex organization in animals, seem also to have a division of labor. However, in insect societies, the physical and biological properties of the organism and the environment are fixed for every type of species-member according to its predetermined biological endowment. In contrast, in human societies, conventional relations that develop as and through language become specialized sets of customs or institutions. Quoting Emerson (1958):

> A society is defined as a group that manifests systematic division of labor among adults of the same sex. Most social behavior of insects is genetically determined, while most social behavior of man is culturally determined through symbolic communication.
>
> (p. 331)

Deferred or postponed exchange is the basis of labor division. The characteristics of labor division determine the distribution and consumption of goods and services according to contingencies that emerge from particular conditions related to with whom, what, when, and where the goods and services are produced and exchanged. The *non-immediate* character of labor division has been possible because of the *simultaneous* development of language as conventional behavior. Language behavior mediates relations between individuals that take place at different times and in different locations (Ribes, 1985). Division of labor in human societies detaches the production and consumption of goods from immediate individual use, and gives them social use to the extent that they are collectively shared in one way or another. This is possible only through language. By speaking or writing, labor acts may be detached from the particular circumstances in which occur, relating them to the practice of other individuals in different circumstances (Bennett, 1989; Ribes, 1986).

Living together allows for the survival of individuals, but living together in society essentially involves interactions that are not *directly* related to survival, and are on occasion completely divorced from survival. Survival in animal groups depends directly on feeding, reproduction, and defense activities. In human societies, most eating and drinking, sexual, and agonistic-like behaviors are independent of any immediate survival demand of the group. Language, as a human distinctive phenomenon, not only allows for the social division of labor, but also for the detachment of survival behavior from original circumstances in which they have taken place (Weiss, 1926). Individual survival behaviors became institutional regulated activities. With language and social division of labor, institutions emerged as shared systems of differentiated relations among individuals.

From a psychological standpoint, institutions are not abstract representations of social structures (Kantor, 1982). Institutions always consist of individuals interacting with other individuals according to collective criteria. When individuals are influenced, regulated, or affected by institutions, reference is made to actual interactions between individuals with different social roles and attributions. Institutions are always actualized in the form of interindividual interactions adjusting to functional criteria that are *descriptive* of the social exchanges in a particular group. Since the social roles and attributions of individuals are conditional to institutional practices, these may change according to settings, time, outcomes, and many other factors. Thus, institutional functions may be conceived of as complex sets of contingencies that involve the interactions of individuals with differential social attributions in particular situations.

Social division of labor is based upon production. The skills and the physical force required in the production and appropriation of goods have historically determined the emergence of power functions controlling the exchange of goods and wealth. The organization of society in institutions reflects the diversity of ways in which the productive and appropriation processes influence activities other than those directly related to exchange of goods. Parallel to the establishment of the State, societies created laws and special institutions to secure the conservation of wealth and power (Lull & Micó, 2007). History shows that politics and law have appeared and have been worked out to support and maintain the social organization based upon a given economic system (Marx, 1884/1946; Weber, 1964). Power, exchange, and sanction are an integral part of human society and should be considered as functional dimensions underlying all human social interactions. Institutions, in addition to their unique or specific social responsibilities, always involve power, exchange, and sanction contingencies. These contingencies determine the social attributions of the behavior of each one of the individual members of institutions and set the functional scope and boundaries of their mutual interactions. Institutional contingencies are the *contact medium* (Kantor, 1924) that enables social interactions among individuals. Living together always consists in a special way of *living together*. Living together is always conditional or contingent to the requirements, criteria, and demands of a given social framework.

Power, exchange, and sanction, as functional dimensions of social institutions, are related to general effects or outcomes. On the one hand, the ultimate achievement of power contingencies is *domination*. From a psychological standpoint, power contingencies deal with the prescription, regulation, monitoring, and administration of interactions and their outcomes. On the other hand, the final achievement of exchange contingencies is *complementation*. Exchange contingencies involve the production, appropriation, distribution, and consumption of goods and services. Finally, the ultimate achievement of sanction contingencies is *demarcation*. Sanction contingencies deal with justification, authorization, or penalization of behavior interactions. The three sets of contingencies do participate in any kind of social interaction, but from a behavioral standpoint each of them should and can be analyzed separately in order to carry out an experimental analysis of their relative influence and course of action.

An experimental preparation

I advocate that the molecular interactions taking place under micro-institutional contingencies are the subject matter of psychology. From this standpoint, social interactions may be conceived as interactions among individuals that comprise at least dyadic behavioral units. It may be expected that the nature of these interactions will be a function of the institutional contingencies that characterize different social systems. In spite of the fact that behavioral or psychological processes may be considered as universal, social interactions between individuals should vary according to the specific features of the power, exchange, and sanction contingencies constituent of different social formations.

Social systems and institutions involve the operation of complex molar processes that, as such, may be impossible to put under the analysis of contrived empirical methods. The historical character of social formations adds another obstacle to the replication of phenomena required by empirical scrutiny or inspection and justifies the outstanding roles played by historical and hermeneutic methods in the understanding of social phenomena. However, in spite of the fact that overall social phenomena cannot be reproduced at will, it is possible to reproduce some of their defining features under contrived conditions, such as the rules of exchange of a specific economic system, the criteria underlying the use of power in a given group, and so on. With the exception of special cases, experimental research does not consist in reproducing analogs of the phenomena under study. On the contrary, experimental research consists in creating contrived conditions that allow for the explicit manipulation of abstract variables. Experimental research is not interested in the occurrence of the concrete natural facts ultimately to be explained. Because of this, individual social interactions framed by power, exchange, or sanction contingencies may be examined under experimental conditions, with psychology assuming the role of the experimental science providing knowledge about the molecular functions involved in social phenomena.

I will describe an experimental preparation designed for the analysis of social interactions in laboratory and quasi-natural settings. This preparation involves at least two *explicit* participants in a dyadic interaction, but it may include more than two participants depending upon the roles ascribed to different individuals. The functional roles in the social interaction are designed according to the three kinds of contingencies previously examined: power, exchange, and sanction. Power contingencies deal with the prescription of behavioral requirements and attributions and with the regulation, supervision, and administration of consequences as behavioral outcomes or products. The prescription of contingencies may be external to the situation or may emerge in the situation itself as a result of interactions exemplifying different power attributions. Exchange contingencies deal with the production, appropriation, distribution, and consumption of goods when fulfilling different requirements. These contingencies are related to traditional issues of altruism, competition, reciprocity, and so on. Finally, sanction contingencies have to do with externally or self-administered outcomes or earnings, and with the correspondence of these with implicit or explicitly prescribed rules. Sanctions and justification of this correspondence or non-correspondence may be manipulated outside or inside the situation, with added consequences for appropriate or inappropriate behaviors.

This experimental preparation allows for real-time interactions between individuals, and distinguishes the behavior under individual contingencies from that under social or shared contingencies. The dyad is the minimal unit of interaction. All social or shared contingencies involve cooperation – that is, the behavior of two individuals affecting each other's behavior or outcomes. Even competition demands cooperation. The experimental setting involves at least two synchronized computers (see Figure 19.1). Computers may be located in the same room or in different rooms, in order to control for social and physical proximity. On the monitor of each computer two displays of a same visual puzzle are presented. One puzzle appears in the left section of the screen, the other in the right section. The puzzle in the left section of the screen has to be completed by the participant working on the computer; the puzzle in the right section has to be completed by the other participant in the dyad, or by a confederate. The computers are programmed to be synchronized in such a way that the performance of one participant, displayed on the left side of his/her monitor, is also displayed on the right side of the other participant's monitor. Therefore, each participant can track the performance of his/her peer in the process of completing the puzzle. The computer system also allows each participant to place pieces into the puzzle of his/her peer. Differential earnings can be scheduled for both participating for placing pieces in each of the two puzzles. To audit the number of points earned, each participant can activate a window that shows the accumulated points for each member of the dyad. Points can be exchanged at the end of the experimental sessions. Any of the participants can finish the session, when his/her puzzle is complete, by positioning the mouse and pressing the left button on a window marked "end."

Different exchange relations can be established depending on the earnings of each participant by placing pieces into the peer's puzzle. Placing pieces only into one's own puzzle (local) corresponds to individual contingencies,

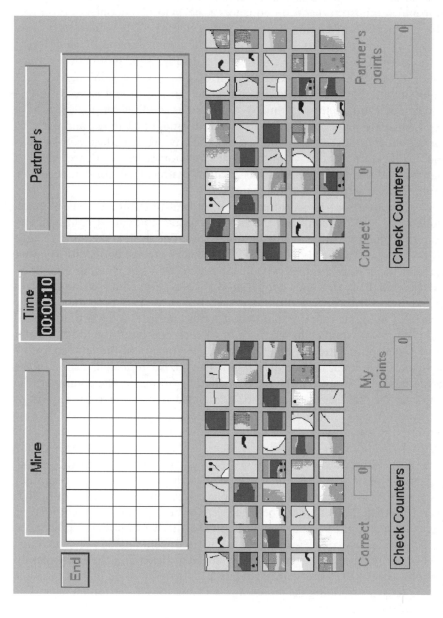

Figure 19.1 Typical arrangement of the computer screen at the start of an experimental session.

but placing pieces into the peer's puzzle (remote) involves social or shared contingencies. If by placing a piece into the puzzle of the peer the participant gets the earnings of such a response, the interaction corresponds to a competition. If, on the contrary, the earnings go to the peer, then it corresponds to altruism. But if both participants obtain earnings, it is a case of partial altruism (traditionally called cooperation). Conditions of exchange can be made inequitable and asymmetrical. Exchange is inequitable when earnings for placing pieces into the peer's puzzle are not the same for the two participants. Exchange is asymmetrical when earnings for placing pieces into their own puzzles are not the same for the two participants.

The choice for a given puzzle can also be manipulated. Responding to one's own puzzle or to the peer's puzzle may be freely chosen, but choosing to respond to the peer's puzzle may be forced in order to be able to respond to one's own puzzle. Responding or not to the peer's puzzle may be induced: (1) by the systematic response of a confederate, (2) by responding to the peer's puzzle as a prompt to the experimental participant to do the same, (3) by being reciprocal with the participant when he/she place pieces in the peer's puzzle, or (4) by being indifferent. It is not only contingencies that can be individual or shared; responses and outcomes can also be so. Placing pieces can be done by each participant on an individual basis, or it may be required that both participants move and place together every piece in any of the puzzles. In the same way, earnings can be an individual outcome according to the earnings obtained by each participant, or be a shared outcome by pooling together individual earnings and afterwards splitting the total earnings into different parts for each participant.

Verbal behavior is also considered in this experimental preparation. Audio recordings are made of spontaneous verbalizations by participants during the experimental sessions, looking for the functional orientation of these verbalizations, and for agreements among participants regarding how to solve the task. Verbal behavior can be explicitly manipulated through written declarations by the participants about their anticipated choice of responding; declarations that can be exchanged between them or not.

It is not irrelevant to mention that special control procedures are taken to ensure that participants understand the experimental task. All participants are exposed to baseline sessions in which they separately solve their puzzle with and without access to the peer's puzzle display. During baseline sessions no earnings are obtained. Additionally, participants are given detailed instructions about the task, and the earnings that may be obtained according to how they place pieces into their own puzzle or into the peer's puzzle. A demo is presented on the screen, showing the procedures described in the instructions, and afterwards participants have to answer some questions regarding the earnings to be obtained according to their responses to either puzzle.

Some experimental findings

One of the major influences on research involving exchange relations has been that of econometric and game-theory conceptions (Axelrod & Hamilton, 1981). These conceptions assume that individuals behave according to rational decisions based upon relative pay-offs, in such a way that individuals always choose the momentary condition that provides "larger" individual – not collective – earnings or benefits. Operant research on social interactions coincides with the former approaches assuming that individuals' responding correlates with the choice involving larger earnings or benefits (Baum, 1973; Shimoff & Matthews, 1975). According to these views, when individuals are faced with two alternative responses, the "cost" for responding to the two alternatives being equal, they will choose the alternative that will provide the greater benefit.

The results obtained in our research program do not support these assumptions. When two individuals interact in our experimental preparation under competition or partial-altruism situations, and have the option of choosing to respond to their own puzzle or to the peer's puzzle, they consistently prefer to respond to the former (Ribes & Rangel, 2002; Ribes, Rangel, Carbajal, & Peña, 2003a). This happens in spite of the fact that they could obtain larger earnings by responding to the peer's puzzle. The preference for individual contingencies to the detriment of social or shared contingencies cannot be attributed to the fact that the points earned are just symbolic. In most of the experiments, points earned were exchanged for "valued" music CDs, and the number of CDs obtained depended on the number of points earned. Most of dyads in our experiments preferred to respond to the local puzzle, in spite of the fact that often they could not even obtain a CD. If dyads had responded to the remote puzzle, they could have obtained two or three times as many points. These results were observed consistently under competition and partial-altruism contingencies, using symmetric, asymmetric, equitable, and inequitable exchange conditions (Ribes et al., 2003b; Ribes, Rangel, Magaña, López, & Zaragoza, 2005).

The preference for responding to the local puzzle was changed by using a forced-response procedure (Ribes et al., 2003c). When participants were forced to respond to the peer's puzzle instead of the local puzzle to obtain individual earnings, all participants chose the remote puzzle. However, when the forced-response procedure was eliminated during the free-choice condition, participants preferred again to respond to their local puzzle in the altruism and competition situations. In the partial altruism situation, participants changed to the remote puzzle during the choice condition, but after one or two exposures to the forced-response procedure. The effects of the forced-response procedure were evaluated in another study in which responding to the remote puzzle was followed by two-fold earnings similar to those obtained in a partial-altruism situation. In this case, all participants continued responding to the remote puzzle when they changed to the free-choice condition.

Some studies were done to evaluate the effects of differential and non-differential individual earnings, compared to shared earnings, on choice between individual and social contingencies (Ribes et al., 2006). The results of four studies evaluating these variables showed that participants chose to respond under the social contingency (the remote puzzle) only when they had made some verbal agreement at the beginning to the experimental sessions regarding where to respond to the puzzle. Otherwise, the administration of differential or non-differential earnings on individual or shared bases had no special effect. Similar results were obtained by Marwell and Schmitt (1975) in a risk situation. These results suggest that explicit linguistic interactions may be a necessary condition for the development of behavior under shared contingencies and would explain trust and partial altruism as distinctive features of human small groups' reciprocity in the context of evolution (Pennisi, 2005).

Reciprocity can be conceived as a continuum ranging from negative to positive outcome interactions. Partial altruism, in which individuals respond for the benefit of the dyad by obtaining earnings for themselves and for their peer simultaneously, is an extreme case of positive reciprocity. The opposite case would be fighting and aggressive behaviors in which each individual acts in such a way as to produce negative effects in the other at the time that maintains reciprocal actions by the peer (Patterson & Reid, 1970). The neutral point in the continuum would consist of reciprocal indifference, when each individual behaves independently of the other. The preference for individual contingencies could be conceived as a case of reciprocal indifference. Several studies in our laboratory support the idea that positive reciprocity and indifference can actually be interpreted as different outcomes in a same contingency continuum.

We evaluated the induction of reciprocity in a choice situation involving individual and partial-altruism contingencies (Ribes et al., 2008).

In one of the studies, using a confederate in each dyad, three different conditions were manipulated: prompting, reciprocity, and indifference. During prompting, the confederate always placed the first ten pieces into the peer's puzzle. Once these ten pieces had been placed, in the modality of reciprocal prompting, the confederate placed a piece into the remote puzzle every time that the experimental participant did the same. In the indifferent prompting modality, the confederate always placed the pieces into the local puzzle, irrespective of where the peer had placed his/her pieces. During reciprocity, the confederate placed a piece into the peer's puzzle every time the peer placed a piece into the confederate's puzzle. During the indifference conditions, the confederate always placed pieces into his/her own puzzle, independently of the placements of the peer. During reciprocity or reciprocity prompting conditions, experimental peers responded mostly to the confederate's (remote) puzzle, whereas they responded to their own puzzle during the indifference and indifference prompting conditions. These data showed that partial altruism can be locally induced through reciprocal responding of one of the participants, in this case the confederate. By the same token, it was shown that indifference, or preference for the local puzzle in a partial-altruism situation, was also a function of reciprocal responding in the local puzzle by the peer.

In a second study, we evaluated the effects of a verbal declaration by each participant anticipating how they and their peer were going to respond to the task. This was done by filling in a questionnaire in which the various response options were included. The declarations were exchanged between participants in a second condition. Some dyads included a confederate who induced reciprocity and indifference in alternate conditions. Half of the dyads verbally anticipated their responding preference, and the other half did not make the declaration. Another group of dyads did not include a confederate and just had to anticipate their responding to the task. None of the dyads that declared their intentions anticipated responding to their own puzzle. The results of this study showed that dyads (with and without confederate) that anticipated their responding consistently chose the peer's puzzle, even when some of those dyads were exposed to an indifference condition by the confederate. On the other hand, those dyads that did not anticipate their responding to the task only responded in the peer's (confederate's) puzzle during the reciprocity condition and chose their own puzzle during the indifference condition.

This study suggests that two functional kinds of reciprocity can be distinguished. One kind of reciprocity is induced by present, momentary, situational factors, as shown by the effects induced by confederates in the prompting, reciprocity, and indifference conditions. Positive reciprocity and indifference seem to be an immediate outcome of previous behavior by the peer in the dyad. However, a second kind of reciprocity seems to depend upon linguistic variables, as shown by the effects observed when participants in a dyad verbally anticipated their responses to the task. In this case, participants chose the peer's puzzle even in those conditions in which the confederate induced indifference. This kind of reciprocity is non-situational and, therefore, does not seem to depend upon fluctuating factors taking place in a situation. This second kind of reciprocity could be conceived as exclusively human and social, whereas the first kind of reciprocity could be considered to be shared with other species in phylogeny. An experiment recently conducted in our laboratory supports this view. Participants in dyads including a confederate were exposed to different percentages of reciprocal responding by the confederate: 0, 25, 50, 75, and 100%, in both ascending and descending series. The data clearly showed that the percentage of choices of the peer's (confederate) puzzle by experimental participants matched the percentage of reciprocal responses by the confederate, either in the ascending or the descending procedures. This finding confirms that when linguistic factors are not present, reciprocity behavior in a partial-altruism situation depends upon the momentary behavior of at least one of the peers.

Future perspectives

Present research on social behavior is basically oriented by rational and economical models, assumed to be universal and timeless in their scope. A market-oriented conception of exchange, and its correlated logic, emphasizes that individuals choose the option that provides more benefits for the individual and not for the group or for other individuals. This conception assumes that individuals are essentially egoistic and, by extension, that biological evolution and social progress are based on egoism and free enterprise.

However, prehistory and history tell us a different story. The first truly human beings, Homo sapiens-sapiens like us, have always lived in small groups. Language as symbolic communication (Mithen, 1996), and a very primitive division of labor, were characteristics of the first primitive forms of social organization typical of nomadic hunters and harvesters. Power relations derived from skill and physical force and exchange relations had to do with effective foraging in the form of recollection and perhaps short-term storage. From then on, with sedentary harvesting first and afterwards with the first farmer and shepherd groups, institutions emerged reflecting the differentiation of social roles regarding the production, appropriation, and distribution of goods and the power relations resulting from them. History tells us about the different economic and political systems developed as an outcome of the progressive complexity of social organization demanded by economic processes: the oriental production mode, slavery, feudalism, and the various kinds of capitalism that formed after the appearance of absolute monarchies in Europe. All these systems, and many others that have had only a short period of micro-existence within others, secured their continuity and operation by building up a complex net of institutions. It would be at least naive to assume that social interactions between humans are independent of the characteristics of these systems and their institutions. The tendency of social scientists to extrapolate questionable interpretations derived from speculative genetics and evolutionary biology to human social behavior, instead of approaching its understanding from the standpoint of the ways in which social institutions shape social interactions between individuals, is also surprising. Elsewhere (Ribes et al., 2008), we have examined the various contingency functions involved in power, exchange, and sanction relations and the complex ways in which these functions are interwoven in institutions and social organization.

The analysis of social interactions between individuals from the standpoint of historical formation of social systems may be exemplified by a recent experiment in our laboratory. We adapted our experimental methods to simulate a primitive economy of nomadic harvesters. The puzzle is functionally equivalent to the site where harvesting takes place. The dyad has a leader (the scout finding the site) and a follower. The roles of leader and follower are ascribed according to how the participants solve a letter-string problem before facing the puzzle task. The dyad has to complete only one puzzle, but every piece has to be chosen at the same time by both participants, and also placed into the puzzle by them simultaneously. When several puzzles are completed in a phase, participants obtain three music CDs. Two of them are for each of the participants. Who gets the third one is decided by the leader of the dyad. Our findings show that the leader hands over the remaining CD to the follower. This is a case of altruism rarely found, if at all, in the experimental literature on social exchange relations. This finding has been replicated between dyads when two dyads solved separate puzzles and the leader of the dyad that first completed the puzzle decided how to distribute the remaining CDs.

In this experimental simulation, power and exchange roles are explicitly examined. Usually, the current literature neglects other social factors in the analysis of micro-economic processes that may take place in social interactions between individuals. Our experimental preparation may be adapted to include increased complexities in the operation of nomadic harvesters and hunters. It can be also extended to simulate the specific relations that characterize other social and economic systems, in order to develop comparative studies of individual social interactions. The studies may help us to increase our understanding about the ways in which social behavior by individuals is shaped and regulated by the net of power, exchange, and sanction contingencies that characterize institutions and social systems.

References

Abelson, R., Aronson, E., McGuire, W., Newcomb, T., Rosenberg, M., & Tannenbaum, P. (1968). *Theories of cognitive consistency: A sourcebook*. New York: Rand McNally.

Axelrod, R., & Hamilton W. D. (1981). The evolution of cooperation. *Science, 211*, 1390–1396.

Bandura, A. (1977). *Social learning theory*. Englewood Cliffs, NJ: Prentice Hall.

Bandura, A. (1986). *Social foundations of thought and action: A social cognitive theory*. Englewood Cliffs, NJ: Prentice Hall.

Baum, W. M. (1973). The correlation-based law of effect. *Journal of the Experimental Analysis of Behavior, 20*, 137–153.

Bennett, J. (1989). *Rationality*. Indianapolis, IN: Hackett.

Emerson, A. E. (1958). The evolution of behavior among social insects. In A. Roe & G. G. Simpson (Eds.), *Behavior and evolution* (pp. 311–335). New Haven, CT: Yale University Press.

Kantor, J. R. (1924). *Principles of psychology* (Vol. 1). New York: Alfred Knopf.

Kantor, J. R. (1982). *Cultural psychology*. Chicago: Principia Press.

Lull, V., & Micó, R. (2007). *Arqueología del origen del Estado. Las teorías* [Archaeology of the origin of the state. The theories]. Barcelona: Ediciones Bellaterra.

Marwell, G., & Schmitt, D. R. (1975). *Cooperation: An experimental analysis*. New York: Academic Press.

Marx, K. (1884). *El capital. Crítica a la economía política* (Vol. 3) [Capital. A critique of political economy]. México: Fondo de Cultura Económica, 1946 (Spanish translation).

Miller, N. E., & Dollard, J. (1941). *Social learning and imitation*. New Haven, CT: Yale University Press.

Mithen, S. (1996). *The prehistory of mind: A search for the origins of art, religion and science*. London: Thames & Hudson.

Mowrer, O. H. (1960). *Learning theory and the symbolic processes*. New York: Wiley.

Patterson, G. R., & Reid, J. B. (1970). Reciprocity and coercion: Two facets of social systems. In C. Neuringer & J. L. Michael (Eds.), *Behavior modification in clinical psychology* (pp. 133–177). New York: Appleton-Century-Crofts.

Pennisi, E. (2005). How did cooperative behavior evolve? *Science, 309*, 93.

Ribes, E. (1985). Conductismo o marxismo? Un falso dilema. *Revista Mexicana de Análisis de la Conducta, 11*, 255–295.

Ribes, E. (1986). Language as behavior: Functional mediation versus morphological description. In H. W. Reese & L. J. Parrot (Eds.), *Behavior science: Philosophical, methodological, and empirical advances* (pp. 115–138). Hillsdale, NJ: Lawrence Erlbaum Associates, Inc.

Ribes, E. (2001). Functional dimensions of social behavior: Theoretical considerations and some preliminary data. *Revista Mexicana de Análisis de la Conducta, 27*, 285–306.

Ribes, E., & Rangel, N. (2002). Choice between individual and shared contingencies in children and adults. *European Journal of Behavior Analysis, 3*, 61–73.

Ribes, E., Rangel, N., Carbajal, G., & Peña, E. (2003a). Choice between individual and shared social contingencies in children: An experimental replication in a natural setting. *European Journal of Behavior Analysis, 4*, 105–114.

Ribes, E., Rangel, N., Casillas, J., Álvarez, A., Gudiño, M., Zaragoza, A., et al. (2003b). Inequidad y asimetría de las consecuencias en la elección entre contingencias individuales y sociales. *Revista Mexicana de Análisis de la Conducta, 29*, 385–401.

Ribes, E., Rangel, N., Juárez, A., Contreras, S., Abreu, A., Gudiño, M., et al. (2003c). Respuestas "sociales" forzadas y cambio de preferencias entre contingencias individuales y sociales en niños y adultos. *Acta Comportamentalia, 11*, 197–234.

Ribes, E., Rangel, N., & López, V. F. (2008). Análisis teórico de las dimensiones funcionales del comportamiento social. *Revista Mexicana de Psicología, 25*, 45–57.

Ribes, E., Rangel, N., Magaña, C., López, A., & Zaragoza, A. (2005). Efecto del intercambio diferencial equitativo e inequitativo en la elección de contingencias sociales de altruismo parcial. *Acta Comportamentalia, 13*, 159–179.

Ribes, E., Rangel, N., Ramírez, E., Valdez, U., Romero, C., & Jiménez, C. (2008). Verbal and non-verbal induction of reciprocity in a partial-altruism social interaction. *European Journal of Behavior Analysis, 9*, 53–72.

Ribes, E., Rangel, N., Zaragoza, A., Magaña, C., Hernández, H., Ramírez, E., et al. (2006). Effects of differential and shared consequences on choice between individual and social contingencies. *European Journal of Behavior Analysis, 7*, 41–56.

Scott, J. P. (1958). *Animal behavior*. Chicago: University of Chicago Press.

Secord, P., & Backman, C. W. (1974). *Social psychology* (2nd edition). New York: McGraw-Hill.

Shimoff, E., & Matthews, B. A. (1975). Unequal reinforcer magnitudes and relative preference for cooperation in the dyad. *Journal of Experimental Analysis of Behavior, 24*, 1–16.

Skinner, B. F. (1962). Two "synthetic social relations." *Journal of the Experimental Analysis of Behavior, 5*, 531–533.

Thibaut, J. W., & Kelley, H. H. (1959). *The social psychology of groups.* New York: Wiley.

Thorpe, W. H. (1956). *Learning and instinct in animals.* London: Methuen.

Weber, M. (1964). *Economía y sociedad* [Economy and society]. México: Fondo de Cultura Económica (Spanish translation).

Weiss, A. P. (1926). A set of postulates for social psychology. *Journal of Abnormal and Social Psychology, 21,* 203–211.

Wilson, E. O. (1975). *Sociobiology.* Cambridge, MA: Belknap Press.

Author index

Subject index